Three Sons for the Kaiser

Three Sons for the Kaiser

A German Family's Sacrifice in the First World War

Hazel Strouts

Pen & Sword
MILITARY

First published in Great Britain in 2025 by
Pen & Sword Military
An imprint of Pen & Sword Books Limited
Yorkshire – Philadelphia

ISBN 978 1 03613 870 7

A CIP catalogue record for this book is available from the British Library.

Typeset by Mac Style
Printed in the UK by CPI Group (UK) Ltd, Croydon, CR0 4YY.

The Publisher's authorised representative in the EU for product safety is Authorised Rep Compliance Ltd., Ground Floor, 71 Lower Baggot Street, Dublin D02 P593, Ireland.
www.arccompliance.com

For a complete list of Pen & Sword titles please contact

PEN & SWORD BOOKS LIMITED
47 Church Street, Barnsley, South Yorkshire, S70 2AS, England
E-mail: enquiries@pen-and-sword.co.uk
Website: www.pen-and-sword.co.uk
or
PEN AND SWORD BOOKS
1950 Lawrence Road, Havertown, PA 19083, USA
E-mail: uspen-and-sword@casematepublishers.com
Website: www.penandswordbooks.com

To Joël

Contents

Acknowledgements

Many people in many different parts of the world contributed to the writing and publication of this book. It started with Yves Dufeil in France who, through *uboat.net*, put me in touch with a kind and generous military historian, Gary Staff, in Australia. He had been working on my grandfather's story for thirty years. Thanks to Zoom, I could see a photo of Grandfather on the walls of his Melbourne home. Thanks also to his kind daughter Emily Hamasaki in Japan who, when, to our great sorrow, Gary suddenly died, sent me some of his material. I was guided through the labyrinth of the German military archives in Freiburg by Sebastian Remus, a map-reading wizard who made a comprehensive collection of reports, maps and aerial photos so that we could track every step of Waldemar's march through Belgium and France in August 1914 and study every encounter on his way to the First Battle of the Marne. We walked the field where, just before dawn, with rifle unloaded, he took part in the bayonet charge which propelled the German troops forward. We also found, near Verdun, the exact trench where, in 1916, the middle son of this trio, Georg, scrambled out and stood at the top of the trench wall, shouting his last order in the face of machine-gun fire. Thanks also to two indefatigable editors, Bernard Phillips and Gillian Davis, and above all, thanks to editor Antonia Leckey who, with great tact, guided me to the present structure of the book. Thanks to Jo Outram, who forged a way through the technology maze associated with transforming family photographs into book illustrations. And thanks to my strongly supportive book club, Cookie Dakin, Bridget Wakehurst, Ursula Ellwood, Ali Ferris, Frances Morrish and Huthrie Copplestone. Thanks, too, to my kind, supportive family, especially to Irmgard, Dietrich and Ingrid Ehlers whose expertise in deciphering handwriting and reading *Sütterlin* (an old German script, largely impenetrable to modern eyes), combined with oceans of patience and determination, transformed Great-Grandfather's handwritten chronicles into legible, modern German. Last of all, thanks to my mother Ursula, who translated one of those Chronicles into English. Profound thanks.

Introduction

'The Past is never quite the Past ...'

Freya Stark[1]

It would be easy to blame the Kaiser. A lot of people did, including Philipp. He said repeatedly that Wilhelm II was a cowardly dog and the cause of everything that went wrong. But that was in the 1930s, when he was putting it all down on paper. By that time, he had reason enough to say so. If you'd asked him what he thought of the Kaiser earlier on, if, for example, you had asked him when Wilhelm had just inherited the crown, then he would have given a very different answer. But that was fifty years earlier. Back then, the Kaiser had been the Great White Hope. The visionary of the Imperial German Navy. Its architect. Its hero. The man to transform it from an inconsequential North German Confederation fleet into a navy to rival the very best. Even Britain's. Even the Royal Navy. Even Nelson's home fleet. And all in just fifty years.

In the process, he would open up new naval pathways for ambitious members of Germany's middle classes. He would transform naval officers, turn them into members of a fiercely proud, highly respected élite corps. He would make sailing the most fashionable of all sports, in Britain as well as in Germany.

Now, if there was anything in the world which Philipp cared about (other than his family), it was the navy. He loved the navy. This meant that of course, he also loved the Kaiser. He and the Kaiser were on the same side. Wholeheartedly so. Lock stock and barrel. Ships ...the sea ...Germany. These were the things that mattered.

Then it changed. The Great War exploded in their faces. Before it began, Philipp had had three sons. Promising, handsome young men. Philipp and Mila thought the world of them. True, the world itself knew little of them, how could it? They died too young to make a mark. But where it did know, the world thought the same.

Yes. They lost all three. Hermann, the eldest, Georg the middle boy, and Waldemar, the youngest. One after the other, in reverse order to that in which they had been born. But no, the Kaiser wasn't to blame, at least, not entirely. What if you had asked him his opinion? He could easily have blamed lots of people other than himself. He could (and did) blame his own mother for some of his troubles. But Philipp insisted on just one person. In 1918, had it not been for the Kaiser, he and Mila, my great-grandparents, would still have had their three boys. As it was, at the end of 1918, the only child left them was their daughter, the youngest child, Lenchen.

My grandfather, Hermann Gercke, was the only boy who had had time to marry. From that marriage, he had four children. The last was born a few weeks after he and his crew of seventy had sunk to the bottom of the Atlantic Ocean. His eldest daughter, Ursula, was my mother. She was almost two when he was killed. One autumn evening, several months after the terrible news, she wandered to the end of Warnemünde's long mole. It runs along the western side of the little harbour, projecting northwards into the grey Baltic. It was the mole from which, in the dark chill of an early February morning, her father's U-Boat had cast off. The mole where her grandfather stood, waving farewell and calling out, '*Komm gut nach Hause!*' (Come safely home again!). Ursula was carrying, in one hand, a stick with a paper lantern at one end. She dangled the lit lantern over the water. Was she watching the flickering light or the sea? She stood there, singing a folksong, a version popular in the great port-cities of north Germany. In Bremen, Kiel, Rostock and Königsberg. In all the cities through which this story passes.

Laterne, Laterne,
Sonne, Mond und Sterne
Brenne auf mein Licht
Brenne auf mein Licht
Aber nur meine liebe Laterne nicht.[2]

(Lantern, lantern, by sun, moon and stars, burn brightly, burn brightly, but don't burn my lantern!)

Around six o'clock in the evening, her panic-stricken mother found her there. Was she waiting for her father to come home? I think she waited for him all her life. His photo sat on her bedside table till the end. No wonder she asked me to write this story.

Well, no. That's not quite true. She asked me to write about her father, forgetting about his brothers Georg and Waldemar. And so we set to work. We ordered catalogues from military book sellers. We pored over them. We crowed with delight whenever we came across Hermann's name. But I never wrote a thing. Then came old age. Liberating, wonderful old age. Time was at last sitting at my feet. This was it. The moment I had been waiting for. First of all, I decided to write about all three boys. How unfair to limit myself to only one. And I would write about the parents who loved them. I wanted to understand the pre-war glory of Philipp and Mila's naval life. I wanted to understand pre-war Berlin, often described as the liveliest city in Europe. A Mecca for artists, theatre-goers, musicians, scientists, for the avant-garde in every walk of life. Then, when war broke out, I wanted to track the boys' separate pathways. They were entering a maelstrom. Each in his own way. I would invade Belgium, walking the routes Waldemar once took. I would walk the trenches on the Western Front which he and Georg both walked. I would stand on that infamous hill, *Toter Mann* (Dead Man's Hill) just west of Verdun, where Georg fell. And, somehow or other, though I couldn't so easily follow a sailor's tracks, I would find whatever traces remained of the life of my grandfather.

But it all starts with Philipp. Philipp in the 1930s. A bereft old man. He tried to make sense of loss. He sat at his desk in an apartment just outside Rostock. He could see the River Warnow from his window to the east, the garden to the south. The tables around him were piled high with books, files and papers. He had kept everything. His own and the boys' childhood sketches. Photos, postcards, family poems. Menus from great occasions (either of family or of state). Concert programmes. Grand invitations. Letters from Important People. I.O.Us from the Kaiser. He tried to focus on the boys, but bits about himself kept straying in, and with good reason. His own life had shaped theirs. The two generations were intertwined. They could not be separated. Nor could the ones to follow. Even I cannot be separated from them.

From time to time, he would glance out of his window, hesitating as he recalled some particular event. There in the garden, Lenchen's three little boys were playing. The sight shook him. A scene from the past. His own three boys. The past and the present have an uncanny knack of sliding into each other. He made an effort and brushed uncertainty to one side. He turned back to his desk and wrote, occasionally in anger, but always with humour. Gentle, derisive humour, mocking the foibles of mankind. He wrote two Family Chronicles. One for Lenchen and her children, and one for the children of his eldest son. A record. A reminder. He wrote so that his sons' lives would not be forgotten. His writings are the basis of this book. The kernel. Around them I weave stories from other family memoirs, from letters, diaries and books. From official archives, both in Britain and in Germany. And from my own direct experience as I walked in the footsteps of my great uncles, through Belgium and France. But the story starts in Moscow.

Part I

Fair Weather Sailing

The Baltic Sea 1914.

Chapter 1

The Starting Point: Moscow

You could say, I suppose, that it began with Ivan the Terrible. He started a trend. He encouraged European merchants to migrate to Moscow, and his successors followed suit. Peter the Great, for example, and his grandson Peter III. The second of these was actually a half-German migrant himself. Born in Kiel to a Russian mother and German father, he was barely able to speak Russian when he inherited the throne and became Peter III, Tsar of all the Russias. On leaving Schleswig-Holstein, he took many Germans with him. Comfort companions. But nothing could save him from his fate. His cheerful and determined wife (Catherine the Great) had him murdered. And so time rolled on till, eventually, in 1855, a German baby, Philipp,[1] innocent of all this history, was born in Moscow, in the German quarter.

By that time, so many foreigners in Russia had originally come from Germany that the word for 'German' in Russian (*nemets)* is exactly the same as the word for 'foreigner'. Never overly keen on outsiders (wherever they came from), the Russian authorities generally settled the incomers in quarters outside city centres. They had their own communities, schools, churches, shops and businesses. Result? Many failed to pick up the local language. And that leads to the third meaning of the word *nemets*: someone who can't speak. Dumb. But Philipp wasn't. He was brought up to speak fluent Russian by his Russian *nanya* and, largely through her, felt a great love for the Russian people all his life. He spoke Russian and sang Russian songs (he loved singing), but as a child he spoke German with his family and went to local German schools. When he was an old man, the two large engravings which dominated his Rostock apartment were by the Russian painter, Ilya Repin.[2] They illustrated both the hardy life of the resilient Russian people and Philipp's deep connection with Russia. This was a connection he passed on to his sons and grandchildren. Sometimes this Russianness of his proved helpful. Sometimes not. Mostly not.

But he didn't stay in Moscow. Leaving aunts, uncles and cousins behind, his family migrated ever further westwards, as if pulled by invisible strings from their ancestral home. By 1863 they were living in Wirballen,[3] a railway town near the Russian border with Prussia. That's where Philipp first fell in love. No. Not with women, but with adventure, military adventure.

In 1863, one of several Polish uprisings against Russian rule was disrupting life in their new home town.[4] It lay in Russian Poland so, for safety's sake, Philipp's father sent his children over the border into Prussia. They would wait things out till the uprising was over. But while in Prussia, the eight-year-old Philipp saw a sight which made his heart stop.

> There, on a walk one day, we see, what can it be? In an open field, something sparkles and shines. To and fro, at a word of command, a rippling shimmer runs, like a fork of lightening. Another clear, sharp command. Again, lightning flickers along that puzzling line which remains otherwise immobile. Every stroke of rippling light is accompanied by a metallic sound. I stand, listen and marvel. I am speechless. Then I understood. These were soldiers. But how different these Prussians were to their Russian counterparts, the only ones I had seen so far. There they stood, a full battalion, moving as one. They were divided into three companies, each equipped and armed with rifles and fixed bayonets. The sun reflected and enhanced every bright surface, particularly their helmets with their sharp metal points. In front of them, their officer sat on a wonderful thoroughbred. My eyes shone at the sight. What in God's name was this? What man was this? What men!

Philipp was eleven when the family next moved. This time, they settled in the Prussian port of Königsberg,[5] and there that sense of thrill overwhelmed him once again. This time it wasn't the army that set him off. In Königsberg, Philipp fell head over heels in love with the sea. The sea became, and remained all his life, second in importance only to his family.

Whenever possible, the young lad ran out of his house and down to the docks. There, walking along the harbour wall, he drank in the sights around him as if tasting the finest champagne. Not that, in those early days, he had the slightest idea what fine champagne tasted like. All he knew was that river craft and sea-going ships lay at anchor; that thickets of masts and yard-arms sprang up above them; that he could see tall ships, schooners, brigantines, brigs and barques; that he could identify them by their rigging and their home ports from their flags. He loved the sight of them. He basked in the magic which lies in the sound of place names which were, to him, exotic and remote, bathed in mystery. Denmark, Norway, Holland, England, Spain. Born deep within a continental landmass, in the seaside city of Königsberg Philipp first understood what the sea was. A miraculous element which united the whole world. That's where he first saw ships which could take him into the heart of it all. For him, the sea was a window on the world.

The sounds he heard in Königsberg, and the smells he smelt, remained with him for the rest of his life. Shouted commands, jokes and laughter. The flap of sails. The thud of rope. Rattling chains. As for the smells, when he remembered Königsberg, he smelt oranges again, piled high in heaps. Herrings in nets on wooden decks. Hemp rope. Dried cod and fresh-sawn wood. Wheat-grain, bones, hides. Above all, he smelt tar.

And the men he saw there? Never forgotten. The harbour master, the pilots, the sailors. He remembered their blue uniforms, the gold braid, the gold buttons with anchors on them. Such people were, to the impressionable young boy, a race apart. How they swanked and lorded it along the quayside. They even spat with authority. Such scenes decided it. When he grew up, he would join the navy. Little did he realize that one day he would wear uniforms far grander than any of the ones he was seeing there. That one day, he would travel further than any of the men he met in Königsberg.

This was a time of huge change for all the world's navies, but especially for the German *Kaiserliche Marine*. In only a few decades, it was to grow from a tiny north German Baltic force into the second most powerful navy in the world. One that could build an empire, supply it and disrupt the long-established empires of others. At the same time, its ships, and ships everywhere, were being transformed. Over the course of the nineteenth century, the three-masted tall ships Philipp so admired in Königsberg gradually disappeared. They were replaced first by ironclad ships [6] and then by steel.[7] The new ships were lighter, longer and wider. They could hold more cargo. And they carried funnels, not at first in the place of masts, but sprouting up in between them. Wind power was on its way out. First coal[8] took over, then oil.[9]

Philipp was one of that generation of sailors who found, as old men, that the ships on which they had trained as boys, three-masted, wooden sailing ships (not so different from those that Nelson sailed), had been replaced by boats of iron and steel; that submarines and torpedoes had been invented; that within a single lifetime, the navy had hurtled forward, several centuries; that the modern naval era had begun.

As the technology changed, so did ideas about the role of the navy. It was becoming clear to the western world that Britain, the greatest sea-power in that world, owed its position to its empire, and that the empire owed its existence to its navy. The two were inter-dependent. No navy? No empire. No empire? No wealth. The new approach was perhaps best expressed in Alfred Thayer Mahan's [10] influential book, *The Influence of Sea Power Upon History*. His work was translated into German in 1898, and the Kaiser made it compulsory reading for all his naval officers. He wanted everyone to understand what he himself also believed: that command of the seas was central to holding significant power in the world, that states should use their navies to acquire overseas possessions and protect trade, that Germany *must* have a significant navy. And, under Kaiser Wilhelm II, it did. As it changed, the Imperial German Navy took on an increasingly important role in the development of the state. Its officers became an élite corps. Some would say that they never carried quite as much clout on the national stage as army generals, but still, socially, they were a race apart. Privileged, admired, respected.

Philipp was only sixteen years old when he left home. It was 1871 and he was going to attend the *Marineschule* (Naval School) in Kiel. Its entrance examinations were notoriously tough. Private tuition was an essential first step, and the best tuition available was in Berlin. That's where Philipp was heading. In Germany's history, 1871 was one of the most significant years. It was the year that the German Empire was born. It was only one year before the birth of the Imperial German Navy. Philipp could hardly have arrived in Berlin at a more critical moment. He was just in time for the birth of nation, navy and empire.

The German Empire took its place on the world stage following Prussia's victory in the Franco-Prussian War (1870–71). During the course of that war, Prussia (with its allies) re-took the provinces of Alsace and Lorraine or, as they are called in Germany, Elsass-Lothringen.[11] These key provinces lie in the borderlands between Germany and France. Inhabited early in history by German-speakers, they had been lost to France's Louis XIV in the seventeenth century. Occupying French forces moved in and many an Elsasser-Lothringener moved out. Those that remained endured the occupiers' policy of assimilation. The German language declined. French flourished. Bitter memories were forged.

So how did Germany wreak revenge? In January 1871, following the French defeat, the new German empire, thanks to the war, now included Elsass-Lothringen. As if to make sure that France understood its total defeat, the German empire's birth was declared in France's Hall of Mirrors at Versailles. All the German great and good attended. Wilhelm I, the newly crowned Emperor, his son and heir, Crown Prince Friedrich of Prussia, and the wily Minister President Otto von Bismarck, whose careful management of alliances had done much to engineer the event in the first place.

It is difficult, from the French point of view, to imagine a more humiliating choice of venue. The German triumph took place in a palace built by Louis XIV, the Sun King, the lodestar of European civilization. Versailles was and is the epitome of grandeur, elegance and style. French greatness expressed in architecture. What was the court of Prussia doing in the Hall of Mirrors? Why, they were forging more bitter memories. More dreams of revenge. Dreams that, alas for Philipp's family and for many others, led to the outbreak of the First World War.

Sixteen-year-old Philipp, newly arrived in Berlin, had no idea of any of this. On 16 June 1871, in the highest of spirits, he set out from his lodgings carrying the young son of one of his tutors on his shoulders. They were going to watch the victory parade from the best place possible. Philipp, like everyone else, was walking on air. He was smiling. The boy on his shoulders was smiling. Everyone was smiling.

They set out early and headed for Unter den Linden, Berlin's most famous street. It led from the Brandenburger Tor at one end to royal palaces and regimental barracks at the other. This was the parade's last stretch and far from its starting point in the Tempelhofer Fields. Philipp wouldn't see anything till the procession reached the Brandenburger Tor, but he knew exactly what to expect. He knew the course of the route. He knew who was in the procession. He knew in what order they would process and when it would begin. It had been brilliantly and precisely organized; everyone knew the plan. First to arrive would be the mounted Cuirassiers. They would clatter into Belle Alliance Platz from the Tempelhofer Fields, followed by the Grenadier Guards, still basking in their victory at Sedan.[12] The royal family would follow, waving and smiling from grand, horse-drawn coaches. After them, generals and statesmen on horseback. From Belle Alliance Platz they would ride down Königgrätzerstraße before arriving at the Brandenburg Tor. Philipp and his charge were ready to wait for hours. And they did.

When there was only half an hour more to go, the crowd began to grow restless. Then, quite unexpectedly, an unscheduled opening act. General 'Olle' Wrangel,[13] eighty-seven years old, on a magnificent stallion, was riding the route on his own. A handful of mounted adjutants rode some paces behind him. Defying both old age and the set programme, he was also, in a way, defying the crowd because, as Governor of Berlin, he was not generally a popular man. He had a reputation for brutality. But this daring, solitary ride worked. Seeing him there, smiling and fearless, the crowd greeted him with a roar of approval. Perhaps it was his defiance which captured their hearts. Perhaps it was everyone's indefatigable sense of joy on that particular day. Wrangel was having his last hurrah. He waved and waved. Everyone enjoyed it, none more so than Wrangel himself. His was the perfect warm-up number to the main event.

Many years later, Philipp wrote:

> Then came the great men, first of all, Bismarck, Roon,[14] Moltke[15] and, fifty metres behind, the Kaiser. He rode by himself, all alone. After him rode the Crown Prince, Friedrich Carl, with field marshals and generals, the general staff and members of the war ministry. Men from the various regiments followed, with captured flags, regimental eagles and standards.

> Next, several horse-drawn carriages (à la Daumont[16]) with the Empress[17] and the Crown Princess[18] in them, as well as attendants. Lastly, the military bands and the troops themselves.
>
> We were silent when the procession first came into sight. It was as if everybody's breath had suddenly failed. As if all our hearts had missed a beat. But once that first spell was broken, we shouted with joy. Actually, more than that. The crowd went completely mad. I stood, rooted to the spot, Hänschen on my shoulders. We were in a throng of thousands. It was hot. It was noisy. The dust was thick. Suddenly, out of nowhere, pickled gherkins appeared. They were passed from the back of the crowd, from hand to hand, till they reached the marching soldiers, who received them with laughter and thanks. Sour gherkins, in their thousands. Where did they all come from? From every house, and from every tub in every cellar of every house, all along the route.

Philipp took his exams the following spring, in April 1872, the year the Imperial German Navy was founded. *General der Infanterie* Albrecht von Stosch,[19] was its first chief. At the time, the navy depended on the army for admirals and regulations. The army was all-important, the senior service, the profession of Prussian landed grandees. They passed their profession on from generation to generation. It was quite different in the navy. Almost everyone there was 'new', including Philipp. He passed his exams with flying colours. Of course he did.

The entry exam had been tough, but the four-year course which followed was tougher. Philipp became, first of all, a *Seekadett* (Sea Cadet) and then a *Fähnrich zur See* (Ensign). He climbed the mainsail every day, ran to the end of the royal yard[20] and thanked his stars that he didn't suffer from vertigo. Years later, Philipp remarked that of his three sons, the only one who could run the yardarm was Hermann.

Philipp's teachers were of the sergeant-major variety. 'Out with your prayer books!' they barked, by which they meant the sandstone scrubbing blocks. Then 'Pray!', by which they meant fall on your knees and scrub. Philipp was determined to succeed. And he did. He ran the yardarm. He scrubbed the decks. And he made it to the end of the course, excelling along the way. He was top sailsman, first oarsman and number one on the cannon.

The last stage of the training programme was a round-the-world trip in a tall ship. Philipp's group set sail in the autumn of 1873 on the SMS *Arcona*,[21] a three-masted tall ship. An old ship and in bad shape, very bad shape. Her first anchorage was in Portsmouth, where a patronizing British journalist visited and reported, with some disdain, that no British engineer would have ever allowed such a decrepit ship to set sail.

That first evening, officers and ensigns gathered in the mess. They were awaiting a visit from the English port admiral. He came on board, met the ensigns and asked about their course. The *Arcona*'s captain, a kind-hearted and good man, replied, 'Round the world from Rio to Melbourne.'

'What! You are going to cross the South Indian Ocean?'

'Yes. We pass the MacDonald Islands.'

The MacDonalds are desolate, remote, uninhabited, sub-Antarctic volcanic islands lying about half way between Madagascar and Australia.

'You'll never see them!'

But they did. Only a glimpse, mind you, and that from a distance. This was because, although falling apart and constantly in need of repair, the *Arcona* was incredibly fast. Really fast. No other ship could keep up with her. They passed the islands in huge seas, with waves fifty metres high. And at the most tremendous speed.

The ship's poor state was widely known. The news seemed to precede her into harbour. As a result, once they anchored, port authorities would celebrate the *Arcona*'s sailors as if, simply by arriving, they had won a most heroic victory. City worthies organized a series of festivities, one after another. Officers and crew were given free rail tickets, theatre tickets, balls, picnics, steamship excursions. And nowhere were they more fêted than in San Francisco. The *Arcona* had to lie at anchor there for longer than usual because she needed a new mainmast. The old one was growing toadstools. It had only stayed upright, wrote Philipp, by force of habit.

Although they had a fast ship, it took them seventy-seven days to sail from Rio to Melbourne. The biggest challenge was rounding Cape Horn. There, the winds howled and the waves towered over the decks, sometimes fifty-five metres high. Their comfort in those wild seas were the albatrosses. They flew alongside as if delighting in both the tempest and the presence of the young sailors.

The ship arrived home almost three years after she had set off, on 19 December 1875. Families gathered around the Hamburg landing stage. Parents wept, cadets wept. Everyone wept. The journey had been long. Here indeed was a taste of a sailor's life. The first lesson was that much depended for your happiness on the character of your commander. Sometimes they were kind, sometimes not. And sometimes, Philipp later found out, to his horror, they were insane. The second lesson was that sailors have to endure long stretches of time far from home. Could he bear it? Could his family bear it?

After what those young men had endured, it's a wonder they didn't all resign on landing. Far from it. The final officers' examinations were held almost immediately, from 27 to 30 December. Philipp graduated. He was a member of Crew 1872, a class of twenty-four young men, of whom five would eventually reach the rank of admiral – von Capelle, von Heeringen, Meyer, Paschen and von Pohl. It means a great deal, for a graduating German sailor, to join a Crew. All *Marineschule* graduates, for the rest of their lives, belong to the Crew of the year in which they entered the school. They form a close-knit society which supports its members, wives/husbands, widows/widowers and offspring in perpetuity. They publish newsletters and keep all informed of the life-journey of the others. A family. Thirty years after the death of her husband at sea, my grandmother cherished her husband's Crew newsletters. After she died, her daughter asked if she too could join. And she did.

On 31 December 1875, at the very earliest possible opportunity, the *Arcona*, the last ounce of life squeezed out of her, was taken out of service. Philipp stood on the threshold of the rest of his life. What would come next? To his surprise, he would spend most of the next five years in the Far East, mainly in China.

Chapter 2

Old China Hand

Cixi, Dowager Empress of China, ruled a huge, unwieldy country stretching from Vietnam to Manchuria.[1] Hers would have been a difficult job at any time, but in the second half of the nineteenth century, facing European powers equipped with fast ships, armed with modern weapons and lusting for empire, it was all but impossible. Her first problem was that, until the 1860s, she didn't have a navy, only a coastal police force. Given the threat to China, mainly from Britain and France, she ordered warships from England and began to establish a navy. But in 1879, China began ordering new ironclads from Germany, although the country was a naval novice and had only recently started supplying her own navy with ships made at home.[2] At that time, if you wanted good ships, the obvious country to which you would turn was Britain, the world's greatest naval power. But suddenly, in relation to China, Germany found itself with unexpected advantages. First of all, Germany, unlike Britain, was not involved in aggression against the Chinese empire. China had recently fought, and painfully lost, two wars against first Britain and then Britain and France: the First and Second Opium Wars.[3] Germany, on the other hand, found that its 1871 victory over France had not only propelled the nation into existence, but also gave it a useful reputation for military success. It was now obvious to all that the victor of Sedan had both the military skill and the weapons needed to win. Flowing from this, Germany was able, in the late 1870s, to enter discussion with China for the production of Sachsen-class armoured ironclad corvettes. Given the timing of Philipp's next assignment, and where he was headed, his new voyage was likely linked to those trade discussions.

He was appointed Officer of the Watch and Navigation Officer on the gunboat SMS *Wolf*. She was berthed in Wilhelmshaven and, on 26 October 1878, set sail for the Far East. Philipp sailed via Malta and Aden, reaching Singapore on 2 February 1879. It would be a gruelling assignment and a long one. He would be away for just under three years.

Almost seven months after she left Germany, the *Wolf* reached Hong Kong, a British colony and one of Cixi's early losses. Britain was perhaps the worst of her enemies, possibly because she had the best of navies, though France was a close runner-up. The First and the Second Opium Wars with Britain and

France had left a humiliated China the subject of what were called 'Unequal Treaties', in which China gave and the colonial powers took. In the case of Hong Kong, China leased the land to Britain in perpetuity. Hong Kong was one of many treaty ports where foreigners were allowed, within a specific area around the harbour, to run their own police force, use their own legal system and civil service, and set up their own warehouses, dockyards, shops, schools and churches. They could exercise rights as if China did not govern this part of its own country. They could even ban Chinese from entry.

In 1879, Hong Kong was the ideal place for the *Wolf* to dock. The crew carried out repairs, took on coal and re-supplied with food and water. Germany had no such place of her own in the Far East. Not yet. This would change, and in only eighteen years time.[4] Until then, Germany depended for supplies, recreation and coaling on the Treaty Ports strung the length of China's seaboard. In such places, European crews enjoyed European-style facilities and the company of other Europeans, both long-term residents and sailors from other ships. Favourite ports for German ships were Chefoo (Yantai), the chief base for the *Wolf* on this particular voyage, together with the port of Tientsin (Tianjin).

Both cities are in the north of China. Tientsin is particularly significant. It is the port for China's capital (Beijing) and sits at the western end of the Bohai Sea, which is connected through the Bohai Straits (which separate the Shantung Peninsula to the south from Port Arthur [Lüsun] to the north) to the Yellow Sea. Tientsin is not only Beijing's port but, in 1879, was also home to the mandarin Li Hongzhang, governor of that province[5] and Cixi's Chief Minister. He was also a man who employed a number of German advisors. In Tientsin, political and economic power went hand-in-hand. Any papers regarding the purchase of new Sachsen-class armoured corvettes from Germany would cross the desk of Li Hongzhang. Philipp's daughter-in-law, writing many years later, said of Philipp:

> He had spent a long time in China and had plenty to say about it. He visited mandarins and used to tell us about their customs. The one the children wanted to hear about most was how you have to burp after a meal. Burps were necessary to show your appreciation of the meal. But most of all, he was impressed with the old empress whom he described as extremely clever, but also cruel and ruthless. He said you couldn't help admiring her.

I can find no evidence that Philipp actually met Cixi. More likely, he only saw her mandarins. She is said to have first met a European male only with the arrival of Prince Heinrich, Kaiser Wilhelm II's younger brother. He visited her in May 1898, from her point of view not the most auspicious of moments. Germany had just seized a slice of the Shantung Peninsula and extracted a ninety-nine year lease on the property from China.

Chefoo was a port on the north coast of the Shantung Peninsula. It looks north across the Bohai Straits towards Port Arthur. It was a treaty port, as were the other ports where the *Wolf* dropped anchor. These included Amoy (Xiamen), Woosung (now part of Shanghai) and Shanghai itself. From Shanghai, in July 1879, the *Wolf* sailed across the Yellow Sea to call at Yokohama in Japan. Germany's relationship with Japan had been established for longer than its relationship with China.[6] By the time Philipp called there in 1879, Japan had already singled out Germany from among the European powers as the one to emulate. Japan wanted to modernize its military and educational systems, and Germany would be its model. Yes, Germany was a successful combatant in Europe, but it was also in the top league when it came to science. The country had became a centre for research, so that, between the inception of the Nobel Prize in 1891 and the end of the First World War, every third scientific prize winner was German. In those days, if you wanted to study scientific subjects you needed to be able to read German. Also, because Germany had sent a trade mission to Japan in 1873, roughly twenty years earlier than it sent one to China, there were more German merchants, teachers and doctors working in Japan than in China. But Philipp's stay was brief. By August he was back in Chefoo. He spent most of that year sailing up and down the coast between Shanghai and Chefoo, spending, in December 1880, roughly two months in Tientsin. And that's where his life improved considerably.

There had been one major flaw during Philipp's first trip to China, a flaw which was, unfortunately, repeated in his second. The Captain of SMS *Wolf* was, in the language of his crew, 'stark staring bonkers'. In the language of his doctor, he suffered from *dementia paralytica*, a condition brought on by syphilis. It must have made life miserable for all of them but, in spite of this (or perhaps because of it), Philipp was given his first promotion on 20 November 1879. He became a *Leutnant*. A year later, anchored off Tientsin, the *Wolf*'s captain was replaced. Just as well, for there was still one year to go before the ship arrived home.

Philipp returned to Hamburg in December 1881. His parents and brothers were once again, at the St Pauli quayside, waving their handkerchiefs and crying.

Now a fully-fledged *Leutnant*, Philipp hoped he could afford to marry, but who would want to share life with a man who was away so often, and for such long periods of time. Did such a woman exist? And if she did, would he have enough time to meet her?

New Year's Eve 1880 was as boisterous as any other, but in the midst it all, Philipp remembered, for the rest of his life, a banal little ditty which a friend sent him that year:

Prosit Neujahr! (Happy New Year!)
I wish you, in the New Year,
A wife to accompany you in the world
And to make you happy whenever possible.

A wife. The word struck home. At the time, he was posted in Wilhelmshaven, near Bremen, and had already caught sight of someone who, with just one glance, had somehow hit his heart hard. He saw her again at the New Year ball. He even plucked up the courage to dance with her. Her name was Emilie Friederike Caroline Seeger (known as Mila). Eight years younger than Philipp, she was the eldest daughter of Bremen's first and, for a long time only, dentist, Dr Julius Seeger. Her long dark hair was parted in the middle and pulled back in a bun. Brimming with youthful confidence, she had full lips and soft grey-green eyes beneath clear, questioning eyebrows. She had a happy, but quiet and self-possessed expression. Unlike Philipp, she had lived in one place all her life and radiated three qualities which Philipp longed for: *Haus, Hinterland und Heimat*[7] (home, a sense of place and of belonging). In many ways, she was his opposite.

In early March, Philipp received an invitation from his Wilhelmshaven commander: 'Navy Director Councillor Berndt and his wife have the honour of inviting Lt. zur See Gercke to dinner on Tuesday, the 8th of this month.' As casually as he could, Philipp asked Councillor Berndt if, at the dinner on the 8th, he could please sit next to Miss Seeger. Councillor Berndt glanced at him with the trace of a smile.

'Aha', was all he said.

At dinner, Philipp was indeed sitting exactly where he wanted, but one person had obviously asked for the same thing. On the other side of Emilie sat a young man wearing white buttons on his uniform. A naval lawyer. Philipp referred to this man, for the rest of his life as 'White Buttons'. He wrote in his Chronicle:

> After that dinner, on the following day, the matter was decided in a very German way.
>
> White Buttons came up to me and said: 'Do you have serious intentions towards Miss Seeger?'
>
> 'Yes.'
>
> 'So do I. Pistols?'[8]
>
> 'No. Let her decide for herself.'
>
> 'Good. Tomorrow I will ask for her hand.'
>
> 'I wish you a very good morning.'
>
> 'Good morning.'

Too discreet to tell us Mila's answer directly, Philipp simply stuck an engagement photo of himself and Mila into his Chronicle. It's dated March 1881. He stands in full uniform (with gold buttons). His left arm rests on the hilt of his *Dolch* (the dagger which all naval officers carried, an emblem of self-respect and rank), and his right arm rests on Mila's back. The two things he cared about most: his family and the navy. She is seated, very upright (her grandchildren remarked on the fact that she always sat ramrod-straight); her hands rest lightly together, on her lap. Both of them look serious and quietly confident. They have each won what they were looking for. At their wedding in October that year, Mila's sister Julie and two cousins strewed their path with flowers. Mila's parents were there, together with Philipp's and a cluster of supporting friends, including Oberleutnant Guido von Usedom, who later became an admiral and served in the Dardanelles in the First World War.[9]

Philipp's decision to marry was daring. He was very junior. Could he afford a wife? In most people's opinion he could not. This is why he was the first and last naval officer of his rank to be allowed to marry. His *Kommissvermögen* (yearly stipend) was only 1,800M. Shortly afterwards, the minimum salary at which an officer could marry was raised to almost twice that sum. Philipp and Mila had squeaked through the door. Just in time.

They were well matched. Her grandchildren described her as patient and loving, with nerves of steel. She needed them. It is difficult to imagine greater stresses than the ones she and Philipp had to face. He would react to stress by falling ill, but she did not. She never wavered, at least not in public. She was the perfect complement to her doting, emotional, romantic and sometimes fiery husband. He liked to say that his wife had never been born but had arrived in her parent's house delivered by angels. He called her his 'For-Ever'. He well knew that his buoyancy was impossible without her; that he wouldn't have survived his worst trials, had she not been there. Their sons understood this too. And their grandchildren.

An impressive presence in any room, Philipp had a youthful energy about him which lasted almost till the end. In most circumstances he took centre stage. He was a born entertainer, a first-class after-dinner speaker, a first-class mixer with all sorts of people. There is only one mention of him faltering. That was when Princess Irene, wife of Prince Heinrich, Wilhelm II's brother, visited him in 1918. The family were living in Warnemünde near Rostock, while the Princess lived in Hemmelmark, near Kiel. In order to arrive in Warnemünde in time for lunch, she had got up at six that morning. She was making the visit in order to offer her condolences to Philipp and Mila at the loss of their last and the eldest of their three sons, also to comfort Hermann's widow, Winnie, the Englishwoman, the enemy, and yet nothing of the kind. She offered Winnie herself as godmother to Hermann's new-born, posthumous daughter. Mila and Philipp had hired a cook for the occasion and entertained her in style. Given the extreme shortage of food at the time, this alone was an amazing feat. But the most amazing feat of all was that Philipp and Mila were able to smile and entertain at such a moment in their lives. Nevertheless, they did. And they did it well. So well that it turned into a long day. After lunch, the Princess stayed to tea. She didn't leave till evening. Philipp kept everything up perfectly until the subject of his grandchildren came into play. His intention was to say that his grandchildren were his great hope for the future, but he found that he couldn't. He faltered. He remained an actor all right, but a bad one. He had just fluffed his lines. Yes, Philipp worked at acting, and so did Mila. They both played a part. His was to entertain, hers to support.

Mila gave and comforted and never asked for anything in return. Her ambition and her achievement, according to her grandchildren, was to make everyone feel safe, well-fed, loved and happy. For their sake, she would survive whatever life threw at her. She made herself remain calm, whatever the situation. She hid her tears, especially from her husband, and did this so successfully that her daughter once accused her of coldness. But she wasn't cold. She *did* cry. Buckets. But, whenever possible, in private. She had married a man who could, on occasion, be rash and impulsive. He went up and down. She stayed on the level. Philipp was the man in Goethe's poem, '*Himmelhoch jauchzend. Zu Tode betrübt*'.[10] One minute buoyant with joy, the next, flattened by grief. Mila understood this. She would always hold steady. Her first thought was how would those she loved react to any situation. How could she help them through? Years later, her daughter-in-law Winnie wrote of her:

> She dressed plainly and usually in black, her hair was coiled back in a bun, because her husband preferred it done in this way. She was the most wonderful woman I ever met. Quite unique. Modest and unassuming. She was the perfect head of the household. No one disputed with her, and her children seemed to know what she wanted, and what they ought to do, without any word from her. She ruled by goodness. They all knew that their friends were welcome in her home and that anyone who arrived would be invited to a meal. A wonderful hostess, she quickly made everyone welcome and at ease.
>
> She was also musical and a woman of many accomplishments though she never pushed her gifts to the fore. She had a delightful touch at the piano, spoke several languages with a soft accent, and had a particular gift for making delectable food. She never dictated or dominated. She was gentle. As were her children.

She was brave too, even stoic, as later events proved. And, in spite of her modesty, and in spite of the strong ebullient character of her husband, she was the strongest influence in the household. If there were family disagreements, she was the one to pour oil on troubled waters. Her presence acted like magic on her husband who was inclined to be quick-tempered and excitable.

'Quick-tempered and excitable'. Yes he was. And good at everything. He also played the piano and sang opera and operetta like a professional. He acted, he told anecdotes, he was funny, he wrote funny books (illustrating them with comic drawings)[11] and he wrote serious books.[12] He was a top-class sailor. He spoke several languages, he loved children, all the more so when they were naughty. He would clap his hands when, in a passion of temper, a grandchild flung his dinner plate to the floor.

'He has spirit!' he would declare.

He entertained one and all, young and old, rich and poor. One grandson wrote (long after Phillipp was dead, and the grandson an adult), that without Philipp he would never have become the man he was. Yet, yet … Philipp sometimes gave way to depression. Every time this happened, Emilie pulled him through. But she was to pay a high price for the love of her life, and payment started immediately.

Mila's first child, Thusnelda, was born on 7 August 1882. The name was unusual, even in the Wilhelmine period when the fashion was to search Germany's past for inspiration. The original Thusnelda was a Germanic princess, wife of Arminius (known in Germany as Hermann), who won a stellar victory over the legions of Rome.[13] Perhaps the victory at Sedan reminded Philipp of the earlier one. Whatever the case, he was associating bright moments in his country's past with bright moments in his family's future. This was not to be. Little Thussi died in April 1883. To make matters worse, two months after her death, a grieving Philipp was parted from his For-Ever.

It was another long assignment to the Far East. Two years. And just when Mila was about to give birth to their second child. They gave up their Wilhelmshaven apartment, and Mila went to live with her parents in Bremen. They would hold her hand.

SMS *Stein,* with Philipp on board, left Wilhelmshaven 16 July 1883.[14]He was once again bound for the Far East, one man in a replacement crew for a ship already out there. This was SMS *Stosch*, flagship of the East Asia Squadron and sister ship to *Stein*. The *Stein* had only reached Gibraltar when orders came for them to stop. The expected route had been through the Suez Canal, but cholera was rife in the Mediterranean. After much argument in Berlin, it was decided that the safest thing was to re-route the ship round the Cape of Good

Hope. A much longer journey. About one month longer. Unfortunately, no one thought to re-route letters from home, and this was especially tough on a man desperate to hear about his newborn child. A telegram had arrived while he was waiting in Gibraltar, but all it said was that the child was a boy and his name was Hermann. Given Thussi's short life, Philipp was worried sick. He remained so for the four long months it took to reach Hong Kong.

The risk of cholera was something the Admiralty could prepare for. Not so the eruption of Krakatoa. Most of this small island in the Malay Archipelago disappeared on 27 August 1883. At the time, Philipp must have been somewhere off the west coast of Africa. The blast and its effects ricocheted round the world. A tsunami followed. The *Stein* was lucky to be where she was. The best place for a ship at such a moment is in deep water with anchor raised. Even so, Philipp must have experienced huge seas and a deep darkening of the sky. The volcano rumbled on till October, but the *Stein* was still able to sail past Singapore and arrive safely, if somewhat shell-shocked, in Hong Kong on 4 November 1883.

Once in Hong Kong, the longed-for letter arrived. Joy! All was well. Little Hermann (my grandfather) had arrived in the world in good form. Five fingers on each hand. Five toes on each foot. But Philipp's joy was soon mitigated. The trouble was, once again, a half-mad ship's captain.

The *Stosch* led Germany's small and new East Asia Squadron. Squadrons could be formed at will and ships added or subtracted as need arose. The following year, 1884, the East Asia Squadron briefly morphed into an East Africa Squadron, when it was joined by SMS *Gneisenau* and SMS *Elisabeth*. But at the beginning, in 1884, the Far East Squadron consisted of the *Stosch*, the *Prinz Adalbert* and a couple of gunboats, *Iltis* and *Wolf*.

Stosch had been anchored in Hong Kong since August, undergoing repairs and waiting for the *Stein*. She was to stay there a long time, till April 1884, long after the replacement crew had arrived. *Stosch*'s commander was Georg von Nostitz, and there lay the source of Philipp's grief. Never one to mince words, he described Nostitz as 'A cowardly dog, a glutton, a bully, a fat pig and a liar. He ran his ship on a network of distrust, fear and hate.' Of all the commanders Philipp met, Nostitz was the worst. One of his crew committed suicide.

Philipp had arrived in the Far East just before the outbreak of the Sino-French War.[15] France was trying to detach Vietnam from the main body of the Chinese Empire and, to this end, was ready to battle the Chinese navy up and down the southern coast of China. Cixi's empire was, in fact, being successfully torn apart by jackals. They came from all over. Not just from Britain and France, but also from the United States, Italy, Spain, Russia and even Japan. This is odd because Japan had its own problems in dealing with greedy would-be colonizers. Yet it too tried to tear pieces off China.[16] Yes, the boats bobbing about in the water alongside *Stosch* came from all over the world. Perhaps not so much jackals, but seagulls squawking for their next meal.

Germany's position at the time was slightly different to that of the bigger players. Because she was a late-comer, Germany was selling ironclads, not attacking the Chinese empire. Its Far East Squadron existed to protect the interests of German merchants ashore, and to show the flag to other would-be colonizers as well as to China. A visible and active fleet meant that Germany was in the game and ready to take advantage of every opportunity. In spite of this, concessions came from Berlin when, at the request of France, it delayed delivery of those two Sachsen-class ironclads to China. They had been ready to set sail, but instead, the *Dingyuan* and *Zhenyuan* stayed in the Vulcan docks in Stettin. They remained there till after the war was over.

On his first trip to China, Philipp had spent most time in the north near the capital, but now, given that the dispute between France and China was over land in the south, Philipp's squadron kept to more southerly ports such as Hong Kong, Swatow (Shantou), Amoy and Shanghai. In the spring of 1884, shortly before hostilities between the French and Chinese navies broke out, *Stosch* sailed from Shanghai to Nagasaki, Kobe and Yokohama, treaty ports in Japan. The German navy used the dockyard in Nagasaki as one of its main East Asia repair bases. In Kobe, *Stosch* officers met the German consul and probably enjoyed Germany's Club Concordia, founded in 1868, the oldest social club in the foreign settlement,[17] while in Yokohama, the well-equipped German Medical Hospital, with its cluster of associated German teachers and doctors, as well as Yokohama's German traders, would have welcomed officers and crew to the foreign settlement.

By July the squadron was back in Shanghai. War was in the offing. It broke out with the Battle of Foochow (Fuzhou) on 24 August, yet another humiliation for China. Over 3,000 Chinese sailors died, while French losses were comparatively trivial. It was a reminder no one could ignore. China needed a strong modern navy. Some foreigners observed the battle at close hand. British and American vessels stood by as their officers watched. The French used, for the first time, spar-torpedoes to ram and blow up enemy vessels. Torpedoes were soon to figure large in Philipp's life and, later on, in the life of his son Hermann. During this battle, the German squadron was generally anchored to the north, at Shanghai, probably concerned about possible riots and the looting of foreign settlements by a furious Chinese population. The squadron remained there, occasionally sailing south down the Chinese coast as far south as Hong Kong. In February 1885 it narrowly missed finding itself in the midst of the next encounter, the Battle of Shipu, on 14 February. But by March, with still one month to go before the end of the Sino-French War, new orders arrived from Germany. The squadron was to abandon its China operation and travel to Australia. Off they sailed, and not with friendly intent.

Australia, or rather New South Wales and Queensland, had eyes on New Guinea. But New Guinea was also one of Germany's target areas for colonization. The north-eastern quarter of the island was already under German protection and was known as Kaiser Wilhelmsland. But the Governors of New South Wales and Queensland considered New Guinea to be in Australia's sphere of interest and objected to German ambitions. So much so that, in March 1883, the Premier of Queensland, unilaterally proclaimed the annexation of Kaiser Wilhelmsland. London was shocked and upset. Berlin even more so. And that is why, in March 1885, *Stosch* had been sent south. They were heading for Sydney to settle the matter, one way or another.

They sailed east of the Philippines, across the Moluccan Sea to Halmahera Island.[18] Papua New Guinea lay to their east and the Celebes (Sulawesi) to the west. After a pause, on they sailed, further south, to Ambon Island,[19] then through the Banda Sea and the Arafura Sea. Lastly, the ships entered the Torres Straits, which separate New Guinea from the north of Australia. What an idyllic cruise. Palm trees. Translucent, turquoise seas. Peaceful islands. Some of them uninhabited except for birds which wheeled and called in the sunshine. If ever there was a halcyon cruise, this was it. But it wasn't halcyon. Not at all. The 'cowardly dog, a glutton, a bully, a fat pig and a liar' was with them. Nostitz was on board.

They sailed down the Great Barrier Reef to Cooktown,[20] Brisbane and finally, on 7 May 1885, they reached Sydney. The journey had taken so long that, by the time they arrived the issue had been settled. Amicably. Proper diplomacy. Gunboats not required.

New orders. The little fleet, with *Stosch* still as flagship, was to transform itself into an East Africa squadron. Instead of manning gunboats in a scramble for the Far East, they were to take part in the scramble for Africa. Trouble was brewing with the Sultan of Zanzibar. Dr Karl Peters, founder of a German colonization society, had arrived on the mainland, off Zanzibar in 1884. He concluded treaties of friendship with local chiefs and laid claim to large tracts of the land lying between the coast and Kilimanjaro (which is about 400km from the sea). This land was nominally under the control of the Sultan of Zanzibar. Dr Peters and the Sultan were at cross-purposes.

While Germany already held a significant amount of territory in west Africa,[21] it had little in the east. Until Peters arrived, that is. *Stosch* was to help persuade the Sultan, by force if necessary, to cede control of this land to Germany.

First stop, Port Louis,[22] Mauritius. This was where Philipp's problems were solved. The squadron's Commodore, Admiral Karl Paschen, ordered his fleet to set sail from Port Louis on a Friday. Now sailors, traditional, superstitious sailors, the kind, of course, which no longer exists, never leave port on a Friday. Nostitz was traditional. Most traditional. And very superstitious. But he had to obey. What else could he do? Result? As soon as his ship left harbour, he keeled over and fell down dead. Some said it was shock, some that it was a heart attack, some said it was fear of having to fight the Sultan of Zanzibar, and others that it was greed. He used to eat in the ship's mess. All had noted that while one piece of food was in his mouth, another was on his fork and he was eyeing up a third for his next forkful. In short, he was a glutton. In addition, he had overdone the cucumber salad the previous evening. Whatever, the reason, the sadistic captain disappeared off the scene, and everyone breathed a sigh of relief.

Philipp's life improved no end, but nothing improved it more than after sailing via Cape Town, Cameroon and the Cape Verde Islands, he arrived home in December 1885 and met his firstborn son, Hermann. My grandfather was two and half years old when he first saw his father.

'*Papa. Raus*!' he said that first evening (Papa. Out!).

The three of them were standing in the bedroom. This was the beginning of a new family life. As if to mark the occasion, in November 1886 the navy transferred Philipp from Wilhelmshaven to Kiel. He joined the 1st Shipyard Division. A new place. A new life.

Chapter 3

Kiel

Kiel is the capital of the flat, windswept, northern state of Schleswig-Holstein. It sits at the base of the Jutland Peninsula, with Denmark to the north. No one is quite sure whether it is more Danish than German, or vice versa. But all agree that it is a sailors' town. A Baltic sailors' town. Looking east, down the broad sweep of the Kieler Fjord, it holds a key position on a quasi-inland sea, one which unites Scandinavia, Russia and the North German Plain. The only sea-route from the Baltic to the rest of the world lies to the north, through narrow and shallow straits (called 'The Sound') which separate Denmark from Sweden. These straits lead, through the gulfs of Kattegat and Skagerrak, across the North Sea to the Atlantic and the rest of the world. The journey from Kiel to the North Sea was, and is, a long one if you sail via The Sound. The distance was halved when the Kiel Canal was cut across the base of the Jutland Peninsula. Once that happened (it was opened on 20 June 1895), German warships from the big naval base in Wilhelmshaven on the North Sea could quickly join the Baltic fleet lying at anchor in Kiel, without having to sail through international waters.

Kiel was and is also a fishermen's town. Every day, local boats bring their catch to quayside markets and fish halls around the docks. But in Philipp's day, the economic and social heart of the city was not its fishing industry but its naval base. Kiel was home to the Imperial Navy's Baltic fleet and therefore also to naval barracks, coaling stations, shipyards and moorings for an array of naval boats – corvettes, frigates, battleships, cruisers, torpedo boats, minesweepers and, eventually, submarines.[1] It was home to the nation's *Marineschule* (Naval School)[2] and *Marineakademie* (Naval Academy),[3] so all officers in the German Navy had, at some point in their lives, to pass through Kiel. And that's where we find Philipp and Mila in 1886. They rented a comfortable apartment, in a large house, at 103 Niemannsweg. They were in an affluent neighbourhood, along with the families of admirals and those about to become admirals. The social hub of their new world was Prince Heinrich, the Kaiser's younger brother.[4] Seven years younger than Philipp, he shared with him a passion for the sea and sailing. They had both made that gruelling round-the-world trip to finish off their training at the *Marineschule*. Both loved the navy. Both had worked with torpedoes. In Kiel, Heinrich commanded the First Torpedo Division. Philipp joined him.

Niemannsweg lies north of the town centre. It runs from Schwanenweg (Swan's Way) in the south, past the Botanical Gardens, Admiralty Headquarters, naval garrisons and the naval hospital, up to Düsternbrook Wood. It was, and still is, in spring, summer and autumn a pleasant, leafy, lively, walkable place. Yes, I have left out winter. That's because in wintertime it is different. The town and the flat landscape around it take on an air of desolation. A biting salt-wind blows in off the sea. It's damp and raw. There's rain, snow, fog, ice. Such weather demands, as an antidote, extra-festive Christmas and New Year celebrations. This was certainly the case at 103 Niemannsweg on New Year's Eve in 1886. They had much to celebrate.

On Boxing Day 1886, a second son, Georg, had arrived in the world, a Sunday's child, round and brown, with shining dark eyes and a merry smile. He was the only child born when Philipp was not away at sea. Hermann, Georg's big brother, peeked round his parents' bedroom door. Mila caught sight of him. Her smile drew him towards her.

'Come *Schätzchen* [darling]. Come and meet your little brother!'

And three-year-old Hermann approached the cradle beside his mother's bed. He gingerly stretched out his hand to touch the shawls around the little form. Georg. The first of his two younger brothers. Philipp had been away so long that Hermann, even as a small boy, had assumed a fatherly role. Seeing Georg in his cradle, a helpless babe, he felt a strong wish to guard this little creature. Not rivalry, not jealousy. Tenderness. Concern.

The birth was celebrated in style two weeks later, on *Silvester Abend* (New Year's Eve). To mark the occasion, two unmarried Kiel aunts (they were called aunts but were actually distant cousins) were invited. Mila's parents were also there. They had travelled from Bremen to celebrate the birth of their third grandchild.[5] But it wasn't just the birth they were celebrating, it was also their first New Year *en famille*. The first when Philipp could assume a role he longed for. Paterfamilias. He would follow the Silvester *Abend* ritual that he himself had enjoyed as child. Late that evening, Mila with the baby in her arms, Hermann, aunts, grandparents, nurse and maid, all gathered round the long rectangular dining table in the ground floor reception room. Philipp stood at the head of the table, a bowl of brandy in front of him and a box of matches in his hand. No one spoke as he lit a match and held it over the brandy. But as soon as the blue flame leapt up, the room erupted in chatter and laughter. Philipp handed round glasses. New beginnings for one and all. Change.

Two years later, and there was another new beginning. A major one, but with few celebrations. It happened in Berlin. At the ripe old age of ninety, on 9 March

1888, Wilhelm I, the Empire's founding Kaiser, died. His eldest son, Crown Prince Friedrich,[6] succeeded him. There was little rejoicing because everyone knew that Friedrich, of whom the more liberal-minded courtiers and government officials had once had such high hopes, was mortally ill. He had cancer of the larynx. He and his wife Vicky (the driving force in the marriage) had hoped that, together, they would introduce a more liberal, English-influenced, constitutional monarchy to Germany. That things would change. But it was not to be.

Only three months after Friedrich's accession, Philipp, recently promoted *Kapitänleutnant* (Captain Lieutenant), was in Kiel. He was just outside the harbour, in the bay, standing on the bridge of SMS *Bayern.* On one side of him, Commander Freiherr von Senden-Bibran[7] held a pair of field glasses to his eyes, and on the other, First Officer Graf Baudissin[8] leant against the rails, screwing up his eyes against the glare of the midday sun. They were taking part in naval manoeuvres. All three were watching the ships in front of them intently. Suddenly, there was a yelp. No one knew where it came from, but all swung round to face the shore. There they saw a black speck on the water. A torpedo boat. It was roaring out of Kiel and coming towards them at top speed. It carried a signal on its masthead. What did it say? No one could make it out. Something of extreme importance. Some major, national shock.

Corvette Captain Graf Baudissin shouted with joy: 'War!'

Yes, that was his reaction. But there was no war. The boat drew nearer. The signal read, 'His Majesty Kaiser Friedrich III is dead!'

The news was not unexpected, yet it transfixed them all. Wilhelm II, only twenty-nine, was now on the throne. They knew little about him except that he was young, energetic and, most important of all, that he loved the navy. Their first thought was that they would at last get new and better boats.

> Our current squadrons consisted of out-of-date ships which we were truly ashamed of. We endured this humiliation by reminding ourselves that at least our seamen were top-class. They were full of enthusiasm. But with the new Kaiser things would definitely get better. At last, better ships!

Philipp underlined those last two words in his Chronicle. Joy! And joy spread quickly through the ranks.

The young Kaiser's naval interest was, in part, due to his mother Vicky. Among the many British ideas which she brought with her to Germany was her attitude to the navy. In island Britain, the navy was the premier service, whereas in continental Germany, the army ruled supreme. Vicky suggested a different emphasis when she sent her second son, Heinrich, to the *Marineschule*, the same school from which Philipp had graduated. A member of Crew 1877,

Heinrich had been the first royal prince to attend. He not only attended, but showed aptitude and enthusiasm for the naval career which followed, becoming known as the Sailor Prince.

Wilhelm had a complicated relationship with his mother. He was full of anger towards her, as well as admiration. Her attitude to him was just as intense and contradictory. She was unable to give him the love she felt she should have given her son, especially her eldest, the heir to the throne. He was, from the point of view of succession, the most important child she had. But the truth was that the difficult birth she had experienced when he arrived had left her traumatized. Beforehand, she had been a hopeful, idealistic 18-year-old. She was confident. She expected to do everything perfectly, but she found that she hadn't. It was a breech birth, and when, after a long labour, Wilhelm was finally, with enormous difficulty, hauled out by the doctors, they found that his left arm had been deformed in the struggle. Vicky couldn't forgive either herself or him. Nor could he forgive his mother. She coped by retiring in her widowhood to lead a sad and lonely life. He, the new All Highest, the peacock on the throne, coped by insisting on a constant diet of praise and admiration. He needed ceaseless reassurance, an aspect of court life that Philipp couldn't stand. The flattery. It was larded on with a trowel: 'Your Imperial Highness' this, 'Your Imperial Highness' that.

In spite of his deformity, his mother insisted on treating him, as a child, as if there was nothing wrong. This led to terrible struggles on little Wilhelm's part. How was he to stay on a horse when he only had one good arm? But, in spite of this, Wilhelm carried a lasting love for some of the things his mother cherished, such as her fondness for art. He drew and painted, as had she, and he was, all his life, a patron of artists. He used art to confirm his image of the new Germany. *His* new Germany. A great power with an empire won and held thanks to Germany's new, strong, well-trained navy. A navy that could hold its own when compared with his mother's, the Royal Navy of Britain. No surprise then, that his favourite artists were marine specialists, especially those who painted warships with the handsome, black and white Imperial Navy flag much in evidence.

But it wasn't just warships he loved. He also loved yachts and competitive racing. He was a German Ratty living in a court, instead of on a British river bank – 'Believe me my young friend, there is nothing – absolutely nothing – half so much worth doing as simply messing about in boats.'[9] Yachts also allowed the Kaiser to show off. They gave him a platform from which to impress fellow heads of state. And, just as important to a man known for his restlessness, they satisfied his need to be constantly on the move. Yes, he was a Mr Toad[10] as well as a Ratty. Senden-Bibran, Baudissin and Philipp had no idea just how important the sea would be to their new monarch, but they were well aware that, with Wilhelm's accession, better days lay ahead.

Wilhelm II could scarcely conceal his joy. Only a few weeks after his father's death, he brought the royal yacht, SMY *Hohenzollern*, out of mothballs. She was going to be central to his new life. She would serve a critical new role, both for him personally and for Germany. She would become a mobile court-cum-embassy-cum-cruise-ship. Officially, she was nothing of the kind. Officially, she was a warship because she carried cannon, but her quarters were the height of luxury, differing little from rooms in the palaces of Berlin.

During Kaiser Wilhelm's reign there were three royal yachts, each with the same name. The first one was a rather old-fashioned but very luxurious paddle-steamer built in 1876.[11] The Kaiser, understandably, was not slow in agitating for a more technologically advanced replacement. The second one (to distinguish her from her predecessor, she is sometimes called *Hohenzollern* II), was launched in June 1892, though not brought into regular royal service till 1893. As soon as the second was launched, the old one had her name changed to *Kaiseradler* (Imperial Eagle). There was a third yacht, *Hohenzollern* III. But she had the misfortune of being launched in September 1914, just after the First World War had brought Wilhelm's sea-going life to an abrupt end. When any royal yacht sailed, she was never alone. She was usually accompanied by a squadron of warships, generally ironclads, and a number of smaller boats. They formed an impressive procession. They caused quite a stir.

Appointing his brother Heinrich as commander of the *Hohenzollern*,[12] Wilhelm ordered four ironclad warships, SMS *Kaiser*, *Friedrich der Große*, *Preußen* and *Deutschland* (each of these carried a full rig as well as funnels), to act as an escort, together with a flotilla of smaller boats. Philipp was on board *Kaiser*. They would all sail on an exuberant and showy summer cruise, partly to establish good relations with other monarchs, partly (where relations were already good) to consolidate an existing friendship. But above all, the trip was to celebrate the Kaiser's accession. The tour set the tone for German court life in the years to come. The Kaiser was to spend much of his time on board the royal yacht. Between 1888 and 1914, if you added up all his time at sea, it would probably have amounted to two complete years.[13] Philipp was on board either one of the escort ships or the royal yacht itself for almost all the Kaiser's sea-voyages between 1888 and 1892. This meant they saw a great deal of each other.

The first visit was to Kronstadt, Russia's chief naval base, lying at the head of the Gulf of Finland, opposite St Petersburg. The Kaiser was to see Tsar Alexander III, a fellow monarch high on Wilhelm's list of people he wanted to influence. Germany feared that if France (hostile to Germany since the Franco-Prussian War) ever wooed Russia, Germany risked being squeezed between two hostile powers. In 1888, Wilhelm hoped that his own personal charm would help to neutralize Russia and divert the Tsar from befriending France. He was mistaken. Alexander III was a no-nonsense, big bear of a man who liked to call a spade a spade. He did not enjoy flummery. He did not enjoy Wilhelm. After that 1888 meeting he described the Kaiser as 'an exhibitionist and a nuisance'.[14] Meetings between the two clearly did not bring an equal amount of pleasure to both sides. From Kronstadt, the Kaiser, with Philipp in tow, sailed on to Sweden to visit Oscar II, King of both Sweden and Norway.[15] Oscar was sympathetic to Germany and a keen sailor. The meeting went well. Afterwards, it was on to Denmark, to see King Christian IX.

As with Alexander III of Russia, Wilhelm seems to have been unaware of Christian's personal dislike of him. But then, it is often reported (and Philipp was one of the reporters), empathy was not Wilhelm's strong point. This is especially evident in the case of Christian IX, whose anti-Prussian prejudice was completely understandable. He hadn't been keen on Germany since the War of 1864, when Germany forced Denmark to cede the duchy of Schleswig-Holstein.[16] Worse still, the King's prejudice permeated his entire family, and the Danish royal family, like Queen Victoria's, had married into significant royal houses all over Europe. One of Christian's daughters was Dagmar, happily married to, and the trusted confidante of, Tsar Alexander III.

Wilhelm II spent much of the first two years of his reign simply celebrating being Kaiser and visiting other important people. In his first year he visited (as well as Alexander, Oscar and Christian) Umberto I, King of Italy, Franz Josef, Emperor of Austro-Hungary, and the Pope, but those trips were by land. In the second year, the *Hohenzollern* took off again, with its escort ships and Philipp on board *Kaiser*. They were received by Leopold, King of the Belgians and, in the Netherlands, by the popular Queen Regent, Emma. Senior officers were part of the delegation. Philipp chatted with both monarchs and was taken aback when King Leopold asked for his views of the Congo.[17] Naval officers had to be well informed. Or at least able to parry uncomfortable probing. But the two most significant trips which the Kaiser made that year were, first, a trip to England, and second, a long voyage in the Mediterranean. The latter was the journey of the 'The Champagne Fleet', sailing from ball to ball, from reception to reception, from one glorious extravaganza to another. The first trip took place in July and August, the second, from October to December.

Glamorous as such visits were, from Philipp and Mila's point of view, the most important event of the year was neither of these. It was the birth in March 1889 of their third son. Small and delicate at birth, he had light-brown hair, merry brown eyes and full lips, just like his two brothers. He was born the same day, and at virtually the same hour, as the first-born son of Prince Heinrich and Princess Irene. They had called their new son Waldemar, an old-fashioned name plucked from a Nordic and supposedly heroic past. At the time of the birth, Philipp was on board SMS *Gneisenau*, part of the Manoeuvre Squadron[18] commanded by Rear Admiral Friedrich von Hollmann.[19] When he got home, Philipp and Mila pondered on a name. They had produced a child who was a twin in time and place of birth to Heinrich's and Irene's. They decided to follow suit with the name, and so on 20 March that year, in Kiel, two baby Waldemars entered the world.

In the summer of 1889, Philipp was on board the flagship, SMS *Kaiser*. He was part of a flotilla similar to but larger than the escort of the previous year. They were heading for the Isle of Wight. The Kaiser was to pay his first visit as Kaiser to his grandmother, Queen Victoria, a woman he admired and valued, and the commander of the Royal Navy. This was an important moment for him, and the fleet knew it. The Royal Navy was the best in the world: it was both a model to be admired and a rival to be outmatched. Philipp was one of many Germans to have ambivalent feelings about Britain.

The Queen was spending her summer, as she usually did during that period in her life, at Osborne House on the Isle of Wight, just a few miles away from the most dazzling social and sailing event in the world, the Cowes Regatta. This was held every year in the week following the last weekend in July. Sensibly enough, Wilhelm timed his visit so he could attend the Regatta first. Then granny.

The glamorous, showy and highly competitive regatta suited the Kaiser down to the ground. He relished competition and took the helm whenever he could. His competitiveness much annoyed the Prince of Wales who, until Wilhelm joined, used to enjoy racing himself.

In spite of the Prince's displeasure, the sailing community welcomed the Kaiser with open arms. On that first visit he was elected a member of the exclusive Royal Yacht Squadron, and, four years later, he won the Queen's Cup, the most coveted prize of all. He, in turn, over the years, established prizes of his own, among them the Kaiser's Cup for the winner of a newly instituted Dover to Heligoland race. Philipp found the enthusiasm contagious. So did the patrician British yacht-racing world, which benefited from the support of someone of the Kaiser's status. Also, of course, that world appreciated the money he spent on new yachts and on racing. On his return to Germany, the Kaiser brought some of Cowes' social brilliance back with him. He founded the Kiel Imperial Yacht Club in 1892 and instituted Kiel's annual sailing regatta, an important annual event to this day.[20] As the anonymous author of a 1907 article in the magazine *British Yachts and Yachtsmen* wrote, both Britain and Germany were 'under a deep obligation to H.I.M Wilhelm II'.[21]

Kiel, with its naval base, had possessed glamour before, but never as much as after Wilhelm II came to the throne. This wasn't solely due to the Kaiser. One of his main supporters was his brother, Prince Heinrich. Milder in character, less prickly, not so quick to take offence, Heinrich was popular. Based in Kiel Castle (right in the centre of town) and later at Hemmelmark (a house he built in the English style), Heinrich happily played second fiddle to his older brother. He was Vice Commodore of the Yacht Club to Wilhelm's Commodore. Heinrich was also keen on planes and cars, in fact, on all kinds of sport. They both were. The two of them were so integrated into Kiel's social scene that Philipp's daughter-in-law talked of seeing Wilhelm playing tennis on Kiel's town tennis courts, and scarcely causing a stir.

On to grandmother's house. In 1889, the Queen, with great acumen, had had the uniform of a British Admiral specially made for her grandson. The gift was offered together with the rank. Though it was customary for the Kaiser and other (usually male) monarchs to exchange uniforms, this gift of the Queen's meant more than usual – 'Fancy wearing the same uniform as Nelson at St Vincent; it is enough to make one quite giddy.'[22] Yes, Wilhelm, like most men in the German navy, Philipp included, was impressed by, if not even in awe of, the Royal Navy.

In return, Wilhelm made the Queen honorary Colonel of the Royal Prussian Regiment of the 1st Dragoon Guards, saying, 'My Army is proud of the fact that, by means of this appointment, it is allowed to number among its officers the Ruler of the greatest naval power in the world.'[23]

The Queen was generous. She invited all the officers and accompanying crews to a review of the Royal Navy at Spithead on 8 August and, the following day, invited everyone back to Osborne House, where she reviewed the German sailors. This was the first time that Philipp met Queen Victoria, but not the last. He saw her again on each of the Kaiser's annual visits over the next three years. He got to know Spithead, Portsmouth and the Isle of Wight extremely well. Twenty-five years later, that knowledge would be worth its weight in gold.

Meanwhile, in Niemannsweg, in September 1889, a happy but fatherless little family walked to school. Mila pushed baby Waldemar in a pram, her three year old toddler, Georg, held the nursemaid's hand, while the eldest, Hermann, walked beside his mother. He had turned six that July. This was his first day at school.

The first day at school is a much celebrated moment in Germany. The new schoolchild holds a brightly-coloured cardboard cone, a *Schultüte*. Hermann held one of these objects in both his arms. His was stuffed with carefully wrapped presents: coloured crayons, a pencil box, note paper, a ruler, fruit and sweets. He was on his way to the local *Volkschule* (primary school), where teachers taught reading, writing, arithmetic and ethics. Ethics? All young Germans were taught the following virtues: duty, diligence, obedience. Many years later, Philipp wrote that his sons 'brought a sound sense of humour to a deep belief in duty. They were serious, diligent and ambitious, but had honest, open-hearted dispositions. They were talented, brave and loyal. And one more thing: they were self-sacrificing.' They were taught to be so. A sense of duty, a belief in the value of diligence and obedience. The bedrock of a sound military.

In family photographs of the three boys, the two younger and shorter ones stand on either side of Hermann, making the little trio look like a three-leaved clover. Philipp described them as a Triumvirate which 'brought us only pure joy'. He liked to joke that their great advantage was that they were brought up by Mila, not by him. The father's absence truly did make a difference. It turned Hermann into a carer. In the afternoons, home from school, the three of them would walk, with their nurse, along the street to play by the stream in Düsternbrook Wood. Once, when little Georg fell in, it was Hermann, not the nurse, who jumped in and fished him out. In the evenings, when they were all tucked up in bed, he would tell the two younger ones fairy tales.

They were supposed to be sleeping, but instead of scolding, Philipp, who was in the next room with Mila, said, 'What's to become of that boy? He's too kind hearted.'

Like his father, Hermann's great passion was the sea. He made no objection when Mila dressed them all in sailor suits: white tops with blue collars in summer, dark tops with white collars in winter. They would walk along Niemannsweg looking so trim that passers-by couldn't help smiling.

Naturally their childless Kiel 'aunts' adored them, often handing out generous presents. They gave little Georg a miniature hurdy-gurdy for Christmas, or was it for his birthday? With Georg, the two dates came so close together no one could remember which presents were for which. Mila helped him slip the hurdy-gurdy strap over his shoulders. She put a large floppy hat on his head, and off he ran, into the street and on to the house next door. He wanted to show off to Marga, the daughter of Adolf Paschen (Crew of 1872), who lived there. When Georg refused to give her his present, she grabbed a book and hit him soundly over the head.

Those aunts were resourceful when it came to gifts. They gave Waldemar a toy Cuirassier's helmet, breastplate and sword. He put them on, aged three. Once dressed, Mila couldn't get him out of them. From that time on he wore sailor suits with great reluctance. The army was for him. And not merely the army, but the Cuirassiers. He wanted a horse.

All the children loved art, but each followed his own artistic pathway. Hermann liked to make models and draw pictures of boats. He drew with great accuracy and absolute concentration. Waldemar painted pictures of birds. He once painted a starling so lifelike you felt you could stroke its feathers. And Georg? No one was more enthusiastic about art than Georg. He was always drawing. As a child of six, he illustrated the stories his mother read them. There in the Chronicle is a pen and ink drawing. Don Quixote, a knight in shining armour. Many years later, in 1916, at Verdun, the artist became the subject.

While Mila was walking Hermann to his first day of school, Philipp was sailing in the Mediterranean. Forty years later, sitting in his Rostock study, he paused at the remembrance. Instinctively gazing east, towards the Warnow,[24] he smiled to himself. He was remembering the Champagne Fleet.

He had spent the last months of 1889 with the Kaiser, wafting through the blue Mediterranean, sailing from banquet to banquet, from concert to concert, from one glamorous tourist destination to another. What wild, joyful days those had been.

Chapter 4

The Champagne Fleet

The Navy called it the Mediterranean Fleet. Philipp called it the Champagne Fleet. It was newly constituted and its job was to escort the Kaiser and his Empress, Augusta Sophia, to the marriage of the Kaiser's sister, Princess Sophie of Prussia, to Constantine, Duke of Sparta and Crown Prince of Greece. The ceremony would take place in Athens. It would be the grandest, most elaborate, most patrician of occasions, the last hurrah of Europe's aristocracy before the Great War. The Mediterranean Fleet had to look the part. It included the usual four ironclads, together with the usual handsome bevy of smaller warships, the royal yacht *Hohenzollern* and the corvette SMS *Irene*, named after Prince Heinrich's wife. Steaming within sight of the shore, it was an impressive show. Those who caught sight of it stopped dead in their tracks, stared and marvelled. Great excitement. Much power. SMS *Kaiser* was the flagship, Admiral Hollmann was Commander and Philipp, Flag Officer. A Flag Officer has to look after the interests of his Commander, including his obligation of hospitality to the Commander-in-Chief (the Kaiser) and to whichever Heads of State and dignitaries he cared to invite on board.

The Imperial party travelled overland to Genoa, by train. First to arrive, Philipp and his colleagues spent their waiting time in the company of Italian naval officers based in nearby La Spezia, the biggest of Italy's three great naval dockyards. Italy was a friendly nation.

The Kaiser was mixing family matters with affairs of state, which meant he could fund the expedition out of the Chancellery in Berlin. After the wedding, the fleet would continue to Turkey for a state visit to the Sultan. The goal was to pull him, economically and politically, firmly onto Germany's side. On the return journey, Wilhelm would visit Elisabeth, Empress of Austria-Hungary, in Corfu[1] and, in Trieste,[2] her husband, Kaiser Franz Josef I. They operated independently of each other.

This was a programme close to the Kaiser's heart. Only two years into his reign, he was doing what he liked best. He was satisfying his wanderlust, flaunting his and his country's power and, hopefully, striking deals. But the expense grated on Philipp and on other naval officers. The Imperial Navy had been founded on the belief that thrift was a great virtue.

Thrift had been the watchword of its founder, Admiral Albrecht von Stosch: 'Thrift, thrift, absolute thrift ... and after that, more thrift'.[3] When Wilhelm II became emperor, an unaware and innocent Philipp wrote in his diary, 'We will show these new court people how well and how cheaply one can live.' As things turned out, it was the other way round; the court taught the navy how to live.

The Kaiser had little understanding of economy. He lived lavishly and spent recklessly. His quarters on board *Hohenzollern* were extravagant, and so were the meals. *Hohenzollern* sailors were soon living like kings, or rather emperors. And they were living like that whether the Kaiser was on board or not. The only price they had to pay was that, when the Kaiser *was* on board, some of them had to behave as if they were footmen, not sailors. Demeaning ... difficult. Sailors knew nothing about courtly Orders of Precedence. Philipp had to train them.

'Always serve the Kaiser first. Always. Always. Serve him first. Got it? If the Virgin Mary herself turns up, ignore her. Whatever happens, *serve the Kaiser first*.'

'*Jawohl, Herr Kapitänleutnant*!'

But at a banquet on board SMS *Kaiser* in Genoa, an Italian admiral turned up who hadn't been warned that it was a civilian dress occasion and arrived '*en grande tenue*'.[4] Philipp was at the banquet table, his view of the Kaiser blocked by a large bowl of roses. All he could see was Lieutenant Freiherr von Senden-Bibran and he was winking and signalling as if something terrible had happened. Peering round the flowers, Philipp saw what he had always feared. The Italian admiral had his soup; the Kaiser had none.

'But Sir,' said the steward afterwards, 'I *did* serve the Kaiser first. I served the Kaiser of Italy.'

While the ship was in Genoa, the real 'Kaiser of Italy' did indeed come on board. King Umberto I arrived[5] together with his strongly pro-German Prime Minister, Francesco Crispi.[6] By that time, fortunately, the steward had learnt his lesson.

A worse test was looming: 22 October was the Kaiserin's birthday. In her honour, Philipp was ordered to have the entire fleet illuminated. But how? Fortunately for him, the Admiralty had already sent for Siemens'[7] top lighting engineer. He duly arrived, armed with cables, lights and generators. He strung bulbs along every bit of rigging. From every mast to every mast. Along every railing. The fleet was transformed into a fairyland. A highly expensive wonderland. Following his orders, Philipp duly sent all bills to the Chancellery in Berlin.

Oddly enough, on the day the fleet was due to depart, the Kaiser left the Kaiserin to sail alone on *Hohenzollern*, while he embarked on Philipp's ship, SMS *Kaiser*. Perhaps he fancied travelling as a man among men? Perhaps he had had a tiff with the Empress?

Once in the Gulf of Salamis, the flotilla docked alongside warships from all the great navies of Europe. Great excitement. Much gossip. Who had a better-looking vessel? Which navy was best turned out? Passengers and officers disembarked, and carriages took them into a celebratory Athens. Its streets were garlanded with flowers and hung with flags. The next few days were crammed with banquets, concerts, receptions, soirées and balls. Then came the day itself, 27 October, the wedding day. Emperors and empresses, kings and queens, princes and princesses, politicians and officers from all the navies in Europe wore their most dazzling jewels, their most lavish dresses, their most stunning uniforms and every medal they possessed. Philipp already held several.[8] In Athens he added one more when King George I of Greece awarded him the Greek Order of the Holy Redeemer.[9] The wedding was sumptuous. Fantastic. Yet it paled in comparison with what came next.

As the flotilla sailed through the Dardanelles narrows, Philipp saw that each of the military forts along the straits raised the German imperial flag in turn, and bands struck up the German anthem. At the narrowest point there was a 101-gun salute. Great co-ordination and very flattering to the Kaiser.

The visit had started well and it continued brilliantly. Sultan Abdulhamid II welcomed the Kaiser and his party, lodging them in a lavish palace specially enlarged for the occasion. Mother-of-pearl and ebony furniture. Curtains of the finest damask. Feasts of exotic vegetables, aubergine and okra, served on gold plate.

The German guests were not only impressed, they were almost overwhelmed, especially the Kaiser. He decided to stay an extra four days.

They sailed in the Sultan's *caïque*[10] up the Bosphorus; they viewed Roman walls, Byzantine churches and Ottoman palaces. Wilhelm was happy, so was the Sultan. Everyone received an Imperial Turkish Silver Medal, specially cast to commemorate the visit. Philipp the charmer received, in addition, the Turkish Order of the Medjidie, 3rd Class.[11] Apart from the dazzle, the Sultan and Wilhelm had agreed business deals: German guns for the Turkish army.

On its way home, the squadron visited the Empress Elisabeth in Corfu (the Kaiser later bought the land she owned there). The next stop was Trieste, where, in December, the Austrian Emperor held a naval review of his fleet and gave a dinner for officers in Adelsberg, followed by a tour of the famous caves.[12] Philipp kept the menu. It was a fabulous travel experience for everyone, not just the Kaiser.

The Kaiser returned home that December, but the Champagne Fleet stayed on, anchoring off British-held Malta in February 1890. And there Philipp was given one final glamorous keepsake of his time with the Champagne Fleet: a handwritten letter from Ludwig, Prince of Battenberg, Commander of HMS *Scout*,[13] inviting him to a last champagne breakfast.

The Kaiser was spending unusually long periods of time away from Germany, and Philipp was spending far too long away from his family. Fortunately, his next major assignment was closer to home. In August 1890, the Kaiser attended a ceremony marking the formal handover of the Island of Heligoland to Germany. The occasion was partly the consequence of Philipp's 1885 cruise with the East Africa Squadron which had been sent to Zanzibar to intimidate the Sultan into abdicating his rights over land claimed by Germany. Five years later, with Britain involved because it too had colonial interest in East Africa, the Heligoland-Zanzibar Treaty provided for a settlement of competing interests. Britain gave Germany Heligoland in exchange for Germany ceding its claims over Zanzibar and other territory in East Africa. The Treaty proved a good deal for Germany. Heligoland was an important submarine base in the war which broke out twenty-four years later. In 1890, when the Kaiser arrived on the island together with his escort fleet, Philipp was on board *Kaiser*.

Shortly after the Heligoland ceremony, Wilhelm, with Philipp in tow, repeated a sea voyage he had first made the year before, and which he repeated every year, right up to and including 1914. After taking part in the Cowes Regatta, he would take a two- to three-week holiday sailing up the west coast of Norway in *Hohenzollern*, a few escort vessels in his wake. This was his annual *Nordlandreise* (Journey to the North). He had fallen in love with the dramatic scenery of the Norwegian fjords, the bracing climate, the rough seas and the mysterious drama of the Nordic legends. He saw the area as the cradle of a hardy Germanic people and himself as their leader and protector. His *Nordlandreisen* gave him a clear sense of his own place in the universe.

Though a man of luxury himself, he was impressed by the tough life of those who lived in little settlements along the coast. Visiting them year after year, a bond grew up between him and the locals. He became a popular figure in Norway, especially when he sent warships to bring disaster relief to one of his favourite little settlements when it was ravaged by fire. He is still, to this day, spoken of well in Norway. His legacy lasted. He brought the area wealth when he inaugurated tours of the fjords. Many have followed suit, and they did so even during his lifetime. Whenever it was known that the Kaiser was present, others would gather, either at sea or on shore. They would ask for autographs and he would affably oblige.

These were not easy trips from the navigator's point of view. The Kaiser liked to travel well beyond the Arctic Circle, to North Cape in northernmost Norway. North Cape is so far north that only the Svalbard Archipelago separates it from the Pole. It is also dramatic. Three-hundred-metre cliffs plunge down from a plateau into a turbulent sea, where currents from the Atlantic Ocean meet those from the Arctic's Barents Sea. The Kaiser, his guests, officers and crew would land, climb to the plateau and wonder at the remoteness of the place, the stunning, panoramic views and the awesome power of the elements. It is an ideal place from which to view the Aurora Borealis, and in summer, to experience the midnight sun.

Philipp was with the Kaiser on these cruises because, following the Champagne Cruise, Wilhelm had personally asked Philipp to transfer to SMY *Hohenzollern*. Philipp became a 'Hohenzollernmann', first as Flag Officer, then Navigation officer, and finally First Officer and Commander.

But Philipp's role was rather broader than his job title suggests. Each year, the Kaiser invited a few select male guests to travel with him: a scientist to make meteorological and oceanographic observations, a marine artist to give him drawing lessons. To while away the time, especially in the evenings, as was usual on cruises, anyone with any entertainment gifts (and Philipp had many) had to lend a hand. Philipp played so many games of skat[14] with the Kaiser on board *Hohenzollern* that, at the end of his life, he had a pile of IOUs all signed 'I.R.' (Imperator Rex).[15] Philipp also sang, extremely well. He was particularly keen on operetta, as was the Kaiser. The latter knew by heart the words of the Admiral's song, 'When I was a Lad', from *HMS Pinafore*.[16] So did Philipp. Imagine, then, how they spent some of those evenings. Imagine who joined in the chorus. Imagine with what relish they sang

> When I was a lad I served a term
> As office boy to an Attorney's firm.
> I cleaned the windows and I swept the floor,
> And I polished up the handle of the big front door.
> I polished up that handle so carefully
> That now I am the Ruler of the Queen's Navee!

The thought that the Queen's Navy had fools in it was a particularly good joke. Much appreciated.

W.S. Gilbert's wit (which comes over so perfectly in that song), often plays with the absurdity of the promotion to high rank of people who are actually blatantly incompetent. Philipp thought the same and he had witnessed it often, particularly in the navy. Several times in his Chronicles he described some of the Kaiser's wartime appointments as 'operetta admirals'. I like to imagine those summer evenings on the *Hohenzollern*. Moored off the fjords, Philipp is singing that wonderful song. Guests are laughing. The Kaiser joins in.

It wasn't just the officers who entertained. Day-time entertainment included ratings diving off a high board fitted to the top deck, above the paddle wheel. They did back-flips and somersaults into the water far below. Sometimes they cobbled together ramshackle one-man-operated, craft. They would hold races in the water or battle each other, to much laughter from the Kaiser and his guests leaning over the rails above. These were schoolboy larks which sometimes went too far. The Kaiser would make his elderly guests take keep-fit classes on deck. As they did their squats, he would creep up from behind and cruelly push them over. At other times, he cut their braces. On board, it was the Kaiser's world.

The Kaiser was someone very difficult to describe. People disagreed about him; some liked him, others did not. In Norway he was nicknamed the 'Travelling Emperor', which Norwegians saw as a positive description. He was a man who loved sailing the fjords and brought prosperity to their shores. Berliners had a different viewpoint. They claimed that I. R., the initials which followed his signature, stood not for Imperator Rex, but for *Immer Reisebereit* (always ready to travel). Not purposeful travel, but random, at the drop of a hat. Travel for travel's sake. You find the same contradictions in Philipp's view of Wilhelm. On the one hand, he and the Kaiser were great friends. The Kaiser always waved when they passed each other in the street, or when the Kaiser, in the royal car, saw Phillip, standing on the back of a tram. The Kaiser never forgot a friend. When things went badly wrong for Philipp, the Kaiser personally asked after him. He asked to be sent reports. And he remembered Philipp's birthday. He always sent him a birthday card, even long after the war was over. Even when the Kaiser was in exile, living at Apeldoorn in Holland.[17] Typical of the Kaiser's thoughtfulness, he sent Philipp and Mila a gift to celebrate their golden wedding anniversary in 1931. It arrived in a cardboard tube, the address written in the Kaiser's hand and the tube sealed with red sealing wax. Inside was a large coloured print of Wilhelm in dazzling military attire. He looked wonderfully imperious. A terrific uniform. Every inch an Emperor. An accompanying note ended with Wilhelm remarking jovially, in a north German dialect, '*und nu rin in die Kartoffeln*!' (A peasant expression meaning 'and now, back to the potatoes', or 'back to work'). A picture of himself? Of the man for whom Philipp's three sons had died? Who was celebrating what? The Kaiser could joke. Philipp could not.

Writing the *Family Chronicle* in 1932, Philipp said the Kaiser was 'A first class actor, an outstanding braggart, an egoist beyond compare, a vain, unstable and incompetent disaster of a man. Worst of all, he was a coward.' But his eldest son thought differently. Winnie wrote, 'My husband was most impressed with an address the Kaiser made to his officers after naval manoeuvres. It was brilliant and showed absolute mastery of the subject.'

The fact is, after the war, Philipp could never assess Wilhelm except through a veil of tears. The image was distorted.

But the man apart, his world, Wilhelmine Berlin, offered everyone in Philipp's family some dazzling moments. Socially, artistically, professionally. Utterly dazzling moments. But they also led to disaster. As Philipp often said, 'Disaster and joy. They lie so close together.'

Chapter 5

Hohenzollernmann

The world could scarcely have been a sunnier place. Three delicious small boys. One loving wife. A comfortable home. A fantastic job. Philipp spent his working life aboard the Kaiser's yacht and, when the Kaiser was on board, which was much of the time between April and October, he was in everyday contact with a man who ruled an empire. The Kaiser clearly enjoyed Philipp's company, perhaps he was even fond of him. Yes, I think I can say that. The Kaiser was fond of Philipp.

In every sense, Philipp had been on a long journey. Remember Königsberg harbour? How impressed he had been by the uniforms, the *savoire faire* of the harbourmaster and his mates? And now? There stood the Kaiser. Few knew better how to dazzle in uniform. And as for *savoire faire*, it was Philipp himself who now possessed it. Every officer was assessed annually by commanders. Their reports went to the Naval Cabinet in Berlin. In 1899, Philipp's report declared that he was a man with top-rate intelligence and great abilities as a seaman. His work was good 'and in some cases, outstanding'.[1]

But a tragedy was unfolding which would engulf them all: Philipp, his happy family and his young, successful country. It started with Germany's feeling of encirclement, a fear which arose from the moment the German Empire was born and retook Elsass-Lothringen. Just as Germany had long been thirsting for revenge, now France felt the same, and relations between Germany and France took a turn for the worse. They were so bad that, in the run up to 1914, Philipp's daughter-in-law reported that the German navy was ordered not to dock in French ports. English ones, yes. French ones, no. The Kaiser feared that a vengeful France might provoke an 'incident'.

When new to the crown, Wilhelm had his grandfather's old chancellor, Otto von Bismarck, to guide him.[2] That was helpful. When it came to Germany's relations with France, he had to thread his way through a metaphorical minefield. Bismarck believed in the creation of networks held together by alliances and treaties. The plan was to isolate France and bind other countries to Germany. Of all the countries which Germany needed on its side, Russia was perhaps the most important; because if France and Russia were to work as allies, they could bring a pincer movement to bear on the nation lying in between them.

Whatever happened, Russia must *not* ally with France. Conversely, France must *not* be allowed to woo Russia.

But the young Kaiser did not like Bismarck. He was old, slow and cautious. He belonged to a different world to that of the new, young, energetic, impetuous Kaiser. Wilhelm wanted to be a hands-on monarch and he believed that he, personally, could guide the ship of state. He thought that he, personally, could forge, or at least influence, international alliances. He thought he could make people like him. Insecure as he was, he had surrounded himself with yes men. Could he do all this? Yes, they told him.

On 20 March 1890, Bismarck resigned. Or had he been pushed? Few knew. And even fewer knew that when Bismarck's resignation came, Germany's relationship with Russia was in jeopardy. Bismarck had negotiated a secret Reinsurance Treaty with Russia.[3] It helped keep that powerful neighbour onside by stating that both Germany and Russia would remain neutral if the other became involved in a war with a third great power. The exception would be if Germany attacked France, or if Russia attacked Austria-Hungary. To obtain Russia's agreement, Germany had made a few minor concessions, but after Bismarck left the stage, the Kaiser was persuaded that these concessions were excessive and the treaty should not be renewed. It was cancelled in 1890.

The field was now open for a possible rapprochement between Russia and France. Germany's reaction was twofold. Firstly, the General Staff started work on a plan to tackle the problem. What to do in the case of a war on two fronts? The consequence was the Schlieffen Plan.[4] This aimed to pre-empt any pincer movement by Russia and France by making sure that Germany struck first. Struck quickly. And struck, in the first instance, France. The German army would march through Belgium along the Channel coast and then swerve south to take Paris. With one enemy eliminated, Germany could then deal with Russia. A key element in the plan was the mistaken belief (deriving from Germany's experience in 1870) that a war could be won quickly with one *Entscheidungsschlacht* (decisive battle).

A second way of approaching the problem was for the Kaiser to establish a cordial relationship between himself and Tsar Alexander III. Solidarity at the imperial, personal level would surely bring security at the national level.

In the early years of his reign, the Kaiser made three attempts to win the Tsar's friendship. All three were made using his yacht *Hohenzollern* as the platform. The first effort was Wilhelm's impulsive foreign visit, only weeks after his father died, to Kronstadt in 1888.[5] Philipp accompanied him on an escort ship. For the next two attempts, Philipp was on board *Hohenzollern* herself. In August 1890, he was First Officer when the Kaiser, the Empress, Prince Heinrich and other dignitaries sailed to Reval (Tallinn), a major Russian naval port on the Baltic.

The German party were guests of the Tsar and Tsarina for several days. Plenty of time for bonding? Well, not exactly. Given Alexander's views of Wilhelm, and Dagmar's views of the entire German nation, no amount of time in Russia would have done the trick.

Things went wrong from the start. The *Hohenzollern* was four hours late in arriving which left a Russian Grand Duke and Reval's city officials kicking their heels with impatience. Fortunately, the Tsar and Tsarina were not among them. They were awaiting the Germany party in the town of Narva, on the south shore of the Gulf of Finland, about half way between Reval and St Petersburg. The German Emperor, his wife and entourage had to take the train to join them, which gave them time to reflect, gloomily perhaps, on how the visit had gone so far. The first intimation that all was not perfect was the fact that the Tsar had not come to Reval to greet them. The second was that they would not be staying in a royal palace, but in the home of a wealthy industrialist and banker. Fortunately, these thoughts quickly evaporated as their carriages rattled along tracks lined with cheering crowds. The Kaiser was happily reminded that the towns along the Baltic coast had such substantial German-speaking populations that these often outnumbered the local Russians and Estonians.[6] And of course, it was always satisfying to be cheered. The Kaiser smiled cheerfully and waved back. He was a great deal more popular with the Balts than with the Tsar and Tsarina. In spite of that visit, later that same year, those talks between Russia and France which the German military so dreaded, got underway.

Nothing daunted, the Kaiser tried a third time. In 1892 he invited the Tsar to Kiel for a review of the fleet. The Tsar had no interest in accepting the invitation, but he had to go because he owed the Kaiser a visit. It was, anyway, a trip he could manage without too much effort because, most summers, he and Dagmar enjoyed convivial gatherings with her informal family in Denmark. From there he sailed to Kiel, leaving his family probably laughing and teasing him about his inability to escape the German Emperor. Wilhelm was waiting for him on board *Hohenzollern*. So was Philipp.

There is a photo in Philipp's Chronicle which shows the Tsar and the Kaiser standing on the bridge of the *Hohenzollern*. It was taken between 4 and 8 June 1892. Philipp, First Officer, stands on the deck below, field-glasses raised to his eyes. He was obviously interested in the review. The Kaiser and the Tsar, not so much. The Kaiser looks detached, and the Tsar, positively glum. But the uniforms are terrific. Lots of gold braid. Many medals. Even Philipp had a good share, a glittering array, all earned in direct consequence of the Kaiser's love of sailing and his friendship for Philipp.

The Kaiser's tactic failed miserably. Ten days later, Russia and France secretly signed a convention which provided for mutual military aid in the event of a

German attack. So much for Wilhelm's charm offensive. It hadn't worked, and the die was now cast. Many historians see this Franco-Russian alliance as one of the long-term causes of the First World War.

Not long after inheriting the crown, Wilhelm had ordered a new yacht. This was understandable because *Hohenzollern I*, as she came to be known by historians, was, after all, an old-time paddle-steamer. Very out-of-date. *Hohenzollern II* would be top-of-the-line, *avant garde*, equipped with the very latest in naval technology and decorated to give all who sailed in her the latest in human comfort and the finest in décor and style. It would allow the Kaiser to feel comfortable vis-à-vis the British competition (a rivalry always at the back of his mind). After paying a visit on 2 June 1891 to see his new yacht under construction, he wrote that he was extremely pleased with the decor and furnishings and that it looked just like an English yacht. The following June, the yacht was ready. She lay in Stettin dockyards, awaiting the usual maritime naming ceremony. The royal party sailed there in the old *Hohenzollern*. The Kaiser gave a speech. The Kaiserin broke a bottle of champagne on her bows and lo, the new *Hohenzollern* was born. From that day on, the old yacht was renamed *Kaiseradler* (Imperial Eagle).

In spite of the new boat, for the remainder of the year, both Philipp and Kapitän von Arnim remained on board the old *Kaiseradler*. This was because the new yacht had yet to undergo sea trials and would not be ready for official use till the following year. Much to his chagrin, the Kaiser had no choice but once again to embark for his *Nordlandreise* on the old boat. The odd thing is that when, in 1893, the new yacht was ready, von Arnim became its captain but Philipp was left behind. He was given command of the *Kaiseradler*.[7]

No doubt about it. Something had changed for the worse. The glory days were over, both for the old boat and for Philipp. It seems a little unfair, for though the boat was old, Philipp was only thirty-eight.

Since shortly after Wilhelm came to the throne, Philipp had worked in close though intermittent contact with him. No longer. He was no longer the star of *Nordlandreise* evenings. No longer the man to beat Wilhelm at skat. Instead, he was in charge of the second best boat, and even that assignment was short-lived. What had happened?

By most measures, Philipp should have become an admiral. He graduated into the navy top of a class of twenty-five men, four of whom did become admirals. Once launched on his career, his seniors wrote an annual report on him and sent it to the Naval Cabinet in Berlin. The same was done for all officers. In 1889, his assessor wrote glowingly about him. 'Exceptional' was the word used. And he wasn't just good at his job. Philipp was well-liked. A popular man. Companionable. A regular sea-dog.

Yes, Philipp had all the attributes for success, except for two things. Two? Maybe three. He was so ashamed of these that he hid them as best he could, even sometimes from himself. Keeping a secret is a hard thing to do, especially if you are gregarious. It goes against the grain. It isolates. Philipp's hidden issues cost him dear.

Firstly, he was colour blind.[8] Seriously colour blind. His grandchildren would laugh at him. Here was this grand old man, who knew everyone and everything. He was the life and soul. Yet grandmother could never ask him to do the simple job of picking strawberries for lunch. He couldn't do it. He couldn't tell which berries were ripe.

Astonishing as it may sound, in spite of its rigorous entrance examinations, there was no test for colour blindness for recruits into the Kiel naval academy. For obvious reasons, this matters tremendously. Green is starboard (left-hand side) and red (right-hand side) is port. Philipp could never tell which was which.

As a young man, using home-made glasses, he carried out secret experiments. Surely, somewhere, somehow, there was a cure for his problem. He tried everything he could think of, manipulating coloured glass and prisms. But nothing worked. He couldn't save himself. There was nothing to be done except avoid being found out. It was a joy for him to discover, on his first job as Officer of the Watch, that his fellow watchman suffered from an even worse case than his own. Well, that's what he says in the Chronicle. In fact, it is difficult to imagine what could have been a worse case than Philipp's. However, the two men laughed away their sorrows. They sat together on the bridge, a blanket thrown round their shoulders, a bottle of brandy in their hands. And that was the second problem.

Perhaps in order to survive the tough world of the navy, long absences from home and a sense of inadequacy, some sailors took to drink. Philipp was one of them. At least, that is how I figure it out. *He* had a different explanation. He blamed his Russian wet nurse. When he was a baby, she once whisked him off to the countryside near Moscow to join in a particularly jolly family celebration. He met his 'milk brother' there (the nurse already had her own child), and to keep the two of them quiet (and free herself to dance and have a good time), she gave both babies the famous 'Russian vodka dummy', turning herself, in effect, into a vodka fountain. As if this wasn't enough to give him an early taste for alcohol, a little later, at the tender age of seven, along came the glamorous, alluring, fun-loving Mademoiselle Jenny, his French governess. Whenever his parents were out, she would take over the dining room. Standing at the sideboard, home to various bottles of this and that, she would conjure up a wonderful alcoholic concoction. It looked like watery milk and tasted of almonds. But when he was a child, he thought it was the most wonderful drink. The perfume alone transported him. It led him to a world he knew of from pictures in his favourite book, *A Tale of a 1,001 Nights*. Gardens, flowers, fountains and sunshine.

And the third problem? This is the one he scarcely mentions, except to say that when he was given his medical exam to enter the navy, the director of the naval school looked at the naked stripling and said:

'You are dark. Where do you come from?'

'From Russia.'

'Aha!'

Philipp was in some senses a foreigner because he was a Russian German, but he also looked, according to the standards of the time, Jewish. He was smallish, dark and with a distinguished nose. It's to his nose that he cheerfully attributes the Kaiser's wish to have him on board *Hohenzollern*: '*Hierbei hat ihm meine Nase gefallen*' (He liked my nose). And the Kaiser did. He used to call him '*Mein kleiner Jude*' (my little Jew) and once, so Mila told her grandchildren, he handed Philipp a decoration he had been given by Pope Leo XIII. Mila said the gesture upset everybody, none more so than the Court Chaplain,[9] a staunch and well-known anti-Semite. It upset everybody except the Kaiser.

Philipp took it on the chin. But he hated being an outsider. He couldn't deny being born in Russia, but he could deny the rest. And he did.

Of all his problems, the biggest was alcohol. He drank under pressure and, on *Hohenzollern* pressure was in good supply. It was a notoriously difficult assignment. The Kaiser, like his mother, was a perfectionist. He demanded that everything be impeccable. A less than perfect mooring, a worn rubber strip: these were crimes of the first order. What with this worry, and that of being colour blind, Philipp felt he was living under the sword of Damocles.

At the end of 1893, Philipp ceased to be Commander of the *Kaiseradler*. It was alcohol. He was so well liked that even when this problem was identified, he was treated with sympathy and even kindness. The Kaiser himself asked the Naval Cabinet for regular reports. How was he getting on? Was he cured? When could he come back? He was told that Philipp had 'undergone a course of treatment to eliminate the nervousness caused by the excessive drinking of alcohol.'[10] Philipp was sent for several treatments called *Wasserkuren* (water cures), presumably because the intention was to flush the system out with water. Lots of it. Philipp mentions one treatment where he was particularly impressed by the doctor in charge: 'Owing to a widespread drought, there was no water. So my doctor prescribed regular glasses of wine. Ah! God the Righteous. What a man that doctor was!'

In the end, he abstained altogether. At least I think he did. Who can tell? His naval reviewers *thought* he had. But they never seemed to be quite sure. In 1894 he was promoted to the rank of *Korvettenkapitän* (Lieutenant Commander).

Perhaps the Kaiser had a hand in this? He wanted to encourage him? Who knows? He was given a series of dismal postings which he didn't enjoy at all as First Officer on board different ships. During one of these postings, on 2 August 1895, his youngest child and only daughter, Lenchen, was born. A father with uncertain job prospects now had one more child to support. But Lenchen turned out to be not only a precious personality in her own right but, in the end, the only child to survive the war and accompany her parents into their old age.

Philipp's last Naval Cabinet report of 1 January 1895 begins promisingly: 'Mentally well-disposed, he has a quick sailor's eye and is rich in service experience and practical aptitude. He manoeuvres the ship very well.' Then comes the killer: 'The old vice of consuming alcoholic beverages to excess during great mental and physical exertion has not been completely overcome. He is therefore not suitable for independent shipboard commands, nor for positions in which he would have to lead an officer corps.' Signed, Admiral Koester.[11]

So it was time to work onshore. In late 1895, he became an instructor in torpedo warfare at the Marine Academy. Early torpedoes were explosive devices mounted on the end of a spar projecting from the end of a boat and used to ram the enemy. Robert Whitehead, working in the Austro-Hungarian port of Fiume for the Emperor Franz Josef I, improved on this by inventing a self-propelled torpedo which could be fired on or under water. After this, the word 'torpedo' came to describe, more or less, what it does today.

At the beginning of his career, Philipp had worked in Kiel's 1st Torpedo Boat Division with Prince Heinrich as his commander, but still, on his new 1895 appointment, he claimed he was no expert. He explained it by saying that although he knew very little, those who appointed him knew even less. ('I thought so little they rewarded me, by making me the ruler of the Queen's Navee'). But in no time at all, he knew enough to write a book. *Der Torpedo* was published in 1898 and it has survived to this day. It was reprinted in 2012.[12]

Philipp's situation looked bad. He didn't enjoy leaving the sea. Mila was worried sick about her husband although, of course, she tried to hide her worry from him. Yet as it turned out, it was all for the best. A few years later came another change. He was offered one of the most interesting jobs available to anyone who cared about the Imperial Navy. And one for which Philipp was peculiarly well suited.

Off to Berlin.

Chapter 6
Berlin

The three boys were taken out of their schools in Kiel, baby Lenchen was wrapped in a blanket, and the family took the train south, to the capital. Philipp had found the perfect apartment for them. It was at 4 Achenbachstraße, west of the city centre in an affluent, newly developed area called Charlottenburg. Houses and apartment blocks in neighbouring streets are built in the light and playful *Jugendstil.*[1] Though Achenbachstraße as such no longer exists, its surroundings still do. The buildings are elegant, wonderful examples of the curvy, innovative, free-flowing style which broke with the past. It suggests movement and change. I hope Number 4 Achenbachstraße was in the style, because the alternative is not attractive. It is the heavy Wilhelmine style, rooted in the past, the architecture of the new Kaiser Wilhelm Gedächtnis Kirche (Memorial Church) just up the road. This church had opened, with much royal and ecclesiastical pomp, only two years before the Gerckes arrived. Its grand, monumental parish offices still stand, opposite what was once 4 Achenbachstraße.

Ten years before the family moved there, Achenbachstraße had not existed. Berlin was growing at a tremendous pace, and Charlottenburg, sitting between the Royal Palace in the town centre and the palaces around the small town of Potsdam to the west, was growing faster than anywhere else. It was an ideal site for the Gerckes. Near to the Tiergarten park and zoo, near to the elegant shops on the Kurfürstendamm, to the Joachimsthaler Gymnasium, which the boys attended, to Charlottenburg Technische Hochschule (Technical High School), less a school and more a top-notch world scientific centre, and near to leading *avant garde* art galleries, which pleased Georg, the artist in the family.

Joachimsthaler Gymnasium was possibly the best secondary school in the country. It was housed in a handsome neo-classical building which exists to this day. Two statues, one of Aristotle and the other of Plato, stand above the main doorway. They are set in a warm, ochre-coloured façade and gaze down severely on little boys who must have crept through the big doors, in awe, on their first day at school. In the entrance hall, elegant round arches and columns stand on an exquisite mosaic floor, around a bronze statue of a young Pan playing his pipes. The building is meant to impress and it does. So did the schoolmasters. They had a reputation for high standards and severity. Philipp's boys all attended. It was five-minute walk from their home. He warned them to stand firm. Not to be intimidated.

Remembering his own experience as a boy when he saw Prussian soldiers exercising, and given little Waldemar's love of the Cuirassiers, one of the first things Philipp did was take his youngest son to the Tempelhofer Feld, the army's exercise area, to see the annual military parade. There they were. Soldiers. First, *Die Grenadiergarde* (Grenadier Guards) marched past, led by bands. Second, the heroes of the hour, squadrons of mounted Cuirassiers, dashing beyond belief. They wore spotless white-leather gauntlets, shiny black riding boots and gleaming nickel-plated breastplates. Their helmets glinted in the sunshine. What a sight, and what a sound! Trumpets trumpeted, flutes fluted, drums banged and hundreds of horseshoes clip-clopped on the cobblestones. Philipp and Waldemar could feel the sound through their feet. Waldemar was eight years old and quite transported.

'*Die sind unüberwindlich*!' he shouted with joy ('They are unbeatable!').

How easy it is, at any age, to get carried away by military show. It happened to Philipp time and time again.

If you couldn't walk from the new family apartment to wherever you wanted to go, you could easily take one of the city's new electric trams. Philipp caught the tram to his office in the city centre, and the whole family took the tram westwards out to the Grunewald on sunny summer weekends. Grunewald was a sandy forest of pine trees, crisscrossed with inviting footpaths and dappled with lakes. The children rented rowing boats and idled away summer afternoons on the water. And if you didn't care for outdoor activity, you took the tram in the other direction. In the city centre you found a wealth of new museums and galleries, many centred on *Museumsinsel* (Museum Island), a concentration of galleries and museums and an idea later copied by Prince Albert when he designed 'Albertopolis'[2] in South Kensington.

But why had they all arrived in Berlin? Because of the appointment of a new Secretary of State for the Navy, Alfred von Tirpitz,[3] appointed in 1897. His influence was tremendous on both the Kaiser and the navy. He believed in big boats, big fleets and big battles. He thought you could win a war in one battle. After one massive naval *Entscheidungsschlacht*. He was now in charge of perhaps the most important of the three naval governing bodies in Berlin.[4] As head of the *Reichsmarineamt* (Navy Office), he advised the *Reichstag* (Parliament) on naval matters, including budgetary requirements. Naval budgets depended on approval by members of the Reichstag. If you wanted more ships, you needed money. If you needed money, you had to have members of the Reichstag onside. The Reichstag was key.

But what did Reichstag members care about the navy in 1897? Not much. The tradition that the army carried all the kudos was deep-seated (then as now). Every schoolchild knew that Frederick the Great's well-trained army had been the foundation stone of Prussia's greatness. That Wilhelm I's army had made the empire. As Bismarck's winning catchword had it, 'Blood and iron'.[5] He wasn't thinking about ships. The army had made Germany great. The navy didn't just take second place; few people even thought of it.

This had to change.

In 1890, in a move strongly supported by the Kaiser, the *Reichsmarineamt* launched a monthly magazine, *Marine-Rundschau* (Naval Review). In 1896, Philipp was invited to become its editor. One of the articles published that year was the first in a serialized German translation of Mahan's *The Influence of Sea Power Upon History 1660–1783*. The message was clear. If Germany was to be great, it must have a strong navy. Everyone should be aware. As usual, Philipp protested that he had no qualifications for the job. This wasn't true. Philipp hadn't yet published anything, but he had a gift for writing.

Marine-Rundschau was so successful that it survived (with intervals for the two world wars) until 1989. But it wasn't up to the job which Tirpitz had in mind. Carrying little of general interest, it was essentially a naval paper. Who other than those already in the navy would read the translation of Mahan's critical book? To win over Reichstag members, Philipp needed a wider audience. Something different.

Tirpitz, like the Kaiser and like Philipp himself, had mixed feelings towards England. He admired Britain for its history and power; he was irritated by the British sense of superiority; and he envied Britain for all that he liked about it. One of the things Tirpitz and the Kaiser admired and envied was the popularity of the Royal Navy. How to make the German navy equally popular?

Tirpitz sent his two daughters, Ilse and Margot, to school at Cheltenham Ladies' College. He spoke fluent English and understood the British way of life. At this time, an exciting feature of life in so many British middle-class households was the *Illustrated London News*. This magazine, founded in 1842, was a runaway success in Britain because its publisher, Herbert Ingram, had had a brainwave. He was the first to realize that pictures sold papers. He filled his new magazine with pictures and focused on stories with wide appeal: stories about the monarchy, stories about heroic British explorers hacking their way through jungle which was either already part of the great British Empire, or was shortly to become so. It was the world's first illustrated weekly magazine.

The plan was for Philipp to publish something similar in Germany, except that its focus would be on the navy. He would produce a weekly illustrated magazine with broad appeal and insert into it as much as he could about the sea and ships. He chose the name himself and was rightly proud of it. *Überall* ('Everywhere'). A highly inclusive title, implying that the magazine was for everyone. It would primarily carry material about the navy, but also about the army and the empire, as well as articles on history and other stories of general interest. Its title, *Überall*, remained the same throughout the magazine's existence, but its subtitle changed, reflecting power shifts between different governmental interests and priorities. It was called, at different times, *Überall, Zeitschrift des Deutschen Flottenvereins* (magazine of the German Naval League); *Überall, Zeitschrift für Armee und Marine* (for the Army and Navy); *Überall, Zeitschrift für Armee, Marine und Kolonien* (for the Army, Navy and Colonies). It was a propaganda organ, and a successful one. Its success lay largely in its widespread readership, developed through its close connections with Tirpitz's newly founded *Flottenverein* (Navy League). The *Flottenverein* (Philipp was a founder member) was born one year before the launch of *Überall* and became *Überall*'s distribution platform. It brought together individuals and organizations throughout the country who responded to the Mahan-influenced argument. Build a strong nation? Then build an empire. Build an empire? First build a strong navy. It was essentially a nationalist approach. After a few years, the *Flottenverein* had 300,000 fee-paying members with a further 770,000 members affiliated through other organizations. By the outbreak of the Great War it had over one million members. All members of the *Flottenverein* received copies of *Überall*. A guaranteed readership.

Philipp's magazine was such a terrific success that in 1901 it was bought out by a private company, Boll und Pickardt, who appointed their own editor, Count Reventlow.[6] Philipp was out of a job. Fortunately, the Count proved a resounding failure, and two years later, Philipp was invited to return. He remained editor until the outbreak of war.

During that two-year gap, to make ends meet, Philipp took a poorly-paid job with a London-based German company, the Heberlein Co. Ltd.[7] It sold old-fashioned railway brakes, which, according to Philipp, nobody wanted. He called it (using English to express himself), 'A Company with a big name and no customers'. The job took him frequently to London and there he met Henry James Pryce,[8] a railway engineer and locomotive superintendent with the North London Railway. At first, this appeared to be an inconsequential encounter. It wasn't.

With *Überall* coming regularly into the hands of a large section of the population, the middle classes became increasingly supportive of the navy, and Reichstag members increasingly supportive of Tirpitz's naval budgets. He was thus able to carry out his ship-building programme, and an arms race with Britain began. Britain kept its lead (by building ever more Dreadnoughts), but the size and power gap between the two navies narrowed, so that neither side dared risk all in what they feared might be an *Entscheidungsschlacht*. During the Great War, Admiral Jellicoe[9] (heading the British Grand Fleet) consistently avoided pitching his ships in a winner-takes-all battle against Germany's High Seas Fleet.

In Berlin, life for Philipp changed a great deal. He had become something he dreaded, a landlubber. Yet his life in Berlin was in many ways better than his life in Kiel. He now lived within the bosom of his family. Clearly, this was somewhere he needed to be. He was a family man. His family mattered to him, far more even than the sea.

Life changed for Mila, too. In naval Kiel, she had led the quiet life of a grass widow, mixing mainly with other grass widows (Kiel was full of them). Perhaps they met to keep each other's spirits up while their husbands were away at sea. Or perhaps they met to share their contentment at having their homes to themselves. Not so in Berlin. Now Mila had a husband who came home every night. He had to be fed and entertained and was ostensibly captain of the household. That's what everybody called him, 'Captain'. He was spontaneous, passionate, idealistic and demanding. Mila and her children always fulfilled his wishes. But her tenderness, humanity and prudence softened Philipp's authoritarian approach.

Each child had a different relationship with their father. Hermann managed best. He was a natural diplomat who got his way through tact. Georg was quietly tolerant and cheerful. He accepted orders by keeping quiet. Waldemar, the brightest one, the most academic (and perhaps Philipp's favourite), got his way by using logic and discussion. Lenchen simply appealed to him as his only and much-treasured daughter.

In Berlin, Mila kept company with the wives of the many admirals based in the city, especially with Luisa, wife of Eduard von Capelle,[10] who was a great friend of Philipp's. Both were members of Crew 1872. Luise and Mila belonged to a weekly *Kaffeeklatsch* (coffee gathering), made up, with the exception of Mila, of admirals' wives. They met for coffee and cake in each other's houses. Also for gossip and mutual support.

In no time at all, the children found themselves thoroughly enjoying Berlin. Entering their teenage years, they were the heart and soul of the family. Every Christmas, they used to present puppet shows for aunts, uncles and cousins, with Hermann acting as writer, director and producer. The others would nag him to write something, but in the end he always gave in. The children presented their shows in one of two ground floor reception rooms, usually separated from each other by large double doors. With those doors wide open, the audience sat in the first row of one room, not far from the puppet theatre in the other. On one occasion, the children presented the dramatic love story of Kunigunde and Adalbert. Georg painted a stormy seascape backdrop. In front of this, Kunigunde, in a small rowing boat with Adalbert beside her, fled from her angry father. The sea was rough. Very rough. Suddenly, she leant overboard (on the audience side) and was violently (and noisily) sick. Waldemar meanwhile, was holding a pipette of water. Standing on one side, hidden by a curtain, he sprayed the first row of aunts with water. Shrieks. Laughter. More shrieks.

This was a time when home entertainment often brought families together. Almost every middle-class family owned a piano, and the Gerckes were no exception. Perhaps they were unusual in that theirs was a Bechstein grand, and everyone in the family played. Lenchen played the violin as well. They all played duets and moaned when the others practised. Grandmother Seeger often visited from Bremen. She taught them card games: sixty-six, piquet, skat, bézique.[11] She wanted them to be brilliant. She wanted them to win, yet when they did, she was shocked to find herself genuinely irritated. Philipp taught them chess. He, too, found he was annoyed when they beat him.

In her old age, Lenchen looked back on that time with nostalgia:

> My three brothers played a big role in my life, and even today, now I am old, I still keep thinking about how they looked after me and influenced my childhood and adolescence. How grateful I am to them. When I wanted to play, one of them always had the time to play with me, when I wanted to romp, I always found a partner. And how we romped! When I cried because of a bump or a broken toy, they comforted and helped me. When I groaned over my grammar or mathematics homework, they stood by me. And as I grew older, they took an interest in whatever paths I pursued.[12]

By the 1900s, new railway lines connected Berlin with spas along the Baltic coast and with mountain resorts inland. It was now possible, and soon became the general fashion, to go on family summer holidays by train. With Philipp back on shore, it was also now possible for the Gerckes to enjoy family holidays. Most Julys, a *Droschke*[13] would take them (accompanied by an assortment of aunts, uncles, grandmothers, cousins and maids) to the station. Once they arrived, they took a phaeton,[14] or sometimes a farm wagon, to reach the pension which Mila had booked in advance. With the help of her *Kaffeeklatsch* wives, she organized the whole caravan, including the choice of destination. Favourite spots were Sophienhof, in Thuringia,[15] in the mountains, and Deep on the Baltic.[16] Wherever they went, Philipp and Waldemar went fishing, while Georg painted and took photographs. He was never without his sketch book, pencils, crayons and water colours. Philipp immortalized some of their holidays in comic drawings and poems. On one such trip, they took a boat ride on the Baltic in rough seas, and the women were seasick. The family's in-house playwright enjoyed this story. He used it in his next Christmas production.

The year 1899 was the last time they went on holiday as a complete family. The following summer, Hermann was leaving for Kiel to take the entrance examinations for naval school, and the children had scarlet fever. Hermann stood in the doorway, waving goodbye, while at the other end of the corridor, his siblings, each standing in their bedroom doorway, waved back. A nestling had fledged.

Perhaps the person to whom Berlin meant most was Georg, the artist in the family. Paris was the centre of the art world, but Berliners, discerning Berliners, were following developments there with rapt attention. Impressionism was new and still, to many, shocking. The old guard, including the Kaiser and the academic world, favoured a realistic (in the sense of photographic) style, preferably with subjects that glorified the regime. This approach is perfectly encapsulated in a single painting: *The Proclamation of Wilhelm I as Kaiser of the new German Reich in the Hall of Mirrors at Versailles on the 18th January 1871.* The picture, painted by Anton Werner,[17] shows the scene (so mortifying to the French), when the German Empire was proclaimed. There were several structures in Berlin which carried a similar message. The Kaiser Wilhelmchurch near the Gerckes' apartment for one, and also the new cathedral,[18] but perhaps the best example of Wilhelm's nationalistic taste was the Siegesallee (Victory Walk).[19] This was a pathway through the Tiergarten, lined with white marble neo-classical statues of Wilhelm's royal Prussian predecessors. The Kaiser adored it. The public, on the whole, laughed at it. Overtly grandiose, it provoked the kind of negative reaction which expressed itself in a growing taste for satire. New satirical magazines such as *Kladderadatsch*[20] and *Simplicissmus*[21] appeared, offering, with their distinctive, modern, single-line graphics, an antidote to the elaborate Wilhelmine style.

Artists need to exhibit, but access to national and international exhibitions was, in those days, closely guarded by academic artists like Anton Werner. They vetted all would-be entrants and excluded those who did not conform. The result was a rebellion, led by Max Liebermann,[22] a Berlin impressionist painter. In 1898, two years after the Gerckes arrived in Berlin, he founded the independent Berlin Secessionist Movement.[23] Artists in this group exhibited in private galleries.

Georg as a teenager had two famous private galleries to choose from. One was just down the road at 12 Kantstrasse, where the architect Hans Grisebach[24] had built a modern gallery in a style which blended the whirling *Jugendstil* with the homely Arts and Crafts movement.[25] When Georg was nineteen, the lease ran out, and the gallery moved to 208–209 Kurfürstendamm, also close to the Gerckes. Popularly known as 'The Secessionist Gallery', this was where Berlin artists such as Max Liebermann exhibited. Members included Emil Nolde,[26] Ernst Barlach[27] and Wassily Kandinsky.[28] The work Georg saw in the Secessionist Gallery followed a wide range of artistic trails. Exciting trails. Daring trails. New and revolutionary. Impressionism and Expressionism were leading movements, but there were many others. Some led to Cubism, some to Surrealism and others to Dadaism.

A second place of refuge for Georg was the *Kunstsalon Paul Cassirer* (Paul Cassirer Art Gallery) at 35 Victoriastrasse, further from home than the Secessionist Gallery, but still within easy walking distance. This was the gallery and home of Paul Cassirer, a cousin of Bruno Cassirer.[29] The two Cassirers had an unerring feel for the modern, Paul focusing on art and Bruno on literature, though they frequently overlapped. They were literary and artistic connoisseurs. Both had been involved in the Secessionist movement from the beginning.

It would be difficult to overestimate the significance of the small Cassirer gallery. Paul Cassirer presented a series of ground-breaking exhibitions there, often bringing in artists from abroad, especially from France. This was where Georg first saw the work of artists such as Cézanne and van Gogh, and where he saw modern German artists such as Paula Modersohn-Becker.[30] Yes, Berlin at this time was heaven for someone like Georg. Not just for the pictures in the modern private galleries, but also, in the case of Cassirer's gallery, for interior design, debate and discussion. The rooms at 35 Victoriastrasse were exquisitely furnished by the Belgian *Jugendstil* artist and architect, Henry van de Velde.[31] The house became a meeting place for everyone interested in things modern.

Like Georg, Waldemar also had a clear idea of what he wanted to do with his life. Not painting. Not the army, or the navy. His interest was in civil engineering. This too, was *à propos* in a city like Berlin where a rapidly growing population demanded ever better infrastructure. The population grew from 41 million in 1871 to 65.3 million in 1911, a rise of more than 50 per cent in only forty years. By the 1900s, new municipal water supply systems provided the city with running water; a municipal sewage system and flush toilets were being introduced; and the city's first electricity supply company (Siemens) powered the new and highly popular electric tram network. In 1902, the same company also supported a new subway system.

Expanding with phenomenally rapidity, Berlin was in constant need of innovation in critical sectors such as transport, energy, water and housing. Philipp used to say that the city had expanded far too quickly. It was achieving in decades what, in other countries, had taken centuries. Berlin needed, more than anything else, a period of quiet consolidation. Time to stabilize.

Waldemar wanted to attend the prestigious Charlottenburg Technische Hochschule,[32] which had produced an extraordinary number of distinguished scientists, including Nobel Prize winners Fritz Haber[33] and Carl Bosch.[34] In the early nineteenth century, the language of science was German.

Of the three brothers, perhaps Berlin meant the least to Hermann because his life would, he was sure from the start, be dedicated to the sea. He had graduated from the *Marineschule* as a *Leutnant*. Two years later, he was an *Oberleutnant* and, in 1908, a *Leutnant zur See*. He used his spare time to teach himself Russian and, with a canny eye to Germany's naval future, made a special study of the Russo-Japanese War. The sea battles of that war were, and still are, second only to the Battle of Trafalgar in terms of their significance to world naval strategists. They were the first between ironclads; the first to use wireless telegraphy; and the first to use submarines, mines and torpedo boats. The war also saw, for the first time, the devastating effect of machine-gun fire. A machine gun could mow down an entire company in a matter of minutes. The Russo-Japanese War was a disaster for Russia, which lost and lost badly. The defeat came as a shock to a racist Europe. The first contest between a European and an Asian power had produced an unexpected result.

Hermann published *Die Schlacht bei Tsuschima* (The Battle of Tsuschima) when he was only twenty-four years old. It was the translation of a book by Vladimir Semenov,[35] a captain in the Russian fleet and one of only a few Russian naval officers to have survived the battle. A year later, he published another translation of Semenov: *Rassplata, Kriegstagebuch über die Blockade von Port Arthur und die Ausreise der Flotte unter Rojestwenski*, a wartime logbook written about the Japanese blockade of Port Arthur and the voyage of the Russian fleet under Admiral Rojestwenski from Russia to Asia.

While the boys were choosing their professional lives and moving towards them, little Lenchen attended a private school and took extra lessons in the violin. Perhaps one day she would teach music. Philipp and Mila were both proud of their children, though in different ways. Philipp wanted them to succeed, which meant that he wanted them to be financially secure. Mila focussed on their happiness. Her biggest problem in Kiel had been the horror of dealing with Philipp's alcoholism, but in Berlin her anxiety was about how her husband would deal with Georg's wish to be an artist. Artists were notoriously poor. Georg was walking a path which could lead to disaster, from some points of view.

Hermann once told Lenchen, having just read Thackeray's *Vanity Fair*, 'If I could only write just one such book, it would satisfy my ambition for the rest of my life.' His attitude exactly reflects that of Georg. Georg wanted to do only one thing, to be an artist. The cost of the chosen goal was irrelevant. He considered himself lucky to be living in Berlin close to modern galleries. He was also lucky because frequent visits to his grandmother in Bremen brought him into contact with the Worpswede artists' colony, a community which shared his views on how and what to paint. Georg and the Worpswede artists, like the Impressionists, believed that painting was best done outdoors and that the best subjects were modest, even humble people and places.

Worpswede lies in the marshy, peat-rich area north of Bremen and east of the River Weser. The houses in Bremen were, at the time, heated by peat fires, and Worpswede was the area which provided the fuel. Peasants dug it, loaded it onto barges on canals or on the Hamme River, and bargemen transported it into the city. Winters were chill. Those fires were a lifeline to the people of Bremen, and even more so to the Worpswede peat-diggers, who lived in small, timber-framed cottages with thatched roofs pitched so steeply that they almost reached the ground. Often shared with farm animals, these building were gathered round a larger farm house or grouped within the village of Worpswede itself. The landscape was flat, the canals dark. Willows abounded along the ditches. Groves of birch trees clustered around villages and farmsteads. In winter, the landscape was bleak. In summer, it burgeoned green. In either season, Worpswede's scenes of poverty had a beauty and simplicity about them which Georg had first sketched as a child of twelve, and to which he returned as an adult.

The rural setting had long appealed to Fritz Mackensen[36] and Otto Modersohn,[37] painters who founded the Worpswede colony in 1889. Among its most famous students was Paula Becker, who later married Otto Modersohn. Of all the painters in the colony, Paula Modersohn Becker is perhaps the most famous. Her style was influenced by spells in Paris, where she studied at the Académie Julian[38] and was inspired by Cézanne and other post-Impressionists. She developed a unique approach, one which appealed to Paul Cassirer, who held a retrospective of her work in 1909, when Georg was twenty-two. It was part of a series of solo exhibitions also featuring Matisse and Cézanne. These exhibitions were the talk of the town.

Philipp's response to his middle child's special gifts was, initially, to find him teachers. He knew many naval artists, all of them from the Kaiser's circle. Marine artists were invited to travel with the Kaiser in exchange for giving him lessons. He was also happy to give them permission, at other times of year, to travel on board his warships, hoping that they would produce work to honour the Imperial Navy. One of these artists was Poppe Folkerts,[39] from the Frisian island of Norderney. His liveliest paintings were not of grand ironclads, but of small fishing smacks, dashing up the North Sea in a haze of sea and sky. In 1904 Folkerts was twenty-nine years old and had just returned to Berlin from trips abroad on Imperial Navy ships.

That year, the Kaiser appointed Folkerts as art teacher to his third son, Adalbert (of his six sons, Adalbert was the one destined for the navy). And Philipp hired Folkerts to teach Georg. The two got on well, but after two years Folkerts moved to Kiel and Philipp had to find another teacher. He hired Arthur Johnson,[40] son of the American consul in Hamburg who was twenty-eight years old when he started teaching Georg and already a member of the Akadamie der Künste (Academy of Fine Arts). This suggests that he belonged to the academic school of art, rather than the breakaway Secessionist movement which Georg loved. Perhaps this drawback was, from Georg's point of view, mitigated by the fact that, at last, here was a teacher not obsessed by marine art. Johnson's style probably changed over time. In 1906, he was best known for landscapes and portraits. Today, he is remembered for the minimalist, linear work he did for the satirical magazine *Kladderadatsch*, and because he was, in the 1930s, closely associated with that magazine's antisemitic outlook.

In 1906, Georg passed his final school exam, the *Arbitur*. This was it. The moment of truth. Would he commit himself wholly to art? Philipp tried hard to counsel against this and sought third-party support. He gathered up a portfolio of Georg's drawings and paintings and asked professionals their opinion. Was the work good enough? Could Georg ever hope to support himself as an artist?

Georg was an attractive, amusing, rather dreamy young man. Women looked at him with interest. One of Tirpitz's daughters, although I don't know which one, was attracted to him. Whatever Georg's feelings on the matter, the prospect was hopeless. As an artist, he would never be able to marry her or anyone else in their circle of friends. The only artists Philipp knew who were not poor were those who lived off family money, men like Max Liebermann and Arnold Böcklin.[41] They could afford the life. Others risked ending up as social outcasts. Many lived daring lives on the fringes of society.[42]

It was always a point of great regret to Philipp that there was no family fortune. All he had were hopes that the *Erbtanten* (aunts from whom one hopes to inherit) might, one day, leave them a great deal of money. There were two such aunts in Kiel, while a third (again, actually a cousin not an aunt) lived in St Petersburg. Though all played an important role in the lives of Philipp's children, it was more a matter of personal kindness than the handing over of large sums of money. In the end, to Philipps's fury, the Kiel aunts left the bulk of their fortune to the city of Kiel, and nothing for the family. He read the letter which brought him this news aloud to his family. It was dinner time and they were all seated round the table. It quickly became obvious that Philipp was working himself up into a fury. Mila and the children girded themselves for the explosion. Only the eldest son Hermann dared face the hurricane. He had lived in Kiel as a cadet and had suffered, as they all well knew, from the indignities of living in a town with no municipal sewage system. He had built his own indoor lavatory, which was constantly getting blocked. He kept encountering problems of the kind that can only be solved with the help of a long pole.

'Well', said Hermann with a wry grin, 'If at least they make it a condition that the city use the money to build a sewage system, then it may mean that people can, at last, have indoor loos!'

This remark succeeded in defusing the situation.

As for the childless Russian widow, she had inherited a fortune from her husband and lived in a palace in the fashionable quarter of St Petersburg. Then came the Revolution, and the house vanished. The possessions vanished too. And so did she. Philipp was never able to find out what had happened to her, or even where her body lay.

Most likely, Georg hoped that he would have none of the difficulties his father foresaw. He hoped, I expect, that if he found the right woman, they would, together, find ways of resolving the sticky issue of funds. Other artists managed. Paris, he knew, was full of impoverished artists with companions. Whatever the case, he would stand by his calling and pay whatever costs were due. And he did. Hermann married when he was twenty-six. Waldemar got engaged at twenty-five. But Georg died unmarried, at thirty.

Philipp's consultations? First of all, he talked to Carl Saltzman,[43] a marine artist and president of the *Akademie der Künste* (Academy of Fine Arts). Philipp had gone straight to the top, to a man he knew from his life on board *Hohenzollern*. Saltzmann, like Folkerts, was a *Nordlandreise* art teacher to the Kaiser. His verdict? Georg was not good … he was very good.

Nothing daunted, Philipp made a second attempt, turning to Hans Bohrdt,[44] another ex-*Hohenzollern* art tutor to the Kaiser. Borhdt specialized in dramatic, nationalistic paintings of the imperial fleet. His verdict? The same as Saltzmann's.

One last try, then. Philipp turned to Willy Stöwer,[45] the self-taught son of a sea captain and, like Philipp, a member of the *Flottenverein*. He was the Kaiser's favourite marine artist. Stöwer confirmed that Georg was very good indeed.

The die was cast, and despite worries and misgivings, Philipp agreed to fund Georg's further studies. Once these were completed, he would be on his own. In 1906, Georg set out for Weimar, home to a famous art school, the Grand-Ducal Saxon College of Fine Arts. When he arrived, a sumptuous modern Art Nouveau building, designed by Henry van de Velde, had recently been built, and a second building by the same architect, with a famous elliptical staircase in the main hall and a statue of Eve by Rodin at its foot, was under construction. The Director of Georg's School was Hans Olde,[46] an enthusiastic supporter of French Impressionism, a firm believer in working outdoors and in choosing humble, rather than grand, subjects. Georg had landed where he belonged.

From Weimar, Georg went to Munich, famous for its Secessionist movement, the first such one in Germany. When Georg was there, the city was buzzing with young painters who have since become household names, among them Wassily Kandinsky, Paul Klee[47] and Franz Marc.[48] It would have been next to impossible to study art in Munich at that time without being drawn into a lively, modern art world which included these three. Kandinsky, Klee and Marc were Georg's contemporaries. The war shattered them all. Kandinsky returned to Russia, Klee returned to Switzerland, while Marc, like Georg, was called up to fight for Germany and found himself painting camouflage tarpaulins in Verdun. It was in Verdun that both he and Georg were to meet their end.

Georg returned to Berlin in 1908, to find that a pretty young Englishwoman had arrived in the Achenbach apartment. Philipp asked Georg to paint her portrait. It was to be a gift for her parents in England. Almost all of Georg's paintings have vanished, but I believe this one may still exist. Somewhere. It came up for auction in October 2004 at David Lay's auction house in Penzance, was sold for £10 and bought by a dealer who sold pictures out of the back of his van. Georg's painting went to whomever happened to be passing by. Somewhere out there, it surely still exists.

The new arrival was Winnie, my grandmother. A spirited, spoilt and attractive girl. A concert-standard pianist. Who could resist?

Chapter 7

Coup de Foudre

Winifred Alice Bessie Pryce[1] was a talented, laughing, adventurous young girl. She had been brought up secure in the knowledge that she was loved. Loved? Much more than that. Her father simply doted on her. Philipp used to say that the two of them reminded him of Bella Wilfer and her father Rumty,[2] not an entirely flattering comparison. Rumty Wilfer is innocent, fatherly and kindly. He has a querulous wife and a spoilt, demanding daughter. In the case of both the imagined Bella and the real Winnie, the daughter adored her father back. And both fell deeply in love (it took Bella more time than Winnie) with the right man.

Henry James Pryce was in some ways quite like Rumty. He was quiet and hard-working, a self-made man. With no formal training, he had become a railway engineer and, in the early 1900s, was senior engineer with the North London Railways, well-known and respected in London engineering circles and a member of the right club, the Institute of Mechanical Engineers. His father was Welsh and his mother Irish. That's another point that Philipp noted. Winnie was a Celt and therefore, in his view, passionate and excitable.

Henry married Bessie Collins,[3] and the couple lived in a handsome, semi-detached house at 54 Filey Avenue in Hackney, together with Winnie and her young brother, Wilfred,[4] a bright and kind boy who spent his entire life cheerfully living in his big sister's shadow. Bessie was elegant but defensive. Winnie described her early life and her mother:

> She kept her pride and charm of manner until the last. She was a proud and pretty stiff lady in many ways. She never once during the London Blitz went to a shelter. She said she wanted to die in her own bed. She was no friend of foreigners, whether they were at war with us or not. But she made a huge exception for my husband. It means a great deal when someone like my Mother, with such insular views, praised a man who wasn't British. In fact, she liked my husband so much that she considered him to be too good for me. I never admitted this to her. But I thought the same.
>
> My parents doted on me, far more so (especially my Father), than on my younger brother Wilfred. He really did get the thin edge of the wedge.

> Maybe just because I was female, I was the apple of my Father's eye. He loved to show me off. Once, as a child of five or six, I did some drawings, which my Father had helped me with quite a lot, and yet he showed them to everyone as if they were my work. Adults have no idea how sensitive children are to this kind of thing. Children's feelings can be inconvenient. I was in agony. Yet I knew he showed me off because he loved me, because he was proud of me.
>
> Music was my real skill and great love. My parents made me practise for four hours every day. It bored me so much that I would take a novel and prop it up on the music stand on the piano lid. We had a fine grand piano. I used to read while reeling off my scales. My mother was never any the wiser. I was six when they first made me perform in public. I was shy and terrified. That is why, in the end, I let the piano become a pastime and not a career.

Winnie didn't rebel openly. She did what was required of her. She practised hard. She went to the Royal Academy of Music. She went to Paris to learn French. She went to the best finishing school in Brussels. The *directrice*, Mademoiselle Mathilde, 'fat, tiny and very ugly', chose Winnie to play Franz Liszt's 8th Hungarian Rhapsody (not an easy piece) at the end of term Christmas concert. She played brilliantly, but never forgot the terror it caused her.

Brother Wilfred went to Haileybury School to become an engineer like his father. Winnie stayed at home, fighting off eligible young men chosen for her by her mother. These episodes were relieved by periods abroad. Her father would whisk her off and deposit her with carefully vetted families in Paris and Brussels, or he took her on holiday with him, to explore Ireland and see her grandmother in Dublin. But all the while he continued to hope she would become a concert pianist. Her gift was sometimes a millstone round her neck, but it could also be a stepping stone to the stars. In 1908, she was a few weeks short of her twenty-fifth birthday. She forced the issue and chose the stars. She would study the piano in Germany. And off she went.

> I was in Berlin to study the piano and learn German. At least these were my declared intentions. When my friends and family saw me off in London, they said, 'Now don't you dare go marrying some German chap! Don't forget to come home!' They were a merry bunch at the station that day. I told them that of course, no such thought was in my mind.
>
> I was met at the Berlin Hauptbahnhof [main station] by a girlfriend who'd given me a few German lessons in London. She took me to the pension where I had arranged to stay. For a short while, it all seemed

dismal. I thought I was going to be unbearably lonely. I had been abroad before (I had studied piano and French in both Brussels and Paris), but I had always stayed in families found by my father. And I always knew he would come and visit me. Often. That moment of despair lasted a fraction of a second. In no time at all, my mood changed.

The first thing I did was buy a street map of Berlin, the second was to look for a piano, and the third was to look for a teacher. I found one quite by accident. He was a very dear man and very old, but his teaching was a revelation, especially after the mechanical, orthodox methods taught in the Royal Academy at home. In London, playing had been largely a question of physical strength. In Berlin, I learnt to abandon myself to the music. And I did. And not only to music.

Soon, I began my round of calls. My father had armed me with a list of contacts and letters of introduction. I called, first of all, on a retired Captain in the German Navy. He and his family lived off the fashionable Kaiserallee. I rang the doorbell. A young maid answered and showed me into the drawing room: there I met the most endearing personality it has ever been my luck to meet – a small, stoutish woman with greying hair and a beautiful, sensitive face. I fell in love with her at once.

She made me welcome, offered me tea and persuaded me to stay for *Abendbrot* (the light German supper, usually pumpernickel bread,[5] cheese, sausages and gherkins). This was so that I could meet the other members of the family.

First, fresh from school, came the young daughter, Lenchen. She was thirteen, a musical girl who adored her three big brothers. She played the violin. Later in the afternoon, the youngest son arrived, Waldemar. He was nineteen. Last of all, the father, a retired naval officer, came home from his office. '4 Achenbachstraße' was his ship. Everyone there called him 'Der Kapitän'.

Waldemar had just passed his *Arbitur* and qualified as a student to serve one, instead of two years military service.[6] He was going to be a reserve officer but, until call-up, he was a free agent. The Captain suggested he make use of his time by showing me the sights. With typical gallantry, that first evening, the Captain himself accompanied me home.

After that, I saw a lot of the family. They took me to the theatre and to operas. The Captain was a great fan of both opera and operetta. He sang himself. He had a very fine voice. Waldemar took me to science museums, I went shopping with *Mütterchen*[7] and I played duets with Lenchen. She on the violin, me on the piano. We all went for long walks and excursions in the pine-wooded countryside around the city, and we rowed on the Grunewald's many lakes.

Why were they so generous and kind? They were comfortably off, but not in any way rich. Their attitude was that whatever was theirs was shareable. During the war, when they were posted to ports on the Baltic, they put their Berlin apartment at the disposal of refugees. It was their own inherent goodness of heart which prompted them. They enjoyed being kind.

My piano studies began to suffer. I had so little time. I dropped the other letters of introduction and gave myself up almost entirely to the cosy warmth and good humour which I found in Achenbachstraße. I was soon invited to move in and very much wanted to accept, but felt bound to at least appear a little bit reluctant. I put forward excuses but, to my joy, none prevailed. The hired piano went back to the shop. I left my pension. And I became a temporary member of the Gercke family.

When I arrived, Waldemar, the youngest of the three brothers, was the only one at home. He was five years younger than me, but very grown-up. He took me to science and technical museums, assuming that, just because my father was a railway man, I too would be interested. His chief love was the new Royal Museum of Building and Transport.[8] It had only just opened and was in a very grand and now disused station. The imposing halls were stuffed full of everything to do with engines. Yes. My father would have been in his seventh heaven, and actually, I was too. But not because of the engines. For me it was thrilling just to be in Berlin and on my own. No mother around, trying to marry me off. No father, forcing me to practise the piano six hours a day. Fabulous. Life couldn't be better.

My excursions were quite different when Waldemar's artist brother, Georg, returned home. The two brothers were very different. They were both brainy, but while Georg was artistic, Waldemar was scientific. His strong suit was maths, economics and management. He was also brilliant at cards. He taught me bridge and tried to teach me 'skat', but soon gave up. He was also good at managing money. We youngsters were all living off small allowances from our parents. Most of us ran out of cash at the end of each month, but Waldemar actually managed to save! This wasn't because he was mean. Not at all. He was always ready to help. Everyone expected Waldemar to make his way in the world. He would be secure. This was quite unlike his brother Georg. Georg's heart was entirely set on becoming an impoverished artist.

The second son was home from Munich and Weimar where he had been painting. He was a most attractive young man, charming, highly intelligent, artistic and very well informed. He was a delight to talk to, and very funny. He spoke English with a slight accent, and Italian too. No wonder that he was fancied by the young women we met, including one of Admiral von Tirpitz's young daughters.

As soon as he arrived, his Father set him the task of painting my portrait, and what a task it was. The Captain was always hovering near, criticising and making suggestions. It would have maddened me, if I had been in Georg's place. The sittings were interminable, and by the end I was heartily sick of it. But Georg kept completely calm. He was a calm kind of person. Nevertheless, the painting went on and on and, from the Captain's point of view was never good enough. Poor Georg.

The reason for the sittings was because my parents were asking me to come back. But the Gerckes protested and asked for me to be allowed to stay. In the end, the Captain asked if he could send them the portrait instead of returning me. Once completed (to everyone's dissatisfaction), it was put into a huge gilt frame (which must have cost a packet) and duly sent off. It did the trick. My parents relented, and I stayed on.

Now I had the advantage of going around the galleries with an artist as my guide. He took me to the big national galleries on the *Museumsinsel*, but the first galleries he took me to were two private galleries, his favourites. The Secessionist gallery on Kantstrasse and the Paul Cassirer Kunstsalon, on Viktoria. I saw the works of Impressionist painters like Max Liebermann, and we attended a large van Gogh exhibition together. These were the artists who did not toe the establishment line. I loved them, but many of the other pictures baffled me. They were so very modern. Cubism, Expressionism and so on. Some were really quite disgusting. I could see no beauty in them.

Back in Berlin, Georg started a course at the Kunowski School of Art, run by Lothar von Kunowski and his highly gifted artist wife, Gertrud.[9] He was more the teacher and technician, she more the painter, Secessionist-style. They both valued applied art and insisted that ordinary objects were worthy of good design.

Then the third brother appeared. The eldest, Hermann. In August 1908, he was about to be transferred to the Kiel Torpedo Boat Division. He had three days' leave in between assignments. Also, his third book, another translation of a Semenov work, was about to be published. Winnie wrote:

No one warned me. I wasn't prepared. I knew that, at some time, he (the eldest) would arrive, but I didn't know when. Perhaps the others didn't know either. He just turned up.

I saw a man, about the same age as myself, enter the room. His face was intelligent and kind. Quiet, interested, handsome. His short dark hair was parted almost in the middle, and beneath it lay this extraordinary, questioning face. I found it hard to take my eyes off him, especially off his full, curvy lips. Kissable in the extreme. My eyes were glued to them, and then, eventually, moved to his eyes. He had dark eyes. They lay beneath strongly marked eyebrows, one more questioning than the other.

I ought to have hidden my heart. But I couldn't. I was smitten from that first moment.

I soon learnt that he was gentle, forthright and frank. He knew what he intended doing. No shilly-shallying. But on the other hand, he never calculated or tried to make a good impression, either among friends or in his work. He was frank. He simply did what he believed was the right thing. And he did it to the best of his ability.

He had just been through several years of hard naval training. As a cadet, he had started every day with a climb to the topsail. Physically, he was fit. That too was very apparent. I was in difficulty before he said a word. But then he spoke. At that point, everything got a great deal more difficult. His voice was low yet bright. Burnished chestnut.

He was home for only three days but immediately took over the job of escorting me around town. We went out that very afternoon. Hermann's English was not much better than my German. So we chatted away, in whatever language came to hand, as we walked and walked all over Berlin. I don't think I was flirting. But I do know that I was utterly transported. And so two days passed.

On the third day, I was playing the piano in the drawing-room while, in the next room (connected by sliding doors), Hermann was busy writing a prize essay on naval tactics, or what he hoped would be a prize essay. He finished the essay and came in to see me. He told me he would be leaving next day and wanted to talk. He asked me to marry him, just like that, after knowing me for two days.

I needed no persuading. And the prize essay? He won. He won an engraving of Admiral Lord Nelson in a wooden frame. The picture hung over his writing table until the very last.

Getting engaged in Germany is a very formal event. Almost as important as getting married. We sent a telegram to my parents and received a non-committal answer. They asked that Hermann come to London for a fortnight. The next day, he left for Kiel, but returned again on special leave after only a few days. Then we went to London, where he was cross-questioned by my father on the subject of money. He was reduced to pointing out that Berlin was less expensive than London. Rents were lower and more favourable to the renter (far more people rented in Germany than in England), accommodation was generally of a higher standard, and entertainment was inexpensive. Lastly, he pointed out that, unlike London, few people in Berlin were very wealthy. Most were of moderate means, as we would be.

My Father was difficult. He didn't want to lose me, certainly not to someone who would take me abroad. How could I even entertain the idea of marrying a foreigner! My mother was worse. She couldn't stand foreigners. Of any kind. From anywhere.

As it turned out, everyone came to love Hermann. Even my mother. In the end, she decided that he was actually too good for me! Before those initial conversations were over, the Captain came over to England to back up his son.

We also had to get permission from the Kaiser,[10] and Hermann had to show the civil authorities in Berlin that he could afford to marry.[11] This was tricky since he had little money. There was even talk, at one point, of him leaving the navy in order to earn a 'proper' salary, but at this point the Kiel *Erbtanten* came up trumps. And then there was the question of a dowry. In Germany at that time, women were expected to bring a dowry. This annoyed my Father no end. But he paid, giving my brother Wilfred the same amount at the same time.

The Gerckes printed out an embossed engagement card and, with Hermann back in Kiel, I was invited to a big dinner party with my parents-in-law, to sort of launch me on the scene. As sometime Captain and First Officer on the *Hohenzollern*, my future father-in-law was well known in naval circles in Berlin. And he, in turn, seemed to know every admiral there ever was. Mila knew all the wives. The wives, Mila included, belonged to a weekly *Kaffeeklatsch* so everyone quickly learnt everything about everyone else. This particular party, on this particular evening, was given by Admiral von Capelle (same Crew as Philipp) and his wife, Luisa. Admiral von Tirpitz was there, so was Admiral von Diederichs and various other admirals and senior officers whom I didn't know. To my incredible embarrassment, I was put at the head of the table.

As an-about-to-be new bride, Winnie was subject to strict German rules of etiquette which stated that the bride always sat in the chief seat. Precedence was also given to any out-of-town visitor or foreigner. Winnie won on both counts.

My health was drunk and all sorts of nice things were said about England and Germany, and about Hermann and me. I think the German Navy was rather in awe of the British. I felt as if Hermann and I, by falling in love and getting married, somehow implied to all round the table that evening closer relations in the future between the two navies. As if I had anything at all to do with the Royal Navy. I didn't!

It wasn't long (thank goodness) before the admirals left me alone and started talking about what really interested them. Russia. When I look back on it, I heard the most amazing conversation that evening. They were predicting a war which actually started only a few years later. They said the ongoing unrest in Russia was so great that the '*Veliki Knyaz*', the Russian Grand Dukes, might well seek a way out by diverting attention through a foreign war. And who would that war be against? Why, Germany! They were particularly concerned because Russia's entente with France would bring France into the war as well.

The date when that war would begin? Sometime before 1916. They all believed that the Russian navy, not the British, was the danger. Their focus was the Baltic.

Virtually all admirals, everywhere in the world, had been riveted by Russia ever since its defeat by Japan. Russia had two fleets, one in the Gulf of Finland and a new one at Vladivostok, on the Pacific. The Baltic fleet had sailed to the Far East to relieve the Vladivostok squadron, which the Japanese had blockaded in Port Arthur. Port Arthur was an isolated Russian port west of the Korean peninsula, west of Vladivostok, and not linked by land with the rest of Russia. The Baltic fleet failed in its mission, suffering massive losses, and Port Arthur was lost. The defeat provoked turmoil within the Russian Empire (assassinations and rebellions became almost regular occurrences),[12] and anxious speculation around Berlin.

The admirals at Winnie's inaugural dinner were wrong about the *Veliki Knyas*. They would not provoke a war to save themselves, because nothing could or would ever save them. In only nine years' time, they would all be gone. Perhaps, in 1908 this thought was too preposterous for these high-ranking German admirals to contemplate, but shortly after the Grand Dukes bowed out, so did the entire German Empire.

Meanwhile, back in the Gercke family circle, there was one person in the apartment who was not overjoyed at Hermann's engagement. This was his little sister Lenchen, twelve years his junior. She was used to having his attention all to herself. She worshipped him. In her old age, she recalled:

[How] he took care of me from the very beginning! Even when I was a howling monster in the arms of our poor mother, he was the only one I

> allowed to detach me from my mother and to comfort me in his own arms ... Later, as a child, he became, for me a figure of absolute authority, especially when he appeared in uniform with his officer's dagger at his waist. I so admired him. I loved his face and his hands. I loved his rousing laugh. I loved the way his presence imbued any situation with energy. I loved the way he was able to concentrate on whatever he was doing, disregarding the chaos going on around him. He could write serious articles, for example, while his toddlers squawked and crawled around on the floor around him. As I grew older, I saw, more and more, what a wonderful blend of wisdom and goodness he was.

Part of that wisdom was handling clashes between Lenchen and Winnie. One was so fierce that a contrite Lenchen wrote to her brother apologizing for her quick temper. He wrote back tenderly: 'Little Sister, you must learn that even those we love have failings.' And he ended with a poem by Goethe:

> Feiger Gedanken bängliches Schwanken,
> Weiblisches Zagen, ängstliches Klagen,
> Wendet kein Elend, macht dich nicht frei.
>
> Allen Gewalten zum Trutz sich erhalten
> Nimmer sich beugen, kräftig sich zeigen
> Rufet die Arme der Götter herbei.
>
> Cowardly thoughts and fearful indecision,
> Womanly squabbles and anxious lamenting
> Won't shift your misery, won't make you free.
>
> Defy forces which try to make you bend,
> Stand fast, remain yourself.
> Call the gods to stand with you.[13]

It was never easy for Lenchen to share her brother with Winnie. Or the other way round. But they managed an uneasy truce.

Winnie and Hermann married in London on 16 March 1909, at All Souls, Langham Place.

> With parental and imperial consent, we married in March 1909. Heinrich Mathy,[14] one of Hermann's fellow officers, was best man and one of the witnesses. The others were my parents and my brother. The registrar

noted that Hermann was an *Oberleutnant* in the Imperial German Navy and lived in Wilhelmshaven. Our reception was in the Langham Court Hotel, where my Father missed most of what was going on because he was crying (so my Mother told me afterwards).

We had no time for a honeymoon. Hermann had used up a fortnight of his leave by living in London before marrying (a legal requirement). We spent our first married night in the Grosvenor Hotel. The next day, we travelled by stages, first to Bremen to see some of my husband's aunts, and then on to our new home in Wilhelmshaven.

My mother-in-law had organised an apartment for us in the 'Villa Irene', on the town's outskirts. We had the upper part of the house, while other, unmarried, naval officers lived downstairs. My husband was flag-lieutenant of a destroyer torpedo flotilla. The commander of this flotilla, Kapitän zur See Hans Eberius[15] (a very striking man) promised us a delayed honeymoon in Kiel, during its famous *Kieler Woche* (Kiel Week).

Soon after our arrival, we began our rounds of official Sunday morning calls. It was a very formal business. Full dress uniform was de rigueur and, as newcomers, we had to leave visiting cards. If we met others (unknown to us) at the door of a house where we were to be guests, the men bowed, said their own name and then introduced their wives. Younger women made a quick curtsy when meeting older women, and men bowed, moving just their neck and head. Yes, there was formality, but also informality. Our social life centred on the Officers' Casino, a club housed in a handsome building. The perfect setting for dances.

Now came my first attempt at keeping house. It wasn't easy. All I had was what every well-equipped young British woman had at such a moment. A copy of Mrs Beeton. I also had maids who I thought, with any luck, would know how to cook. The first one didn't, but the second one did. She did everything, all the housekeeping, all the cooking and even the entertaining. She would cook, carve and decorate dishes with great artistry, while my husband's batman served. When the maid had the day off, alas, I had to take my turn. But Hermann, who came rushing home after work, as happy as a sand-boy, ate everything I cooked. He always declared it delicious. At the time, I believed him.

I was pretty hopeless. I couldn't find butchers' shops or fishmongers. I expected their wares to be displayed outside, on the pavement, as they were in England. And they weren't. With the baker, it was different. I didn't have to find him. He found us. Hot, freshly baked rolls were delivered to our front door every morning, in linen bags, with our names embroidered on them. We supplied the bags and hung them outside before going to bed.

Our milk was pasteurized and also delivered daily.[16] There was nothing like that in England. At least, not at the time.

While we were in Wilhelmshaven, my Father came to stay. My Mother couldn't come with him. She was with her own mother in Ireland. He was, I suspect, rather happy to be on his own. He loved being with us and we loved having him. The day of his departure arrived. We saw him off at the train station. He was going to Hamburg and catching the boat train to England at around midday. Later that afternoon, who do I see out of my window, smiling to himself and approaching our door, but my Father. He had simply been unable to go. So he just turned around and came back. He stayed another few days.

Captain Eberius kept his word about Kiel. In June, we sailed north from Wilhelmshaven, entering the Kiel Canal at Brünsbüttel. Never sailing faster than 8km an hour, it took eight hours to reach the Holtenau locks. But it was worth it. I wouldn't have missed *Kieler Woche* for the world. It was one great round of sea, sun, sailing and, dare I say it, sex (marital of course). There were yacht races, meals in restaurants by the water, receptions every evening and dances, or *Bordfeste*, held on naval ships, one after another. Since the whole fleet seemed to be in harbour, that one week simply wasn't long enough. We needed a year.

While we were in Kiel, my birthday came around.[17] I woke that morning to the sound of an orchestra and choir outside my window. It was what they call a *Ständchen*, or serenade. At the time, only better-off couples could afford this, but in our case, it wasn't expensive at all, for the men outside my window were officers and sailors from Em's[18] torpedo boat flotilla.

All day long, flowers arrived. Soon, huge arrangements stood on every table and window ledge. I had to start putting them on the floor. Germans love giving flowers. Both my father-in-law and husband always met me with a bunch of flowers in their hand.

One day, I received a book from my brother Wilfred in England. It was called *The Riddle of the Sands* by Erskine Childers.[19] It fascinated us all because the events it describes took place in the waters and neighbourhood of Wilhelmshaven. We devoured it with wonder. Was anyone in it real? Not as far as we could see. In the end, we dismissed it as entertaining nonsense. Part of the story is about the east coast of England, where Wilfred's fiancée, Christine Stevenson, lived. Her mother (who had several unmarried daughters) used to invite as many German naval officers (docked with the Imperial Navy in Grimsby) to her home as possible. She hoped one or more of them would marry one or more of her daughters. One of her visitors was my husband's friend, Lothar von Arnauld de la Perrière.[20] He escaped Grimsby still a bachelor. There were, at the time, very good relations between the English and German navies.[21] The Kaiser permitted his navy to enter British ports, but not French ones. He feared an 'incident'. He knew the French were still smarting from the German triumph in 1871.

Lothar was another very handsome man, especially in uniform (looking back, perhaps they all were). When not in uniform, he taught me to roller-skate, but for Em and me, our favourite sport was cycling. The countryside round Wilhelmshaven is flat. Everyone cycled. Hermann and I would cycle at weekends, stopping at inns or farmhouses for tea.

Thinking about books, this was the year Hermann published the fourth of four translations he made of Russian books. Three were translations of a Russian sea captain's works, a man who had fought in the Russo-Japanese War, and the fourth was a translation of letters to his wife, written by someone in that fatal war who did not come back.[22]

Our first son, Hermann Harry,[23] was born on 11 September 1911. When he was about six months old, I upset the very high pram and Harry fell out. Both baby and I were in such shock that, instead of dealing with the situation, I ran in panic to the nearest sailor and asked to him to fetch my husband immediately. Such silly things I did! Poor Hermann. Another Sunday, when Hermann was away, our best man, Oberleutnant Heinrich Mathy, came to take baby and me out for a walk. Heinrich was always jolly and full of fun. He enjoyed the un-officer-like occupation of wheeling a pram, especially when he met a company of his men. He would salute them with a grin, and without taking his left hand off the pram handle.

Wilhelmshaven itself was a dreary town. The exciting part was the naval base, the shipyards and the long waterfront. The local refrain was '*Immer an der Werff entlang*' (Always to the long wharf!). Everyone loved watching the big ships come into harbour.

Things were different in Kiel, where we moved in 1912. Hermann was taking a two-year postgraduate course at the Marine-Akademie. That first year we had a very severe winter. It was cold, but great fun. Deep snow brought with it sleighing parties, often organized at night, with sleigh bells and lanterns. We drove in groups of two or three out to country inns to dance. And in summer time? Just as much fun. Friends and relations sailed with us on the windswept Baltic. It was such a carefree life. Halcyon days. Enchantment. But there were shadows. One such we saw in August 1912. We had decided to cruise all afternoon off the coast and were somewhere near Rügen when my husband pointed in the far distance to a small grey speck. The sun was shining so strongly and reflecting off the sea, it was

> difficult to catch sight of anything at all. I screwed my eyes up and finally saw a thin smudge of smoke in the distance: 'What is it?'

It was a French battleship and it was taking President Poincaré[24] to St Petersburg to see the Tsar and his Foreign Minister Sergei Sazonov.[25] That ship boded ill for Germany: encirclement, potential war on two fronts. The one thing it dreaded beyond all others. Hermann speculated that President Poincaré's visit was to consolidate and strengthen France's alliance with Russia. He was right. But the danger to Germany was much worse than that. It wasn't just the two of them, France and Russia, who were ready to gang up against his own country. The Entente included, in Poincaré's eyes, Britain as well. Hermann had no idea. Not a clue. No one in Germany had a clue. It was a deathly secret and a useful one to Poincaré. Britain had just agreed, with France, to fight on her side in the case of war with Germany,[26] or so Poincaré thought. It soon turned out that there were different interpretations of the agreement. Although sworn to secrecy, Poincaré wanted Russia to know about Britain's involvement so that it would be more robust in its dealings with Germany. It was no longer a question of two against two (France and Russia against Germany and Austria-Hungary), but of three against two (France, Russia and Britain against German and Austria-Hungary). Perhaps Poincaré saw that longed-for moment approaching. The moment when France would retake Alsace-Lorraine.[27]

> My husband's spirits sank. He realised our halcyon, carefree days were numbered. Russia was turning against us. War was uncomfortably close. That's why he was studying torpedoes and wireless communications. It was why he was studying Russian. It was why, the following year, with only one week's notice, Hermann was suddenly given a new job in Berlin. They wanted to train him to be a spy. A spy in Russia. My second child was due at any moment. But off we went. The removal men packed our things and I got out my oil paints. I painted a picture of our Kiel living room – its French windows, the balcony, the sea beyond. Our heaven.

Chapter 8

Spying in Russia

In 1909, Georg knuckled down. He could avoid it no longer. He would put his art to one side for a year and face his military service. He joined *Das Königin Elisabeth Garde Grenadier*[1] (the Queen Elisabeth Grenadier Guards). Their regimental barracks were in Charlottenburg, near the family flat. The following year, Waldemar followed suit. Uniforms with twisted wool piping on the epaulettes. To their surprise, neither of them found their year of enslavement to the military anything other than an amusing, and welcome, one-year holiday.

Regiments in those days were drawn from specific areas, so men like Georg and Waldemar found themselves serving alongside their mates from high school. Freed from all decision-making, all that was required of them for one year was that they attend courses and take part in exercises. Not over-taxing. In fact, the physicality of life in the army was a welcome change, especially for Waldemar, who had been tied to his school desk for years, while Georg had been out and about, painting in the countryside. Neither found it difficult to spend his days scrambling about in the sand dunes with the army, and their evenings with their comrades, either out on the town, or at home, making merry in Achenbachstraße. Sometimes they did both. Philipp reported, with great pleasure that they used to bring their friends home late at night and raid the larder. On other occasions, they came to the apartment earlier and enjoyed an evening at home, with music and song. Georg played the guitar, Waldemar, the mandolin and ocarina.[2] Sometimes, Lenchen would shyly join in on the piano. Georg and Waldemar were on the threshold of life. Everything lay before them, including, for Waldemar, stiff entrance examinations for the Charlottenburg Technische Hochschule.

The day Waldemar's results came out, the phone rang in Philipp's office.

'Kapitän Gercke here.'

'Waldemar here. I have passed my exams. With distinction.'

'This doesn't surprise me, my boy.'

And that was that. Both of them hung up. Neither was given to superlatives, but both were bursting with pride.

Waldemar's principal professor at the Hochschule was Professor Heinrich Müller-Breslau.[3] He held the chair of structural engineering and was famous world-wide. Scarcely a bridge was planned anywhere in the world (so Philipp tells us) without engineers first running their plans past Müller-Breslau. In addition to being knowledgeable, he was kind and caring. He looked after his students and was particularly good to Waldemar. On graduating, it was thanks to Müller-Breslau's recommendation that Waldemar walked straight into his first job, working as a civil engineer for the *Gemeindeverwaltung* (Municipal Administration) of Berlin.

I don't know in which section of the city's municipal offices he worked. Winnie suggests it was bridge-building. But I do know for sure that the city had broad infrastructure requirements. It needed top-class water and sewage systems, modern energy supplies and up-to-date communications and transport systems. The job meant Waldemar had landed, immediately, on his feet. Exactly as everyone expected him to do.

On graduating from his term of military service, Georg also had to find a job. Or rather, in his case, a way of gathering enough funds from this or that in order to survive a little longer. He needed just enough to survive until that big break into the art world, a break which was, he hoped, bound to come some time or other. His first paid work was producing illustrations for an edition of a popular fairytale. This was *Der Zwerg Nase* (The Dwarf with the Nose), written in the eighteenth century by Wilhelm Hauff.[4] It was a good start. Books sell widely, and their illustrations are more widely seen than any painting hanging in a gallery or in an exhibition. Book illustration is a good way to build an audience. Georg's engravings for this story were drawn in the romantic, medieval tradition generally associated with German fairytales.

Perhaps some of the *Zwerg Nase* books found their way onto the bookshelves of a Bremen bookseller, Franz Leuwer.[5] He was an important figure in Bremen's artistic world and had turned his bookshop in the old city into a cultural hub by combining the business of bookselling with holding small art exhibitions. He was, in a way, a miniature, Bremen-based, Paul Cassirer. He had a gift vitally important to artists. He knew how to make art pay.

Leuwer got in touch with Georg and suggested an exhibition. He had an idea. The Free Hansa City of Bremen[6] was, like Berlin, growing rapidly as rural populations abandoned the countryside in search of better living conditions in town. Many of them went further and emigrated. Bremerhaven, Bremen's port on the North Sea, was one of the main North German departure points for millions of emigrants pouring out of Europe, not just Germany, and heading for America. More than seven million emigrated through Bremerhaven between 1800 and 1915.[7]

Leuwer had an idea which might make money for poor impoverished artists like Georg and capitalize on the needs of those vast numbers of miserable, soon-to-be-homesick emigrants leaving Europe's shores for ever. His idea was to provide them with keepsake pictures of the city they were leaving. They could ease their loneliness and misery in the New World with pictures of the old. He asked Georg if he would work with his brother-in-law, Max Neumark,[8] and produce a series of engravings showing the intriguing, romantic corners at the heart of the great medieval *Hansastadt* of Bremen. Leuwer himself wrote a note to advertize the new exhibition and placed it in the big bow windows of his bookstore:

> This exhibition is for those who are planning to emigrate. It will give them a memento of their beloved old home. And of course, it is also for those who remain here. It provides all with a true picture of our fine old city. And it will provide generations yet unborn, with evidence of the unique charm that weaves its way around our beautiful old streets.

As it turned out, after the Second World War bombing of Bremen, these are now among the few pictures which survive to tell the story of *Alt Bremen*.

For the duration, Georg moved to Bremen and stayed with his aunts (his grandmother died in 1906). This was familiar territory for him. He loved Bremen and was delighted to be back. He spent hours wandering round the town, especially the old quarter and Bremerhaven. He sketched fishermen mending their nets and cleaning fish. And of course, he was often back in his old Worpswede haunts, sketching cottages, canals and barges and drinking in the beauty of the flat landscape, the willows and the birches.

Georg's circle of friends grew. They were mainly artists, but among them was Carl Schünemann,[9] an important Bremen curator and impresario. Schünemann had many contacts in the art world, both within Germany and beyond. He knew modern artists hoping to sell their work and major collectors ready to buy. He knew 'everybody', and did things on a grand scale. A very grand scale. He was planning a major international exhibition, and his choice of venue was none other than the city's main exhibition hall, the *Kunsthalle Bremen* (Bremen Art Gallery). Some of the works to be exhibited would be loaned by collectors, but most would be for sale and presented directly by the artists themselves. The exhibition would be in three sections: oil paintings, drawings and sculpture. Nothing but the very greatest names in each section. Schünemann was like Cassirer in that he was not simply taking part in a commercial venture, but involving himself in something dear to his heart. He invited a handful of promising young German artists to exhibit alongside established greats. He would give them a leg-up. Would Georg care to join in?

At last. That break. Georg was utterly delighted, but first of all he made the important decision not to tell his parents. He knew that, in order to win his father's approval, he had to show that he really was capable of making his own way. He decided to wait to tell them till he was firmly and fully established, an acknowledged, successful, self-supporting artist. That decision very nearly hid from view the crowning achievement of Georg's career. Philipp knew nothing of it. It is not mentioned in his Chronicle. How to know it ever existed?

Nearly all of Georg's work has since vanished. He left most of it in Paris when war broke out. It has probably since been auctioned off or even just lost. But while writing this book I found, in the Victoria and Albert Museum Library, an incredible clue to Georg's achievements. I found a catalogue. It told me that Georg once took part in an international art exhibition, along with most of the great names in the modern art world. A hundred years after Georg was killed, I climbed the museum's broad, stone stairs. They lead to a high-ceilinged, medieval-style library holding one of the biggest collections of art and art-related books in the world: a hidden treasure. Among that treasure, a pearl of great price: the 1914 catalogue for the *Internationale Kunstausstellung* (International Art Exhibition) held in the Kunsthalle Bremen from 1 February to 31 March 1914. Printed by Carl Schünemann.

It wasn't impressive. A modest, dog-eared catalogue, a little smaller than an exercise book. Its cardboard cover is decorated with Regency stripes, alternating blue and cream, with leafy, scroll-type patterns running along them. An unprepossessing exterior. Inside, the world of *Jugendstil* springs from every page – the lettering, the font, the spacing. The catalogue lists the names of every artist who exhibited in that exhibition: Vincent van Gogh, Paul Cézanne, Pablo Picasso, Otto Modersohn, Edvard Munch. And Georg Gercke. Triumph! I held the catalogue in my hands. Joy!

Georg exhibited three drawings, each priced at 60DM. The show's catalogue lists exhibitors alphabetically, so Georg's name lies between Gauguin and van Gogh. Gauguin's work is offered for 600DM and van Gogh's for 2,000DM. In the section on oil paintings, Georg exhibited one painting, *Landschaft* (Landscape). It was offered for 600DM (about £550 today). Nearby, van Gogh's *Regen* was for sale at 45,000DM, as well as his painting *Das Irrenhaus* (The Madhouse), which was priced at 25,000DM. In comparison to the greats, Georg's work was relatively cheap. But no give-away. His prices compared well with those for members of the Worpswede community, five of whom showed pictures in the same exhibition. Otto Modersohn, already well-known, was selling for 1,500DM, and Hans am Ende,[10] not so well known, for about the same. A third

Worpswede member, Heinrich Vogeler,[11] was selling for close to Georg's price, as were two other Worpswede painters, Walter Bertelsmann[12] and Friedrich Blau.[13] I like to think that these artists were friends of my Great-Uncle Georg. This was his first great international exhibition. And also his last.

The exhibition was a huge success. It brought joy to many, but to none more so than Georg. Philipp often mentions in his Chronicle how close disaster can lie to joy. This moment in March 1914 well illustrates the point. Georg's exhibition took place four months before the borders between France and Germany closed, and they remained closed for the next five years. Art exhibitions continued during the war however. Cassirer continued to exhibit in Berlin, and in Paris, gallery-owner Daniel-Henry Kahnweiler[14] also continued for a while. He launched Cubism on the world in 1916 by exhibiting *Les Demoiselles d'Avignon* in Paris. But the movement of art between warring sides stopped, and artists who found themselves in the wrong place had to relocate. Kahnweiler, a German living in Paris, for example, moved to Switzerland, and van der Velde, a Belgian living in Weimar, went home.

That spring, a buoyant, optimistic Georg moved to Paris. The move suggests that he had sold enough pictures to allow him to take the plunge. He was moving to the artistic centre of the whole world and had probably been hoping to study there for some time. Perhaps, so far, he had lacked the funds to do so, or maybe he lacked the confidence. Many of his friends had already studied there. Most attended the well-known Académie Julian, a school which was especially appreciated by the non-French. Unlike the best known school in Paris, l'École des Beaux-Arts, Académie Julian did not require students to pass an exacting French-language exam in order to enter. Better still, while l'École des Beaux-Arts was rigid and stuffy, Académie Julian was liberal, both towards students and in its attitude to art. Installed in a small studio in Paris, Georg had reached his Seventh Heaven.

It was a time for reaching Seventh Heavens. Waldemar had also found his. He found it soon after settling into his new job with the Berlin Municipality. He got engaged and blinded Philipp and Mia with the unexpected news. Philipp wrote:

> The astonishing thing for Mila and I was that, shortly after landing his first job, Waldemar announced his engagement to Christel Flaischlen. We were stunned. We had no idea. Not a clue. What a dark horse he turned out to be! Apparently, she also worked for the municipality. She was a bright girl, the daughter of Dr Niklaus Flaischlen, a well-known Berlin gynaecologist. Her family, like our own, were immigrants, but no surprise there. More than sixty per cent of us Berliners were either immigrants or the children of immigrants. But while we came from Russia, her family

> were from Transylvania. They were Siebenbürger Saxons[15] and she was, well she still is, a lovely girl, a beautiful, composed, modern girl, though now she is married to someone else. [16] I am glad for her that she has found someone. It is no life, being a war widow.

They announced their engagement in June 1914. Two months later, they were separated, more or less, for ever.

Hermann's life in the two years leading up to the outbreak of war was very different to that of his two brothers. This was not surprising. They were civilians. He was not. In 1912 he had been sent on a two-year course at the Naval Academy in Kiel. After only one year, he was ordered to cut short the course and return to the Admiralty in Berlin. He was to be trained as a spy. These were early days in an industry which has since become much more refined. Nevertheless, the world that Hermann was entering, and the things he was taught, are uncannily reminiscent of the world of James Bond.

The British Secret Service Bureau, a combination of what later became MI5 and MI6, was founded in October 1909. It came into being at a time when spy stories were already quite the rage. They were fascinating and enthralling the public, but it was some time before they also caught the interest of government. Lord Northcliffe, proprietor of the *Daily Mail*, said rather bitterly that spy stories were 'well suited to the average Briton's liking for a good hate'.[17] One of the most popular was Erskine Childers' story, *The Riddle of the Sands*, published in 1903, about an imagined German invasion of the east coast of the British Isles. Wilfred sent Winnie and Hermann a copy. 'It amused us tremendously, so much so that we lent it to friends and they in turn, passed it round. In the end, it was read by just about the entire naval base at Wilhelmshaven, causing huge excitement. But of course, it was quite absurd. Unthinkable.'

Winnie was right. A German invasion of England was unthinkable. But the spy world was real enough. The Imperial Navy's spying section was called the *Nachrichten-Abteilung* (the Intelligence Bureau) and had been founded thirteen years earlier, in 1900, before Childers published his book. It had been founded by Admiral Otto von Diedrichs, one of the guests at a dinner party to launch Winnie onto the Berlin scene. Its offices were at 70 Königgrätzer Straße (today's Stresemannstraße), though these were known simply as 'N'. Its director, entering into the spirit of a James Bond world (or was it the other way round?), signed papers with an 'N', followed by the first letter of his own name. The head of that office was, from 1900 till March 1914, Commander Arthur Tapken (later a Rear-Admiral), a man whose wife, like Hermann's, was English. I do not know if Winnie ever met her or him.

British spies were professionals, so to speak, combining their mission with some other job and doing both at the same time for as long as they could. And they worked for an entity dedicated entirely to spying, MI5 or MI6. Not so in Germany. The *Nachrichten-Abteilung* (Information Division) was directly integrated into the *Admiralstab* and recruited men mainly from the Imperial Navy. They served for a limited period of time and then returned to their regular naval jobs. They were therefore never as professional as their English equivalents. The primary target for the *Nachrichten-Abteilung* was, of course, the British Royal Navy, the Imperial Navy's greatest rival. For this purpose, the organization recruited two types of agents: *Berichterstatter* (fleet observers, generally navy men), and *Vertrauensmänner* (trusted men), generally drawn from outside the navy. The former gathered intelligence on foreign naval strength, technical abilities, defensive positions and movements, while the latter took a more general approach. Spies were provided with codes, wireless telegraphy equipment, invisible ink and all the other paraphernalia required by agents in the early twentieth century. It was a world in which John le Carré would have felt at home.

Britain was one target. Russia another. Britain was spied on as a competitor. Germany wanted to understand the strength and technical ability of ships in the Royal Navy because it wanted to build ships with comparable capabilities. The Russian fleet, on the other hand, was spied on with a view to an expected war. What were its strengths and where were they? What defence systems guarded approaches to potential key targets in the case of war? How were harbours or port cities protected, especially the capital, St Petersburg?

Within the *Nachrichten-Abteilung*, different units handled different geographical areas. Hermann was appointed to the unit responsible for the Nordic countries, Sweden, Denmark and Norway, but its main focus was Russia and its empire (which included Finland, guardian of the northern approaches to St Petersburg) and the southern Baltic region of Russia which shared a frontier with Germany. That area today includes Lithuania, Latvia and Estonia. It was easy to recruit agents in Russia's Baltic Empire because this was an area with a large German-speaking population. Sympathy for Germany was high. The Nordic unit worked closely with the Swedish navy. Sweden was strongly sympathetic to Germany but, during the war, officially neutral. Many so-called neutral countries were neutral in name only. There was a great deal of co-operation between the two countries during the war. Winnie, for example, depended on her Swedish contacts to keep in touch with the family in England.

If, in 1913, you worked in the Nordic unit of the *Nachrichten-Abteilung* and were looking for someone who spoke Russian, had a good understanding of its recent naval history, and, ideally, had family still in Russia, what name would have come to mind?

Whenever Winnie talks about Hermann's work between 1913 and 1914 she says he was appointed a *descernant* (observer) and seems to have been perfectly at ease with what he was asked to do. He starts taking Danish lessons and she joins him. She takes a Russian course as well. He works on codes and brings the work home in the evening. They pore over ciphers together. They had fun. It was a challenge. She loved it. Yet at other points in her memoirs, when she discusses spies, she is strongly against them. With Hermann, it was all right, but otherwise, no. A deceitful occupation.

Hermann's new job was to report on Russia's naval preparedness both at sea and along the Baltic coast. Winnie recalls:

> Of the languages involved in his new job, Hermann spoke only Russian. He immediately set about learning Danish and Swedish. He also studied cryptology and brought exercises home in the evening. We used to practise decrypting together. I, too, began to take lessons in Russian. I can still speak it, to this day.
>
> We settled down to a glamorous life in Berlin. Our apartment was at the junction of Hohenzollerndamm and Sächsischestraße and that's where little Georg[18] was born. Beyond us lay open country, so we could take him in the pram, with Harry trotting alongside, for long walks in the country. As soon as I was fully recovered, we started an energetic social life. As a naval officer, Hermann was offered preferential tickets to the opera. We were invited to numerous soirées meeting Terribly Important People while discreet *musique de chambre* played in the background. It was like a scene out of a Russian novel. Glittering guests flirted, drank champagne and gossiped.
>
> In October 1913, Heinrich Mathy came to see us. He had arrived for little Georg's christening. He was to be one of his godfathers. Our apartment was on the southern edge of Berlin and just north of the village of Wilmersdorf, so the christening was held in Wilmersdorf's beautiful new church, the Auenkirche (Church in the Meadows).[19] Heinrich had joined the Fleet Air Arm. He was working on Zeppelins and taking an airship training course. It made us all nervous. Airships were notoriously unsafe. He had only just begun this course when the latest model, the L-2, blew up.[20] It was a sunny Friday. It was a new ship and Hermann and I were following its launch with great excitement. Then, suddenly, bang. Everyone on board was burnt to death. Our hearts sank for Heinrich. Thank God he wasn't onboard.

After Georg's christening, we walked home from the pretty Auenkirche and sat down to lunch. There were thirteen of us at table. I remember a blank feeling as I looked around and counted. I couldn't help remembering the superstition. An unlucky situation. Of course, I know it's silly. All superstition is silly. But all the same. You see how the memory has lingered.

Hermann never wasted time. After work, he wrote for naval periodicals such as *Marine-Rundschau* and *Überall*. The last of these two was edited by his father. He could easily earn 50 marks from just one evening's work. Not bad at all. Our naval income was modest and it wasn't really enough, partly because Hermann used to buy me extravagant gifts, like tremendous hats and silk stockings.

As '*Descernant*', Hermann had to travel and, to my delight, I could go with him. I was thrilled to realise that I wasn't just there as a companion, he needed me. I would be his cover. Our first port of call was Russia. We were going to visit relations. At least that's what we said.

One freezing February day in 1914, we boarded a small freighter in Stettin to sail to the Russian port of Libau.[21] Libau, on the southern Baltic shore, is the nearest Russian port to the Russian/German frontier. It is the first in a string of ports along that shore, all leading up to the entrance to the Gulf of Finland. When we left, I had a cold, a cough and a high temperature. Hermann said we should give up the trip entirely. But I insisted. So there we were, standing on an icy deck, leaning on deck rails festooned with icicles and gazing at the approaching harbour of Libau. I kept sneezing, coughing and blowing my nose into a handkerchief. This turned out to be an important harbour for us. Two years later, my husband was there again and escaped death by the skin of his teeth. But on this, his first visit, life was comfortable. We stayed at the Hôtel de Rome, the principal hotel, and drove every day, bundled up in furs in an open Droschke, to visit our growing number of new 'friends'.

Next, we went further north, along the Kurland[22] coast, and then sailed east, through the Irben Straits and into the Gulf of Riga. Riga[23] itself lies deep in that Gulf. It was picturesque, but hotels and houses there, as in Libau, had a peculiar smell. It came from the peat used in their stoves, and from poor ventilation. There was a little round circle, about seven inches wide, cut out of the glass in the upper part of each window. It contained a small fan which swivelled round, or at least which was supposed to swivel round, and bring infinitesimal amounts of fresh air into the room. The windows themselves were never opened. Quite the opposite to Germany, where bedroom windows are opened every night, regardlesss of the cold.

Then we travelled by night train to Reval,[24] an important port for the Russian Baltic fleet. There was no electric lighting in our train, only candles, so the carriage looked quite spooky. I think spookiness was on our minds. As in Libau and Riga, most of the people in town were German-speaking Balts. I remember trying to decipher names written in Cyrillic script above shop windows. I would enunciate each letter to myself slowly, making a huge effort, and then found that the name I was pronouncing was an ordinary German name I knew. Nothing exotic at all. We stayed in an old-fashioned but comfortable hotel on the Ulitsa Gogol (Gogol Street), and ate outside, in restaurants. Once again, we visited 'friends'. We met the German Consul, a fine old man called Herr Koch. He had white hair and looked like a biblical patriarch. One morning, Hermann went out early and alone, and saw a man shot dead in the street, right in front of him. No wonder most of the people we met were unhappy with Russian rule. Another day, giving a heavy bribe to the watchman, Em walked slowly all around the naval dockyards. It was very risky. But thrilling. And it was what he was there to do.

From Reval we went on to St Petersburg, arriving, once again, after dark. In Russian winters, dark arrives not long after midday. And midday itself is not long after dawn. I should think it difficult to arrive anywhere in winter in Russia without darkness overtaking you before you get there. Hermann's aunt lived in a beautiful 'hotel', a large private house, in the city centre. She was a kind, elderly widow, immensely rich and with a retinue of servants, including a major-domo. She was the only true relative that we had there, nevertheless, each day we made 'family visits', while, in the evening, we were invited to what people called *Mittagessen*. The word means the midday meal, but starting around 10 in the evening it was anything but. Not only did it begin extraordinarily late, but it was huge, I mean huge. It began with Russian hors d'œuvres, which are called *Zakuski*. They were served in a swarm of dishes each loaded with pies, meat rarities, fish and vegetables, all prettily set out on a long table. I would stare at it all in despair, because I knew that the main meal was to follow.

It would be quite a relief, next day, not to eat anything at all. The city is beautiful. I thought the Nevski Prospekt[25] one of the widest and finest streets in the world. The museums and cathedrals which we visited were handsome and peaceful. So were the streets. But things were not what they seemed. Nor, for that matter, were we. I was particularly nervous of the policemen. They looked terrific in their magnificent, swinging overcoats and their astrakhan hats. But did they know what we were up to? On the other hand, the Droschke drivers, perched on the driver's seat, were surely harmless. They were buried deep beneath rugs and furs. They looked less like human beings and more like mole hills.

Our life continued happily enough until, after a few days, we received word from the German Ambassador, Count Friedrich Pourtalès,[26] that we were being followed. He said that on no account were we to call at the German embassy. Punishment for spying in Russia, as in England and Germany, could be death. I had seen many uniformed policemen, but it turned out there were many more not wearing uniform.

Hermann wanted to explore the naval base of Kronstadt. He decided on a clever ruse. We would develop a sudden and amazing appetite for ice sailing. We took a Droschke to Stealka[27] on the Gulf of Finland. To reach it, we drove past the naval base,[28] past the guns and forts, and past masses of boarded-up *dachas.*[29] And once in Stealka itself, we hired a *buknia* (sailing sledge or ice boat). I lay flat on my stomach on a boat-shaped plank. It had a sail attached to it and some kind of mechanism for controlling the sail. Hermann lay behind me, with a tiller in his hands. We were going ice-sailing and, amazingly enough, Hermann very cleverly gave the impression of someone who knew what he was doing. Perhaps he did, for we dashed, at hair-raising speeds, all over the frozen Gulf of Finland. You were supposed to steer so as to take large cracks in the ice at right angles, but it seemed to me that we were on the crack long before we ever knew it was there. Of course, Hermann, perhaps from his yachting life, managed well. We flew so fast, and so far out from shore, that we could scarcely see the land. And all the while, it was piercingly, piercingly cold. I have never been so cold. I was wearing two fur coats, but I needed three, possibly four. I don't know if any of those plain clothes detectives who were supposed to be following us survived. Possibly not. As we drove back to the hotel that evening, we were, both of us, exhilarated. Hermann because he had seen all the military installations he wanted to see, and I, because I was still alive.

We set out for home via Finland, travelling by regular sleigh over the frozen Gulf. As we flew through the snow, Hermann screwed up his sharp eyes and counted the gun emplacements lining the shore. In Helsingfors [Helsinki] we stayed in a modern, comfortable hotel and, thinking we had thrown off the agents following us, visited the German consul and his wife. This was a mistake. Back at the hotel, we discovered that some darkly clad Russians, all male, and all looking very much like they were not on holiday, had not only moved into our hotel but onto our corridor. Just a few rooms down from our own.

This was when I discovered why Hermann had insisted that we lug our skates all the way with us from Berlin. I wanted to leave them behind. They are such bulky things to pack. In Helsingfors, out came the skates, and off we went, skating along the picturesque Helsingfors shoreline. Quite by chance, we skated past all the Finnish naval installations. Was this perhaps a little bit too risky? Next morning, I woke to find Hermann with our suitcases open on the bed. We were leaving. Immediately. I protested. I thought it a mistake to appear to flee but, of course, I did exactly as he said. We went to the station, bought tickets and walked to the platform. But instead of getting onto the train, we hung around, had a cup of coffee, and after a suitable delay (and long after the train had departed), we walked back into the station and took another cab, back to another hotel. The second place wasn't such a glamorous affair as the first, though it was still, as everywhere in Finland, impeccably clean. No one had followed us. Next day, at Hangor (Hanko, another naval base), we boarded a ferry bound for Sweden.

With an icebreaker freeing a passage in front of us, we set out on a journey which would take at least 20 hours. So we ate. And there it was. A large table on one side of the dining room, laden with another *Mittagessen*, only now the *Zakuski* table, considering this was a Swedish boat, had turned into a smorgasbord. Once we had got through the pies and so on, as in Russia, the main meal began. We got to Stockholm. I was stuffed.

In Stockholm, we stayed at the Royal Hotel, overlooking the harbour. I breathed a sigh of relief. Our spying days were over. They had been fun. But a little goes a long way in that business. The warmth of our reception in Stockholm suggested to me that Sweden and Germany were on the same side. Or even, that Hermann had been working for Sweden as well as for Germany. We attended dinner parties and receptions. We met admirals galore and other high-ranking officers. Among them were Admiral Henning von Krusenstierna[30] and Lieutenant von Bahr[31] and his handsome wife. She remained, throughout the war, a firm friend and helped me keep in tiny touch with my parents. We also met the King's aide de camp, a Captain Lindstrom.[32] We were having dinner with him when he told us not to turn around. There were two Russian agents at the table just behind. How on earth did they manage that?

Next day, we took the train-ferry home, from Trelleborg[33] to Sassnitz[34] and Hermann reported to the *Nachrichten-Abteilung*. Shortly afterwards, the Swedish government made Hermann a Knight of the Royal Swedish Order of the Sword, First Class.[35] It was a beautiful decoration on a yellow, moiré silk ribbon, with blue bands on the sides. The Kaiser, who for once didn't seem to mind being outdone, gave him the Order of the Red Eagle, 4th Class.[36] It, too, was a handsome piece, hung on a grey, moiré silk ribbon, with red bands at the edge. Both medals were for valour. I think I should have got a medal too. For surviving.

Chapter 9

Spying in Britain: the June–July Crisis 1914

June and July 1914 were frenzied months for the world, for Europe, and yes, also for the Gercke family. In late June, Winnie was in England for a month's holiday with her two boys. Hermann had been sent by the *Nachrichten-Abteilung* on a second spying expedition, again to Russia, but this time to Baku in the south. And the following month, independently of the *Nachrichten-Abteiliung*, Vice-Admiral Hugo von Pohl,[1] Chief of the Admiralty Staff, sent Philipp on his first ever spying mission. He was to go to England not once, but twice: first, at the end of July, to check on whether, following a review of the fleet in Portsmouth, British naval reservists had been kept on duty or sent home; and a second time in August, to check (as far as possible) on sailing orders for the British submarine fleet.

Of all the family's espionage adventures, none was more dangerous than this last one. Philipp, taking Mila with him as cover, left for England on the day hostilities broke out between Serbia and the Austro-Hungarian Empire, the day Russia started mobilizing its reservists. They returned after Germany had declared war on France[2] and only a few hours before Britain herself declared war on Germany. From beginning to end, they were taking enormous risks. They escaped by the skin of their teeth.

To start at the beginning – June. Hermann had done an outstanding job in the Baltic. Now his spymasters sent him to the southern part of the Russian Empire, to where he would again find a large German-speaking population together with its support network: Lutheran churches, German schools, German shops and German newspapers. There would be no shortage of potentially useful contacts in Baku. Many German families were working there for the Berlin-based Siemens Company, which had extensive interests in Baku's petroleum industry[3] and its power stations, in copper-smelting and in the extraction of gold, silver and cobalt.

Already marked by the Russian secret police, Hermann needed good cover. Really good cover. And this time, not Winnie. He needed someone whom he could send home from Tiflis, before he reached the derricks and oily grime of Baku. His Muscovite aunt, Julia Karlovna?[4] Perfect. And she was more than happy to accept the opportunity for an adventure, especially one with such a handsome nephew. Officially, Hermann was in Russia to take her on holiday. He bought tickets for a cruise down the Volga. In summer, boats leave Moscow regularly for the south. It was, and still is a popular trip. They were going as tourists to the popular holiday city of Tiflis. They would spend a few days there, and then Julia would take the train home to Moscow and Hermann would continue alone, by train, to Baku. Once his work was done, he could return to Germany by ship, sailing from Yalta on the Black Sea.

Winnie, meanwhile, accompanied by the children's nurse, Fräulein Käthe, took Harry and little Georg on an extended summer holiday to her parents in England. They had almost a month of it, first in Dawlish, where they idled away long summer days on the beach, and later back in London, at her parent's house on Filey Avenue. Then a bolt from the blue – the assassination on 28 June of Franz Ferdinand, Archduke and heir to the Austro-Hungarian throne, together with his wife. The couple had been on an official visit to Sarajevo, capital of Bosnia-Herzogovina, a territory over which Austria-Hungary had only recently gained control. The change in overlordship had not gone down well with Serbian nationalists, men like Gavrilo Princip, the Bosnian Serb who killed them both.

Winnie, her parents, her uncle and aunt, her cousins, her two boys and Käthe were on the beach in Dawlish when it happened. They thought little of it and continued building sandcastles. Hermann, on the other hand, had just arrived in Baku. He hesitated when he heard the news, but kept on with the job in hand. But the situation worsened. On 23 July, Austria-Hungary sent an aggressive and hostile ultimatum to Serbia, the country it held responsible for the assassination. This was when the world finally realized that a global conflagration was probably inevitable. Investors rushed to cash in their investments. Stock exchanges slid. Interest rates rose. Everyone knew that Austria-Hungary was allied to Germany, so that if the first became involved in a war, so would the second be; that Serbia was close to Russia, so that if Serbia was attacked, Russia would likely join in; and that if Russia went to war, then so did its ally, France. And if France? Well ...The final key question was whether Britain would join France and Russia. If she did, then the situation could easily become a worldwide conflagration. Britain was the issue. The last thing the Kaiser wanted was to find himself at war with the United Kingdom. Poincaré's goal was the opposite.

And so the tug of war began. Who would gain the hand of a coy Britain? Poincaré thought that, thanks to the 1912 secret agreement, in the event of a German attack, Britain would stand with France. Some members of the British Cabinet held that the agreement had done nothing to guarantee British involvement, while Germany, completely unaware of the agreement, simply hoped to keep Britain neutral.

Over the next few days and weeks, telegrams flew between the different European capitals. Phone lines hummed. Politicians and diplomats worked deep into the night. Berlin hoped that Britain would stay neutral in the event of a continental war, but was unable to obtain a commitment from Britain to stay out of it. To help settle the matter, the German Chief of the Admiralty Staff, Vice-Admiral von Pohl, sent for his old classmate, Philipp. Von Pohl, like everyone else in the naval community, knew of Philipp's British daughter-in-law and his British contacts, made when he worked for the Heberlein Company. Would he please now go to Britain and spy out the land?

That month, Britain was holding a naval review-cum-mobilization rehearsal off Spithead. The First Lord of the Admiralty, Winston Churchill, had announced it in Parliament. King George V was to join the fleet. Fifty-five battleships, four battle-cruisers, twenty-seven cruisers, twenty-eight light cruisers and seventy-eight destroyers. The review would run from 18 to 20 July. Churchill failed to mention that an unknown number of aeroplanes (in the newly formed Royal Naval Air Service) would also take part, as well as an unknown number of submarines. These last were serving with the Royal Navy Submarine Service, formed only fourteen years earlier.

The German ambassador in London since 1912 was Prince Lichnowski. He knew all about the review, and so did his naval attaché, Kapitän von Müller, but neither could answer von Pohl's question.[5] He wanted to know if, at the end of the review, British naval reservists were sent home or if they were ordered to remain at base, on a war footing. It was a strategic question which disclosed perhaps too much about the questioner's line of thinking. It was best dealt with outside official channels.

In 1914, spies caught in Britain could be hanged. This was indeed the fate of one German merchant naval officer caught spying later that year.[6] Understandably, Philipp was not at all enthusiastic about the assignment. However, he knew his duty and he had his pride. He took the ferry to England, the train to London, and surprised Winnie and her parents by calling unexpectedly at Filey Avenue. He stayed a few hours, then took the train to Portsmouth.

> The harbour was chock-a-block with sea-going naval ships. There were masses of gunboats in Haslar Creek; the barracks on land were bursting with reserve crews; the coastal batteries were all manned; the streets were crammed with sailors. So I had to question and question. I went to all sorts of pubs where there were sailors, but the English crews were well instructed and withheld any news. At the station, I saw a whole train of reservists about to leave, only to discover that they were going to Sheerness, another naval harbour on the Thames. A couple of very intelligent radio

men turned the joke on me. They didn't let me question, but forced me to drink their frightful bitter beer and tell them where I came from and what I was doing there. Well, luckily for me, I am often mistaken for a Spaniard. I don't look like your average German. Also, I have a good imagination. I can make up stories. So I did. And I escaped unscathed.

As I could get nothing from the sailors, I now sought my business friends, namely those who worked as photographers for *Überall.* From these, as their editor, I could surely get answers. I met a certain Mr Brandenbourg, owner of the firm West & Co. He was a photographer particularly susceptible to flattery. When I told him that his pictures were the best and that I would like to have the photos he had just taken of the Fleet review, he thawed visibly. I was invited to his home where, with his wife and daughter, I had to drink the customary tea and go for a walk.

He wanted to drag me around all the barracks and see the artillery. I had trouble in refusing him. I had other fish to fry. Ships and sailors. I had little time. Yet Mr Brandenbourg became more and more confiding and, in spite of my vigorous protests, insisted on photographing me (he sent me the photo after the war) with the ships. Then he told me that Hohenzollern blood flowed in his veins (hence his German-sounding name) and, at last, he mentioned that his daughter's fiancé, a naval reservist, had been called to the test mobilization. He, like all the others (or so I thought), had been sent home at the end but told to remain on stand-by. An urgent telegram might arrive calling everyone back. Mr. B. was ready to chat further, and possibly give me ever more details about the English Navy, but I had no time to get to know him better. I had what I was looking for. I sent a telegram back to Berlin. The answer to their question was yes, the reservists had been sent home, but had to remain on stand-by. What was going on a blind man could see. War.

In fact, Winston Churchill, First Lord of the Admiralty, wrote that he had sent out an order on 26 July that reservists were not to return home. Perhaps his order was only partially fulfilled. Perhaps some reservists were kept on board and some returned and told to remain on stand-by, just as Brandenbourg reported. The important message, as Philipp said, was not whether the sailors stayed or left, but that the Royal Navy was preparing for war.

On 28 July, the day Philipp arrived safely back in Achenbachstraße, Austria-Hungary declared war on Serbia, and the Kaiser, only four days into his annual *Nordlandreise*, returned to Berlin.[7] Philipp reported his findings to von Pohl, and von Pohl reported to the Kaiser. It was after that meeting, and possibly at the Kaiser's request, that von Pohl asked Philipp to return to London a second time. He was once more to walk into an inferno. An even hotter one. Von Pohl, or perhaps the Kaiser, wanted to know in which direction Britain's E-class submarines were sailing, once the review ended. If it was westwards, then war with Britain was not imminent. If eastwards, then it was.

Philipp less keen than ever on this spying life wrote:

> Von Pohl thanked me on my return to Berlin and said, 'You must return at once to Portsmouth.'
>
> I replied half-jokingly and half in earnest, that a second journey would bring me uncomfortably close to an English gallows.
>
> 'Well, if you don't want to go …'
>
> 'Of course I'll go.'

Hermann was also back in Berlin. He had found a telegram from the Admiralty waiting for him in his Yalta hotel. He was to pretend that, for family reasons, he had to leave immediately. Taking the first boat available, he sailed with a heavy heart. He had two major worries, firstly, for his wife and children who were in England, and secondly, when he learnt of von Pohl's orders, for his father.

Winnie's family had similar worries. Her parents were actually worried sick, but neither dared broach the subject with their headstrong, determined daughter. She was in love. She was happy. She adored her life in Berlin. They hid their feelings, perhaps too successfully, and handed the task of talking to her to the family lawyer. Winnie wrote:

> He took me to lunch in London and warned me that, with the assassination of the Archduke, war between Germany and Russia was almost inevitable. He thought it very likely that Britain would be dragged into the conflagration. He said life could become very difficult. I didn't believe him.
>
> My husband had been sending me exotic postcards from his trip through Russia. Then, unexpectedly, he wrote to me from Berlin. He had been ordered back early. He said he longed for me but that I was to think carefully about what might lie ahead. He knew I was very attached to my parents. Imagine, he said, what war might mean.
>
> Unlike Hermann, I never really believed the danger was serious. I don't think any of my family did either. A very jolly party gathered at Liverpool Street station to see me off that hot July day. My Father wore a boater with a striped red and white ribbon round it. He looked in the best of health. He smiled and hugged me. I am so grateful that neither of us knew it was the last time we would see each other. There were many people on the platform that day, besides my Father, whom I never saw again. The

> children, Fräulein and I got on the train. I opened the window. I leant out as the train pulled away. I waved and waved. And so did they.

Winnie crossed the Channel, narrowly missing almost the entire British Fleet which was sailing straight up it from south to north. Fifty-five battleships, four battle-cruisers, twenty-seven cruisers, twenty-eight light cruisers and seventy-eight destroyers (the submarines stayed behind). The fleet sailed at night, without lights. I don't know whether Winnie was also sailing at night, but whatever the case, she and her little group made it safely back to Berlin, while the fleet, sailing close by, made it safely north to Scapa Flow.

Winston Churchill had his own way of telling his part of the story:

> As early as Tuesday, July 28, I felt that the Fleet should go to its War Station. It must go there at once, and secretly; it must be steaming to the north while every German authority, naval or military, had the greatest possible interest in avoiding collision with us. If it went early it need not go by the Irish Channel and north-about. It could go through the Straits of Dover and through the North Sea, and therefore the island would not be uncovered even for a single day. Moreover, it would arrive sooner and with less expenditure of fuel.
>
> At about 10 o'clock, therefore, on the Tuesday morning I proposed this step to the First Sea Lord and the Chief of Staff and found them wholeheartedly in favour of it. We decided that the Fleet should leave Portland at such an hour on the morning of the 29th as to pass the Straits of Dover during the hours of darkness, that it should traverse these waters at high speed and without lights, and with the utmost precaution proceed to Scapa Flow. I feared to bring this matter before Cabinet, lest it should mistakenly be considered a provocative action likely to damage the chances of peace. It would be unusual to bring movements of the British Fleet in Home Waters from one British port to another before Cabinet. I only therefore informed the Prime Minister, who at once gave his approval. Orders were accordingly sent to Sir George Callaghan, who was told incidentally to send the Fleet up under his second-in-command and to travel himself by land through London in order that we might have the opportunity of consultation with him.
>
> We may now picture this great Fleet, its flotillas and cruisers, steaming slowly out of Portland Harbour, squadron by squadron, scores of gigantic castles of steel wending their way across the misty, shining sea, like giants bowed in anxious thought. We may picture them again as darkness fell, eighteen miles of warships running at high speed and in absolute blackness

> through the narrow Straits, bearing with them into the broad waters of the North the safeguard of considerable affairs.
>
> Although there seemed to be no conceivable motive, chance or mischance, which could lead a rational German Admiralty to lay a trap of submarines or mines or to have given them the time to do so, we looked at each other with much satisfaction when on Thursday morning (the 30th) at our daily Staff Meeting the Flagship reported that the whole Fleet was well out in the centre of the North Sea. The strategic concentration of the fleet had been achieved with its transfer to Scottish waters.[8]

Winnie was home, but Philipp was about to leave. Before his father set off on his second trip to England, Hermann went round to Achenbachstraße to offer advice. He had been trained as a spy. Philipp had not. Worse still, Philipp wasn't well. He had bronchitis and was suffering from stomach pains. His health had been so bad that, long before his first summons from von Pohl, he had been planning a trip to Karlsbad[9] for a cure.

Another family emergency meeting. The three of them, Philipp, Mila and Hermann, sat in the *Berliner Zimmer*. Philipp slumped back in a large velvet-upholstered armchair. Mila perched at the dining table, her back and head parallel to the straight back of the dining chair on which she sat. Hermann sat at the other end of the table, leaning forward on his arms, his hands clasped together before him. How to handle this situation? They soon realized that the safest way forward was for Mila to accompany Philipp. She would be his cover, just as Winnie had covered for Hermann earlier that year. The Karlsbad cure was cancelled; an Isle of Wight cure took its place. Mila was nurse. The only silver lining anyone could find in this desperate situation was that at least Philipp was going to a place he knew well. Early in the reign, he had visited Osborne House, Portsmouth and Cowes several times, together with the Kaiser.

On 1 August 1914, they set off.

> So I was to go again to Portsmouth. I had to find out in which direction the English E-class U-Boats were sailing as they left the fleet review. If eastwards, war soon. If westwards, war later.
>
> My health for this Karlsbad-in-the-Isle-of Wight cure was convincingly bad. Thank God I was with my brave little wife. Has she ever let me down? No. Never. And she didn't then. In that moment of crisis, she stood by me.
>
> The express train from Berlin was overflowing with English people returning home, and in Queenborough the harbour bar was already in place. We were searched (only superficially) by a government official. We had difficulty at the reception in the Hotel Cecil in London. There were

unpleasant stares and many unfriendly remarks from fellow guests and staff. But I was exhausted so we had to spend the first night there. The next morning, we went on to Portsmouth, straight to the harbour. A yawning emptiness. *Quoi faire*? We took the ferry to the Isle of Wight and found ourselves near Sandown Bay in the Hotel Carlton, with magnificent views. From the music pavilion we could see the harbour, the anchorage and quays. But no submarines. Wait a minute. What are those white and pale grey spots just passing the Spithead Forts? Out with the pocket telescope. Good God! Submarines. Class E. And they are steering eastwards. Hurrah! An answer. Not a good one. But an answer. '*Mutter! Nach Hause*' [Mother! Home!] But first to the Post Office with a telegram.

It's a strange feeling sending such a message, however apparently harmless (it was in code), from enemy soil. And yes,without doubt,we were in enemy country. When we got back to London, we found it in a very military mood. There were double sentries everywhere, with guns at their side. All the stations were overflowing with Germans returning to their homeland. Military Policemen called out to those departing, 'Don't go back there. We'll beat you. You'd better join our army!'

It was Monday, 3 August. All was hustle and bustle. The Union Jack was flying from the Houses of Parliament. Every bit of transport was reserved, either for the army or the navy. All this business, and yet it was a bank holiday. Before going home, we went to the embassy to obtain entrance permits for Germany. Mila waited in the car at the embassy's main entrance. A policeman spoke to her. She pretended she didn't understand. Meanwhile, I was talking to the Naval Attaché, Captain von Müller. He clasped his head in both hands. 'Would you believe it?' he said. 'Prince Lichnowski still doesn't believe that the British are going to war!'

To the station! Aha! It's a Bank Holiday. No trains. Find the nearest good hotel. We book a room, but the hotel staff greet us with such hostility that we take a cab to London Zoo and spent our last day there, with the animals. I was drinking litres of milk in an effort to soothe the pain which had now spread all over my body.

At last. Time for our journey. There were nineteen of us, men and women, crushed into one compartment on the train. Almost all of us Germans. Finally, we reached Folkestone and boarded a Dutch steamer. There were searchlights scanning the waters as we passed Dover. A flotilla of destroyers was anchored near the harbour. Everything, everywhere, was on a war footing. But Mr Lichnowski couldn't see it.

Back in Germany, there were military transports all over the place, taking troops westward. Excited crowds thronged station platforms. Many

> 'Hurrahs', much singing of the *Deutschlandlied*, refreshments for soldiers (but also for us), confidence in victory, trust in God, delirious patriotism, unity, the scent of victory. And so on and so on. We finally got home.

Philipp and Mila could scarcely have cut it finer. The day they left London, the German ambassador, Prince Lichnowski, also left. At one hour before midnight, England declared war on Germany. Fortunately, by that time, Philipp and Mila were safely on their Dutch steamer and well out of Folkestone harbour.

Philipp blames Lichnowski fair and square for not publicly acknowledging the imminence of war. So did Kapitän von Müller. They both thought him blind. Philipp and von Müller were military men. They understood confrontation. Prince Lichnowski was a diplomat. His job was to avoid confrontation. But it was also to read the public mind, and this he failed to do accurately. In spite of the double sentries, the troop trains, the flags flying all over the place, he spent those last days of July and early August clinging to hopes for peace. 'Would you believe it? Prince Lichnowski still doesn't believe that the British are going to war!' Among German anglophiles, he was not alone. In Berlin, on the same day that Philipp was in the London embassy, Prince Heinrich told Winnie that there would be no war with Britain. Perhaps he was only reporting what he had heard from Lichnowski.

Whatever Princes Heinrich and Lichnowski thought, Britain was indeed hurtling into war. All the alliances were falling into place. Everyone stood on the threshold. Global war.

Part II

By Land and Sea: the Three Brothers at War, 1914–1916

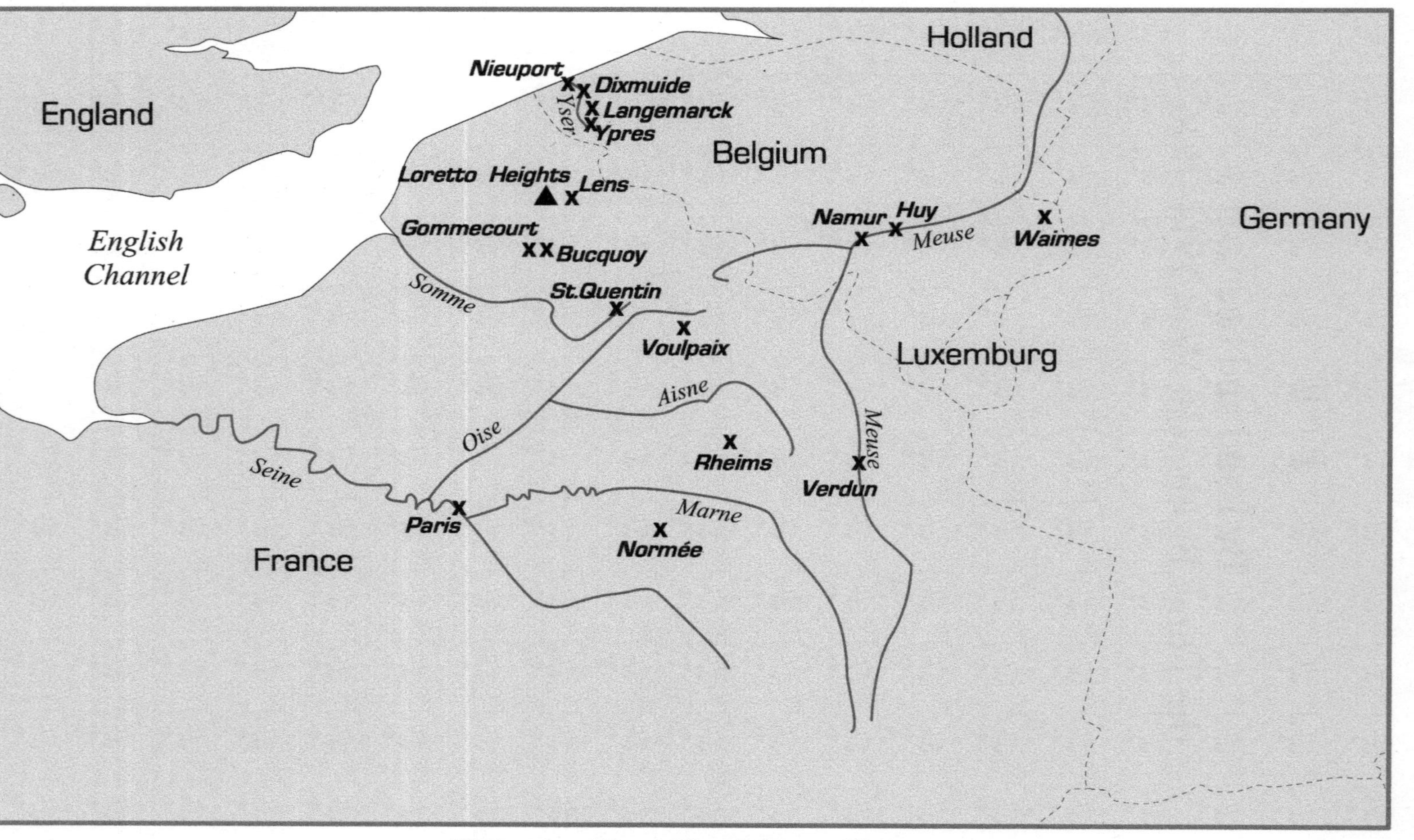

Waldemar's and Georg's War in Belgium and France.

Chapter 10

War in the Baltic

My husband came to fetch us from the Berlin Hauptbahnhof. It was the last day in July. I looked about me as we drove home. The streets were washed and tidy. The town smelt clean. Everything was fresh and spruce. How could this ever change?

A few days, no, a few hours later, I realised that the city looked normal, but actually the population was in a state of nervous tension. It was as if the entire nation were involved in a high-wire act. Would we reach the other end safely?

The next day, 1 August, Germany was at war with Russia. The German Army was fighting on the Eastern Front, and the naval war was in the Baltic. Prince Heinrich,[1] the Kaiser's brother, was appointed *Oberbefehlshaber der Ostseestreitkräfte* (Commander-in-Chief of the Baltic Fleet) and Hermann was his *Admiralstabsoffizier* (Staff Officer). The naval enemy was Russia. Britain's position was uncertain. Everyone waited with bated breath.

Prince Heinrich, like Prince Lichnowski and so many other German Anglophiles, was finding it next to impossible to contemplate war with Britain. He had, through family and friends, many close and valued ties with England. His mother was English. His grandmother was the Queen of England, and he had none of his elder brother's hang-ups. No jealousy. No envy. Not so much insecurity. At the time of the July Crisis, he was in Britain on a golfing holiday. The crisis forced him home at speed. When Winnie reached Berlin, the Prince was also there. He and Hermann were both at Admiralty headquarters, taking part in discussions on how war in the Baltic should be conducted.

It was 3 August. I was waiting outside the Admiralty in a taxi. On Hermann's instructions, I had packed two suitcases. He was leaving for Kiel that afternoon.

When the prince learned that I was at the door, he sent his aide-de-camp down to speak to me. I was to take heart, he said. There would never be a war with Britain. Then Hermann arrived. He took the cases, kissed me goodbye and told me to apply for a pass to join him.

> Next day, I met a retired general in the street. He was quite broken with grief. We had just invaded Belgium, crossing a frontier[2] which we ourselves, along with Britain and other countries, had guaranteed. We had broken our own pledge. 'We had to do it,' said the general, 'but it is a terrible, terrible decision to have made.' It was indeed. Everyone was thinking of Britain. What would she do now?
>
> On 5 August, I woke to learn that the very worst had happened. Britain had declared war on Germany and Austria.
>
> I was frantic. Leaving my little boys with the nurse, I rushed out of the flat and ran into the street. I ran on and on, through the Tiergarten, through the Brandenburger Tor, down Unter den Linden, turning right on Wilhelmstrasse.

Winnie was instinctively running to the British Embassy.[3]

> I stopped. Something was wrong. The embassy was silent. All the doors and windows were shut. There was no one about. They must have known before the rest of us.

Britain had actually declared war the evening before, at 11.20 pm.

> I felt abandoned. I stared, speechless. Then I turned and walked home. What else could I do? That evening, a girl we had met in Libau earlier in the year turned up on my doorstep. She was German and had just fled her home, travelling on top of a hay cart. So this is what lies ahead? The first refugee I had ever met. I took her to my parents-in-law's apartment. They put her up.[4]

The next day, the Russian Army, massed in the Libau area, invaded East Prussia. The girl had fled just in time. Those living in her part of the world, where national boundaries and cultural loyalties did not coincide, were to experience invasion and counter-invasion, by one side or the other, throughout the war, and after.

The mood in Berlin changed from high anxiety to wild patriotism. 'Defend the Fatherland!' was the cry. Groups of young people marched down the street singing rousing nationalistic songs. Flags appeared everywhere. Men volunteered in droves, and rumours abounded. Winnie was told that there were spies running around the city dressed as nuns and that the water supply had been poisoned. People started stockpiling. Shortages were bound to happen. Britain (ruler of the waves) blockaded Germany from the first day of the war, not by surrounding Germany's ports but by using the British Isles themselves as a giant breakwater.

The Isles blocked Germany's exit to the sea. She had two ways through. One lay to the north, between Shetland and Norway, and the other was through the English Channel. These two exits were now mined, and all international shipping round Britain was checked against a restrictive list of what Britain unilaterally declared as 'contraband of war'. That list included foodstuffs. The policy was designed to deprive Germany not only of material for its defence industries but also of the means to keep starvation at bay.[5]

Many countries, including the United States, complained that Britain's move was high-handed and a breach of international law, but most neutral merchant vessels complied. They had no choice. They docked at British ports, agreed to inspections, submitted to the removal by force of any cargo deemed illegal under the new British definitions, and accepted, probably with some relief, an escort through British minefields to a destination approved by the British.

Although a continental country, Germany was dependent on imports by sea. In 1913, Germany imported almost half of its iron ore from Sweden. Without iron, weapons manufacture would have halted. Food and manufactured goods were imported from all over the world for the civilian population. There would soon be shortages of almost everything: sugar, coffee, tea. Over time, the government offered replacements. Ersatz coffee, ersatz tea, ersatz sugar, and a disagreeable product known as *Kriegsbrot* (war bread), partly made from sawdust. With no imports of cotton, cloth was woven from nettles, and shoe manufacturing all but ceased. People started to hoard. That first week of the war, Winnie joined the crowd. She bought endless boxes of quarter-pound packets of tea. These lasted her until the end of the war, providing tremendous solace on the way.

> Almost one month after the outbreak of war, I received a message from the Admiralty that my request for a permit to join Hermann would be granted. I could join him wherever he was stationed.
>
> I gave my provisions (except for the tea) to neighbours. I took my children to my mother-in-law. I went to the Admiralty. Our old friend Kapitänleutnant Arnaud de la Perrière[6] was working there. He gave me my permit.
>
> Packing only one small case so I could carry it myself, I walked to the station. A journey to Kiel usually takes five hours; that day, it took twenty-five. The railways were in chaos. Every train was a troop train and running an emergency route. Frequently, the engine came to a halt. We had to wait for hours on platforms where volunteers handed out cups of tea and coffee. There were only two civilians on the whole train. I was one of them.
>
> I found Hermann living and working in the headquarters. I was to stay in a villa near Düsternbrook, home of the Prince's aide-de-camp.

Obviously, this wasn't the kind of arrangement we'd hoped for, but I was given a permanent pass and this admitted me to the castle whenever I wished. I attended dinners there, along with everyone else on the Admiralty staff, and their wives. Presiding over every occasion were the Prince and Princess. Every evening, guests and staff gathered at one end of the long drawing room, while the Prince and Princess arrived from the other. This was a court, as well as headquarters for the Baltic fleet.

How to make sure I did the right thing? Hermann told me not to worry. 'Just be yourself', he said, and then added as if he wasn't quite sure that that would suffice, 'Always follow the others.' I remembered Mademoiselle Mathilde and my finishing school in Brussels. She had insisted we learn court etiquette, which I had always thought a complete waste of time. Well. I was wrong.

When Prince Heinrich first spoke to me, he spoke in English. I, being a silly girl and wanting to show off, replied in German. I soon realised that this was a mistake and apologised. His reaction was typical. He said he had deserved my rebuke. We were at war. He should have spoken German. He had chosen English because he wanted to show me his love for England, for the English and for the English language.

The fourteenth of August was his birthday.[7] He threw a huge birthday dinner in the castle for everyone on his staff and their wives. It was a very grand occasion. To my utter horror, I was seated beside him. I think he was being kind. He wanted to honour England. To show he had no personal enmity. There we sat, in the centre of the longest table and everyone was listening to what we said. Or so I feared. Of course, we talked about the war. I could tell from the shininess of his eyes and the faltering of his voice, that he felt the situation deeply. I mean as far as England was concerned.

On normal days, luckily for me, I could leave dinner in the castle early and join my husband. The only drawback was that, before leaving, I had to walk alone, up the huge *Saal* (dining hall), curtsy to the Princess, ask her permission to leave, and then walk all the way down again. I felt as if everyone's eyes were boring into my body. '*Die Engländerin*' (the English woman), they were saying to themselves, but not with prejudice. I was a curiosity. Meanwhile, the soul of Mlle Mathilde was whispering in my ear, 'Head up. Back straight.'

This situation went on for some time until Prince Heinrich's chief of staff said, 'We must not keep these two lovebirds apart', and he gave leave for both of us to live together, outside the *Schloss*. Hurrah!

One evening, gathered with the ladies after dinner, I was asked to join my husband and the Prince. They had gone off by themselves and were having a tête-à-tête. As I entered the room, I hesitated. I saw my husband. His back was towards me and he was telling the Prince that he wanted to be relieved of staff duties in headquarters. He wanted to take up active service. I stepped closer. The Prince saw me. 'Your husband is most ungrateful. He is asking me to let him leave for a more active post. I am very hurt. It had been my special wish to have him with me, but I suppose there is no help for it. I shall have to let him go. Really. It's too bad of him to let me down like this. What do you think? Shall he have his way? He smiled as he teased.

Prince Henry was tall, slim, good looking and kind. 'It's for you to decide', I said. Thank God I did, for it was the right reply, but then, what else could I have said? It was a phrase I was to use again, four years later, when I lost my man forever. On the day of this conversation, 21 August 1914, Admiral Ehler Behring was appointed Detached Admiral[8] to the Eastern Baltic. The day after, Hermann was appointed Behring's *Admiralstabsoffizier*.

Hermann was to serve with the Baltic Fleet from 1914 to 1917. Its headquarters were in Kiel, where Prince Heinrich oversaw forces based in a number of ports strung along the Baltic's southern shore. Chief among these were Warnemünde, Danzig, Königsberg, Swinemünde, Memel and, after their capture in 1915, Libau and Windau.[9] Apart from those last two, Winnie was able to join her husband whenever he was in any of these places. And she did. At first, she flitted from Berlin to places like Danzig, but later, as the boys grew old enough to attend school, she rented apartments close to where Hermann was stationed, Swinemünde, for example. She became a nomad, a habit she never threw off.

Once Hermann left Prince Henry's staff, I returned to Berlin, closed up our flat and moved, with the children, to my in-laws' apartment. From there, I flitted to and fro, between Berlin and the Baltic, whenever I got news that Hermann was ashore.

It was in Danzig that I saw him next.

At the beginning of the war, for four days, the German navy was fighting only Russia. Now, with Britain involved, it was fighting the Royal Navy as well. The main fleets on either side did little. The British Grand Fleet spent most of the war parked out of harm's way in Scapa Flow, while the German High Seas Fleet was anchored to the south, in the Jade Bight, near Wilhelmshaven. Both countries had other fleets, though Britain had far more ships than Germany.[10] The most significant encounter between the two sides was the 1916 Battle of Jutland, when the outcome merely confirmed attitudes among senior naval officers on both sides that a naval *Entscheidungsschlacht* (an all-out battle to determine the fate of the war as a whole) was risky and unlikely to decide anything anyway. The Grand Fleet was larger than Germany's High Seas Fleet but that alone did not determine victory. The British Grand Fleet's commander, Admiral Jellicoe, cautious and risk-averse, was determined to maintain his main fleet as a strong, single unit.[11] The Kaiser felt the same. He would, as far as possible, keep his High Seas Fleet intact.

The war in the Baltic, away from the 'High Seas', was different. Here, apart from in the dead of winter when much was ice-bound, there were daily encounters between the two warring sides. The German Baltic fleet had four objectives: to protect the German coast; to protect Germany's Baltic trade (especially imports of iron ore from Sweden); to defeat the Russian Baltic fleet; and to threaten St Petersburg in the eastern Baltic, at the apex of the Gulf of Finland. This could force Russia out of the war and solve Germany's problem of having to fight on two fronts.

These goals would not be easy, because Germany's Baltic fleet was smaller and weaker than Russia's and because early in the war, Germany made one stupendous blunder. That blunder condemned Germany to fight its Baltic war with one hand, so to speak, tied behind its back. It condemned the entire German naval effort, all over the world, to the same fate. That blunder was a disaster for Germany and also for Hermann. It led directly to his death.

Russia's fleet had been tried, tested and found wanting in the Russo-Japanese War, but that was nine years ago. Time enough for the experience to be viewed less as a drain on the Russian navy's morale and more as an advantage. Russian sailors and commanders were battle-hardened and experienced. The Russian Baltic fleet was large and included battleships, ironclads and submarines. But it was ageing, underfunded, and (for the first few months only) its intelligence services were poor.

The German Baltic fleet was also underfunded. It also consisted of ageing vessels, though these were lesser in size and power than those of its opponent.[12] Its biggest ships were light cruisers, it had no ironclads. Several of the German ships were former training boats, and one of its submarines, the *U-3*, ran on paraffin and had to be towed into position before delivering an attack. This situation may come as a surprise, given Germany's recent massive naval budgets. And yes, the navy as a whole was indeed well-funded and well-equipped. But not the Baltic fleet. German top-of-the-line ships were busy in Wihelmshaven, doing not very much at all.

Throughout the war, Germany's main opponent in the Baltic remained the Russian navy rather than the British. This was because Admiral Jellicoe thought it too risky to send in his surface ships. The entrance to the Baltic lay through

'The Sound' (between Sweden and Denmark) and was too narrow (4km wide at its narrowest), and too shallow (7m deep at its shallowest). It was dangerous even for submarines but, at a pinch, submarines still *could* get through, so Jellicoe sent in his long-range E-class boats, the backbone of the British submarine fleet. Not all arrived unscathed. Two arrived in October 1914, three in August 1915. Four smaller C-class submarines also reached the Baltic, travelling there overland by way of Archangel and Russia's northern rivers. They were not fully operational until late 1917. The British submarines were based in Reval and operated under the command of the Russian Baltic Fleet. The impact of the arrival of the E-class boats was substantial. They were technologically more advanced and far more powerful than anything available to the German Baltic fleet. They carried five torpedo tubes and no deck guns. Also, since submarines were new, no one knew how to deal with them. News of their presence caused great alarm on the German side.

The first year of the war was the golden age of the submarine. The top predator, it was next to impossible even to know when a submarine was present. Lookouts would constantly scan the waters for a thin, dark periscope riding just above the surface. But in a huge ocean, with constant waves, what chance did they have of spotting it? It was easier to check for the white wake which followed the periscope. Even when one was sighted, what to do? Commanders could ram the submarine (provided it didn't dive), or sit over it (if it did). Depth charges, hydrophones, submarine nets – all these were yet to be either refined or invented.

Hermann had resigned a relatively safe post at headquarters to work with Behring, who was someone he didn't know. But he did know, from what his father had told him, that for a successful career in the navy, much depended on the relationship between you and your Commanding Officer. Hermann was lucky. *Detachierte Konteradmiral* (Detached Rear-Admiral) Ehler Behring was just the kind of man to appeal to Hermann. He was good-humoured, bold, dynamic, an innovator and a risk-taker. He was a great admirer of Nelson,[13] seen in the German navy (as in the British) as the prototype for all innovators. Behring saw risk as an essential element in war. He once said, 'Where there are no risks, then success is out of the question.'[14] This very much distinguished him from many other wartime leaders. Time and again, Philipp would complain to Hermann that the Kaiser and many of his generals lacked a willingness to take risks. This is not to say that Behring was foolhardy. On the contrary, he was meticulous, full of caution, but also avid for challenges and hard-work. He made tremendous demands on his crew, and the men responded well.

The Baltic war was by no means a miserable experience for German sailors. Writing about it afterwards, they used phrases such as *frisch-fröhlich* (fresh and happy). Even allowing for rose-coloured hindsight, these men seemed to have enjoyed their work and appreciated the commanders for whom they served. Not that their task was easy. Not that they didn't put their lives on the line every day and sometimes every night as well. Not that it was without challenges. They enjoyed it because it *was* challenging. And because they were doing a job they were used to. Sailors in the German Baltic navy were, by and large, professionals, not volunteers or conscripts as in the army. The sea was their métier. Normally, their challenge came from the sea and the weather, now it came from the enemy as well. But challenge was what they enjoyed. They recalled their time with Behring and Hermann with – dare I say it? – delight.

Hermann's experience of the war was very different to that of his brothers. Both Georg and Waldemar served in the army, and the army worked with massive numbers, men in tens of thousands. Such numbers lent a certain anonymity to the individual. The army also required endless marching, much hanging around at crunch points and participation in desperate battles in which the casualties were measured in tens of thousands, and the after-effects were visible to all, for days, for weeks, for months, even for decades thereafter. A sailor, on the other hand, escaped such numbers and the anonymity which went with them. He also escaped the carnage. The worst disaster in the Baltic cost the lives of 670 men and, once the boat had sunk, the waters soon covered the scene of the slaughter so that nothing remained visible. Somehow a sailor's sense of freedom and independence shines through Hermann's wartime story even though, when he became a U-Boat Commander, this freedom was increasingly diminished by unknown and unknowable perils.

One officer, Kapitän zur See Franz Wieting, who served onboard with Behring and Hermann wrote:

> The conduct of the (Baltic) war was fresh and cheerful. Our long distance operations to reach the enemy's waters involved a wonderfully invigorating degree of risk. We had enthusiastic officers and crews. And we had an excellent leader in the person of Rear Admiral Behring. He believed in taking the war to the enemy.

Describing Behring's behaviour under fire, he said that Behring paced up and down the command bridge with unhurried step. 'When the first heavy shells exploded close off our bows, he doffed his cap to them as they fell.'[15]

And a gunnery officer also on board wrote of Behring and Hermann: 'Both men were held in high esteem by all aboard the *Augsburg*. The men took them to their hearts.'[16]

On another occasion, in November 1914, in total blackness and close to the enemy coast, Wieting again talks about the way that Behring coped with danger. Behring and Hermann were standing on the bridge of their boat, which was sinking. There had been two massive explosions and they thought they had been torpedoed by one of the newly arrived British submarines. A direct torpedo strike should sink a boat quickly, but they were sinking slowly. The crew, facing out to sea, stood in a line on the listing deck below them, everyone staring into the night, hoping to sight a rescue boat. The silence was suddenly broken by the sound of Admiral Behring's voice. He was talking to Hermann, but his bass tones boomed down from the bridge. No one could miss his black humour or his defiant tone.

'Well, my friend Gercke,' he said, 'there's one consolation we can take with us to the bottom. These English torpedoes, they're good for nothing!'[17]

Behring and Hermann became firm friends. Between the two of them, they set the tone for the war in the Baltic. They were at a numerical and mechanical disadvantage in an asymmetrical war, yet their relentlessly aggressive spirit put the Russians squarely on the defensive and they remained there throughout the war. As Admiral von Mantey later wrote, 'Rear Admiral Behring and Admiralstabsoffizier Kapitänleutnant Gercke were the ones who, with absolute dedication to the job, maintained German naval supremacy in the Baltic Sea. They continually kept the Russians in check.'[18]

To Behring and Hermann, the relatively small size of their boats was not altogether a disadvantage. Both disagreed with Admiral Tirpitz's obsession with big ships. Tirpitz wanted to compete with the British Dreadnought programme. He wanted massive battleships and favoured an obvious, typically male competition. But Behring and Hermann thought the future belonged to the nimble, unobtrusive, smaller boat. They wanted small, fast, armed vessels, useful for short-range scouting, for mine-laying and mine-sweeping. They wanted boats which were cheap to build and cheap to operate. They wanted the light cruisers and torpedo boats which, as it turned out, they had. Hermann's major triumphs in the Baltic were all achieved by smaller, and sometimes very small, boats.

In this way, Russian naval superiority was transformed in German eyes from a disadvantage into a welcome challenge, a challenge matched by the weather. In winter, the eastern Baltic can be ice-bound from December till April, and at all times it is liable to sudden fogs, which arrive without warning. They can be so dense that you cannot see from one end of a boat to the other. These were challenges indeed, as were the many shifting and highly treacherous Baltic sandbanks.

Behring and Hermann worked together from August 1914 till May 1915. For their first mission, Behring opted to take two light cruisers and some torpedo boats deep into the heavily mined Finnish Gulf. They were heading straight into the lion's den, for the Gulf leads to Russia's main naval base at Kronstadt and to St Petersburg. It was surrounded by Russian territory and viewed by Russia almost as an inland Russian sea. The Germans planned to lay mines inside it. The idea was bold and would have succeeded but for nature (fog and shifting sandbanks), compounded by human error (outdated equipment and incompetence).

On the night of 26 August, the first night of Behring's sortie, they had just entered the Gulf when patches of dense fog suddenly appeared. Behring was on his flagship, SMS *Augsburg*, with Hermann beside him. They were accompanied by SMS *Magdeburg* (another cruiser), by the *U-3* (an antiquated, paraffin-fuelled submarine), and by some torpedo boats. In the fog, shortly after midnight, the *Magdeburg* ran hard aground on Russian-owned Odensholm Island only some 300m from Odensholm lighthouse and signalling station. Try as they might, the cruiser could not be freed. In such a situation, the captain is supposed to order his crew to plant explosives, abandon ship and blow it up, making sure that the code books perish in the explosion. But before completing this work, the fog suddenly lifted to reveal two Russian warships bearing down on them. The Russians opened fire, which set the demolition charges off prematurely. Panic.In that panic, no one was sure what happened to the codebooks. All that was known for sure was that some men had drowned, that the commander of the boat had refused to abandon her and that he, together with fifty-seven members of his crew, spent the rest of the war as prisoners. But no one was sure about the code books. Had they or had they not been destroyed?

Behring feared the worst. Prince Heinrich feared the same. He reported the potential loss to Berlin. But, strangely, the Admiralty did little in response. Throughout the war, when it came to codes, the Admiralty in Berlin had a blind spot. Were they over-confident? Did they believe their codes to be impenetrable? Or was it just a refusal to face the worst-case scenario, making it a dreadful, costly case of cowardice? The Navy carried on, business as usual. But the code book,[19] together with German maps of the Baltic, had indeed fallen into Russian hands. Worse still, the Russians forwarded a copy to the British, and bright people in both countries soon discovered how to use them. Although there were other occasions when German code books fell into Allied hands, this meant that from the start, British and Russian intelligence knew what German boats were saying to each other; what they were saying to home base; and what home base was saying to them. This event was responsible for the entrapment of many German ships and U-Boats, and for the loss of countless sailors' lives.

Berlin occasionally changed the codes, but did so in a cavalier manner, using potentially compromised codes to explain the new one. The view of some in the London Admiralty was that Germany's vulnerable codes may have cost her the war. The Head of its decoding centre described Britain's decrypting ability as 'the kingpin of everything'.[20] The seeds of the final disaster were sown right at the beginning, on 27 August 1914.

Typical of Behring, despite the loss of the *Magdeburg*, he continued the mission. The following evening, together with his torpedo boats and the venerable *U-3* (which had been towed to the Finnish Gulf), they met two Russian armoured cruisers and came under fire. Behring had given the *U-3* orders to position itself in a certain spot while he, feigning damage, would lure the Russians into the submarine's line of fire. But the *U-3* was old. It had to surface to steady itself for firing. The Russians saw it and they fled, standard procedure at the time on sighting a submarine. Behring and his depleted flotilla returned to Kiel.

The Germans never learnt that the Russians and the British had set up secret code-breaking rooms. They never discovered till long after the Second World War that their messages were being read by the enemy. In the Baltic, from this time on, the Russians remained on the defensive, but they were able to effectively parry every German offensive, no matter how innovative, no matter how daring. They knew what was coming. They pinned large charts divided into squares, exactly the same as those used by the Germans, onto the walls of their operational headquarters. As decoded messages came in, they marked the position of the German ships in red, and of their own in blue.

Chapter 11

Waldemar's Battle of the Marne

Mobilization in Germany began at midnight on 2 August, the day after Germany declared war on Russia and the day before the beginning of its war with France. Waldemar was drafted back into his old regiment, the Königin Elisabeth Garde Grenadier, in which both he and Georg had undertaken their military service. The Queen Elisabeths were part of the Gardekorps, an élite military unit headquartered in Berlin. Its 2nd Division included four infantry regiments: the Augustas (Number 1), the Franz (Number 2), the Queen Elisabeths (Number 3) and the Alexanders (Number 4). Unlike most other regiments, they referred to each other by name rather than number. Throughout the course of the war, the four regiments more or less stuck together. Waldemar was in the 2nd Infantry Division, 3rd Regiment, 1st Battalion, 4th Company.

The Gardekorps was the favoured destination for old Prussian aristocratic and military families; it was, in fact, the favourite of the House of Hohenzollern itself. The Kaiser's second son, Prinz Eitel Friedrich, was a Gardekorps commander, and the Colonel-in-Chief of the Elisabeths was the Kaiser's sister, Queen Sophie of Greece. She was in England at the time of the July Crisis and, just like Prince Heinrich, she rushed back to her brother's capital and on 3 August, reported to regimental headquarters. She was there to wish her Regiment all the success in the world. The Regiment was, naturally, honoured by her visit but it was such a rushed, last-minute business that only twenty-two officers were there to receive her.

A few days later, in the morning of 8 August, the Elisabeths' Regimental Commander, the avuncular Oberst (Colonel) Böhm,[1] gathered his battalions together in the regimental exercise yard and gave them a good pep talk. In the afternoon, their Brigade Commander, General von Petersdorff[2] (less fatherly, more like a schoolmaster) did the same thing. And the next day, in the Tiergarten, Waldemar's battalion was given a third pep talk by the Kaiser himself (a formal exhortation, riddled with platitudes).

On 9 August, little more than a week after war was declared, and little more than a month since they had become engaged, Waldemar and Christel said their goodbyes. She, Philipp and Mila stood on the station platform. He was in a troop train bound for the Belgian frontier, a Leutnant in the 1st Battalion, 4th Company. One thought was in everyone's mind: when would they see each other again?

The Gardekorps was to form part of General von Bülow's Second Army.[3] The First Army, under General von Kluck,[4] had already invaded Belgium and was taking the northern coastal route, as recommended by General von Schlieffen in his great Plan. But the Second Army was taking a new route, one devised by Wilhelm II's Chief of General Staff, General Helmuth von Moltke,[5] whose biggest claim to fame was that he was the nephew of a military hero with the same name. The two are distinguished today by calling one 'the Elder' and the other 'the Younger'. The Elder had led the country to victory in the Franco-Prussian War (that touchstone in Wilhelmine Germany for all things good), while von Moltke the Younger had done more or less nothing at all, except to have the grace to try to avoid the job he was offered by the Kaiser. He admitted, as Philipp pointed out, that he was not cut out to be a Chief of General Staff. He didn't have the necessary steel. But the Kaiser got his way. Objection overruled.

The new route for the Gardekorps was through the High Ardennes, which lie along the border between Germany and Belgium. It was, and still is, a twisty, mountainous route, where narrow, cobbled roads wind their way up steep hillsides. High, dark forests lower on either side. I saw them myself when, roughly one hundred years later, I followed in Waldemar's footsteps. The route they took is as favourable a setting for ambushes as ever there was. Apart from the tall trees on either side, the road makes frequent bends, zigzagging uphill so that, to get from the bottom to the top, you repeatedly turn dark corners and walk twice the distance that the crow flies.

Yet the route had one great advantage. Because it was so obviously unsuitable for anyone wishing to invade, no defensive forts had been built along it. Belgium's High Ardennes were undefended, a fort-free zone. The temptation was too great. Von Moltke wrote his plan, and so Waldemar landed in the High Ardennes, marching many unnecessary extra kilometres.

The Gardekorps was divided into two parallel streams, four regiments in each, and both made their way into Belgium by the High Ardennes route. Once through, they would regroup as the Second Army, march into France and join the First Army, which had set out along the coast ahead of them. Together, they would swing south to reach the area just north of Paris for that massive, long-desired, conclusive *Entscheidungsschlacht*, a winner-takes-all battle. With France defeated, about turn for the second target – Russia. If the 1914 invasion of France had followed the pattern set in 1870, when France was ruled by the weak Emperor Napoleon III, this plan might have worked. What the Kaiser and his generals had not considered was that, for one side to win, the other side has to give up, and there was, in 1914, no Napoleon III ready to concede to Germany at the first blow.

Headquartered in Berlin, the Garde drew recruits from Prussia, with some men coming from Elsass-Lothringen which had been designated, since 1871, as 'Imperial lands'. The Elsass-Lothringians were at a disadvantage because few in the rest of the regiment were sure which side they were really on. Waldemar was also at a disadvantage because he was a reserve officer and not, like most of his brother officers, a professional. Apart from that, he came from neither an aristocratic nor a military family, and his father had not fought in the 1870/71 war. It didn't take him long to realize that the fathers of so many other officers had, and that their grandfathers and great-grandfathers had fought Napoleon. Or so they said.

At the beginning of the war, companies were led by officers of the lowest rank, *Leutnant*. They led companies of about 250 men, though these grew smaller and smaller as the war progressed. And they led from the front, which meant they were always the first to get killed. The First World War became known as *Der Krieg der Leutnants* (the War of the Lieutenants). In August 1914, there were plenty of professional *Leutnants* to command not only every company but also every platoon (a small group of about six men operating as a quasi-independent unit within the company). As a result, Waldemar was at first an officer with no special position, but only four months later, so many lives had been lost that there were no longer enough professionals for these positions. In November 1914, Waldemar was appointed to lead a platoon.

In the Gardekorps, two Regiments formed a Brigade, two Brigades formed part of a Division, and the two Divisions formed the Gardekorps (Berlin). In addition to the infantry, there were artillery brigades, sappers, cavalry divisions, flying units (aircraft for reconnaissance purposes), bridge-building units, telephone engineering units, mobile munition units, field-hospital units, many, many horses (one for each officer, others for the cavalry and extra heavy horses for pulling the artillery), veterinary units, cobbler units, mobile kitchens, mobile baking units, plus waggons for the transport of mountains of baggage.

On the road, the invading infantry and its entourage was so enormous that it resembled less a military parade than a *Völkerwanderung*,a folk migration, the kind which took place in the Iron Age when the Franks moved westwards en masse. But this was the twentieth century. It was a great shock for those being invaded to see so many foreigners on the road. It took the best part of a day for the entire Division to pass any given spot. And the spots they were passing were, at first, almost entirely quiet and rural. The army was marching across Belgium's and France's sparsely populated countryside, through villages of some twenty or so houses. When they arrived, farmers were cutting corn in the surrounding fields or digging vegetable plots, cows were grazing, women cooking (their kitchen door open in the summer heat) and children playing in farmyards. All was quiet and peaceful when suddenly distant dust clouds warned them that something was amiss. Villagers scarcely had time to gather at the *Mairie* before the land was crawling with thousands of men in uniform marching four abreast, officers riding alongside. The air was full of the tramp of boots, the jingling of harness, the snorting and farting of horses, the clank and rumble of artillery, the creaking of wooden wagon wheels, the noisy engines of a few motor cars. And the smells? Intense. The incredible, undiluted maleness of it all. It must have been alarming, but also intriguing. The kind of horror show you watch through almost closed fingers.

From the soldiers' point of view, the worst thing was the marching. They were ordered to cover sometimes 40km a day or even more. Men like Waldemar weren't used to this, but all had to obey. Speed was of the essence to meet the requirements of the Schlieffen Plan. They had to get that *Entscheidungsschlacht* over with as quickly as possible so that they could turn round and protect Germany's eastern borders. Boots were a man's most precious possession: they had to fit and they had to be kept in good repair. Naturally, the cobbler units were much in demand, and a spare pair was flung over each infantryman's shoulder, part of his 30kg of kit. That kit also included a food pouch with his 'iron rations' (emergency food for when the kitchen unit failed to keep up), a water bottle, a coat, a blanket, a waterproof sheet (which served as a kind of tent) and, of course, his weapons (a rifle and a short side-dagger). Officers carried pistols.

In 2022, when I was there, it was a brilliant summer, just as in 1914. Once in France, the pine-gloom lifted and the countryside opened up. I too was marching in August. It was hot and dry. Harvest-time. Puffs of grey and white cloud drifted across a bright blue sky, and the golden stubble of recently harvested corn-fields stretched right up to the horizon. Brilliant gold. Sparkling blue. My spirits lifted. Waldemar's must have, too.

'*La Douce France*' lay all around me. Nothing but fields and woodland punctuated by the occasional sleepy village. A church, a *Mairie*, a school and a handful of houses. In almost every village I saw ancient, walled, fortress-like farmyards. Places where Waldemar and his men once bivouacked. In one village I saw an oak tree well over a thousand years old. Waldemar saw it too. He bivouacked close by and must have strolled past it in the evening, before turning in for a night's rest.

He then. I now. We were both on our way to the Marne valley. That's where the weather broke for both of us, but for him it wasn't just the weather which broke. Everything did. The whole war broke. That spirited surge which had carried the men forward suddenly came to a full stop.

Waldemar was twenty-five years old when he went to war. He wrote letters to Christel at every opportunity. At the end of the war, she gave all Waldemar's letters to Philipp save one, the very last one. That last letter, she treasured all her life, even though, after the war, she married someone else. Some of his letters follow:

Waimes,
12 August 1914

Dearest, dearest girl,
What can I say? Who would have thought this would happen so quickly? First of all, thank you so much for coming to see me off. And thank you for your precious gifts. I have your photo in my pocket. All the time.

The train trip was interminable. Very slow. There were endless stops and hold-ups. It took us thirty-seven hours. The railways are one mass of crowded troop trains. Huge armies are on the move. Look at our own. All four of our regiments were travelling to the same spot and there are 16,000 men in our Division alone. Hats off to whoever is doing the logistics. Please stay away from the railways for the duration of the war! Not that we all travelled on the same train. We and the Alexanders arrived last night. We are in Waimes, close to the Belgian border. Somewhere in these hills are the Franz and the Augustas.

I can't say I'm overly enthusiastic about Waimes. There is a certain gloom about the place. The houses look severe. They are built of rough sandstone with dressed stone round doors and windows. There's not much in the way of decorative trim. Perhaps it suits the place. Perhaps the architectural style is a reflection of the dark pine forests which cap the mountains and line the roads. Yes. We are in the High Ardennes. This and all the other villages, as far as I can see, are tucked away, deep in the bottom of narrow valleys. Green fields rise up at almost forty-five degrees on either side. I can see cows grazing on steep slopes.

We've been spread between a number of different villages, but all the same, there are lots of us in any one village, and our arrival was sudden. No one was expecting us. It must be quite a shock to the locals. And, of course, as well as the men, there are also our horses, the artillery, the cavalry, the baggage train and our mobile kitchens. The mobile kitchens are a new thing. Apparently, the Kaiser saw them in use in the Russian army so now we have them too. Not a bad idea, provided they keep up with us.

We've been billeted with local families. I write this in a small room, in a small house, where four children stare at me wide-eyed with curiosity.

They and their parents are very kind. So is everybody. Complete strangers in the street wish us good luck and thank us. God knows why. We haven't done anything at all. Our men are in good humour. It's nice to be fêted and made much of. Why not enjoy it? It won't last. Tomorrow we cross the border into Belgium. I somehow think our reception will be different there.

We spent yesterday wearing in our new boots. They're a bit slippy. Thank God for the cobblers in the baggage train, and for our spare pairs. The regulars are used to marching, but for us reservists it's tough going. The plan is to march 40km a day. And as long as we are in the High Ardennes, it'll be up and down hill all the time. The men have to carry 30kg in kit, though officers are spoilt. Our kit goes in the baggage train, but some of the regulars tell me it's best to carry your own gear, just in case the baggage train gets held up. You don't want to get caught bivouacking at night without blanket or tent gear. We carry large ground sheets which, if propped up in the right way, can serve as a rudimentary sort of tent. The roads here are good, but hard to walk on. Unforgiving. They are all cobbled. So far, they have been wide enough for us to march four abreast. The officers ride. Yes. Guess what? At last I have a horse.

If everything goes according to plan, this should be over in about six weeks or so. Now let's see. If we take 11 August as the start date, I should be back with you by the end of September. Awful. But it could be worse.

Dearest girl. I love you very much. Ever your own Waldemar (Yes. Leutnant!)

Near Huy,
16 August 1914

Dearest Christel,
We are in Belgium! Amazing. How easy it was. There was no resistance of any kind. There was the border (or so we were told) and we just stepped over it. We marked the moment with our usual 'Three Hurrahs' and we sang the *Deutschlandlied*.[6]

Then we had a truly massive, glittering, military review. All the top brass and the entire Second Army, assembled near Stavelot, a handsome, eighteenth century Belgian border town. Tall, elegant houses line numerous town squares. There are stone fountains and water troughs everywhere. Our horses loved it. But the streets are narrow so, for safety, we gathered in the fields outside. The bigwigs stood on a reviewing platform and took the salute. Von Bülow himself was there. Everybody who was anybody was there. And the entire Division marched past. It was a huge morale booster. Not just for them (!), but also for us.

We rode or marched, led by bands and followed by artillery. It took hours and hours for us all to pass the platform. I don't know what the locals made of it. Not much, I suspect. By the way, the smiling faces and cries of 'welcome' and 'thank you' have ceased. Surprise, surprise. Few citizens came out to watch. I have to admit that our attitude has changed as well. We are nervous and distrustful which, given the situation, anyone would understand. This nervousness applies to all of us, even to those of my fellow officers who come from illustrious military families. Yes, even they are nervous now. It's all quite logical really. They may be professionals, but they've never marched in enemy territory before, nor have they seen real-life combat. Their fathers fought. They didn't.

After that review, we met the first tentative resistance. It was in Trois Ponts, where we found a random mound of tree trunks and cobblestones blocking one of the bridges. A rough and ready job if ever there was one. Our sappers dismantled it in no time at all.

Do not worry about me at all, dearest girl. I am all right. Sleeping rough is, in some ways, quite fun. I shall be home soon anyway. We can make plans. What a wonderful life lies before us. Once this war is over.

Your ever-loving Waldemar

One of the reasons the parade took such a long time to pass the reviewing stand is that it included the artillery. Germany was showing off its new siege guns for the first time, howitzers with a 42cm bore, the largest ever made. They could penetrate even reinforced concrete. But they were not just large, they were also mobile. They were carried in sections on limbers (two-wheeled carriages) pulled by teams of eight extra-heavy carthorses.

The howitzers had been designed to take down forts in Belgium and France and were critical to Germany's success. They had been developed in top secrecy in the Krupp armaments factories and were nicknamed 'Big Berthas', probably after the owner of the firm, Bertha Krupp von Bohlen und Holbach. These hitherto secret weapons were the key to Germany's speed; these and the resilience of the marching soldiers. Massive forts guarded the river crossings. They would all have to be taken, one after the other, on the way to Paris, and they had to be taken quickly. There was no time for a prolonged siege. This was an army in a hurry.

Waldemar refers to a blockade he found on a bridge in Trois Ponts. It turned out to be the only occasion, in the whole of the regiment's 400-odd-kilometre march south when there was any attempt at blocking a bridge. This was amazing. The army had to cross several major rivers, the Sambre, Meuse, Oise, Aisne and Marne. Each crossing was a potential choke point and an ideal place for an ambush. At each crossing, the assembled mass of regiments, cavalry, artillery and all the rest milled around the bridgehead for hours. A highly vulnerable moment in the advance. Generals approached every bridge with maximum care, sending planes ahead to check if any enemy troops had been deployed on the far side. Except for the Sambre at Trois Ponts, not once was any bridge blocked or damaged. Not once was there an ambush at any crossing. Even so, contingency plans were laid, and at every bridge there was a slight pause while everyone, including the generals, held their breath.

It was tempting to imagine that the French had not destroyed the bridges because they were in too much of a hurry. Perhaps that is indeed part of the explanation. Another possibility is that the French were deliberately luring the invaders ever deeper into France. They were, after all, successfully blowing up railway bridges and tunnels, so it is clear they could have blown up the bridges if they wanted to. But they didn't want to, for the deeper into France the invaders came, the further they were from their supplies. Later in the war, Germany re-supplied its troops by rail, extending the German rail network at Waimes so that it connected with the Belgian and French lines. And they repaired blown-up bridges and tunnels. But this work did not get underway till later in August and wouldn't be completed till September or October. That was when German supply depots could move forwards. Until then, supplies arrived mainly by horse-drawn wagon.

As soon as the regiment crossed the border into Belgium, the men became nervous. Sentries on duty at night were particularly prone to fear, if not terror. In the dark, any sound, the cracking of a twig, the hooting of an owl, the rustle of dry leaves, or indeed any noise which was not immediately explicable, caused fright, especially when heard by a sentry on his own, standing in enemy territory and feeling the weight of responsibility for his sleeping comrades in the camp behind him. Was it a squirrel, or was it an enemy sniper? Was it an owl, or was it an enemy signal? There was one case, near Hamoir in Belgium, when in the middle of the night a sentry thought he saw the shadowy forms of enemy soldiers advancing over the fields. He started firing and others soon joined in. One man even used a machine gun. Next day, they discovered that they had been shooting into a field of haystacks. Another time, in France, after a day-long march, the men had just sunk into an exhausted sleep when, at midnight, in panic, the bugle boy sounded the alarm. The whole camp jumped into action. That, too, turned out to be a false alarm. The soldiers were edgy in enemy territory.

Part of the nervousness was caused by the rumour mill. Once, not long after they had crossed into Belgium, it was rumoured that some 3,000 Liège factory workers had armed themselves and were marching against them. It caused panic but it wasn't true at all. The officers were hard put to it to calm the men down and get them back to their billets for what they most needed – a good night's sleep.

The regiments avoided towns, preferring to bivouac in isolated villages, preferably on raised ground and in a good defensive position. Waldemar's first night was in the tiny village of Rahier. It was remote, on high ground, and it commanded a good view over the surrounding countryside. It was also home to several fortress-like traditional Belgian farmsteads. You found them in every village. Each had a large, rectangular, cobbled courtyard surrounded by thick brick walls and had only one entrance. Farmhouse, stables, barns and cowsheds stood along the walls facing inwards. They overlooked the vast, paved farmyard, which had a well or pump at its centre. Such places were ideal for billeting large numbers of horses, as well as men. The fortified farms could accommodate several companies. That first night, Waldemar bedded down on straw in a Rahier barn, along with his men.

North of Huy,
20 August 1914

Dearest Girl at Home,
I knew it would happen. I thought I'd have a go at marching, just to see how tough it is on the men. Now I've worn holes in the soles of my boots. I patched them up using scraps of leather I found in Acosse, the last, tiny hamlet we passed through. The cobbler unit had fallen far behind. Worse still, so had the kitchen units, including the bakery section. In Acosse, which is really minute (a church, a school, a *Mairie* and a few farms), the locals were ordered to produce bread overnight for 4,000 men. They baked 400 very large loaves. Not enough, but a truly amazing effort. Another problem is water, especially for our horses. A place like Acosse has only one central village pump. Difficult.

We are now marching through a transformed landscape. It's opened up. We get broad vistas, large fields and cultivated crops, as well as pasture. It's continuously sunny. Guess what? In spite of the war, our spirits lift. It's harvest time, or just after. Most of the wheat fields have been reaped to leave sheets of golden stubble. I saw corncrakes running about in them. The turnips, potatoes and maize are still unharvested. I'm afraid the men don't hesitate to help themselves.

At Huy we saw our first major fort. Impressive and dominating. A sheer cliff rises up, high above the town and on top of it the massive walls of

Huy Fort rise up even higher. It guards a bridge over the Meuse. What an engineering challenge, to take a fort like that! Fortunately, we didn't even have to try. News reached its defenders that, thanks to our howitzers, Liège had just fallen. The citizens of Huy decided to capitulate. That was fortunate for all, including your own, loving,

Waldemar

Waldemar's regiment was taking a route which skirted north of Namur. Once west of the city, they swerved south, marching between Namur to the east and the French Fifth Army to the west. The idea was to stave off any possible attempt by the French to help the Belgians in Namur, which was under attack by another section of the Second Army. The taking of Namur would be a tough task. The main fort there was itself defended by a ring of nine smaller forts, each made of reinforced concrete and all connected by trenches and barbed wire. On 25 August, the Second Army succeeded, thanks to its Big Berthas. Namur fell. Waldemar and his regiment were encamped to the west. They escaped the battle.

To help the Belgians (and themselves), the French had invaded Belgium from the west. Failing to stop the German advance, their goal was to slow it down by carrying out a kind of guerrilla war. As the German front line progressed, the French retreated but left behind a scattering of their men, often Zouaves,[7] to act independently and harass the invader wherever and however possible. A classic controlled retreat strategy. Rearguard French troops hid in woods, farmhouses and town houses. They shot from behind trees, from behind open doorways, from first-floor windows. But whatever they did, they melted into the landscape whenever German soldiers came to check on where the shots were coming from. By the time a German search party arrived, all they found when they entered the house was a Belgian family and possibly the family guns (used for hunting). At this point, it was impossible to tell whether the Belgian civilians had been firing, or whether it had been French soldiers who had since vanished. This mattered. A civilian firing was called a *franc-tireur* and could be shot. A soldier firing was only doing his job. The rules of engagement were governed by the Geneva conventions;[8] these hadn't existed long, but they were in force. If a soldier was captured he had to be treated according to the rules; he could not be shot because he was doing his job. On the other hand, *franc-tireurs* were *not* protected. They could be treated as murderers, tried as such and shot. In the German view of the Conventions (there were other interpretations) everything depended on whether or not the person firing the gun was a soldier or a civilian. But who could tell? For safety's sake, and being nervous, the Germans often arrested Belgians they found in the houses from which the firing had come, then took them before a military court. Many were shot.

At first, when Belgian civilians heard that the German army was on its way, they remained at home, stood in the doorways, smiled, offered bread and helped with the wounded. But after a while, following numerous unjust arrests, great anger grew among the civilian population. They soon learnt to flee.

Near Cerfontaine,
25 August 1914

My own Christel,
Now we are in Cerfontaine. We have had some adventures getting here. This letter is to say that, for all that, I am well. We are close to the border with France and the countryside is beautiful, though parched by constant blazing sunshine. In spite of this, there is an autumnal feel to the air. The swallows are gathering. You see crowds of them darting around farm buildings. And flocks of lapwings. The men pick shiny ripe blackberries from the hedgerows as we march past. I don't have much to report, except that I miss you dreadfully. I rather hope that you miss me! We got our first *Feldpost* (field postal delivery) the other day. Two letters from you at once. Thank you, from all my heart.

Ever and ever, your Waldemar

Waldemar is reluctant to talk about his regiment's first battle, their first losses and the awful revenge which followed. This was the Battle of Jemeppe on 21 August.

Jemeppe lies close to a strategically significant bridge over the Sambre. There was no protective fort by the bridge. The 1st Battalion was sent into the town ahead of the others and ordered to stay there while the rest of the Division positioned itself on higher ground to the north.

As Waldemar and his comrades entered, they saw French bicycle troops, scouts, escaping in haste from a church tower, field glasses in hand. They jumped on their bikes and pedalled away like fury. But the Belgian civilian population did not run away. The inhabitants, mainly women and children, were friendly and curious. They came out of their houses smiling and watched the 1st Battalion enter. Some offered the men bread. Some told them about the French cyclists and in which direction they were going. Just as the Germans were beginning to relax and enjoy their easy passage, rifle fire and shelling came in from the far side of the river. Some of that fire may have come from within the town itself. No one was sure.

Now the mood changed dramatically. People vanished off the streets. Shutters came down. Doors closed. And Waldemar's company commander was shot in the left lung. His fourteen-year-old bugle boy, standing beside him, was killed.

ila's and Philipp's engagement photo, Bremen, 1881.

The three boys. (L to R) Georg, Hermann, Waldemar in summer sailor suits, Kiel, 1893.

The three boys. (L to R) Waldemar, Hermann, Georg in winter sailor suits, Kiel, 1894.

The Kaiser (centre) with officers and crew on board SMY *Hohenzollern*. Philipp is on the far left. The crew wear straw hats, the crowns bound in black ribbon. *Hohenzollern* is written on the front, between two flags. Black streamers hang over the brim at the back.

The Kaiser on the bridge of SMY *Hohenzollern*, Tsar Alexander III to his left. Below, Philipp raises his field glasses to watch the review of the fleet, Kiel, the first week of June 1892.

The Joachimsthaler Gymnasium (now part of Berlin's University of the Arts), where the three boys wer
to school.

Charlottenburg Hochschule, alma mater of Nobel Prize-winners and of Waldemar. Now the Technical University, Berlin.

Self portrait of Georg, 1912.

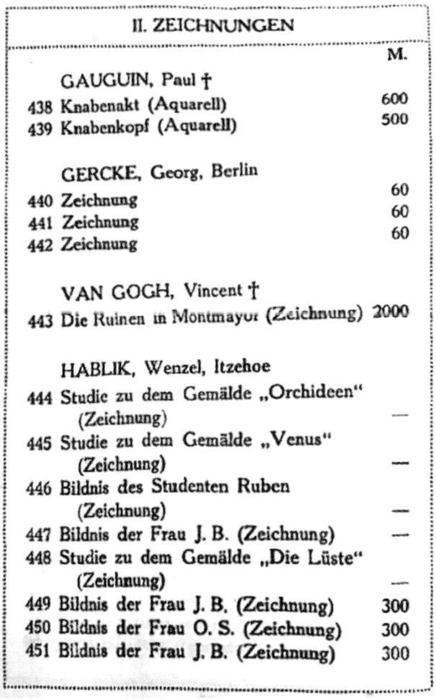

II. ZEICHNUNGEN

		M.
	GAUGUIN, Paul †	
438	Knabenakt (Aquarell)	600
439	Knabenkopf (Aquarell)	500
	GERCKE, Georg, Berlin	
440	Zeichnung	60
441	Zeichnung	60
442	Zeichnung	60
	VAN GOGH, Vincent †	
443	Die Ruinen in Montmayor (Zeichnung)	2000
	HABLIK, Wenzel, Itzehoe	
444	Studie zu dem Gemälde „Orchideen" (Zeichnung)	—
445	Studie zu dem Gemälde „Venus" (Zeichnung)	—
446	Bildnis des Studenten Ruben (Zeichnung)	—
447	Bildnis der Frau J. B. (Zeichnung)	—
448	Studie zu dem Gemälde „Die Lüste" (Zeichnung)	—
449	Bildnis der Frau J. B. (Zeichnung)	300
450	Bildnis der Frau O. S. (Zeichnung)	300
451	Bildnis der Frau J. B. (Zeichnung)	300

Page from Bremen's *Internationale Ausstellung*, 1 February–31 March, 1914, the National Art Library, Victoria and Albert Museum, London.

Winnie Pryce and Leutnant zur See Hermann Gercke. Their engagement photo, Berlin, 1908.

Hermann, Admiralstabsoffizier to Admiral Hopman, Danzig, 1915.

Lt. Waldemar Gercke, 1st Battalion, 4th Company, Queen Elisabeth Grenadier Guards, November 1914, his Iron Cross ribbon in his buttonhole.

Arched entrance to an enclosed armyard, Strée, Belgium. The erfect defensive environment.

A seemingly impregnable fortress guards the cathedral city of Huy, Belgium.

Marble fireplace in the Chateau Gommecourt, France, the only surviving feature from the time that Waldemar was there.

Waldemar's grave, Neuville-St-Vaast, France.

Georg's sketch of Esen Church, near Dixmuide, Belgium, October 1914. The sketch book was punctured by a shell fragment at Loretto Heights, France, 28 May 1915.

General von Seydewitz stands behind his staff. (L to R) Adjutant von Frantzius, Lt. Gercke, Major von Wedekind, Staff Dr Legahn. Georg's head is shaved against lice. Houthulst Forest, near Langemarck, Belgium, 24 April 1915.

In the ruins of Langemarck, Belgium, 26 April 1915. The bereft staff of the 201st, after General v Seydewitz's death. Dr Legahn is standing, and seated on the table is Georg, to his left, Major von Wedeki and Adjutant von Franztius.

eorg’s sketch of a confident French woman surrounded by German officers. Adjutant von Frantzius holds cigarette, while a bearded Major von Wedekind stands arms akimbo. Carignan, France, 1915.

Hermann wearing his Iron Cross, with Winnie and son Harry, skating in Swinemünde, winter 1916/17.

Hermann, U-Boat Commander, 1918.

Philipp boarding one of the Deutschland Class (cargo) U-Boats, possibly Hermann's, Warnemünde, 191

ermann, Ursula, Georg and Harry in the garden in Borby, near Kiel, 1917.

U-154 in exercises off Kiel, January 1918.

U-154 in the Atlantic, taken from *U-153*.

he first boat *U-154* encountered once its mission began in March 1918, a handsome old Norwegian our-master. Her papers were in order, and she sailed on.

e last photo of Hermann. He leaves *U-153*, 9 May 1918.

Korvettenkapitän Philipp Gercke wearing his Iron Cross ribbon and back in service, *c.* 1917.

Philipp in retirement, Rostock, 1930.

Regiments had a soft spot for their drummer and bugler boys. They were younger than everybody else, between twelve and sixteen years old. They were allowed to join young because they were buglers, not fighters, but ironically, their job was actually one of the most dangerous. They had to stand by their commander, in this case, the company commander, and relay his orders by bugle blast in the heat of battle, when shouts would have been drowned out by shelling and rifle fire.

In Jemeppe, fearing that the Belgians themselves were to blame for at least some of the firing, the Germans searched the houses for *franc-tireurs* and took suspects before a military tribunal. Waldemar never discovered what happened to them. But he did discover, later that evening, how the army would take its revenge.

Shells had been coming in so thick and fast from the further side of the Sambre that the 1st Battalion was ordered to retreat to the town's northern edge, where the rest of the regiment stood. The cost of battle? Waldemar's battalion had lost fourteen officers and men killed, with thirty-eight wounded. Local men came out of their houses to help battalion doctors collect and treat the wounded.

Up to that day, the regiment had had an easy time of it. They weren't used to losses. The Battle of Jemeppe was a severe shock, and the army took revenge. They fire-bombed a town where, only a few hours earlier, smiling people had given them bread and locals had helped with the wounded. It was a terrible sight. Standing on the hill to the north, Waldemar could see civilians, lit by the flames, fleeing their burning homes in the darkness. They were running for the bridge over the Sambre. They were running to the next town. After the Battle of Jemeppe, whenever news came of the regiment's approach, the civilian population fled.

Next day, the men crossed the Sambre with no opposition. They marched on, in a south-southwesterly direction, towards the border with France. Marching along a narrow country lane, they arrived in the tiny and remote French village of Eppe-Sauvage. Still no opposition.

Near Erloy,
28 August 1914

Dearest Christel,
We have crossed into France! Our three hurrahs went up, though none of us were sure where the border actually was. There was no mark. We were marching on a remote country road. The fields on either side of the frontier looked exactly the same. So did the cows. So did the chickens.

Now we are here, but where is the French army? Where on earth are we going to engage in this famous and final *Entscheidungsschlacht*? Time is slipping by.

Well, we have left the Ardennes, where the rivers flowed northwards to the Meuse. Now we are in France, the rivers flow west to join the Seine. This is a very different landscape. The villages are more prosperous. Everything looks more prosperous. Most of the cottages have small, but well stocked, vegetable plots. Yes, once again, I'm afraid we raid them.

It was just after we passed the town of La Chapelle that we got our first good view of this new world. We found ourselves on a ridge looking south. We were overlooking the great Plain of Picardy, the heart of France. In the distance, the medieval city of Laon, with its twin-towered cathedral. To the left, in the even further distance, the long, low, blue-green ridge of the Chemin des Dames. And on the plain, straight in front of us, wide, open, unfenced fields full of over-ripe maize, its leaves bleached white in the sun. You know how Georg loves France. Well, at last I can see it too. It is beautiful. He is so right.

Our next crossing is over the Oise. Our pilots report that the further side is clear.

I long for your next letter. Please write!

Your loving Waldemar

Two days before Waldemar wrote that last letter, von Moltke, misinterpreting the easy run which the German army was initially enjoying in France, transferred troops from von Kluck's First Army and sent them to the Eastern Front. This was a mistake. Von Schlieffen planned for a major decisive battle with the French before there was any thinning of the ranks.

News of this withdrawal reached the ears of General Joffre, Commander-in -Chief of the French forces.[9] It may have encouraged him to call a halt to the general retreat, to make that vital, final, decisive stand. The German troops had just crossed the Oise, and with that behind them, they risked being trapped. The French Fifth Army, led by General Lanzerac,[10] stood directly in front of von Bülow's advancing Second Army. Joffre ordered Lanzerac to attack '*sans s'occuper des Anglais*' (without bothering about the British – who were to the north of him). He was to ignore their needs and get on with the opportunity he now had to beat the Germans. And so the French launched the Battle of St Quentin.[11] On the face of it, everything was in their favour, particularly when it came to numbers. Lanzerac's Fifth Army had eleven divisions. Von Bülow only had six.

The battle took place over a large area of countryside which stretched from the town of St Quentin (occupied by Germany) towards the village of Voulpaix, about 45km to the east, where the Elisabeths were stationed. The Elisabeths and other regiments in the *Gardekorps* were to hold the left flank of the German battle line.

Voulpaix is not a place to write home about. Not then. Not today. It consists of about thirty houses which stand on sloping land to the north of a stream. Three short village streets run parallel to that stream, while two north-south lanes cross those streets at right angles. They run through the village, down the slope and cross the stream over two small bridges. One bridge lies immediately south of the village centre, the other to the south-east, on the village outskirts. On the further side of the stream, green fields rise towards woods on a hilltop. That is where the enemy were sheltering on 28 August 1914.

The fast-paced Elisabeths reached Voulpaix first. Soon the Alexanders, Franz and Augustas caught up. They dug in on higher land, north of the village. The battle started with the French opening fire. By evening, the Germans' situation was so bad that the generals discussed the possibility of retreating north of the Oise. They decided against it, but to hedge their risks, ordered seven pontoon bridges to be made ready, just in case.

The 1st Battalion, as at Jemeppe, was ordered into the village first, while the rest stayed to the north, on higher land. The 1st Battalion was to spend the night in the village and make sure the French were kept out, while the others dug a second trench to the north of the village. If the worst came to the worst, and the 1st Battalion had to retreat, this trench would be their refuge.

The new order put Waldemar in harm's way because his company, the 4th, was to barricade the bridges, and to do so quickly, before it got dark. Once at the bridges, it was obvious that barricading them wasn't enough; the stream itself was so narrow that the enemy would be able to cross it without bothering about the bridges at all. Sappers were sent for, and they built a dam downstream to raise the water level. No one could now jump the stream, but it still wasn't the safest of situations, although the best that could be done before dark.

By nine that evening, one platoon was put in charge of each bridge, while the rest of the battalion sheltered in village houses and barns. Waldemar was on the bridge in the village centre. Those lone bridge-guarding platoons came under fitful rifle-fire all night long. The men got no sleep and they had had nothing to eat for the last 24 hours. As soon as the sun rose, they faced a full-blown artillery barrage from the south. Three and a half hours went by. Then the further bridge fell. That was it. The French would now be able to cross the river and attack those on the central bridge from behind. However, by 10.30 no one had been killed, and everyone, including Waldemar, was scrambling through the village, back to that newly dug frontline trench. And so the French reoccupied Voulpaix.

You might think that was the end of it, but it wasn't. By this time, the Garde's howitzers were in place and started to hit the rear line of the attackers. Once again, those relentless, pounding guns turned the tables. They so often did. They sapped the enemy's fighting spirit and by 1.30 pm. the French retreat began. The German artillery fired at their red trousers[12] as they scrambled back up the slopes south of Vouplaix. A little later, a pilot reported that the French were in general retreat.

The Elisabeths were elated, but not for long. It had been a hollow victory. The 1st Battalion's 250-strong 4th Company had lost one-fifth of its strength, and the regiment had lost its two doctors (one killed, the other wounded). In the evening of 30 August the band tried to jolly the troops up with happy tunes, but there was little to be happy about. The enemy had retreated in relatively good order. There had been no *Entscheidungsschlacht*. Neither for Lanzerac, nor for von Bülow.

The French were even more depressed. Shortly after the Battle of St Quentin, for safety's sake, they moved their military headquarters further west, from Paris to Bordeaux. The German High Command, on the other hand, must have been feeling positive. On 30 August, they also moved Command Headquarters further west, from Koblenz to Luxembourg, closer to the battle lines, but still too far away for easy co-ordination.

Waldemar and his comrades soon had other reasons to feel happy, as he wrote to Christel a few days later.

Near Vertus,
6 September 1914
Early in the morning

My own dear darling girl,
We crossed the Aisne, unopposed. We saw Rheims. I could just make out the twin towers of its cathedral in the valley below. We marched past fields of sunflowers. Fields of potatoes. We marched past harrowed land. The brown soil was turning milky. Chalk. We were in the valley of the Vesle River which flows through Rheims.

Not long after, the slopes of gentle hills rose up on either side of our road, from valley floor to bosky hilltop. Those slopes were dense with rows of vines. Dark green vines. Peasants stood between the rows with wicker baskets on the ground beside them. They took no notice of us on the road below. They were picking luscious, fat, round grapes. Dark mauve, shining through a misty bloom. We all picked as we passed by.

We are in champagne country. Can you imagine our delight? Our hearts rose. The landscape is so rich, so comfortable. The houses too. In Montigny-sur-Vesle they were built of a glowing, cream-coloured stone. I could scarcely believe the names we read on notices along the road. It was like reading a catalogue in a Berlin wine merchant's. Veuve-Cliquot, Bollinger, Moët et Chandon. Our generals have brought us to paradise. At least, it would be, if you were here.

Then we came to the town of Épernay. It sits where a bridge crosses the River Marne. Of course, as ever, we crossed unopposed. Épernay is the centre for many, many champagne businesses. I saw jeroboams, rehoboams, a methuselah and even a nebuchadnezzar (twenty bottles worth of it). We had had another 40km march that day and reached our last stop very late, 11 pm. Did our exhausted men slump immediately into their tents? No. They scampered off to find champagne stores. It was the early hours of the following day before they turned in.

Now we are in Vertus, our last stop before descending from champagne paradise. We are going down to the great Marne plain. Oh, and by the way, we are enjoying the first proper rainfall since we left Berlin. It's coming down in sheets.

I hope you are safe and dry my own Christel. I daren't look at your photo. It'll get wet. I kiss you.

Your Waldemar

Sunday, 6 September was the first day of the Battle of the Marne.[13] Marshal Joffre, Commander-in-Chief of the French, had decided that the Marne plain would be the site for that decisive battle. He prepared his men with a ferocious pep talk, telling them to choose death rather than retreat. This was going to be it.

The German army was well aware of French preparations. Their generals had gathered on top of Mt Aimé, about 30km south of the Marne River and a well-known lookout site, famously used during the Napoleonic wars. General von Winckler, commander of the Garde's 2nd Infantry Division, was among the generals gathered on Mont Aimé. Looking south, he could easily see the ranks of Joffre's troops strung out along a 160km front. They were encamped to the south on the broad Marne plain. The British stood west of the French. On the German side, the First Army would hold the centre and right flank, while the Second held the centre and left, with the Saxons (the Third Army) on the far left and the Gardekorps stationed to the right of the Saxons.

A day before the battle began, the Garde's 3rd Brigade, with the Elisabeths as its left wing, deployed across rough turnip fields westward and reach the hamlet of Clamanges. The Elisabeths (always the first to get anywhere) reached Clamanges at 10.00 am and saw signs of a recent, hurried French departure. They found a roughly constructed military chapel, but nothing else. The hurried departure of the French encouraged the Germans to make haste also. Waldemar's battalion wasn't given time to fill water bottles or even to snatch a quick drink from the spring.

Although retreating, the enemy was keeping up intermittent fire, which killed several officers and men, among them Leutnant von Wienskowski, the younger brother of a more senior officer in the regiment. The elder brother buried the younger. He found a letter in his pocket addressed to their mother which read, '*Ich habe immer gewünscht, für eine große Sache zu sterben.*' (I always wanted to die for a noble cause). Hopeful words. He was buried close to a spot where one of his ancestors had fallen during the Napoleonic wars. Some parts of Europe are destined to be battlefields.

South of Clamanges lay a linear village running along a stream. This was Normée. It consisted of a handful of farms, a church, a school and a *Mairie*. Its main features were farm buildings opening directly onto the one and only village street. Once again, the Germans found defensive-style, walled courtyards with barns built into them, accessed by a single set of large gates. The buildings were the object of the first battle. Once captured, they would provide shelter for fighting the next day. The Germans fought hard, and by early evening, the village had fallen; Waldemar and his regiment occupied Normée. The men lit small fires and, taking water from the stream, cooked whatever they could find. This was their first and last meal of the day.

Immediately to the south of the line of Normée farmsteads stretched about 2,000m of cultivated land. It rose gently southwards, towards a wood on a low hill. That's where the enemy was encamped. A railway line ran along an embankment in the middle of this cultivated land, about half way between the village and the wood, and a line of enemy trenches ran along it. The trench line was punctuated with lookout posts on the northern side, but their view of the German troops in the village barns and behind, was poor, which was why Waldemar and his friends were allowed to light small fires that night.

Digging trenches the next day was a tough job. In spite of the rain, the ground was still as hard as nails. But the men dug with energy because, should things go wrong, these trenches would be their refuge. And things might go wrong, because German pilots had warned that, judging from the numbers, the French were planning to concentrate their counter-attack on the Second Army's left flank, exactly where Waldemar stood. The Elisabeths and the Alexandras were to lead the assault, the Elisabeths working from the western end of the village with the Franz and the Augustas behind them as a second wave. The aim was first of all to take the field south of the village street, then the embankment and the land beyond and lastly the wood. Once out of the barns, the regiment would be exposed and downhill of the French. They would be fighting uphill. As General Robert E. Lee is supposed to have said at the Battle of Gettysburg in 1863, 'Never fight uphill, me boys! Never fight uphill.'

It had been a heavy day. Lots of firing. Lots of incoming shells. Lots of digging. By midnight, the men of the Elisabeths' 1st Battalion were sunk in the sleep of the utterly exhausted, but at 3.30 am on 7 September they were woken not by a bugle call but by whispered orders. The assault would be that very morning, before dawn, in a few hours' time. The idea was to counter the disadvantage of attacking uphill by making a fixed-bayonet charge in the dark.

Before sunrise, to eliminate the possibility of anyone spoiling things by opening fire early out of terror, they were all ordered to unload their rifles. As quietly as possible, they removed the cartridges, slipped them into their pockets and fixed bayonets.

At 5.00 am, in that extra cold moment just before dawn, Waldemar and his comrades left the shelter of the barns and stepped out into the mist-covered field across the street. The grass was wet with dew. It soaked right through the men's boots. Bending forwards to offer less of a target, their rifles grasped tightly in both hands, they advanced towards the embankment and the French lookout posts. It was a very dark night with no moon, yet easy to see where the embankment lay. Bushes along its top were silhouetted against a platinum sky.

Each man listened to the soft brushing of his boots through the grass. The minutes it took to reach the embankment felt like hours. Hearts were in mouths. Just before they arrived, the company commander straightened himself up and shouted '*Los*!'(Charge!) Then he fell, shot by a shocked sentry. The sight of a comrade falling galvanized the rest. Roaring with rage, they rushed up the embankment and, without firing a single shot, fell on the men in the trenches with their bayonets.

The Frenchmen in the trenches had been sleeping. They had no weapons in their hands. Their reaction to the sudden assault was to fling their hands up in horror and run. Waldemar and his comrades fought like men possessed. Once the embankment was taken, they prepared to charge across the next bit of field to reach the wood, but instead of clambering out of the trench, Waldemar fell back into it. In the melee he had been shot through the right thigh. All he could do was lie there, together with many, many others, both French and German, both dead and wounded. He had to wait for the battle to end. That's when the regimental band, who turned themselves into stretcher-bearers during battle, would be able to rescue him.

The attack was an unbelievable success. Much more was gained than had originally been set as the goal. By evening they had not only taken the wood but also the land beyond. They had even taken the next village to the south. It was an extraordinary, amazing victory. Stunning. Beyond all their wildest dreams. Allied forces had seventy-two divisions in the field. The Germans had only fifty-one. Allied casualties were about 270,000, German casualties, around 260,000. Not that much different. They had fought with raw fury and had succeeded. But at a cost.

Waldemar's company commander was killed, while Waldemar himself, badly wounded, was carried back behind the lines to the military *Lazarett* (field hospital). He knew, as they carried him back, that the French were in full retreat. Instead of choosing death, as Joffre had asked of them, the French were streaming back to the town of Sézanne, only about 100km east of Paris.

By 9 September, the 1st Battalion, minus Waldemar, had taken the village of Fère Champenoise. They bivouacked in a field south of the wood. By this time, the field artillery was with them, as well as machine guns and even the field kitchen. They were preparing to take the next village to the south, Conantry. They had lost many comrades in bitter fighting, but they had prevailed. Their hearts were high. Paris was, at last, within reach.

It was not to be. At 1.05 pm on 9 September, an order arrived from German General Command in Luxembourg. Retreat. Von Moltke's order shocked officers and men to the core. In the twinkling of an eye, it transformed everything. One minute, the French were utterly demoralized and the Germans riding high. The next, the opposite. The order hit the German army like a bolt of lightning.

But by this time, Waldemar was out of it. He was on a train bound for Berlin.

The military lazarett, Normée
9 September

Dearest Christel,

I am on my way home. I leave by train tomorrow because I have been injured, but not seriously. I am useless to the army till this leg mends. We shall soon talk face to face, arm in arm and heart to heart.

For ever, your Waldemar

On returning to Berlin, Waldemar was at first confined to hospital. After about ten days, he was allowed home. He sat in the *Berliner Zimmer*, his right leg resting on a pile of cushions on the chair in front of him. Philipp had time to be with him because he had just put the last-ever edition of *Überall* to bed. His farewell editorial pointed out that, in wartime, monthly magazines about the military don't work, because secrets and censorship are essential. The best way for citizens to get news was simply to read the daily newspapers.

Philipp was dying to talk about the progress of the war with his son. Above all, he wanted to talk about von Moltke's loss of nerve. What on earth had happened? But he couldn't, at least not at first. He was under strict instructions from Mila not to pump the patient for stories about what was happening at the front. So he sat with Waldemar, talking about the weather and playing chess. For Mila, life was simple. She bit her lip, kept quiet, and busied herself cooking all those dishes which she knew her youngest son liked best. Luckily for her, food was not yet rationed. She was busy anyway (she always was), since Christel had moved in. She had been given Georg's room and joined her future mother-in-law in tending to the needs of the man they both loved. Christel's presence was in itself the best medicine possible. Waldemar came to life whenever she entered the room.

Everyone was thrilled to see him, and their delight was unbounded when, after about a month, the patient found he was able to hobble about again. Eventually, he could walk, albeit with a limp. By this time, Philipp's vow of restraint had been well and truly broken. The two of them had talked for hours about the war. Neither could be sure of what had happened, but it did appear, on the face of it, that von Moltke had, quite simply, found himself unable to take the strain. He was a nervous man. Risk-averse. Whichever direction he moved in, advance or retreat, he foresaw casualties and disaster. After ordering the retreat from the Marne, he allegedly told the Kaiser, 'Your Majesty, we have lost the war.'[14] This military disaster was followed, a few weeks later, by the loss of the naval codes with the sinking of SMS *Magdeburg*. Both disasters, at the Marne and on the Baltic, were the result of German mismanagement, not enemy action. September 1914 was a bad month for Germany. No. Worse than that. It was utterly disastrous.

Philipp shook his head in despair. He wrote in his Chronicle:

> Von Moltke was an amiable man. I got to know him quite well on board the *Hohenzollern*. He was a capable officer but no Chief of General Staff. That is something he himself would be the first to admit. He didn't want the job. But Wilhelm II insisted. As it happened, events at the Marne overwhelmed him. He simply could not take on that much responsibility. Besides, he was ill.

He was indeed ill. He suffered a nervous breakdown, resigned and died two years later. He was succeeded as Chief of Staff, German General Command, by Erich von Falkenhayn.

Waldemar was awarded the Iron Cross, Second Class, for his role in the Battle of the Marne, but no one in the family was mollified by this. There was a strong feeling throughout the country that the army had been betrayed.

After a little over a month recuperating, and still limping badly, Waldemar took a last farewell of his Christel. She was at the station when, once more, he climbed aboard a troop train. Philipp and Mila were also there. No one knew what lay ahead.

Chapter 12

The Pied Piper's Regiments

Georg was in his Paris studio on 1 August 1914. On hearing the news, he dropped everything and implemented a plan which he had dreamed up some days earlier, as the July Crisis deepened. He ferreted out his cash box (luckily there was just enough in it to pay his landlady four months' rent in advance). He slipped this into an envelope with a short note: *Je m'excuse. Je reviendrai* (Forgive me. I'll be back). Running downstairs, he left the envelope with the concierge and ran back up to his garret. He packed a few things; he wouldn't need much. The army would provide his uniform, and he'd be back soon anyway.

He left his paintings stacked against the walls of his studio.[1] The canvas he was working on sat on his easel. His drawings and sketch-books lay on the shelves. His brushes, paints, palettes, pastels, pencils and pens were all left where they were. His artist's coat hung on a hook behind the door. He had rented the studio only a few months earlier. Glancing round for the last time, what thoughts raced through his mind? His friends in Germany? His friends in Paris? With a quick intake of breath, he blocked out all regrets and sadness. He locked the door. And caught the next train to Berlin.

War had crashed its way into his life at the worst possible moment. All that he had ever hoped for was in Paris, where he had arrived riding a wave of success following the Bremen exhibition. Now, just when he stood on the threshold, someone had slammed the door shut. Half of him despaired. Half of him clung to hope.

Georg never saw his studio again. Most of his work vanished. It is *possible* that one of his oil paintings still exists – the portrait of Winnie, which he painted at Philipp's request, the one painting by Georg which was sent to England, the one painting which may have survived. I have never seen any of his paintings, though some engravings still exist, especially those he worked on in Bremen, when he was wandering the old town's narrow streets, the Bremerhaven wharves and the Worpswede marshes. Quaint, crooked houses, narrow streets. Fishermen mending nets. The steep-pitched thatched roofs of Worpswede cottages, standing among birch trees. And I have one of his pastels. Two young, silken-skinned female nudes. They stand half turned towards each other. As I write, opposite on the wall, above the piano, I can see some of his pencil drawings. His mother, father and elder brother. And some of his wartime sketches have been published. They survive as illustrations in the regimental history. So little. So tantalizing. I long for more.

For reasons unknown, Georg was not sent to fight in the regiment he had served in as an *Einjährig Freiwilliger.* On his return from Paris, he must have showed up at his Charlottenburg barracks a day or so after Waldemar. Perhaps, by the time he got there, it was too late. Perhaps the regiment had already reached its full complement. There were tens of thousands of untrained volunteers. The army, at first, didn't know what to do with them. Georg hung about, fulfilling various temporary assignments. He briefly headed a bicycle unit until mid-September when, more than a month after war had been declared – the same month that von Moltke had declared it lost, the month the German naval codes were stolen – Georg was drafted into one of the newly created, so-called 'Reserve Regiments'. The horse had bolted. The stable door shut. Georg went to war.

Many of the volunteers were young students, full of idealism, full of hope and without wives or children to make them think twice about what they were doing. The new reserve regiments would be run by professional officers, with a scattering of those who, like Georg, had recently completed their military service. Georg was assigned to the general staff of the new 201st Reserve Regiment.

Around a quarter of the men in this regiment were under the age of twenty. Many were students. Almost all were Berliners. The 201st was, in fact, one of the famous *Berliner Studentenregimenten* (Berlin student regiments). The significance of the student regiments was that they consisted of bright young men, Germany's future, who were sent with insufficient equipment, insufficient rifles and insufficient training to fight professional soldiers. Virtually weaponless in the face of the enemy onslaught, they were reduced to singing the *Deutschlandlied* by way of a plucky defiance, or so the legend goes. Hitler later twisted the story, presenting it as a case of heroic youth taking on a superior force. He entirely ignored the real issue, which was disastrous management by Berlin army headquarters. They were dispatched (not led, as in the fairy tale) by a modern-day Pied Piper. Few returned.

Why did the generals send them out when they weren't ready? The answer to that question brings us back to the Kaiser's new Chief of General Staff, Erich von Falkenhayn.[2] A few weeks into his new job, von Falkenhayn made a rash promise to the Kaiser, that the reserve regiments would be trained, equipped and in the field by 10 October 1914. Bang! He had boxed himself in. The timing he proposed was impossible. But rather than admit the mistake, he and the generals charged with approving the regiments' readiness, sent the men out as they were. Unready and ill-equipped. It was the easiest path forward, from their point of view.

It began well enough. In September, Berlin volunteers assigned to the new 201st Regiment were sleeping on straw mattresses in their Friedrichstraße barracks. They dined on peas and bacon at lunchtime and, of an evening, sitting on the ledges of their open barrack windows, flirted with their girlfriends in the street below. Their greatest fear was that the war would be over before they got to the front. On 18 September, they were moved from the city to the army camp at Döberitz, about 20km west of Berlin. Here, life was even pleasanter. Now they enjoyed the relative luxury of bunk beds. On weekdays, they marched to sand dunes outside the barrack gates and played war games. On Sundays, mothers arrived with parcels. Clean clothes and cake.

How long should a training period be? It varied in different countries, though for all combatants, as the war progressed, it became shorter and shorter. Germany's peacetime system of national service required one to two years' training. In 1914, the French High Command aimed at six months' training. By the end of the war, Germany was sending men to the front after only a few weeks. And the student regiments? They were trained from 18 September till 10 October. About three weeks. But this wasn't their only problem. They were sent out before all the necessary officers had been appointed and before sufficient uniforms and equipment were available.

Ten days before departure, the 201st had no Brigade Commanders, while rifles, bayonets and ammunition were in short supply. There weren't enough uniforms to go round. Some men were issued with bonnets instead of the regulation *Pickelhaube* helmet, and with blue uniforms instead of the standard grey. At the front, such gear looked remarkably like that of the enemy, and some wearing it were shot by their own side. What else was in short supply? Boots, knapsacks, ground sheets, tents and provision pouches. There were no spades at all.

A few days before Falkenhayn's deadline, General von Loewenfeld,[3] *Stellvertrender Kommandierende Gardekorp* (Acting Commander of the Guard Corps Headquarters, Berlin), arrived at the Döberitz camp. For his benefit, the first and only full brigade exercise took place. Recruits heard machine-gun fire for the first time and, again for the first time, watched the simulated effects of enemy artillery. General von Loewenfeld quickly saw that these soldiers were ill-prepared. In his report, he said that the men had, unfortunately, been trained by old soldiers who did not understand modern warfare. He issued one and all with a small handbook he had written himself, *How to be a Soldier*. And then he approved their deployment.

He was right about the senior officers. Many were older men brought out of retirement. But whether they were any good or not did not necessarily depend on their age. The 201st's first Commander was *Oberst außer Dienst* (Colonel, retired) von Kuczkowski,[4] who proved a disaster. He was eventually replaced by an even older man, but one who was a success. Von Kuczkowski's top assistant was *Adjutant Leutnant* von Frantzius[5] and his second assistant, *Ordnanz Offizier* (Ordnance Officer), was 'our' Georg. This position is peculiar to the German army. His job was to liaise between the commander and battalion commanders, assist with intelligence, oversee maps and ride ahead to find comfortable quarters for regimental staff. He needed to be good with people and if he could speak French, so much the better. Georg filled the bill; he was the youngest in staff headquarters and the only one, along with the regimental doctor, who was neither an aristocrat nor a professional soldier.

Two months earlier, Georg had been standing in front of his easel. He wore an artist's smudged white smock, carried a palette in one hand and a brush in the other. Now he wore the uniform of a lieutenant in the 201st Reserve Regiment and carried a pistol. Winnie had always thought that someone with Georg's relaxed, liberal temperament would not look good in a military uniform. But when he came home on leave, she was surprised. He wore it with a natural elegance.

On 10 October, the 201st marched out of Camp Döberitz. Georg was Ordnanz Offizier to the Commander of the 201st Reserve Regiment, in the 85th Brigade of the 43rd Division. The 43rd was part of the XXII Reserve Infantry Corps.

They embarked on what was called a troop train but was actually more like a cattle truck. Bound for Belgium, they would join von Bülow's Second Army. The Schlieffen Plan had been to take Paris within about six weeks but, as we know, this hadn't happened. There was no attempt to produce a new plan. The generals simply stuck to the original goals but allowed themselves more time to achieve them.

By late October, the 201st was close to Dixmuide, a small Belgian town on the east bank of the River Yser. The Yser flows north, through Dixmuide, to join the English Channel at Nieuport. The Germans were advancing from the east. The generals sent the 201st forward in the mistaken belief that the Belgian army, with French support, was retreating west of the Yser. This would, they hoped and expected, leave Dixmuide unoccupied. Perhaps the long series of French retreats in August had led to complacency. The German generals were unwise in their expectations. There was to be no easy advance. Perhaps if those in Berlin had realized this, von Falkenhayn would not, as the 201st marched out of Berlin, have delivered an order similar to the one Joffre gave his men before the Battle of the Marne: 'Advance', he said. 'Advance regardless of cost!' Schooled in the virtue of obedience, the hopeful and loyal young reservists took von Falkenhayn at his word.

Meanwhile, in Dixmuide, a professional Belgian army, strengthened by French troops, dug in and prepared. In the flat Flanders landscape, they built lines of trenches to the east of the town and positioned observers on church towers and windmills in and around it. Every high point was occupied by enemy soldiers, field-glasses in hand and telephones at the ready. The eastern landscape, into which the Germans were advancing, lay before them like an open map, a patchwork of little fields separated by hedges and barbed-wire fences. The fields were soggy from recent rain. The area is known as the 'wash basin' of Belgium. Many fields contained unharvested turnips and beet. The Belgian observers in their towers and windmills watched everything the Germans were doing and reported it by phone to their comrades in the trenches below. In this way, they could ensure accuracy of fire, which the Germans could not – they couldn't even see where their enemy was. Whenever the Germans attacked (and they did so several times) the Belgians and French defended the town with determination, intelligence and strength. This was the Battle of Dixmuide, part of what later became known as the Battle of Yser.[6]

The 201st made three disastrous attacks on Dixmuide. Each failed, and with appalling losses. The first came on 21 October. The night before the planned attack, the Belgian and French defenders kept the invaders awake with artillery fire. In the morning, that same fire prevented the kitchen units from coming forward to feed the troops. The student soldiers were about to launch the first attack of their young lives after a sleepless night and with nothing in their bellies. And what an attack! It was to be full-frontal, in the old style, as if taking part in the Battle of Waterloo. There was no preparatory artillery bombardment. There were no trenches (How could there be? They had no spades). It was to be made in broad daylight, all the men charging simultaneously, rifles at the ready (these would make it difficult to run, though it would have been difficult even without rifles because of the terrain). If the first wave fell, there was no reserve wave to follow. The 201st were launching their first assault using an outdated and ill-thought-out strategy. And so it began.

'*Los*!' (Go!) called the officers, and the young men ran a few steps but soon staggered, sank in mud or fell over turnip stumps. It was an obstacle course, not a military charge. Snipers in their towers or hiding in trenches (which were invisible to the attackers) picked them off one by one. Machine guns decimated their ranks. It was all too easy for the enemy. Companies broke up into platoons, and platoons broke up into groups. Groups dissolved, leaving only isolated individuals to survive or die on their own. It was every man for himself.

In no time at all the fields were strewn with the dead and dying; when the bugle sounded the retreat, few could respond. Some battalions lost almost half their men. Entire companies all but vanished. After that first assault, one battalion's four companies had to be combined into two.

It was impossible to count the dead. All you could count were the gaps in the ranks at roll call. Those who were not there, the dead and those described as 'missing'. Everyone knew that 'missing' meant they might well still be lying out there somewhere on the battlefield, in desperate need of medical help. In the following days, patrols went out at night to search for the 'missing'. Five days after the fighting was over, one patrol found six wounded men in a group. They were close to enemy trenches but, amazingly enough, still alive. Six days after the battle ended, another patrol found three men together, severely wounded and barely alive.

The second attack was on 23 October. This time, the generals took greater care, but still not enough. They ordered a preliminary artillery bombardment, a staggered assault and the use of the regiment's three machine guns. That attack also failed miserably.

Fortunately, at this point, Commander von Kuczkowski was sent home and a new regimental commander, Generalmajor von Seydewitz,[7] took his place. He was sixty-five years old and had fought in the 1870 war against France. Even older than his predecessor, he was nevertheless, more understanding of his men and a better soldier. Seydewitz greeted his Ordnance Officer with a warm smile: '*Na, Junge*!'(Well, boy!). Georg, utterly shattered from the two previous assaults, could scarcely bring himself to smile back.

A new divisional commander was also appointed and he, in turn, finally appointed brigade commanders. Up to this point, there had been none. Things were improving, especially as better weapons arrived, trench mortars and *Schnellbrücken* (temporary bridges), which were essential in an area riddled with dykes and ditches. Most importantly of all, there was a large delivery of spades. For the first time, they could dig trenches.

On 31 October, Seydewitz launched the third attack on Dixmuide. He would advance not only from the east, but also from the west and north, and ordered some of his units to cross the Yser north of the town. That night, two battalions crossed and started to dig in, but as they dug they found the water level, already high, rising ever higher. Soon they were knee-deep, and still the water rose. It turned out that Belgium's King Albert[8] had, only a few days before, ordered the flooding of the polders south of Nieuport. On 29 October, a rush of water flooded Nieuport itself, all the fields south of it and the area north of Dixmuide where the 201st were trying to dig in. For a moment, it seemed to Georg and his companions as if everywhere was flooded. The third attack was abandoned.

A fourth assault was planned. Seydewitz's command style was consultative and personal. With the help of the Adjutant and his Ordnance Officer, he kept in close contact with his three battalion commanders and asked for their views. Once new orders were issued, he made sure that all commanders understood and that their company commanders were fully informed. Most importantly of all, he kept an eye open for any change in circumstances. Georg, a sheaf of maps tucked under his arm, trotted beside his general as they walked from one battalion commander's dugout to another. These were all in the forward trenches. Communications trenches, at right angles to the battle trenches, now linked the battle line with regimental headquarters to the rear.[9]

The fourth attack was planned for 9 November. It was to be made from a base position of several forward trenches, all as close to the enemy's front line as possible. Seydewitz wanted his men to fire their new trench mortars directly into the enemy's front trench. They started digging as soon as it was dark on 8 November. But after an inspection in the early hours of the 9th Seydewitz found the trench wasn't far enough forward. Another was dug. Scarcely had this been done when news came that the enemy had vacated their front trench.

At a hasty meeting in a dugout by the light of a tallow candle, Seydewitz, his Adjutant and Georg met all battalion commanders. There were still a few hours before dawn. All agreed, though not without grumbling, to make a third attempt at a well-positioned front line. Yes. They would dig yet another front trench. The trouble for Major Freiherr von Wedekind, commander of the 3rd Battalion, was that he was stout. To reach his four company commanders, he had to feel his way in the dark along narrow trenches, his stomach constantly brushing against damp mud walls. They started digging at 3.30 am. As the morning mist rose, those in the newest front line could now peek over the top and see the enemy only a few metres from them. Beyond lay the town of Dixmuide.

The assault started with an artillery bombardment. Explosions came thick and fast. Black, parachute-shaped puffs of smoke rose where the shells hit home. When they struck the railway embankment they threw sleepers high in the air, as if they were matchsticks. Then, as planned, mortars opened fire straight into the enemy's trenches. Boards and beams flew all over the place. For the first time, enemy soldiers ran to the rear. Last of all came the infantry charge. At one o'clock, the three battalion commanders shouted '*Los*!' and off the men shot, sprightly as jack-in-the-boxes, springing out of trenches and running forward, half-propelled by their own shouts of '*Hurra*!'

The assault was quick and easy. In less than half an hour, they reached the railway embankment where they waited for the artillery to change its range. Then onwards, right into the heart of Dixmuide.

The town had to be cleared house by house. Belgian and French soldiers (and among the French, many North Africans[10]) were hiding in cellars. Hand grenades were the order of the day. Until this battle, hand grenades had been reserved for use by sappers. That had been a mistake. They proved to be one of the best weapons available to men running forward. You can't aim and fire a rifle when running. Nor were rifles much help in an urban setting where there was little space. Rifles, in fact, were of little use in any close-combat situation. Hand grenades, so they discovered at Dixmuide, were the answer.

Late that afternoon, the three battalions of the 201st met in Dixmuide's now ruined market place. General von Seydewitz, congratulated his men. '*Jungens*,' he said, beaming broadly, 'You did well', then off he went, accompanied by Georg, to inspect the bridge over the Yser. It was a dangerous place to be. The bridge was now the front line and the site of much wild shooting from the rag tags of an infuriated, defeated enemy. Georg suggested that this was perhaps not the best moment to view the bridge. Seydewitz insisted. Almost inevitably, a shot caught the General in the leg. He staggered. Georg put his arm around his waist and eased him, limping, to shelter under a large tree near the bridge head. About 100 metres separated them from the nearest house. Their attacker was firing out of a cottage window on the other side of the river. Georg took out his revolver, aimed at the arm resting on the window ledge and fired. The assailant withdrew. With the General limping at Georg's side, the pair reached the safety of the nearest house and from there, the field hospital. Amiable and kind-hearted Major Freiherr von Wedekind took over. An unruffled, gruff and popular old soldier, he was to become a good friend to Georg. He was with him, right to the end.

Seydewitz could have taken sick leave and gone home to recuperate, but the stalwart old general refused. He would stay with his men. On their last Sunday afternoon in Dixmuide, the regiment paraded in the ruins of the old market place. The band played jolly tunes. The divisional commander stood on the viewing platform. He distributed Iron Crosses. One of them (second class) went to Georg.

After Dixmuide, the regiment moved to the Belgian city of Menen, close to Ypres. The men served intermittently in trenches round Ypres,[11] though most of their time was spent training, partly because, following their heavy losses at Dixmuide, they had been joined by many new recruits. At Menen they studied how the artillery and the infantry should work together. They studied combat formations, the importance of observation, and how to use mortars and hand grenades. The Adjutant looked on scornfully: 'Yes, you can learn all these things in Menen. But the best teacher of all is war.' So far, war had proved an excruciatingly expensive teacher, and it was about to prove even more excruciating. Germany was looking for the right moment to introduce a dire new weapon.

Chapter 13
Zeppelin Interlude

It was waving Waldemar goodbye at the station that did it. A potent reminder that his sons, all three of them, were offering their lives for their country. It was more than he could bear. Philipp decided to volunteer himself. Apart from periodic stomach pains, he was fit enough. Not as strong as he used to be, but then, that's old age. Not that he was particularly old. Only fifty-nine. A bit rotund perhaps. But mentally spry. He was accepted, and in October 1914 the Admiralty posted him to Dresden. He was to work with a team managing the army's Z-11 airship. They needed naval help.

Mila sighed. What could she do but encourage and support him? Perhaps it would do him good to feel useful. At home he played the role of grandfather to Hermann's two boys. As Winnie bobbed to and fro between Berlin and the coast, the boys were living with their grandparents. Philipp loved it. He would take them on his knee and draw pictures to order – a ship, a plane, an aunt. He loved to draw comic scenes. Giggling, the children coloured them in.

Airships were a new weapon which both the army and the navy claimed as their own. The Army was particularly frustrated in its claim because it depended on the navy for pilots. It couldn't manage without them. But the Z-11 project, which Philipp joined, was an army venture. Its crew was recruiting naval pilots so that the ship could navigate over the North Sea and reach London. The ideal candidate needed a good knowledge of both. The goal? To bomb the enemy's capital.

An obvious candidate was Hermann's best man, Heinrich Mathy. He had stayed in London with Hermann in 1909 and, shortly before war broke out, had joined the naval airship unit. There is no record of whether he was considered for the Z-11 job because, as Philipp scornfully reports, instead of going through with the plan, all the pilots, both army and navy, upped sticks and left. They were attending a conference in Frankfurt am Main, a talking-shop on Zeppelins chaired by the great man himself, Count Ferdinand von Zeppelin. He had been developing rigid-body airships since the 1890s and was 'The Authority'.

When the Z-11s' commander returned to Dresden, he told Philipp that everyone at the conference had talked a great deal about everything, except for the one thing which was important for the Z-11, namely, bombing London.

The Kaiser was opposed to it, so nobody dared raise the issue. Apparently, the Kaiser was nervous in case any of the British royal palaces were hit. He didn't want to find himself responsible for the death of his own relatives. He cast around for support in his views (he always needed support), and, of course, he always had the necessary yes-man in place. The man in this instance was Admiral Georg Alexander von Müller,[1] Chief of the Imperial Naval Cabinet and one of the men Philipp styled as the Kaiser's 'Operetta Admirals'. Müller was popular with the Kaiser but unpopular with everyone else. The ratings called him *Tantchen* (Auntie), while officers called him *Das Miespeterchen* (Minnie the Moaner). Thanks to 'Auntie', the plan to bomb London was shelved. It would be resurrected later, once the enemy, as Philipp pointed out bitterly, had had time to plan an effective defence.

And so, once again, as after the First Battle of the Marne, indecision, hesitation and half-measures won out over daring and risk-taking. The Z-11 was moved to the eastern theatre of the war and, more dejected than ever, Philipp caught the train home.

Chapter 14

The Sinking of the *Friedrich Carl*

The title of 'Flagship' is a temporary designation. For a brief period, while it suits, the flagship is the lead ship in any flotilla, the one used by the Admiral in command. As long as he is on board, the ship flies his flag and the crew smiles. This is because Admirals bring a certain kudos with them. An Admiral on board raises everyone 's spirits: all feel more important. The flagship needs to be large enough to host meetings of all the captains in the flotilla, as well as their key staff. They need space for maps and a large table. Finding a ship with this kind of accommodation wasn't easy in a Baltic fleet where the biggest vessels were light cruisers. For their first expedition in August, Behring had used the *Augsburg*. His next flagship was the slightly larger SMS *Friedrich Carl*. She was big enough to accommodate two sea-planes on deck. One night in November 1914, with Behring and Hermann on board, she was sailing towards the Russian port of Libau.[1]

Libau was a spa town with sandy beaches and a busy fishing industry; during the early 1900s, it was a major embarkation port for Russians emigrating to America. Direct shipping services linked it to the United States. It was also Russia's closest port to Germany. There was a string of Russian ports similar to Libau along the Russian Baltic's southern and eastern shores. Libau, Windau,[2] Riga, Reval. They guarded the southern approach to the Gulf of Finland and would all have to be taken if Germany's final goal was to threaten St Petersburg. But first Libau, the nearest.

From late 1914 until 1915, the Baltic fleet constantly bombarded Libau. Tsar Alexander III had built a military harbour north of the town's commercial port and had lined the shore there with barracks and block houses. In 1912, Alexander's successor, Nicholas II, founded Russia's first training school for submariners in Libau, which is why, in October 1914, when the first two British E-class submariners, the *E-1* and the *E-9*, arrived in the Baltic, the German navy expected them to serve out of Libau.[3] On the *Friedrich Carl*, all eyes were on the water, scanning the surface for that tell-tale black periscope or for the white ripple which followed. Everyone knew there was no effective way of dealing with a submarine (apart from ramming it). Everyone knew that one strike by a submarine's torpedo in the right place, and your ship sank. Quickly. Very quickly. The navy was nervous and on full alert.

It was a cold on the night of 17 November. The *Friedrich Carl* was alone on her journey to reconnoitre Libau. Around midnight, when no one stood a chance of sighting a submarine in the dark, a huge explosion near the forward torpedo room rocked the ship, and she shuddered as if giving up the ghost. Hermann and Behring were standing on the bridge; they looked at each other. A British submarine! Then a second, louder explosion. A second torpedo. The ship started to sink. She began to slide backwards into the water, putting her deck and the bridge at an increasingly sharp angle. How long did they have? No one knew. Would the rate of sinking remain steady? No one knew that either. Most expected it to speed up as the list grew. She soon had a 14-degree list to starboard and some 2,300 tons of sea-water flooding on board. There were still four hours to go before dawn.

A desperate wireless operator arrived on the bridge. He reported that the blast had destroyed the wireless system, which meant of course that they could not call for help. Without saying a word, Hermann, accompanied by the wireless operator, wriggled his way down to the damaged radio room.

'It's finished, Sir,' said the operator. 'Look.'

He pointed at the tangle of wires hanging from the ceiling. Hermann stood thinking for some seconds, with water lapping at his feet. Then he set to work with total concentration. It was the same sort of concentration that Lenchen once remarked on when she saw him writing articles for *Überall* of an evening at his home in Berlin. His children squabbled and crawled about his ankles, yet it was as if nothing else in the world existed except his work. It was the same that night on the *Friedrich Carl*. He worked in silence, the wireless operator beside him, offering him this wire or that, as need arose. It took around ten minutes for Hermann to reconnect the system, although not perfectly. They could make one call. Only one. And they would not be able to receive any at all. They would never know if their SOS had been picked up unless or until a rescue ship arrived. And how long would that take? They were 102km north of the nearest German port. There was nothing for it but to wait and hope for the best. What would come first? The boat sinking or its rescue? They prepared for the worst.

Hermann took his place back on the bridge next to Admiral Behring. They stood in silence. Both were surprised and marginally relieved to find that, in spite of the torpedo strike, their ship was still only sinking slowly. The crew stood below in a long line on that part of the deck which was still above water. They too were silent.

That's when Behring's friendly booming voice rang out: 'Well, my friend Gercke, there's one consolation we can take with us to the bottom. These English torpedoes. They're good for nothing.'[4]

That same night, Hermann's great friend Gernot Goetting was on board the SMS *Augsburg*. They were sailing north of Memel[5] off the Russian coast. He recalled:

It was the middle watch. The hardest watch of all. Just past midnight. We were in Russian waters. A handful of officers stood on the bridge. Lookouts leaned on the railings. Forward gunners stood in the protection of their gun shields. You could see only their silhouettes. All lights were out. All was quiet. The only sounds were the occasional whispered word, the tin rattle of a coffee pot somewhere nearby, and the soft rustle of the sea as the stern threw it back, along the ship's sides. Suddenly, a shout went up: 'Wireless report!'

The signaller hands it to an officer on the bridge. He takes it to the chart-house, where the Navigation Officer studies it.

'Lord God!' he says. 'Another!'

His words sent everyone's heart racing. It was a wireless message from our flagship, the *Friedrich Carl.* It gave the ship's position followed by three words: 'Immediate help needed'.

The Navigation Officer's hands flew across the chart, plotting the reported position, and then, with dividers, he tried to determine the distance between us and the stricken vessel. It was considerable. We were worried. Would we get there in time?

That slow, middle-watch atmosphere vanished as the news spread like wildfire throughout the ship. The turbines turned. Two cutters, with rescue buoys and life jackets, were made ready for launching. As we worked, our thoughts were with the endangered crew. Two names in particular kept coming up: Admiral Behring and Kapitänleutnant Gercke. Both were held in high esteem. Until recently, they had been aboard the *Augsburg*, for our own ship had recently served as the Admiral's flagship. Fears were high as hour after hour passed and not once did the *Friedrich Carl* answer our wireless calls.

After three hours, we arrived in the reported area but found no ship. Nothing. Not a single shaft of light penetrated the blackness. We probed the darkness with a blinker lantern and then with searchlights. Finally, from the darkness ahead, a white star shell shot high in the sky.

We went ahead at high speed. 'Searchlight on!' And then we saw it. Our fatally wounded flagship. Unforgettable. She lay with a strong starboard list, the aft deep in the water. Water was already spilling over the stern. By the mainmast lay the debris of a broken aircraft (an artillery observer for our planned bombardment of Libau). Between the funnels, dense white clouds of steam wafted upwards.

Along the port railing, the ship's crew was standing, side by side, in deep silence. High on the port bridge wing, we saw the Admiral, with his *Admiralstabsoffizier* and the boat's commander. The barrels of the stricken ship's heavy port artillery were swung out to port-side. We could see down the muzzles of the guns. In the faint light of very early dawn, the spirit and discipline of those men on the *Friedrich Carl* was stunning. Their electric system had long since collapsed, their ship was sinking, her list was steadily increasing. Yet the crew stood there in the dark, orderly, quiet, in rows, on the higher side of the boat. They had been standing there for hours. Below, in the ship's interior, a damage control party was waging a bitter and losing battle. Their best hope was to postpone the inevitable.

In the waters between us and the flagship, two cutters, the only small boats our ships carried at that time, bobbed about on the waves. Each had a coxswain and a crew of ten. They were launched so that, in the event of the ship capsizing, they could use flares to mark the position of those in the water.

Our captain called out, 'Hold the cutters! Both engines half speed astern! Clear to put alongside on starboard.'

With brilliant manoeuvring, he laid the *Augsburg* along the higher side of the sinking ship.

In a few minutes, almost the entire crew was aboard the *Augsburg*, except of course for those heroes in the stern forward torpedo room. They had died immediately, on impact. But there was one man missing. My good friend Hermann. I boarded the *Friedrich Carl*, calling his name as I clung to the railings to stop myself from sliding down the deck. I thought of his young wife. I thought of his two boys. Then, suddenly, his form appeared in a stairwell. He shouted and scrambled up to where I was. He had been making doubly sure that all who could leave had done so. What relief I felt on seeing him.

The *Friedrich Carl* had not been torpedoed. She had hit two mines. If that was the case, then we too were in danger. Maybe there was an unknown mine barrier nearby. So far, we had managed to manoeuvre without hitting anything, but this was nothing more than good luck.

Admiral Behring ordered the *Augsburg* to run into Memel[5] at high speed, so we turned to make an easterly course and as we did so, we saw the *Friedrich Carl* suddenly slip beneath the waves. We had rescued the crew one quarter of an hour before she sank.

The idea was to disembark the rescued crew in Memel so that we in the *Augsburg* could continue with our mission. We had been on our way to Libau when the emergency call reached us. As we set out on our new course, we raised the Admiral's flag. A good moment for all. The dear old *Augsburg* was, once again, a flagship. Then, suddenly, from the speaker tube came the news, 'Ahead, to port, three vessels!'

Who could possibly be at sea at this early hour? Three boats were sailing directly towards us. In the grey drizzle, it was impossible to make out who they were. Was it the minelayer responsible for the new barrage?

'Alarm!' We went to battle stations. I was in the conning tower and gave preparatory commands to the guns.

It is odd that our opponent has not yet seen us, for the ships continue directly towards us. I choose the largest of our opponents. The gunners have him in the crosshairs of their aiming telescopes. We await the salvo gong to open fire. I ran to have a look through the range-finder. Perhaps then I might have a chance of identifying these boats? A few seconds later, the largest of the vessels suddenly stood perpendicular in the water, her bow stretching up to the heavens. She sank like a stone. We stood, stupefied. At this, the two remaining small vessels turned so we could see that one was the Memel pilot steamer, and the other a large motor yacht. They began to rescue survivors from the third vessel which had struck a mine. All three had been sent to rescue the *Friedrich Carl* crew by the Intelligence Officer in Danzig. He, too, had heard that urgent call for help.

The *Augsburg* slowed. We pondered our situation. Ahead of us? Mines. Behind us? Mines. Were they from a connected barrier, or were there several, separate barriers? One thing was certain. The stretch of water behind us was clear.

'Turn about! Run back along our course and then, in deep water, back to Neufahrwasser and Danzig.'[6]

Winnie soon heard the news:

Shortly after I returned to Berlin I was called back by a telegram. The Admiral had changed flagships. He and Hermann were now on the *Friedrich Carl*, and the *Friedrich Carl* had just been sunk.

I rushed to pack some clothes for him, and a new uniform. He had lost everything. Well, except for what he was wearing at the time, and that was soaked in sea-water and torn. He met me at Danzig station. He carried a large bunch of flowers in his hands. What joy danger brings if you escape its clutches! He was still alive. I still had my husband to embrace. I still had Hermann.

I stayed in Danzig for almost a week. It was a fine medieval city, full of beautiful old houses and quaint corners. We stayed in the fashionable Hotel Kaiserhof, but went out in the evenings to cosy restaurants, tucked away down narrow streets. Hermann's comrades would join us and we'd sit at bare, scrubbed tables which, because we were near the countryside, were piled high with delicious food. Yes, there was a war going on, but at that particular moment we were well-fed and very happy.

It was only a few miles from the front line so I was given strict instructions on what to do if the Russians invaded. We were told that we must not, under any circumstances, take up arms against the enemy. Fighting was only for soldiers in uniform. Sniping and underground activities were prohibited. Those who disobeyed could, under international law, be shot.

I didn't need persuading. I think most of us were only too glad to do exactly as we were told. That was Hermann's first brush with death. There were others.

A second came only two months later.

Chapter 15

Siege on the Somme

Until the First Battle of the Marne, the German army had been waging a *Bewegungskrieg* (war of movement). After that battle, it became a defensive war, a *Stelllungskrieg*. Siege warfare, in other words. From the German point of view, it was no longer a question of when Germany would beat the French, but when the French would give up, and the British.

It may seem odd, with Germany the occupying power in France, that the German soldier saw himself as being on the defensive, but he was. His job was to a hold a line marked by trenches. True, occasionally (especially at the beginning, when the generals had not quite given up hope), he was asked to attack. This would mean an advance into no-man's-land, followed by a retreat after a counter-advance by the enemy. It was a war of attrition, of minimal gains. Sometimes it was extremely boring, at other times, active and hellish.

At the end of 1914, the Elisabeths were positioned at the most westerly point of the German front line in France. They and the Alexanders were in the village of Gommecourt, near the small town of Bucquoy, close to the Somme. That November, Waldemar arrived from Berlin by train. What did he feel? Possibly, some pleasure. He was now part of the violent, stressful life of his comrades in the 4th Company. He belonged more to them, perhaps, than to those he had left behind in Achenbachstraße. He must have realized that things would never be the same again. He carried a letter in his top inside pocket. It was addressed to Christel and inscribed, 'In case of my death'.

Waldemar's new rest quarters were in Bucquoy. He spent three days on duty in the trenches at the front, followed by three days off relaxing in Bucquoy. There they had their own common room, their own newspaper, *Die Liller Kriegszeitung*[1] (the Lille Wartime Newspaper), their own shops and their own canteen. But their greatest delight was the bath-house. They were all infested with lice and how they hated them. Lice were in their hair, under their nails, in the seams of their trousers. In Bucquoy, they washed and slept, not outdoors in the rain, crumpled up on a ledge hacked into a trench wall, but in proper beds. They could stretch out their whole bodies. Luxury.

Bucquoy was an odd choice as a rest place. The front line was only 10km away, so the town was within range of the French guns. At the front, in Gommecourt, the area which the Elisabeths were defending was also an odd choice. It was triangular in shape. Two sides of the triangle projected westwards into no-man's-land, and the base faced Bucquoy. It was not easy to defend. You needed men all along the two projecting sides.

The village of Gommecourt itself was tiny, a small cluster of houses and a little church. It stood close to the fine, symmetrical, eighteenth-century, brick *Chateau de Gommecourt*, front-line headquarters for the Elisabeths. When not in the trenches, Waldemar and his fellow officers would chat in its elegant salon, their backs to a fine grey marble fireplace. To their right, they looked through French doors towards a garden edged by a ha-ha. Beyond that lay pasture, where a few cattle grazed.Beyond the cattle was a wood, and hidden deep in that wood were their trenches. The front trench was studded with dugouts and backed by a parallel support trench. Zigzag communications trenches were dug at right angles to the front line. They led back to the chateau. Beyond the wood lay no-man's-land and within it, the ruins of a few abandoned farmsteads. Ownership of these ruins was hotly contested by the two sides. One day, they belonged to the Germans, the next, to the French. The two sides were engaged in a constant, expensive and useless see-saw struggle. Beyond no-man's-land lay the French front line and a couple of villages, including Hannescamps, to the north-west.

The chateau in the middle of the Gommecourt triangle was eventually reduced to ruins. When I reached it, about a hundred years after Waldemar, the house was still by far the largest in the village, but no longer eighteenth-century. A French couple had bought the ruins and rebuilt it in a different style. Now elderly, the lady of the house came out to greet me, a stranger staring at her house for no apparent reason. Full of goodwill, understanding and hospitality, she invited me in and listened to my story. Madame then produced the best lunch I had eaten in many weeks of hard trekking and, with her charming, amusing husband, we drank wine, feasted and talked about the past. I thought then, as I do now, about how much I loved France, and the French.

Madame told me that only one object remained from the original house. They had found, buried among piles of rubble, the grey marble fireplace which had once stood in the main reception room. They had put it back. I stood beside it and ran my hand along the cool, smoothly moulded sill. Then I turned my back to it and looked out, through handsome French windows (new ones), over lawns, a ha-ha and parkland, towards the woods where the trenches still lie. Waldemar's 4th Company occupied the northern section of the triangle, the part which looked north-west across no-man's-land towards the village of Hannescamps. That's where the enemy had some particularly big guns. Consequently, Waldemar and his comrades dug a particularly deep concrete well in their frontline trench. A metal ladder ran down the wall which had its back to no-man's-land, and rooms and corridors branched off the central well. There it is. An extra-deep cement bunker, the iron ladder still attached to the wall nearest the front, but its walls now covered in ivy. This was where those First World War soldiers first learnt to live as troglodytes.

The chateau had been abandoned before the Elisabeths reached it. Previously, it had been the home of Baron Lallart de Gommecourt's two daughters but, with their father dead, the enemy advancing and their male servants (including the chauffeur) drafted into the army, without either of them knowing how to drive, they packed their things into the family limousine and headed south. Amazingly enough, they reached Toulouse safely, thereby giving rise to a legend of verve and panache which lasts in their village until this day. Their last act before leaving was to ask their elderly gardener to build a brick wall in the cellar and hide the best wine. That wall didn't last long. Nor did the chateau. Nor did the wine.

Life in Gommecourt was very different to life on the march. Gone was the endless diet of beans and bacon. Here, resourceful soldiers ate well (as did I). They killed grazing cattle and sheep, shot pigeons, chased down squawking chickens, and prepared feasts for the whole regiment. They also (as I did) drank wine. Food and drink were in good supply, but otherwise life in the trenches was sodden, cold and dangerous.

The men tried to conjure up some degree of homeliness by pinning pictures and photos to trench walls. They furnished underground rooms with chairs and tables stolen from the chateau. They put flowers on makeshift tables. The biggest difficulty was finding a dry place to sleep. They leaned against the trench sides or bundled themselves onto shelves in the walls. Sometimes, they slept on all fours, using their hands and knees to keep their bodies out of water. The wet was a menace but could be, if not cured, then at least alleviated. Soon, sappers built drains and laid duckboards. But they couldn't cure the cold. As November turned into December, sleet, hail and snow exacerbated the misery.

The biggest danger of all was neither the cold nor the wet, but incoming shrapnel shells, hollow steel projectiles filled with metal shot. They screamed and whistled their way towards the front line. When they hit, they exploded, scattering deadly projectiles over a wide area. These brutal weapons were now causing far more casualties than rifle fire. To counter them, sappers built strong roofs over their trenches and dug ever deeper foxholes and dugouts.

Bucquoy,
Saturday, 28 November 1914

Dearest Heart,

Thank you for the send-off. Thank you for the flowers. Thank you for the lovely times we have had together. I arrived safely and am settling into a routine. The fact that there is a routine at all is something new. We no longer march 40km a day. Excellent. This is our new *Stellungskrieg*. We sit still. They sit still. There is a sortie. It's repulsed. Then everyone sits still again. Not good. Often boring.

I have been appointed platoon leader but only, I'm afraid, because we're running out of more senior officers.

Ever and ever, and ever and ever, your loving Waldemar

That was the penultimate time that Christel heard from her Waldemar. On New Year's Eve 1914, he went to church in Bucquoy. It was packed for *Silvester Abend*. New Year's Eve is not traditionally celebrated this way in Germany, but in 1914 it served as an excuse to bring the men together. They wanted to mark the end of the first year of a war which was supposed to have been over long before Christmas.

They sang an old New Year's hymn, '*O komm du Gott der Warheit, und kehre bei uns ein*' (O come, God of truth, stay with us). The priest rose to speak, but hesitated. He, and everyone else, could hear that well-known sound, the hissing, whistling noise of incoming shells. One landed close by. The service came to a hasty end.

The main door of the church was at the west end, and the men were told to return to barracks immediately, everyone for himself. As they left through the two big doors (which, incidentally, faced the direction of enemy fire), a shell hit a corner of a neighbouring building. It exploded and a shower of iron shrapnel sprayed those exiting the church. Carnage. Suddenly there were eighty men dead or dying on the church steps, on the pavement and in the street. Among the dead was Oberleutnant Stein von Kamienski. He had just been appointed leader of the 4th Company. He was killed instantly. Next to him fell his new platoon leader, Waldemar, with a bad head wound. He was taken to the *lazarett* in nearby Achiet-le-Grand. He died there, in the early hours of New Year's Day, and was buried with full military honours nearby in Ablainzeville's little cemetery. It lies on the edge of the village, almost surrounded by fields. Waldemar joined a community of bodies, most of them French. Before lowering him into his grave, his batman removed a letter to Christel from the inside pocket of his jacket. She never gave it to Philipp. We can only imagine the tender farewell of a young man to the woman he had hoped to marry. I am sure he thanked her for her love. I am sure he told her to be as happy as she could, for his sake as well as her own. I am sure he asked her to remember him.

When Philipp wrote about his youngest son in his Chronicle, he ended by saying:

> So. In brief. Your life shone so much more brightly than my words can ever shine. I lack the ability to conjure up your qualities as they should be remembered. I have planted a sacred grove for you in my heart. There I dwell with you. And there I will dwell with you, forever.

One Hundred Years Later

In the late 1970s, the *Volksbund Deutsche Kriegsgräberfürsorge* (War Graves Commission) moved his body, or rather his skeleton, to a vast new military cemetery in Neuville-St-Vaast, where he now lies, alongside 44,829 of his comrades.[2] I went there in trepidation, some one hundred years after his death. At the entrance there is a list of those buried. No Waldemar. Only acres of dark crosses stretching out in long straight lines. A few scattered Scots pines relieve the symmetry. A stone memorial sits in the centre. Its inscription reads, *Ich hatt einen Kameraden* (I once had a comrade), the first line of that moving soldiers' song so often sung as a friend was laid to rest. On another side are the words, *Sei treu bis in den Tod* (Be true even unto death). He was.

With so many graves, there was no chance I would find him. I needed at least some indication of where, among the 44,829, he lay. Home in Kent, I wrote to the Commission. Apologies. By some freak accident, everyone whose surname began with a 'G' had been omitted. They would correct the situation. I went back.

It was a hot summer's day. I was standing there in silence, by Waldemar's cross (one he shares, as they all do, with three others), when the graveyard cat appeared out of a hedge. He came towards me. He rubbed the length of his whole body against my bare legs. In his soft warmth, past and present were united. The touch of this quiet cat spoke eloquently: 'The past (is) expressive, articulate, not dumb and forgotten.'[3]

* * *

Man is a rope stretched between the animal and the Superman – a rope over an abyss. A dangerous crossing, a dangerous wayfaring, a dangerous looking-back, a dangerous trembling and halting. What is great in man is that he is a bridge and not a goal: what is lovable in man is that he is a prelude and a transcending force.

Friedrich Nietzsche, *Thus Spoke Zarathustra*

Chapter 16

Steering into Sandbanks

Winnie wrote:

> Early in January 1915, we heard the terrible news of Waldemar's death. It was a deep blow to the whole family. Partly to digest this, Hermann took leave and suggested a skiing holiday. He wanted to go to a remote inn more than a mile outside a hamlet called Drei Annen Höhne in the Harz Mountains. But I had just sprained my ankle so Hermann went off with his father instead. His father wasn't well either, but decided to risk it. He didn't want to lose any opportunity to be with his son.
>
> After a few days, my ankle was much better and anyway, I too couldn't bear the thought of missing time with Hermann so, without being able to let them know beforehand, I set out to join them. I arrived when it was dark and snow lay thick on the ground. I asked the station master for a taxi but there was none. There wasn't even a road to the inn. The station was isolated – just a couple of cottages and a deserted platform. The station master found someone to walk with me and carry my suitcase. It took about an hour along a mountain track and we passed not a soul on the way. He told me his family history and I told him mine and so the time passed pleasantly. We arrived at the Drei Annen inn just in time for the evening meal. Hermann and the Captain scolded me. I suppose, looking back on it, I ought not to have been so rash. I was, you see, pregnant. Little Ursula was on the way, but they didn't know that, and nor did I.
>
> The next day, we hired skis and set off. The grandeur of the snow-covered mountains and the silence of the forests healed, just a little, the wound of Waldemar.

A few days after his skiing trip, Hermann was back on board the latest of Admiral Behring's flagships. It was an armoured cruiser, the *Prinz Adalbert*. Wintertime was always severe on the Baltic. There were times when spray froze in the air, right in front of your face. Men coming in from watch on deck had to spend their first ten minutes indoors chipping the ice off their coats before they could take them off. On 22 January 1915, the *Prinz Adalbert*, with Behring and Hermann on board, was sailing in sleet and snow, along the Russian shore, eastwards, in the direction of Libau. Some torpedo boats preceded them, acting as mine-sweepers, and two smaller vessels sailed alongside. The idea was to bombard the military installations in Libau, approaching along a route which was deep and mine-free. Somehow or other, they found themselves uncomfortably close to shore where the water was *not* deep. At around 5 am on 24 January, the *Prinz Adalbert* ran aground on a sandbank, almost opposite the small Russian port of Steinort. Philipp, when he learnt what had happened, swore that the Navigation Officer must have been insane.

There she was. Stuck fast. Stranded. Close to enemy territory and with only a few hours of darkness remaining. A sitting duck. Even in the dark, the Russians realized the German flotilla was present and started firing. The first thing to try was to use the boat's engines in reverse, but the body of the boat lay too deep in the sand. She wouldn't budge. Then the other boats tried to tow her off the bank backwards. That also failed. Then the crew lightened the boat by jettisoning everything superfluous into the water. They tried to tow her backwards once again. But again, she was sitting too low to move. That's when Hermann had a brainwave. He ordered two of the accompanying torpedo boats to sail, at top speed and in tight formation, parallel to and past the stranded ship. He hoped the swell they created would lift the boat. At the same time, they would jam the ship's engines sharply into reverse.

It was shortly after 6.00 am and still dark when they tried. The ship rose, but not enough. They tried a second time. She rose slightly more, just enough for her engines to engage in water and draw her backwards. She was clear. As always in the German military, three hurrahs for Hermann. Behring led the cheers.

At about the same time that Hermann was dealing with sandbanks, his father was looking for another way of contributing to the war effort. He found a job as Director of the Naval Supply Depot in Swinemünde. He would be in charge of the harbour as well as the supply station. Mila went with him. It was exactly what they both needed. A sense of usefulness. Busy-ness. A new lease of life. They never talked about Waldemar, either to each other or to anyone else. It was easier just to carry on. Mila wrote to Georg to tell him what had happened. Philipp didn't.

Chapter 17

A Change in Direction

General Seydewitz returned from his sickbed still reluctant to modify his behaviour for safety's sake. One of the many modern things he had no time for was the cry, '*Fliegerdeckung*!' (Hide! Aeroplane in sight). He *did* conform, but he didn't enjoy it. A true soldier, he thought, shouldn't have to run because of some remote plane. He wanted to ride, in the old tradition, fearlessly, on his fine grey, at the head of his regiment. And that is, by and large, what he did. Georg rode behind him, at a respectful distance, always ready to take messages or relay orders.

Once, leading his grey and coming out of hiding after a plane had been spotted, the old General looked at the empty road behind him and asked, 'Good God, where's the regiment?'

'*Noch* (still) *in Fliegerdeckung, mein General*,' replied Georg.

The regiment was in Menen[1] for several major celebrations: Christmas, New Year, the Kaiser's birthday[2] and Bismarck's centenary. Of all these, Christmas was the biggest. The entire regiment went to church, sang lustily and then gathered for a feast. Long tables were set up in a hall and covered with bright red cloth. Apples, nuts, *Lebkuchen*[3] and presents sent by Berlin schoolchildren had been carefully laid out in the middle of the table, just like a family celebration at home. Old Seydewitz, the regimental father, sat at the top table. Swags of evergreen garlands hung above him. Georg was close by. He looked at the festive scene before him but remained pensive. He was thinking of the next day, 26 December, his birthday. He would be turning twenty-eight. In his mind, he saw a succession of scenes from five months earlier. He saw his old studio in Paris. The paintings stacked against the wall. His easel. He thought of happy times sitting at pavement cafés. Chats with friends. What had happened to them all? Seydewitz glanced at him and nodded to Wedekind.

Wedekind leant across the table towards Georg and raised his glass: '*Na, Junge. Zum Wohl! Dein Geburtstag!*' (To your birthday, young man!).

To celebrate General von Hindenburg's victory at the Battle of the Masurian Lakes,[4] the Kaiser's birthday and Bismarck's centenary,[5] the army assembled in the market square. Garlands, flags, bunting, brass bands, marching and reviews.

What the locals made of all the German flags isn't difficult to imagine. Nor what Georg made of it. The locals must have winced, but Georg observed it all with a growing indifference. He had heard, in late January, of his young brother's death in the small hours of New Year's Day, in Achiet-le-Grand. That was only 90km from where he was now. The news came in a letter from his mother, brief and to the point. As Georg read her words his mind grew numb. He realized that while he was raising a glass to the New Year, his brother lay dying in hospital. That when he was getting up on New Year's Day, his brother was being buried. Not a word from his father. Of course not. He would have been quite unable to put pen to paper.

The regiment stayed in Menen partly to assist with the planned launch of a secret new weapon – poison gas.[6] Tear gas had been used by the French in August 1914, but the weapon was inept: it didn't kill effectively. The Germans hoped that their new version would work better and give the army the chance it needed to close the Ypres Salient. The Salient was a bulge in the line which protruded from the Allied-held town of Ypres into the German lines arched round the town, on higher ground, to the east and north-east. A bulge of this kind made the Allies vulnerable yet, so far, they had held their ground. The situation seemed to invite the Germans to squeeze the bulge. It should have been possible. They intended to do so, helped by the shock effect of poison gas.

Everyone around Georg was nervous. What if the wind changed? What if it blew the gas back on their own men? Eventually, on 22 April, weather conditions were exactly right, and the attack was launched. That day, the 201st was sent by train to the nearby village of Langemarck at the northern end of the Salient. A fellow *Studentenregiment* had been attacking the village for months, while Belgian and French soldiers (many from Algeria) were defending it. The attacks had been a disaster, as had those early attacks on Dixmuide. The difference between the Dixmuide assault and that on Langemarck was that, in Langemarck, a stalemate had set in. Neither side was able even to advance into no-man's-land at night to collect the dead. The job of the 201st in April 1915 was, building on the shock effect of the gas attack, to support a final effort and take Langemarck.

Their journey began with a train trip, followed by a night march to camp among the trees of Houthulst Forest. The gas attack had shaken up everybody, not just the French, who had indeed retreated, but the place was buzzing. French aeroplanes kept flying overhead. Lots of *Fliegerdeckung*. The next day, 24 April, the men woke to the regimental band playing one of Georg's favourite Bach chorales, '*Wie schön leuchtet der Morgenstern*' (How brightly shines the morning star). He looked up at the sky. Rainclouds. For some reason, he suddenly thought of his young brother and drew in his breath.

They hung about all day, waiting and waiting for Seydewitz to give them their marching orders. They smoked. Georg had long been a smoker but, since the war started, he was rarely without a cigarette in his mouth. In the afternoon, he, Wedekind and Dr Legahn, the regimental doctor, sat on the ground smoking and playing *skat*. Whenever they glanced upwards they could still see, through the treetops, French planes overhead. The order finally came at 6.30 pm. The sky was at last tranquil. Not so the terrain that lay ahead of them. The land was enemy-free, but in their hasty retreat a couple of days earlier, they had left behind them a nightmarish mess of dense wire entanglements and water-filled trenches. The men of the 201st were walking (marching was out of the question) through a post-apocalyptic landscape. Lest anyone were to forget that the enemy wasn't far away, the odd stray shell still hissed over their heads.

They were on their way to another forest, just south of Bixschoote.[7] It would be their last stop before Langemarck. Fortunately, with such difficult ground to cover, there was a full moon. The moonlight lit up the pools of water and the tangles of barbed wire. It turned the ruined, deserted villages through which they passed into the ghostly scenery for some eerie play.

As if to resist the desolate mood of the scene around them, Seydewitz mounted his grey with more than his usual vigour. But however determined he was, it was soon clear that the going was impossible for a mounted man. He dismounted and led his horse. Georg did the same. At 9.45 pm, a burst of machine-gun fire suddenly rattled angrily through some roadside bushes. No one ever learned whether the attack was intentional or just a matter of chance, but the fire hit the good old General straight in the stomach. He fell, and his horse with him.

He had been well-loved. Wedekind, who took over as commander once again, described von Seydewitz in his funeral eulogy as 'a model of personal fearlessness; a man dedicated to service and to the care of his men.'[8] And so he was. The regiment was traumatized. No one felt his loss more keenly than Georg. You can see loss and shock in a photo of the regimental staff taken the next day.[9]

The next day, 25 April, was bright and sunny again, and at last they caught sight of Langemarck. The enemy had abandoned the village, so no further fighting was required and the regiment was, for a moment, uncertain what to do next. The first thing they had noticed was an unbelievable and overpowering stench. The smell of dead bodies, long-dead bodies. Where was it coming from? All they could see between the village and the old German front line was a lush green field dotted here and there with red poppies and sunny charlock. A pretty scene which hid a grisly truth. Among the tall grasses, the nodding poppies and the yellow charlock lay the bodies of French and German soldiers. Some had lain there since November, when the battle began. Now the corpses were decayed beyond recognition, and with shock Georg saw that their uniforms had survived better than the men. Their clothes were still intact. The soldiers of the 201st dug a mass grave and, covering their noses with rags, started gathering up bodies from both sides, black and white, French and German. They hadn't got far when they heard the low drone of aeroplanes. The French pilots dropped bombs (pilots could rarely resist the temptation), but none hit their mark (they rarely did). Everyone knew what would happen next and rushed to shelter in concrete dugouts. Then it began. Well-aimed, incoming artillery fire. One shelter took a direct hit. More bodies. More graves.

The next port of call was an area near the village of Pilkem, west of Langemarck. It was only about 3km north of Ypres. Following the gas attack, the Germans had won trenches there, but the enemy recovered them remarkably quickly. The 201st's job was to counter the counter-attack. On 1 May, in the black of night, and thanks almost entirely to hand grenades, they succeeded, but on 6 May the French were relieved by the British and they opened fire with the vigour of newcomers, bringing more losses to the German side.

But for this continuous, steady British defence, the Germans might well have taken the bulge out of that Ypres arc but, as it was, German losses were so overwhelming that the High Command decided the taking of Ypres wasn't worth the cost. Between 1 and 11 May, the 201st Regiment had lost almost a quarter of its strength.

The Schlieffen Plan had not been strictly followed, since the scheduled time limit had been overrun. The Plan had allowed the German army six weeks to conquer France. That time limit was passed on 14 September 1914, but only in May 1915 was the Plan effectively scrapped. In May, Falkenhayn decided not only to accept a stalemate on the Western Front, but to plan for it. He was going to transfer troops to the east. The focus was on Russia. Russia first, France second. The exact opposite to what Schlieffen had proposed. Falkenhayn ordered those divisions left in the west (100 of them, including Georg and the Gardekorps) to hold their ground against France's 150 Divisions. Such a disparity in numbers was too great a temptation for the French. A major French offensive began.

General Ferdinand Foch,[10] France's Assistant Commander-in-Chief for the Northern Zone, approached his responsibilities with zeal. It wasn't simply that he introduced new tactics and techniques, but he developed and intensified what was already in use. There had been artillery barrages before; now these were extended to last many hours. The machine gun had been in use since the beginning, but now it was gaining pre-eminence. The infantry had attacked in waves before; now such assaults were mounted repeatedly, with utter disregard for the cost in human life. Shell splinters had filled the air before; now they were the prime cause of death.

War was becoming ever more brutal, more intense and more terrifying. With the new extended artillery bombardments, deadly slivers of metal and ricocheting rock fragments whirled in clouds of smoke and dust above the battlefield. Men had to endure eardrum-shattering explosions and a sense of dislocation and vulnerability as the earth shook beneath their feet. They *felt* as well as heard the noise. They had to endure all this, knowing that, largely thanks to the reconnaissance work of pilots, aim was now so accurate that French artillery fire could flatten the defensive barbed-wire entanglements they had strung across no-man's-land. It could even flatten the wattle breastwork (defensive screens) which lined the front of the German trenches. Slaughter was taking place on an increasingly industrial scale.

Georg and the 201st were sent to the Loretto Heights in the Artois region.[11] The men at the front watched Foch's new infantry attacks with a kind of furious resignation. They watched and waited in deeper dugouts and stronger concrete shelters. Only the poor lookout stayed in the open trench. He peered over the top, often looking through branches which he had piled up in a pathetic attempt to conceal his presence. If he was lucky, he had a periscope.[12] He was watching for the next infantry assault. These came in predictable waves, always in threes. As the first began, he would yell, '*Sie kommen!*' (They're coming), and his comrades poured out of their bunkers and took up positions. Each wave had to overcome, first of all, the barbed-wire entanglements (bombarded by the French during the day, but rebuilt by the Germans at night). Those that were trapped by the wire hung there helplessly for the duration and beyond. Those that escaped rushed onwards, their faces contorted with fury and their voices howling in an unknown tongue. At Loretto Heights, almost all the men used by Foch were black troops from the French colonies.[13] The sight was, at first, very frightening, especially for young men who had never seen a black face before. But as with any new strategy or weapon, the shock didn't last long. The German infantry stood in their front trench and leaned forward on the earth wall, semi-crouching, heads down, noses level with their guns. Once the foe was within range, they fired. When a last few remained running towards them, they jumped out of their trenches and flung hand grenades. If, even after that, some remnants were still advancing, it was daggers, bayonets and rifle butts. Stabbing, jabbing, smashing. Then the second wave. Then the third. After that, all night long, they heard the wails, groans and screams of those hanging in the barbed wire in no-man's-land – 'Comrades, have pity!' 'Water!' Those cries also took their toll. War was becoming a test of nerves.

The Loretto Heights in Artois are an upland area dominating France's northern plain. Early in the war (October 1914), Germany had captured this plain, important for its coal mines. On moving troops to the east, Falkenhayn said that, whatever happened in the west, the French should not be allowed to regain control of their coalfields. Georg and his comrades were part of that effort.

When the 201st arrived, the German defence was going badly, so badly that the Sixth Army had actually been dislodged from the summit of the Heights and driven part of the way down the slopes. They dug temporary defensive trenches as they went. A defensive position on a slope is notoriously difficult, but the 201st was ordered to mend and hold the slipping trenches.

Georg and the regimental staff set up combat headquarters in a small village near the town of Lens. From there, a series of communications trenches led to battalion staff dugouts at different points along the front line. The communications trenches were clearly visible from the air. The Loretto Heights are of white limestone, and the paths running up their slopes appeared as bright white threads shining in the general blackness. Such vulnerability made moving from the frontline to the rear, and vice versa, much like a game of Russian roulette. Many died on the journey. It was so dangerous that Wedekind told his men to leave their knapsacks behind so they could dive aside more readily if shelling began. He also got rid of their helmets. The Loretto Heights battle was the beginning of end of the *Pickelhaube*. It was proving an embarassment. As men crouched to run along trenches, keeping their bodies out of sight, their helmet spikes remained visible and became targets, much as German sharp shooters had been targeting the red trousers of the French. *Pickelhaube* leather was, anyway, useless in protecting men from flying pieces of metal. Wedekind ordered his men to leave their helmets behind as well as knapsacks. It seems incredible but, during this period, when the *Pickelhaube* was discarded and before the metal helmet came in, men fought with their heads unprotected.

Those in staff headquarters always had an easier time of it than the men at the front, but as a courier Georg was constantly running the gauntlet. He had to carry messages from the front to the rear and back again, and along the line between one regiment and another. He too had to leave his *Pickelhaube* behind.

On 23 May, *Oberstleutnant* (Lieutenant Colonel) von Zimmermann, who had replaced von Seydewitz, took sick leave. He went sick frequently, which caused much muttering among the men – not that they minded too much, for whenever he was absent, Georg's old comrade Wedekind took over. Meticulous, careful and good-humoured, Wedekind led the regiment during some of its worst moments in Artois.

On 24 May, the battalions of the 201st were in the front line. They fought all day, and at night carried the wounded to the rear and sent food, drink and replacement men to the front. That day, enemy guns destroyed so much of the barbed-wire defences that the area in front of the 12th Company's trench was left undefended and the enemy came through it. Regimental staff called for help from a neighbouring regiment, but in the end it was other companies in the battalion which saved the day. They formed commando groups and (fighting within their own trenches) made flanking attacks on the enemy until they had cleared them all out. By that time, only twelve out of the two hundred men in the 12th Company were surviving. Things were definitely not going well.

Four days later, 28 May was even worse. In the hurly-burly, the 201st's regimental staff took charge of the entire brigade. The enemy had taken down the phone lines, so all orders went by word of mouth. Georg had to run flat out. The regiment was attacked so ferociously that part of the German line gave way yet again. Wedekind again ordered commando groups from adjacent battalions to use hand grenades in a flanking attack to retrieve the lost trench, and again they succeeded. But it was, as ever, at great cost, to Georg. Running and ducking between one post and another, he was struck by a shell fragment over the heart. Over that heart there was a pocket. In that pocket sat a thick sketch pad. Shrapnel embedded itself in the pad. One of his damaged sketches was later used as an illustration in the regimental history.[14]

To everyone's surprise, late in the evening of 20 June, the men were loaded onto trains. They arrived, some hours later, in a quiet spot behind the front. Recovery time. They mended their clothes, cleaned their weapons, rested their minds and basked in the pleasure of inaction. Officers were offered something extra: 'Coffee kitchens'. They suddenly appeared in battalion headquarters, and the men joked that they would surely have to pay for such a luxury. What fresh hell would they be sent to next?

On 13 July, in the pouring rain, at the dead of night, they were once more loaded onto trains and, to everyone's amazement, arrived in the pleasant, leafy town of Carignan, close to Sedan. From the regiment's point of view, the most important thing about that lovely town was its river. As soon as they arrived, the men rushed to its banks, tore off their clothes and sank their whole bodies, heads and all, in the cool water. Lice. They were infested with them. Abhorrent guests. Georg hated them. He told Philipp that they were worse than the enemy.

There had been heavy losses in Artois. New recruits arrived, and Wedekind supervised their training. The men were relieved to find firstly, that the great value of hand grenades in close combat was now officially acknowledged, and secondly, that the machine gun was also acknowledged as invaluable. It was far superior to the rifle. Unfortunately, supplies were limited.

Georg was known to other officers as 'Our Georg'. The possessive pronoun gives you a sense of the affection he inspired in others. Perhaps he was popular because of his quiet, calm nature, or maybe he was liked simply because he had survived. He represented, just by being alive, the 201st's combat history. Only three officers remained since the regiment had left Berlin nine months earlier: Leutnant Gercke, Commander von Wedekind and Oberleutnant von Frantzius. All of them were on the Regimental Staff. It was clearly the safest place to be.

Von Wedekind, a professional soldier, gruff and good-natured, was older than most, and not ambitious. Perhaps he was looking forward to his retirement. Von Frantzius, the Adjutant, also a professional, was in every respect the opposite. Considerably younger, he gave the impression that he dreamed of advancement. He was caustic and a little superior. Georg, on the other hand, was always ready with a smile and had no military ambitions. He was an artist, dislodged from his chosen path. In this sense, he was in the same position as most of the others. He was making the best of a bad job.

Everyone knew where they could find Georg of a Sunday in Carignan. He would be sitting on the banks of the River Chier, sketchbook in hand, trying to make sense of what he saw. Speaking good French, he used to strike up friendships with locals. He offered to sketch them, or their houses. He gave them his work. One of his Carignan sketches shows a Frenchwoman sitting on a wooden chair on her doorstep. She clasps her hands together and looks up confidently (not a trace of fear) at a group of German soldiers standing on either side. She has a cloth over her left wrist. Is she a housewife, or a cook? The only woman in the picture, and the only one seated, she is clearly in command. The bearded and burly-looking officer on her left is von Wedekind, with arms akimbo. Aggressive, defensive. Von Frantzius, the Adjutant, on her right holds an elegant cigarette in his hand. He seems to be drawing closer to hear what she has to say. What was she saying to them? Surely she is telling them what she has prepared for their supper.[15]

That October, the regiment found itself once more on a train, only this time in broad daylight. Most unusual. They were passing through friendly territory. Georg looked out of the train windows to see the great rolling plains of Hungary. They were on their way to the Eastern Front. Not to fight the Russians, but the Serbs.

Chapter 18

Will-o'-the-Wisp: the Serbian Campaign

In 1915, the Kingdom of Serbia was very different to the Serbia we know today. It stretched from Belgrade, close to the Hungarian border, all the way southwards to the border with Greece. Apart from the northern river plains, the country was made up almost entirely of mountains kept apart by the Great Morava river valley. The Great Morava flows north to join the Danube near Belgrade. There were few roads. To travel south, an army could take the road along the river valley, but if it did it would be exposed to attack by an enemy taking refuge in the mountains on either side. Or it could follow tracks high up in the mountains. These were safer, but they were also very narrow and not clearly marked. In drier weather, the paths were rough and stony, but rain washed earth off the mountain sides and turned them into a quagmire. As for finding the correct route, that was not easy. There were a few maps and most were unreliable.

Politically, Serbia was in difficulties. Austro-Hungary was no friend. It had, after all, been a Bosnian Serb who had killed the heir to the Austro-Hungarian throne, the assassination which had precipitated the war in the first place. Serbia's neighbour to the east was Bulgaria, which favoured the German side. To the west, Albania was a shaky neutral.

Georg and the 201st Reserve Regiment were sent to Serbia in September 1915 as part of a combined German and Austro-Hungarian invasion force. Subscribing, as always, to the belief that Prussia had a genius for war, Philipp was relieved to learn that the leader of this combined force was *not* Austro-Hungarian, but Prussian.[1] He was the fierce, authoritative, moustachioed *General Feldmarschall* August von Mackensen, who wore his Hussars' uniform with aplomb, even braggadocio. He was recognizable anywhere by his high fur cap with a clutch of feathers rising above a large skull and cross bones.

Before setting out for Serbia, Georg took the train back to Germany, to the north, to Swinemünde, walking one evening into the apartment of his astounded, happy and nervous parents. They hugged and kissed him. They hadn't seen him in over a year and, during that time, there was one son fewer for them to hug and kiss. All three of them were thinking of Waldemar during that meeting, but no one spoke his name. This might have been the moment for Georg to tell his parents about his Bremen exhibition. But he didn't. He made no conscious decision not to. He just didn't. His career as an artist had somehow become a sideline. Success had become irrelevant; survival was all. They talked of everything they could think of that was not important, and then he left. He would be far away, and for a long time.

The Serbs meanwhile, were hoping for help from Britain and France. Both countries had promised them support troops. They were expected to land at Thessalonika in Greece. From there they would march north, entering Serbia from the south. In other words, their help depended, to a large extent, on easy access through Greece. This was hardly likely to come, since Greece was ruled by King Constantine I and his wife Queen Sophia, sister to the Kaiser and Commander-in-Chief of the Queen Elisabeth Grenadier Guards. The last thing she had done before returning to Greece in 1914 was to wish her regiment success.

The 201st arrived in October 1915, with Georg still Ordnance Officer. They camped near the capital, west of the two rivers which flow around its walls, the Danube and its tributary the Sava. Winter was coming. It would be heralded by the icy Kosava wind.[2] Every year, this wind whips up great waves on both rivers, so the invading force had to cross quickly.

Using pontoon bridges, the 201st transported baggage, weapons and horses across the rivers, while other regiments took the city. It fell quickly. Soon the black, white and red flag of the German Empire flew over Belgrade Castle. But this was a Pyrrhic victory, for Serbia's King Peter had fled, and so had the entire Serbian army. They had set out on a long trek south, hoping to meet those promised Allied troops.

Mackensen ordered his forces to catch the Serbian army and crush it, although he and his generals knew that this was no easy task. The Serbs had the advantage. They knew the route. The invaders, fearful of ambush, decided to take the narrow mountain tracks which led south, marching two abreast instead of the usual four.

Transporting weapons and baggage was a major challenge of its own. The 201st assembled a band of forty Bosnian ponies with panniers and drivers to carry provisions. Limbers carried their heavy guns, and the kitchen unit was to be pulled initially by cart horses. When the rains came and the horses' shoes were sucked off in the mud, these were replaced by oxen. Machine guns were placed in specially built two-wheeled carts and pushed by hand.

And so the circus moved south. Oberleutnant von Zimmermann had returned from sick leave and was back in charge. He and his Adjutant, together with Georg, took the lead. The first and second battalions followed. Major Freiherr von Wedekind, leading the third battalion, brought up the rear. They were heading for Kraljevo,[3] a town which lay on the West Morava River on the western side of the central valley. Its waters flow east, to join the Great Morava. Kraljevo lies at the junction of the West Morava with its tributary, the Ibar, which flows into the West Morava from the south. Kraljevo offered a narrow route south, along the Ibar, as an alternative to the main central valley. It was also an important link in the Serbian railway system. If King Peter and his army were heading south, it would almost certainly be to Kraljevo. The one direction in which they would not be heading was west. West of Kraljevo stood the mighty Albanian Alps, with no roads running through them.

Throughout that long journey, the Serbian army kept out of sight, but just ahead, of the Germans and Austro-Hungarians. The last thing they wanted was to fight and risk annihilation. As it turned out, travel was so tough that sometimes the invaders felt that they were the ones who risked annihilation, not by the enemy, but by geography and climate. It was especially hard for the kitchen unit. The rockier, the steeper and the narrower the track, the harder it was for the kitchen to follow. The cooks complained bitterly, especially when the rains came, turning the track into a quagmire. Mud sucked the boots off the men's feet as well as the shoes off the horses' hooves. Every now and again a shout would ring out, 'The ropes have broken!', and the whole unit would grind to a halt. Georg would make his way to the back as fast as he could (which wasn't fast at all), to see where the problem was and how it could be fixed. Even the little two-wheeled carts carrying machine guns, which under normal circumstances a young lad could have handled, were impossible to move. Georg told the men to dismantle the guns and carry them by hand.

Commander von Zimmermann rode with his compass in one hand and his reins in the other. He was a nervous man and feared that the regiment might find itself on the wrong route. Georg found it difficult to reassure him because he too wondered whether they were going the right way. Over a year into the war, and he had had, as Ordnance Officer, much experience reading maps, but in Serbia it was something else. He didn't trust the maps they had. It was a relief when Zimmermann backed out, yet again. Another sick leave. Wedekind took over.

Marching at around 400m above sea level, rain turned to sleet. At night, the men bivouacked in hillside cow sheds and warmed themselves against the cows' bodies. And the regimental staff? They too bedded down with the cows. Their day began at 5.00 am when the weather was at its coldest. The cows would get up without any trouble, but not the men. They shook their legs, stretched their arms and groaned a good deal before they could stand, hoist their gear on their backs and march off once again. As for the cook, he had given up the struggle entirely, so Wedekind ordered everyone to live off their iron rations.[4] More groans.

Finally, they reached a hillside where, looking south, they could see the West Morava valley and the town of Kraljevo. Even in the morning haze, they could make out the railway station to the north of the town. It was chock-a-block with tents and people. There was the most tremendous amount of activity going on. It turned out that the entire Serbian Army was at the station, and the King as well. The German attack would be launched early next morning.

A bridge below them crossed the West Morava and led to a railway embankment and the town. Shortly after midnight, on 6 November, the invading army positioned its howitzers to cover the bridge and embankment area. Wedekind sent observers forward to climb trees and phone back reports so that the howitzers could find their range. He wanted accurate firing.

There was still a thick mist. Perfect weather for an attack. The infantry moved down to the bridge and found that the Serbs had made a half-hearted attempt to damage it. Three metres were missing in the centre. At first, Georg and others stood where the bridge was broken, holding lanterns to light the way for the infantry to scramble over, but soon the sappers arrived. They cobbled the two sides together so that artillery could cross and the horses could be led over by hand. None of this was easy, because Serbian soldiers hiding behind the railway embankment opposite kept up constant fire. Crossing under fire would have been almost impossible were it not for the howitzers on the hillside behind. With the help of the observers, the gunners found their range.

When the mist lifted, the Germans noticed that there was still feverish activity in the rail yards, but only an hour later, when they reached those yards, no one was there at all. Empty. Deserted. Not a soul, but an awesome stash of valuable equipment remained: machine guns, ammunition belts, aeroplanes, motorboats, floodlights, ammunition, petrol, paraffin, medical supplies, food. Yes, the Serbian army had fled but it had left most, if not all, of its equipment and provisions behind.

With the Serbian army gone, the fighting was over. It was still early morning when von Wedekind and Georg walked into the market square. A small group of bare-headed local men came towards them with two German soldiers on either side.

'*Herr Major*!' said one of the armed guards, 'These men would like to surrender.'

The leader of the little group stepped forward and bowed with great respect to von Wedekind. He read, in German, from a piece of paper which he held in front of him:

> *Herr Kommandant*! Up to this very moment, I was the mayor of Kraljevo. I now hand over to you, this same town. I have the honour to inform you that we will submit to your orders and will readily obey your regulations. I

> am firmly convinced that the army of your civilised country will maintain the peace and order of the town; that you will protect our lives and property, and that you will allow the population to devote themselves to their usual orderly and peaceful lives.[5]

It was signed by the mayor of Kraljevo and stamped with the town's seal. It was 8.45 am Georg and von Wedekind considered the attack had been a success, but Mackensen didn't. His objective was not the taking of Kraljevo, but the destruction of the Serbian army. It had not been destroyed. Turning itself into an uncatchable will-o'-the-wisp, the Serbian army, together with King Peter, had fled. They had managed to stay just in front of the advancing German and Austro-Hungarian forces throughout the journey south. When they realized that there were no Allied forces to help them and that the game was up, instead of surrendering, they set out, in the depths of bitter winter and leaving most of their provisions behind, to cross the high alpine peaks which separate Serbia from Albania. The Albanian Alps, since 1915, have an additional name. They are now known as the 'Accursed Mountains'.[6] Few Serbs survived that trek.

Wedekind and the 201st went back to Belgrade, taking the same route as the one by which they had arrived.

Georg had long felt that being part of the regimental staff was a soft option, and of course it was. Everybody knew that it was the company commanders who bore the brunt of the fighting in every battle. Everyone knew that it was no accident that only three officers remained from the original quota, all of them with the regimental staff. Georg asked to be transferred, and his wish was quickly granted. Mackensen's army was resting and training in Neu Karlowitz,[7] when one of the 201st's company commanders fell sick. On 16 December 1915, after one week's training, Georg took his place. He was now commander of the 9th Company, 3rd Battalion, 201st Regiment. Fortunately for Georg, the 3rd Battalion was commanded by his old friend Wedekind. He understood what Georg was doing (who could miss it?) and he swore to himself that he would protect Georg as much as he could whenever possible. But he well knew there was actually little he could do except offer friendship.

Three days later, Georg had a chance to see what it was like to command men. He led the 9th Company in a parade in front of the Kaiser himself. Wilhelm had arrived in nearby Nis for talks with his new ally, King Ferdinand I of Bulgaria, and he used the occasion to visit his troops. He gave them a pep talk, heavily laced with praise: 'You young soldiers fight better even than your elders … I see here Prussian order and discipline.'[8]

He did indeed. Georg and his comrades were standing in front of him, their blistered feet crammed into half-wrecked, patched boots. They had just marched over 300km and spent three months sleeping in the open. It was a pain to goose-step. But though their boots were old, their uniforms were new. They had been specially issued for the parade. Unfortunately, there had been no time to de-louse the men first, so the soldiers stood there, stock still as the Kaiser spoke, but they were not listening to his words. Their minds were fully occupied with the thought of the lice, which were at that very moment busily burrowing into fresh new seams.

High Command was sending the 201st to Verdun,[9] a battlefield with a bad reputation. It was known as 'the meat-grinder'. The chances of surviving were slim. Georg's unit took the train to Verdun, but he took leave of absence and went to visit his parents in Swinemünde again. However, they weren't there. Philipp had been sent to a military sanatorium in Bad Homburg vor der Höhe. Stomach pains again. It was his way of dealing with grief. Mila managed differently. The day she heard that her youngest son was dead, she dressed in black from top to toe and wore black for the rest of her life. Apart from that, she just got on with it. She looked after those who had been spared.

Winnie was also in Swinemünde, with her two boys and her new baby, little Ursula. She wrote:

> In April 1916, Georg came home on leave. He was recently back from Serbia. It was wonderful to see him again. The boys loved him. They played trains with him on the floor and he took them down to the sandy beach. They took off their shoes and walked along the sea's edge. Cold water on bare feet. He taught Harry how to click his tongue against the roof of his mouth and Harry never forgot this little trick. Not even when he was a grown man.
>
> Most of the time, when with the children, Georg was totally engaged yet, every now and again, you caught him looking absent. His eyes, previously so merry, were now sober. It wasn't difficult to guess why. He had seen things no one should ever have to see. He showed us his campaign sketchbooks from Serbia. Some of these were shredded by shrapnel. We saw drawings of places and people. Wild and primitive, but friendly.
>
> There are few people I liked more than Georg. He was a typical artist in his interests. He also had great charm and a subtle wit. There was nothing cynical about him. He was so gentle and artistic that, up till that moment, I had not been able to visualise him as a soldier. Soldiering wasn't his thing. But now I understood. He looked terrific. He wore his uniform with natural elegance.
>
> He was on his way to Verdun. Far too clever to deceive himself, he was aware of the likely outcome of this next battle and maybe, even of the war.

> On that last visit, his main concern was for Mütterchen. He wanted to shield her. He wanted to build a protective wall around her, but he knew he couldn't. She had been devastated by Waldemar's death, and perhaps they both knew that worse was yet to come.
>
> He kissed the four of us and told me to give Hermann his love. Then he left. We were sad to see him go. A soft melancholy pervaded his old glamour.

Philipp made a similar comment in the Family Chronicle. He said that when he and Mila saw Georg for the last time, in Bad Homburg vor der Höhe, 'There was a look of sorrow in his eyes. Our merry boy from Niemannsweg was gone.'

Chapter 19

Tales of the Unexpected: The Baltic 1915–1917

Was it the work of Prince Heinrich's enemies? Most likely, yes. On 20 April 1915, the Admiralty in Berlin inserted a new player in Germany's Baltic war by creating a new naval position, *Admiral der Aufklärungsstreitkräfte der Ostsee* (Admiral of Reconnaissance Forces in the Baltic). The new admiral was answerable to the Admiralty in Berlin, not to Prince Heinrich, as Behring had been. Berlin was taking back control. The new post was to be filled by Admiral Albert Hopman.[1] Behring took offence and resigned. Hermann stayed. He was now *Admiralstabsoffizier* to Albert Hopman.

Hermann was in Danzig when Hopman arrived to take up his appointment. To Hermann's relief, they liked each other enormously. Reading Hopman's diaries, you get the impression that some of his happiest days in the Baltic were spent in Hermann's company.

As soon as Hopman arrived, Hermann put forward a plan that he'd been hatching for some time. The primary German motive in the Baltic was to threaten St Petersburg and take Russia out of the war, but ports on Russia's southern Baltic seaboard barred the way. Plans to take the first Russian obstacle, the port of Libau, were already in hand. About 200km north east of Libau (as the crow flies), lies the Gulf of Riga. The low-lying Kurland Peninsula separates the two. If the Germans were to approach the Gulf of Finland from the south, the port of Riga, sitting within the Gulf, would have to be taken first. But what did they know about Russian defences there? In particular what did they know about defences around the Irben Straits, which guard the entrance to the Gulf?

Hermann and Winnie had visited Riga in 1914, but they had not looked at the land around the Irben Straits, nor at the little island of Runö which lies within the Gulf, opposite Riga. Runö was an ideal spot for a signalling station.

Hermann now planned to check Russian defensive positions around the Straits and on Runö. As Behring had once sailed straight into the enemy-held Gulf of Finland, so he now proposed sailing straight into the enemy-held Gulf of Riga, but in very small boats, even smaller than Behring's light cruisers. Hermann's preference always had been for small boats. As an old lady, Lenchen wrote:

Hermann realised, very early on, that in the navy the future lay with the small boats and not with what he called 'the great big tubs'. That's why, from the beginning, he applied for the torpedo boat section. Father was not keen on this, but what could he do against an eldest son who knew how to convince him without wounding him in any way? Hermann could wrap his old man around his little finger."

Could he do the same with his new Admiral?

In April 1915, he presented his plan to Hopman and asked for only two torpedo boats, the *V107* and *V108*.[2] He proposed an intelligence-gathering operation and the destruction of enemy lighthouses and telegraph signalling stations, plus the hope that the operation might so alarm the Russians that they diverted some of their troops, currently mustering on Germany's eastern frontier. The German Army authorities approved Hermann's plan. So did Prince Heinrich. Hermann was to lead the expedition.

In the morning of 30 April, he put to sea from Memel. Travelling under the escort of a light cruiser, SMS *Thetis,* and another torpedo boat, *S148*, by 9.00 pm the *V107* and *V108* arrived at the entrance to the Irben Straits. *Thetis* and the S*148* anchored outside the Gulf, while *V108* and *V107* entered. The night was clear, the wind calm. No lights on either side, no guard vessels, no moon. Shortly after midnight, the outline of the island of Runö appeared. *V108* and *V107* rounded the northern tip and dropped anchor. It was un-garrisoned. Hermann and his little group saw a lighthouse and a warden's cottage. A light shone in the window. Leaving the sailors by the boats, Hermann crept forward in the dark using both hands to help him scramble up through the rough terrain. On reaching the cottage, he flung the door open with his left hand and, brandishing his Browning in his right, he shouted in perfect Russian, '*Ruki werch*!' (Hands up!)

The warden was astonished. He had been sitting quietly at a table, reading yesterday's newspaper. He stood up, very surprised indeed, raised his hands and said, with admirable *politesse*, 'Good evening, sir.'

Hermann's men destroyed the lighthouse mirror, burned the petroleum stores and took captive four lighthouse officers of military age. On their return journey, they did exactly as planned. They bombarded lighthouses at the Straits and destroyed signal stations. They arrived back in Memel harbour at 8.00 pm on 1 May. Later that month, in acknowledgement of his courage, Hermann was awarded the Iron Cross, 1st Class.

The Russians were pushing hard on East Prussia and the German army was pushing back just as vigorously. It was a see-saw process, well-illustrated by the experience of the small German port of Memel. This last town in Germany before the Russian frontier was attacked by the Russians in November 1914, taken back by the Germans three months later, attacked by the Russians again the following month, then almost immediately taken back by the Germans. The wisest local inhabitants kept their heads down and their mouths shut. Perhaps the very wisest left. But by May 1915 things had improved and, anyway, von Falkenhayn now prioritized the war in the East. The German army started to plan how to take Russian ports along the southern Baltic shore.

Their immediate goal was Libau, only 70km from the German border. Hopman was informed on 1 May of a joint army and navy attack planned for 7 May. Time enough for the Russians, who were carefully charting German plans on their wall maps, to prepare for the assault. They upgraded the minefields in and around Libau harbour.

SMS *Prinz Adalbert,* an armoured cruiser, was Admiral Hopman's flagship. She and the *Augsburg*, together with other units under Admiral Hopman, anchored around but not in the military harbour, while Hermann, in a torpedo boat and with an escort of two others, sailed to the harbour entrance. There he disembarked and boarded a small dinghy. His plan was to row into the harbour in a light craft which would be unlikely to strike any mines, but which would still give him an idea of a relatively safe route to shore. At the same time, his presence in the harbour would, he hoped, test whether there was any opposition stationed in the buildings there. And this is what he did. He found a mine-free route and he found it without coming under fire. The only damage was to one of the escort ships at the harbour entrance. It struck a mine and had to be towed back to Memel.

Hopman and Hermann thought it likely that the Russians had left the harbour buildings, but how to be sure? Hermann sailed in again, this time with two small boats with engines, each towing a jolly boat with a crew of ten. Within 800m of the beach they came under machine-gun fire. There was the answer. Hopman and the ships anchored outside the harbour started firing back. Hermann and his two boats returned safely, and the bombardment of Libau began, the army joining in from the landward side. Shells flew from both directions. By the end of the day, the Russians had raised the white flag. Libau was taken.

The German army took charge of the town, while the navy sent a mine-sweeper flotilla to clear the harbour. There was some nervousness among senior naval officers about coordination with the army, because the two services had different views on the usefulness of the town. Hopman, Hermann and colleagues wanted to use it as a working port for future activities. It would be particularly useful as they proceeded against Riga. But the army disagreed. A top-level meeting was essential. Hermann went ashore, found those in charge and organized a meeting for that same day. He returned to the *Prinz Adalabert*, picked up Commander Michelsen, the Navy's spokesperson, and sailing in the *V107*, returned to shore. The boat hit a mine almost immediately and sank with great speed. But Hermann's luck was holding. He was rescued. So were those with him. This was the second ship sunk from under him.

To crown their good fortune, Hopman and Hermann got exactly what they had been hoping for. Libau became their naval base for the rest of the war, and this was particularly satisfying for Hermann. Libau had one very good hotel, the Hôtel de Rome, where he and Winnie had stayed the year before. Between 1915 and 1916 Hopman and his officers spent many happy evenings celebrating there. The first was on 7 May, 1915, the day the Germans took Libau.

Libau was a spa town, with all the concomitant advantages: board walks, parks, beaches, elegant houses along the front. They would walk through the waterside park, swim off the sandy beach and play bridge of an evening in navy headquarters. Libau became an oasis for Hermann, a little bit of luxury, a refuge where officers could get to know each other, share their anxieties about the war and their families at home, and snatch moments of laughter from a life which otherwise consisted of extreme danger. Hopman grew as fond of Hermann as Behring had ever been, if not more so. On 30 July he celebrated Hermann's thirty-second birthday by buying him a champagne lunch, where else but in the Hôtel de Rome. When Hopman got back to his rooms that night he wrote in his diary, 'I hope this great and capable man stays with us.'[3] The remark seems to presage doubt and departure. Had Hermann already mentioned his concern about the future?

Given that the Russians had broken the German naval code, it was well-nigh impossible for Hopman and Hermann, or for anyone in the German navy, to triumph in the longer term. It is amazing that they achieved as much as they did, and with so few vessels. The Russians remained on the defensive and the Germans remained the aggressors, but their plans were always being thwarted. German plans were each stamped '*Streng geheim*' (Top Secret), but in fact little, and possibly nothing, was.

On 1 July, one of Hopman's flotillas was dispatched on a planned sortie without the participation of the Admiral, Hermann and the *Prinz Adalbert*. But of course, the Russians knew of the plans and were ready and waiting. They dispatched a small flotilla which included the hidden treasure of the Russian Baltic fleet, one of the British submarines, in this case, the *E-9*. When Hopman's flotilla realized there was a Russian ambush waiting for them, they signalled for assistance from shore. Out sailed the *Prinz Adalbert* with Hopman and Hermann on board. No one on the German side saw the *E-9*'s periscope. The submarine fired straight at the *Prinz Adalbert*, and a torpedo struck the flagship fair and square, but miraculously, she did not sink ('Good for nothing

English torpedoes'?). She would have sunk, though, had a second torpedo also been launched. Fortunately for Hermann and his comrades, the quick-thinking commander of one of their accompanying vessels, alerted to the submarine's presence, saw the periscope, steered straight towards it and sat over it. His action saved Hermann's life and the lives of all but ten of the seamen on board the flagship that day. The *Prinz Adalbert* carried a large complement, around six hundred seamen. It was indeed a lucky day for all of them, but not for the boat. She was shipping so much water that she had to limp home to Kiel, the only harbour deep enough to take her in that state. With the *Prinz Adalbert* out of commission till September, Hopman and Hermann found a new flagship. They transferred to a torpedo boat, the *V9*. The *Prinz Adalbert* was the third boat sunk under Hermann. He was getting a reputation for leading a charmed life.

After Libau, Germany's next goal was the small port of Windau, on the northern shores of the Kurland Peninsula. It lies close to the Irben Straits and was home to an airfield. Planes from Windau controlled shipping in both the Straits and the Gulf as a whole. If you wanted to capture Riga, you had to take Windau first. The army did the hard work of capturing the town while the fleet stood offshore, keeping Russian ships at bay. Windau fell on 18 July. Riga next. A far bigger prize.

A major joint army and navy assault on Riga was planned for 8 August 1915. Units from the High Seas Fleet in the North Sea were brought in, through the Kiel Canal, to assist. Overall control of naval forces was, for the duration of the assault, in the hands of Admiral Erhard Schmidt,[4] commander of the 'big tubs'.

Russia's naval staff, once again, knew everything: the date of the attack, the time, the battle plan. And they mounted a clever response, making use of mine barrages as well as their British submarines. They kept the Germans at bay without difficulty, and in the end, after repeated attempts, Germany gave up. But only for the time being.

Between the failed attack of 1915 and the successful attack which followed in 1917, the Gulf of Riga became the main theatre of war in the Eastern Baltic. It was the focus of incessant harrying attacks by the Germans, and incessant counter-attacks by the Russians. The objective on both sides was to lay mines and blow up enemy ships, while stopping the enemy from doing the same to you. Looking back on it now, it seems a crazy, nonsensical game. But brave men like Hermann risked their lives playing it.

The Russians were sailing in small boats, battleships and armoured cruisers. The Germans used only small boats for three reasons: because they were operating in Russian waters and it was easier to keep out of sight in small boats; because boats with a shallow draft are less likely to trigger mines; and because small boats were all they had. The Russians were expert at mines. Mines were their number one means of defence. In 1915 they had protected the Irben Straits with at least 5,000 of them. These were laid at night by the Russians and swept for and disabled by the Germans during the day. Both sides did it; the Germans also laid mines at night and the Russians also sent out sweepers to disable them. Both sides were locked in a futile cycle. The only way to break it was to do something completely out of the ordinary. What was needed was the unexpected. Hermann turned the problem over in his mind for weeks.

Of the two sides, the Germans had the harder task. The Gulf of Riga was Russian. It was surrounded by Russian territory. Russian gunships patrolled their mine barriers by night. Their defensive onshore gun emplacements kept guard during the day. The Germans, on the other hand, could not patrol the Gulf. It wasn't theirs to patrol. And as for their mine- layers and -sweepers, it took them two to three hours from the German-controlled port of Windau just to reach the target area. Once out there, they were extremely vulnerable. First of all, they were on their own, for while day shift mine-sweepers might hope for a modicum of protection from German planes in Windau, the night-working mine-layers had no protection at all, neither from planes nor from escort ships.

Hermann's friend Max Bastian (also a member of Crew 1902) wrote about work in the Gulf of Riga:

> The German forces were using commercial motorboats from Hamburg harbour in the narrow Irben Straits and, for two long years, the Baltic war was conducted with these boats playing a critical role.
>
> The small boat men were tireless, fearless and selfless in their work. They were baptised in oil and sea-water. Their base was the north Kurland harbour of Windau, where a broad-beamed motor boat tender welcomed them back from their work each day with its warm stove. Their leader was the indefatigable, undeterred, Kapitänleutnant Franz Weidigen. Day in, day out, ever cheerful, he led his sweeper-men into the deadly minefields in the early morning. Their small motor boats danced out onto the Baltic waves, soon lost to view in sheets of spray. It took them two to three hours just to reach the target area. Then they started work.
>
> The Russians laid their mines close to the surface, so although the sweepers' boats had little draft, they still had to be wary. They trawled a sweeper cable to catch and sever the cables which anchored Russian mines. But for one reason or another, they could never guarantee a clear channel. The Russians invented what we called 'bucket' mines. These were set, like a bunch of balloons, on the sea bed, with only one at a time floating near the surface. If this one mine was detonated or its line cut, then, triggered

by a timer device, another would rise to the surface, sometimes hours later, sometimes days.

Often, on the northern horizon, the well-known silhouette of a Russian gunboat would appear, and our little boats would be bombarded with shells. They had little protection except for the bobbing of the waves and our naval airmen. We used to call them 'flying seamen'. They would take off from Windau airfield and try to bomb the Russian gunships. They nearly always missed. The greater risk was that the bomb would fall on the minesweeper men and turn them into more, but involuntary, 'flying seamen'. Sometimes Russian planes arrived and dogfights took place over the Irben Straits.

Minelayers returned to the Straits at night, without lights, and carrying only three or four mines at a time (more would have been too heavy), they laid a chain on either side of the cleared channel. It wasn't unusual for them to meet the foe during the process, but if they did, a particularly noisy and unpredictable artillery battle ensued when no one could see anyone else. The men could fire only in the direction of noise and flashes of light. Unlucky shots risked hitting a mine.

Our minelayer and minesweeper men were under unrelenting physical and mental strain. You could tell by the way their hands trembled when they returned to Windau. Even so, they had to fill out charts to show where they had laid or found mines, which routes they had mined or cleared, and send the report to our headquarters in Libau. Only then could they go to bed and rest.

Work at headquarters continued till very late. It ended only after the Admiral, Hermann and other officers had gathered in the Admiral's office, leant over charts and plotted the next day's events. After that meeting, no sooner had the watch officer sunk onto his bunk, when, like as not, his telephone would ring. Someone in a North Kurland observation post had heard suspicious motor noises coming from the sea. This meant (almost without a doubt) that Russian minelayers were busy wreaking havoc with our maps of where the mines lay. Plucking up as much courage as he could (and he needed a lot), the watch-officer went into the lion's den, which was, of course, the Admiral's bedroom. He woke the Admiral (always when he was in the deepest of slumbers) and told him the news. In a matter of minutes, we were all once again sitting around large-scale charts, appraising the altered situation, forming new plans. These of course, had to be sent to Windau, so Weidigen, poor man, was in turn woken from his slumbers. At such moments, he had a particularly amusing and rich vocabulary.

To break the inevitability of this cycle, my friend Hermann put forward a proposal to mine a new area, the one small area which Russian minelayers had, so far, left mine-free. This was what we called 'the manoeuvre sack'. It was where their minelayers turned about. Hermann was an especially capable man, an original thinker, but this would be, as everyone knew, an extraordinarily dangerous operation. Our men, working without any backup and sailing in noisy, unreliable motor boats, with sparks flashing from their exhausts, would have to sail past the Russian barrage system and locate a very precise spot, well within the Russian operational area.

As we all knew he would, Hermann took the lead. His pluck and bold resolve had already earned him great respect from both officers and men. It surprised no one when our small boat crews cheerfully and willingly, agreed to go with him. Such an operation could only be undertaken on a particularly dark night, or in a pea-souper of a fog. Wind direction was also important. Noisy engines and the smell of oil fumes would betray everything.

To afford at least some degree of offensive capability, Hermann fitted a torpedo tube to the bow of his lead boat, turning it into a miniature torpedo boat. Travelling at the head of three or four other boats, it became a tiny 'flagship'. If their flotilla were attacked, he, in the flagship, would counter-attack and give the others time to retreat.

One of the many problems he faced was that his main job was in Libau, working for the Admiral. To overcome this, he continued working there, but kept in close touch with Windau by phone. Careful not to alert the enemy, he used code words to learn about weather conditions.[5] If an encouraging code word came back, the teleprinter orderly brought over the leather map, and we officers would all study it together. Then, ten minutes later, Hermann was in a plane and on his way. Many times his flight ended in failure because weather conditions changed. They could change quickly and they had to be exactly right. One night, they were.

Waiting for his return, those of us left in the Libau headquarters were extremely nervous. What a gamble; we well knew the outcome could go either way. The Admiral, officers and men, we all gathered together, hoping against hope that he would succeed. Then the phone rang. Our teleprinter orderly was a plodding sort of chap. He never moved fast. But that night, he shocked us all by actually running to take the call. We had never seen anything like it. He picked up the printed paper, our eyes were glued to his face. His expression would tell us what we wanted to know. And it did. A look of joy spread across it. Success. The news travelled like wildfire round headquarters.

When Hermann and his men returned, everyone thronged around to hear the story. He told us that one of his boats had had engine trouble and struggled all the way. At one point, he feared he would have to abandon it. He went to help the stricken craft and, as he did so, its motor suddenly backfired, sending a huge shower of sparks spewing out from its exhaust. At that very moment, only 100m away, two dark shadows loomed. Two Russian torpedo boats. Had they heard? Had they seen?

With motors switched off, the men in the small boats held their breath. They expected, at any minute, to see a flash from Russian guns. Hermann had one finger on the torpedo firing button. But he waited. He had to fire at exactly the right moment because he only had one torpedo. Nerves were strained to breaking point. Then, almost unbelievably, the big boats passed by, vanishing silently into the darkness. Allowing time for the Russian ships to run a respectable distance, our sweepers hurriedly laid their mines and returned home, their 'sick' boat in tow.[6]

A few days later, a powerful explosion was seen from one of the German coastal observation posts. Painstaking bearings were taken. A large boat was sinking. German sailors could see Russian vessels hurrying to help. An effort was made to tow her, but it failed. Later, a lifebelt drifted ashore. '*Dobrowoletz*'.[7]

This news brought Hermann no joy. Seamen are seamen. He went home to Swinemünde for a break and for the first time met his little Ursula, like Georg, a Sunday child. She was born the day of the failed attack on Riga, 8 August. He didn't return to work till October but when he did, Hopman celebrated once more with champagne and, once more, with a game of bridge. He and his fellow officers had missed Hermann a great deal. But those he had left behind missed him most:

Swinemünde is another of those glorious spa towns which are strung, like a necklace of pearls, along the Baltic coast. Most have promenades, piers, grand hotels, parks and good beaches. Swinemünde is one such. It stands guard over the important port and dockyards of Stettin which lie upriver, but the two towns couldn't be more different. The latter is smoke and industry, the former, fresh air and holiday. The Kaiser used to visit Swinemünde once a year.

We took an apartment there in 1915. It lay on the elegant and newly built Kurparkstrasse, which runs parallel to the beach and overlooks a park. On 8 August, the same day as the planned attack on Riga, at number 16 Kurparkstrasse, our first daughter arrived. Little Ursula, a determined child from the start.

Winters in Baltic watering places are always cold, but in Swinemünde in late 1915 I have never felt so cold in all my life. Our house was near the sea and rather exposed. Spa visitors had long left. Except in the town centre, most places were boarded up. It was desolate. All the same, we had some happy moments. There was skating and tobogganing and, one day, with Hermann with us, we went for a sleigh-ride along the coastal road to the seaside village of Heringsdorf, about 22km to the west. Well wrapped in furs and rugs, our two small sons sat between us, and Ursula was bundled under my shawls.

There was a thick blanket of snow everywhere. The only noises were the muffled clip-clop of the horses' hooves on compacted snow, and the tinkle of sleigh bells. To the left, we saw a seemingly endless, flat landscape and to the right, the ice-covered Pomeranian Bight. Heringsdorf was almost deserted. But one inn was open. That was all we needed.

When Hermann was away, and the wind less bitter, I used to walk with my two boys, Ursula in my arms, along a path through snowy pine woods. It was just outside town. Tall, dry bulrushes grew high on either side. We couldn't see over them but we could hear, and what we heard was singing. The distant sound of hundreds (or was it thousands?) of strong young male voices. They were singing soldier songs, sometimes jolly but more often sad and longing. They must have been men from some nearby training camp. They were, in every sense, marching along an unseen path towards an unknown future. The cold, brittle rustling of the bleached brown bulrushes, the bitterness of the winter, the beauty of the snowscape and the yearning of those singers. We stood there, just the children and I, transfixed by a sense of desolation and glory.

The *Prinz Adalbert* was back in service in September, but on 19 October, Hopman transferred his flag (and Hermann with it) from *Prinz Adalbert* to SMS *Roon*, sending *Prinz Adalbert* to patrol the Baltic. On 23 October, as she steamed some 30km west of Libau, she was intercepted by the British submarine *E-8* (which was of course expecting her). The submarine fired a spread of torpedoes, one of which hit the ship's magazine. A massive explosion followed. Six hundred and seventy-two men drowned.[8] It was the single biggest loss of life in the Baltic war.

That November 1915, Philipp was transferred from Swinemünde, where he was naval depot manager, to Libau, where he took up the job of harbourmaster. Once Windau was captured, he was sent there, again as harbourmaster. Libau and Windau were both towns in newly conquered territory. They were not considered safe for civilians, so Philipp went alone, leaving Mila behind. She decided to moved further west, to Warnemünde. Winnie and the children went with her. The two women tried to steel themselves for whatever lay ahead.

Chapter 20

Verdun[1]

On 7 April 1916, Georg took the train from Bad Homburg vor der Höhe to the small French town of Stenay in Lothringen. The Crown Prince was in charge of the Verdun campaign, and his headquarters were in Stenay. From there, Georg rode west into the countryside. The 201st's initial training area was the rural and peaceful estate which lies around the handsome Chateau de Belval. Officers had taken over the chateau itself, its kitchens and most importantly, its cellars, a tacit acknowledgement perhaps that they were fighting in a civilised country which knew how to live well. The men slept in the farm buildings. The regiment was there for pre-deployment training, a necessary feature of the Verdun assignment because this was a new kind of war. On the rest of the Western Front, trenches and stalemate were the central feature. In Serbia the regiment had spent months on end chasing the will-o'-the-wisp of a Serbian army. But Verdun would be different. The battle would be a non-stop offensive against a fiercely resistant, highly professional, highly motivated, highly nationalistic enemy. One that was ready to sacrifice itself for France (or so its officers hoped). One that would make fierce and repeated counter-assaults. The German army was prepared for this. Its men were deployed with a new weapon and a new item of uniform, and their generals were using new tactics. The new weapon was the flame-thrower. The new item of uniform was the steel helmet. The new tactics were the use of *Sturmtruppen* (storm troopers) and greatly-extended artillery barrages. Barrages at Verdun could last non-stop for two solid days. The battle in Verdun would be a test of nerves as never before.

The cathedral city of Verdun lies in north-east France, on the west bank of the River Meuse, a north-south river which empties into the sea, almost 500km further north, at Rotterdam. Earlier that year, the Germans had already taken land to the east of the city, but if they wanted to take the city itself they also needed to approach from the west. The 201st's job was to take a strategic hill to the north-west of the city bearing the ominous name of *Toter Mann* (Dead Man).[2] It has two summits about 100m apart, almost, but not quite, the same height. When Georg arrived, the French held both summits, and the German front line lay about three-quarters of the way up the northern slopes of *Toter Mann*. The 201st and its sister regiments would be attacking uphill, trying to dislodge the French from the two summits.

From their training ground in Belval, the regiment marched to their new base camp. This, too, was rural, pastoral, even idyllic. It lay hidden in a beech wood capping a hill-top, just north of the small, farming village of Dannevoux. The village sat on the gentle, northern slopes of the Forges valley, a hollow carved out by the little Forges stream. As it wended its way eastwards, to join the Meuse, it skirted the northern slopes of whale-backed *Toter Mann.* This was a landscape sparsely scattered with small farms, each with a herd of cows, each growing corn. Green meadows and cornfields were demarcated by hedges. Dun-coloured cattle grazed or sat, chewing the cud, in dappled sunlight beneath solitary oaks.

It looked quiet and peaceful, but of course it wasn't. From the distance came the continual roar of battle: exploding ordnance and the thudding boom of artillery. Some sixteen kilometres lay between the hill where the battle was being waged and the camp where the men were resting.

The village of Dannevoux itself had been devastated by fire earlier in the year. It had burned as the invading German army drove the French south towards *Toter Mann.* The marks of devastation were plain to see to the newly arriving regiment. Deserted stone houses stood roofless; in some, only a few charred joists remained, while in others, bits of tiled roof had collapsed inwards. The one exception was the church. Somehow or other, its roof had survived. Its slated spire was still intact. Georg passed that church the day he arrived. He was marching with some pride at the head of his 9th Company. They marched north to the edge of the village, where a rough, stony track, with green fields on either side, led straight up the low hill to their camp in the woods at the top.

Berlin seems to have given little thought to psychology in the First World War. There was little or no government attempt to hide death, either from German citizens at home, or from its soldiers at the front. My grandmother noted with horror how the death notices in the Memorial columns in Berlin newspapers grew in number day by day. You could scarcely miss them, she wrote, especially as Germans tend to place more extensive notices than is customary in England. So, too, Georg noted, when he arrived at the foot of that track near *Toter Mann*, that the first thing he and his men saw was a new German cemetery. Their comrades. Those caught in this infamous meat-grinder. And there were many. It was the only approach road to the camp, so no one arrived or departed without this painful reminder. At the cemetery entrance, a tall wooden crucifix stood over a large mass-burial mound. Dark spruce trees had been planted in a semi-circle around it. Beyond were rows of individual graves, each marked with a wooden cross.

Gallows-humour comments from his men were inevitable. But on they marched, straight up the stony track to the top of the hill and the wood. It was a hot sunny day, and under trees at the wood's edge they could already see soldiers relaxing in the shade overlooking a green meadow. A recreation zone. Men were idling, some sitting on the grass, some standing to chat, some smoking, others playing cards. Further south, on the meadow, they were grooming horses. And all against a backdrop of this cheerful deciduous wood. This was Dannevoux base camp.

The closer they got, the more their spirits rose. It was about midday. The sun shone, the sky was blue. Unlike the desolate village they'd just marched through, this place was buzzing with life. In the wood, a leafy canopy hid much business. The 43rd and 44th Divisions were both encamped there. Eight regiments, including the 201st and the 202nd, together with their infantry, artillery, sapper units, cavalry, kitchens and tents.

From the top of the hill, looking south towards the Forges valley, you could see the object of the whole enterprise, *Toter Mann.* A second eminence, Hill 304, stood to the west. Both rose up on the southern side of the Forges stream. Both hillsides were completely bare and, being limestone, were threaded, as on Loretto Heights, with wispy, white paths, which vanished just short of the summit. The vanishing point was the front line.

There was little woodland apart from the trees among which they stood and a few clumped here and there on the further hillside. A ribbon-like wood followed the Forges stream, and on the Dannevoux side of that stream stood the Forges wood. That day in April, when Georg first arrived, the leaves were at their youngest, a light lemon-green, neatly crimped, their tips still unfolding. The green of leaves and of young men. In spite of the rumble of war from the southern hills, in spite of the parachute puffs of smoke which hung in the air over the bare hillside, Georg and his comrades responded to the sunshine, to spring and to the human business of the camp. As long as they could shelve any thoughts of the future they were, in fact, happy to be there.

Georg ordered his company to set up their tents under cover of the wood and settle in. He was enjoying his new job. Instead of being a glorified errand boy, he was now responsible for some 200 men in his 9th Company. He soon got to know them all, as well as other company commanders in his battalion, the 10th, 11th and 12th. The leader of the 11th Company was Waldemar Ritzmann. He, like Georg, was new to the job. Together, they learned how to be fatherly to men not much younger than themselves. They became good friends and never went to the front without first shaking hands and wishing each other well. '*Kamerad*', they would say, and they were indeed comrades. Companies generally had several Lieutenants so that if, or rather when, a commander fell, another took his place.

A battalion's four companies always acted together. They were either all at rest at Dannevoux, or all at the front. Those allocated to the stand-by second-line trenches charged following the first assault. Obviously, it was far safer to be in the following waves than in the first.

In theory at least, soldiers spent five days at rest and five at the front. After that, another battalion took over, while you and what remained of your company stumbled back down the hillside. As you stumbled you passed those coming up to relieve you. An embarrassing moment, it was. The men coming up averted their eyes.

The grass field south of Dannevoux camp served both as 'village green' and as a training area. Everything practised in Belval was rehearsed here. Von Frantzius, the 201st' Adjutant, headed a group teaching men the new way of fighting. How to be a stormtrooper. The technique was based on the 201st's experience at Dixmuide, where force of circumstance had broken companies into groups or platoons, each operating on its own. Such groups consisted of only a handful of men. Three or four. They would discuss their objectives beforehand because once in the assault, there was no time to give orders. Everyone pursued the agreed goal in whatever way the individual thought best. Friendship bound them together. A common purpose drove them, and it was this drive, focus and fury which so shook the enemy. Theirs was a dangerous job but a highly successful one. Stormtroopers became a significant feature of the war.

A new weapon? A new piece of kit? The first was the flamethrower; the second, the steel helmet. The man with the flamethrower had a can of highly flammable fluid strapped to his back and held a leaping tube, gushing fire, in his hands. He did so while standing alone, before his own front line, facing possible machine-gun fire, rifle-fire or a hail of hand grenades from the enemy. He faced all this knowing that one well-lobbed grenade would put paid to him – and if it hit his fuel tank, also to many others behind him. The flamethrower's job was, theoretically, to burn a path forward for the infantry to follow. In fact, his value was primarily in creating terror, although this declined rapidly as the enemy understood the flamethrower's vulnerability.

Poison gas, not brand new, but newish, was also used extensively at Verdun. Its shock value had diminished. Men were now equipped with gas-masks, so that the value of the weapon switched from delivering death to bringing inefficiency and delay. Soldiers fumbled as they took their gas masks out to strap them on. And once wearing masks, they found their field of vision limited. It was the mask, rather than the gas, that impaired a soldier's performance.

Leutnant Kurt Schweitzer, 9th Company, 3rd Battalion, 201st Regiment, was a friend and comrade of Georg. He wrote an account of the fighting on *Toter Mann* in late April and May 1916:[3]

> Every minute spent in our sun-dappled, leafy base camp was a gift. We all felt the same. On those endless hot, sunny days, I remember Georg saying, as we sat, smoking and chatting on the green field, 'What an amazing,

beautiful day!' And he would look up at the sky lost in the glory of the immediate present.

Any optimist might say that, on 30 April, the 9th Company was lucky. Yes. We had just been ordered to the front. But no. We were not going to the front line. We were sent to the second. The 11th and 12th (poor souls) were in the front. One of those two companies returned with only forty remaining of its original complement of 200. Another company lost every single one of its platoon leaders.

Whenever it was our battalion's turn to serve, we would march up *Toter Mann* as a company but settle into our trenches as platoons, only three or four men to each group. Each group united. Brothers. It was the best way to survive and the best way to get a job done. In all our experience of the war, we had never attacked in closer quarters than those we found on *Toter Mann*. And we had never suffered more from the mortal effects of machine gun-fire. One machine gun could obliterate an entire company, in minutes, if not seconds. We, the attackers, had rifles with bayonets, hand grenades and small daggers. They, the French defenders, had all these plus well-established, well-protected machine-gun nests, set at critical points along their front line. These were what we dreaded most. Preliminary artillery fire was supposed to take those guns out, but how could it do this when only some 100 metres separated their front line from ours? We had good artillery men, but were they that good? Georg and I both said we would rather be killed by enemy machine-gun fire than by fire from our own side. Friendly fire is the worst thing of all.

It was so intense up there, and hot. What a hot spring we had of it that year. There we were, stuck on a bare, stony, unforgiving hillside, raked by shell-fire. We cowered in our trench on the northern slope, while they, the French, above us, fired down. In between us and them was a tangle of barbed wire scattered between overlapping shell holes, constantly, thanks to fresh shelling, undergoing rearrangement. We treated those shell-holes as enemy-sponsored emergency dugouts. When we charged, we jumped from one to another, using their walls as protection.

That attack on the 30th failed, but then our attacks were always failing. This wasn't surprising, because we were fighting uphill. The enemy kept to their trenches. They had trench walls to protect them. We had to leap out of ours and charge uphill with no protection. We used anything we could find, including even the stacked-up corpses of our own comrades, to shelter behind. It was a hopeless situation but still our generals wouldn't budge. Repeat the attack, they said, time and time again.

Then, one day, miracle of miracles, they produced a new plan. Hill 304 was causing us trouble. The enemy, who held it, were decimating us on

Toter Mann with flanking fire. The new plan was to take both Hill 304 and *Toter Mann* at the same time.

3 May was scorching hot. It started with a super-massive, incredibly long-sustained, rolling artillery barrage. Over 36 hours of it. Many thousands died. By the end of it, those remaining on both sides were stunned. More dead than alive. The regiments on 304 were ordered to make a *Sturmtruppen* assault, which they did, and by the end of 4 May Hill 304 was ours. But *Toter Mann* was not. As usual, our generals ordered us to try again.

On 4 May at 4.45 pm we attacked. Failure once again.

Almost two weeks later, our battalion was ordered to the front. This time we were not support troops but the frontline. This was it. The dreaded and the inevitable. Worst of all, the 9th and 11th Companies were in the lead. That's Georg's company and Ritzmann's. Georg smiled softly at us as he gave us our orders. We couldn't smile back.

Of the two Companies, the 9th was given the most dangerous position of all. We were to stand to the west of our line, in the section closest to the enemy. That is to say, we were facing that section of the enemy which our artillery guns would have the greatest difficulty in reaching (without catching us as well). We were so close, we could hear them talking in their trenches. We were to hold the right flank. If the 9th failed, it would undermine the entire assault. As Georg told us the evening before we left, we were the key link in the chain.

Saturday, 18 May was yet another bright and sunny day. The Dannevoux wood was at its glorious best. Dappled sunlight everywhere. Our military camp was a positive fairyland, a scene from a militarised version of *A Midsummer Night's Dream*. The woodland floor was covered with an unusual little plant. It holds a single dark-blue berry upright on a green stalk. We were all looking at it, and I saw Georg pick one. He asked me what it was called. I had no idea. Later, I learned it was Herb Paris.

We were ordered to gather on the green meadow on the southern edge of the wood. Our padre was holding a field service. He stood in front of a makeshift altar, his back to the wood.

We stood in a semi-circle in front, our backs to *Toter Mann*.

'Today', he said, 'let us consider, every single one of us, the meaning of the word heroism.'

Heroism? We just wanted to live. Ourselves and our mates. We sang well known hymns and, after the service, wrote letters home. 'Liebe Mutti, lieber Papa'. Georg wrote to his parents. Part of his job was to help everyone in his company write those difficult letters home. And he did.

Late that evening, we assembled again in the meadow, four abreast. Someone started singing, and soon we all joined in. We sang our favourite old soldier songs as we marched down the hill, passed our little cemetery with its wooden crosses, passed the ruins of Dannevoux, up towards the hamlets of Gercourt and Drillancourt. From there, it was on to Forges Wood, where our heavy guns were hidden. At that point we were still almost, but not quite, out of range of the enemy's guns. In spite of this, the trees gave us the illusion of safety. We passed our command post. It was hidden in a hollow in the southern part of the wood. We passed our observation post further to the south, at the foot of the wood. This was where our latest regimental commander, Major Hayner[4] (Zimmermann fell sick once too often), stood. He would watch our performance through field glasses.

Leaving the wood, we nipped over the little Forges stream at the foot of *Toter Mann*'s northern slope. Its bed was so roughed up by the shelling that the water wasn't sure in which direction to flow. We crossed swampy ground, treading on the uneven brushwood which our sappers had laid. No one lingered. We were now under constant fire, even at night. We reached our designated battle strip. It stretched from the stream up to near the northern peak of *Toter Mann*. We had been ordered to take both peaks, the one nearest our front line trenches and the one a few metres further south and three metres higher.

We started up the Lipperweg[5] to reach T-Wäldchen. This was the name we gave our last support post (both military and medical) before the front. Our Battalion Commander, von Wedekind, was there. A good old boy if ever there was one. He greeted us with exactly the same kind of goodwill as he would have offered had we met by chance, on a street in Berlin. He slapped Georg firmly on the back. '*Na, Junge*', he said. '*Viel Glück*!' (Now my boy, good luck!)

Shortly after T-Wäldchen, the Lipperweg reached an unexpected marshy patch. It was a spring. We had all been warned that, however much we were tempted by it, we were not to drink its water. It was polluted and quite undrinkable. It could kill us before we ever got to the front line. In spite of this warning, many men were so hot and thirsty that they were quite unable to resist. They must have been quite desperate. I saw one man drinking through thick green slime while a bloated corpse bobbed about nearby.

On and on we marched, to the front line. As we went we passed those we were replacing. I was never sure how to greet them. Everything I thought of sounded hollow.

Our front line was a trench just below the northern summit. We were to stand between Points 153 and 154.[6] Ritzmann and his 11th Company were in the trench next to us. The enemy was to the south. A tangle of barbed-wire lay in the pock-marked space between them and us.

And so it began. That night, the night of 18/19 May, our long-distance artillery started firing at the enemy positions. They slowly altered range to bring the barrage forward. It progressed at a snail's pace but with grim inevitability. The French were being driven forward into their front lines. We stayed put, but we too were being driven. Driven out of our minds. Shells whizzed and roared above and around us. Explosions thudded. The ground trembled. It felt as if there were an earthquake beneath our feet. It seemed as if the whole hill was being ripped apart. And above our heads, a hurricane. Slivers of iron, rubble and rock whirled in columns of dust, some rising over 800m into the air, and black smoke drifted about everywhere, aimlessly. Our bodies and minds trembled.

The barrage continued all next day, on and on. Would it never cease? At 1.30 am on 20 May, it suddenly got worse. Then, inexplicably, it ceased. The silence was unnerving. So were the flashes of red lightning which split the sky, so was the eerie sound which, after a few minutes, broke the silence. A sort of slow howl which came from somewhere far, far, far away.

20 May. Dawn. The day was shamelessly sunny. Our artillery started firing again. Georg and Ritzmann both sent patrols into no-man's-land to cut a path through the barbed wire. We would be attacking at 4.00 pm, and a long wait stretched ahead. The enemy was quiet. No artillery. No machine guns. Were they silent because they were dead? Or were they holding their fire and waiting?

No one had slept for about forty-eight hours. Little had been eaten. On both sides, we were all waiting. The 9th Company waited. The 10th Company waited. Georg's eyes were fixed on his watch. There it was. 4.00 pm.

'*Los*!' he cried, and the flamethrower led the scramble out of the trench. As soon as he appeared, a French machine gun started up. There was the answer to our question. No. They were not all dead. At least one machine-gunner survived.

As the 9th Company scrambled out, that one machine-gunner raked through us all. Three quarters fell. A shattering sight. But the worst sight of all was the flamethrower. He was standing in front of the emerging front line when a hand grenade hit his fuel tank. It exploded and he with it. A sheet of flame, where once our comrade stood. A human torch. We were not mentally prepared for this. The shock of such a sight was paralysing. For a fraction of a second, the assault's momentum hung in the balance. That's when Georg, already up on the bank, half turned towards his friends behind. Could he see us or was he in a dream? He raised his pistol high in the air. '*Vorwärts*!' he yelled. His bellow, his determination, his spirit

> and his momentum broke the spell. The men surged forward, as they had always planned to do.
>
> But the machine-gunner continued firing and he hit Georg in the stomach. He fell. Ritzmann too. Now the men were enraged, vengeful. My small group leapt into a crater. Then, jumping from one to another, just like children playing hopscotch, we reached that one machine-gun nest. In fury, we hurled in our grenades. It fell silent as everyone roared forwards. We stormed that day as no one had ever stormed before. We roared and stormed. It was one of the most successful assaults ever made at Verdun.

Senior officers observed the action through field-glasses from Forges Wood. They were delighted.

'It looks fantastic,' said one officer to Hayner. 'How your people jump and surge! Fantastic!'[7]

Oberleutnant von Frantzius later wrote:

> The storm on 20 May crowned a difficult 33-day period on *Toter Mann* with victory. Every regiment has some battle names which resonate in its regimental memory for ever. For us, in the 201st, it is *Toter Mann*. The memory of *Toter Mann* is, like its double-domed summit, twofold. We remember firstly the earlier struggles, the stalemate, the horror. But then, secondly, our hearts lift because we remember the heroism and victory of the assault on 20 May.[7]

Von Frantzius was, understandably, rather pleased with himself. The horrors which had preceded the assault are dismissed. He concentrates on the victory, which was, indeed, largely due to his *Sturmtruppen*. He said that many, many people had contributed to that victory; that there were many, many heroes, too many for him to be able to mention each by name. Yet, right at the very end of his essay on Verdun, he names one hero:

> We fulfil a comradely duty when we mention the leader of the 9th Company, Lt. d. Res. Gercke, by name. Through his quiet heroism, he showed us all what a sense of duty is, and what it means to love the fatherland.[8]

Georg. Our artist. Our Francophile. The man who had an apartment waiting for him in Paris.

Victory that day ended a long stalemate. The French were finally dislodged from *Toter Mann*. After that long bombardment and the ferocity of the assault, their nerves failed them. In their confusion and distress, they didn't know what they were doing. Some rushed backwards. Some rushed forward. Many were killed by artillery fire from their own side. But the German battle line moved inexorably south. They overran the enemy's forward trenches. They overran the northern summit. They overran the southern summit. They went further still, charging far beyond the goals set for the day. They roared down the southern slopes of *Toter Mann* so that, by the time twilight arrived, German soldiers at the bottom of that slope could see the outline of the city of Verdun in the distance.

If the commanders had wanted to take that city, then this was the moment to do so. But they didn't. As at the Marne, Germany once again snatched defeat from the very jaws of victory.

General von Gallwitz was in charge of the attacks on both Hill 304 and *Toter Mann*. He had been watching the battle from the Dannevoux camp and met the Crown Prince that evening to discuss the day's events. Instead of basking in triumph, the two of them held a desultory conversation. They talked not about glory but about the dim future ahead. They complained bitterly that the Allies were unreasonable. They would not sue for peace. Neither mentioned any wish to take Verdun. The tone of their conversation suggests that they both believed Germany was losing the war,[9] and if that was the case, then the whole Verdun exercise was simply an effort to strengthen Germany's negotiating position.

Falkenhayn wrote in his memoirs that his purpose at Verdun was 'to bleed the French Army white'.[10] Germany succeeded in this. Verdun left the French army so weak and demoralized that the following year, briefly and unsuccessfully, it mutinied. But the German army had also been bled white.

Philipp wrote in his Chronicle:

> Georg wrote us his last letter on the 18th May, and on the 20th he fell. He fell while leading his company in an assault to take *Toter Mann*. Machine-gun bullets had so ripped his body apart that it was difficult to recognise our brave son. Now he rests near Verdun, unburied and in an unknown place. Do not cry or mourn, all those of you who knew and loved our Sunday child. He found himself alongside the best of comrades. Ah, you dear, dear boy.

His words hide the fact that Philipp had found it close to impossible to handle this, his second loss. When Georg was killed, in late May 1916, Hermann was working in Libau and Philipp was harbourmaster in Windau. This was where the news reached him. On hearing it, Philipp crumpled to the ground. He would not rise. He refused all food. He let no one near him. His faithful assistant feared he would die and phoned Hermann, who immediately drove over from Libau. Somehow, he managed to pick his father up, pack him into the car and drive him to the hospital in Windau. Philipp was heavy and obstinate.

How Hermann succeeded, especially having at the same time to bear his own grief, nobody knew.

Next, he called Baltic High Command and obtained an entry permit for his mother so that she could travel to Windau and take her husband home. A few weeks later, Philipp was relieved of his duties in Windau and transferred to Warnemünde, where, once again, with Mila at his side, he was chief of the local naval supply depot. The two of them stayed there for the rest of the war, and beyond.

One Hundred Years Later

One hundred years after the end of the First World War, I wandered through the Dannevoux training camp where Georg wrote his last letter. It was as entrancing, leafy and sun-dappled as it must have been in 1916. A beechwood, full of woodland flowers. Herb Paris, its single stem holding up a single blue berry. It was scattered all over the woodland floor. Among the flowers I found many unexplained lumps and bumps. Ancient pieces of iron lay here; bits of cooking equipment and iron ovens over there. A great deal of concrete. A concrete cistern was covered in moss and ivy. The curved concrete arch of a shelter was now all but buried.

The green meadow, where their horses once grazed, still spreads out at the edge of the wood. Looking south, I saw the roofs (new ones) of Dannevoux, and beyond I saw a patchwork of fields. These were overlooked, at the horizon, by a long, low hill – *Toter Mann*. Once naked. it is now covered in trees. Once black, it is now a dark blue-green. The track from the wood to the village, took me past the German cemetery. Dark spruce trees still grow there. I looked at lines of black iron crosses. But Georg wasn't there, nor is he mentioned in the book at the entrance. The German war graves commission only mentions those whose bodies are recovered. Georg's and the bodies of so many others were not. Too fragmented. What a marvel that the men carried any of their officers' bodies down at all. A gruesome and a dangerous task. The 10th Company found Ritzmann's body more or less in one piece. Here he still lies. Waldemar Ritzmann.

On I went, past the little village of Dannevoux, through the hamlet of Gercourt, till I reached the two farms which make up tiny Drillancourt. Wild carrot was in bloom and purple thistle flowers lined the track. Here is Forges Wood. Here, the place where the commanders stood to watch the battle. Out of the forest and down to the stream. I crossed its now clear water and walked up to *T-Wäldchen*, an enormous fortification where vast concrete mounds are covered in earth and overgrown with trees. Torn fragments of metal leaned against tree trunks. Shrapnel was everywhere. Up and up, along the *Lipperweg* I went, until I suddenly heard the sound of piglets squealing and grunting on the path ahead. Wild boar! On the dry slopes of this stony hillside, they were wallowing in a patch of mud. The pigs, even more frightened of me than I was of them, scampered off to leave behind a gently moving slough of muddy water. Here it was! That infamous, deadly spring, the one from which desperate soldiers once drank. Onward and upward, past old foxholes, some now used by real foxes. Then, a sharp left and I reached a well-maintained, modern, woodland path. I had entered *L'Homme Mort* park. A boardwalk runs along the top of the northern wall of the German frontline trench. Here is Point 153 and there, Point 154. This is where Georg once stood with all his company, and there is where his friend Ritzmann once stood. This is where they waited for 4.00 pm.

On the summit of the southern peak, an information board has been erected by the French authorities:

> In the latter half of May 1916, Germany's 43rd and 44th Divisions were ordered to advance from the northern peak of Dead Man's Hill to the southern one. Both Divisions had already suffered significant losses. Ludwig Gold, author of a German account of the fighting at Verdun,[11] depicted the first few minutes of one regiment's attack on 20 May as follows: 'And it is 4 o'clock, over the top we go! Thank God the artillery has taken out those deadly machine guns. Only one of them is still firing … but one is enough! As soon as the first wave of the 9th Company jumps out of the trench, three quarters of them are lying on the ground … The flamethrower gets hit and explodes. The people watch in horror as the man carrying it is engulfed in flames. The company commander, Reserve Lieutenant Gercke, jumps out of the trench, pistol in hand, yelling '*Vorwärts*!' The next second, he collapses to the ground with a fatal shot to the stomach.[11]

Dear Georg, the list at the entrance to the German graveyard didn't mention your name, but look at this. The country you loved. The country where you had just settled before war broke out. The country which inspired your art, where you left your paints and pictures. Where you left your painting coat hanging on a hook behind the door. Where perhaps (who knows?), you also left your heart. That country acknowledges you. The enemy. France.

* * *

The arts are not a way to make a living. They are a very human way of making life more bearable. Practicing an art, no matter how well or badly, is a way to make your soul grow, for heaven's sake. Sing in the shower. Kurt Vonnegut, *A Man without a Country*

Part III

An Odyssey

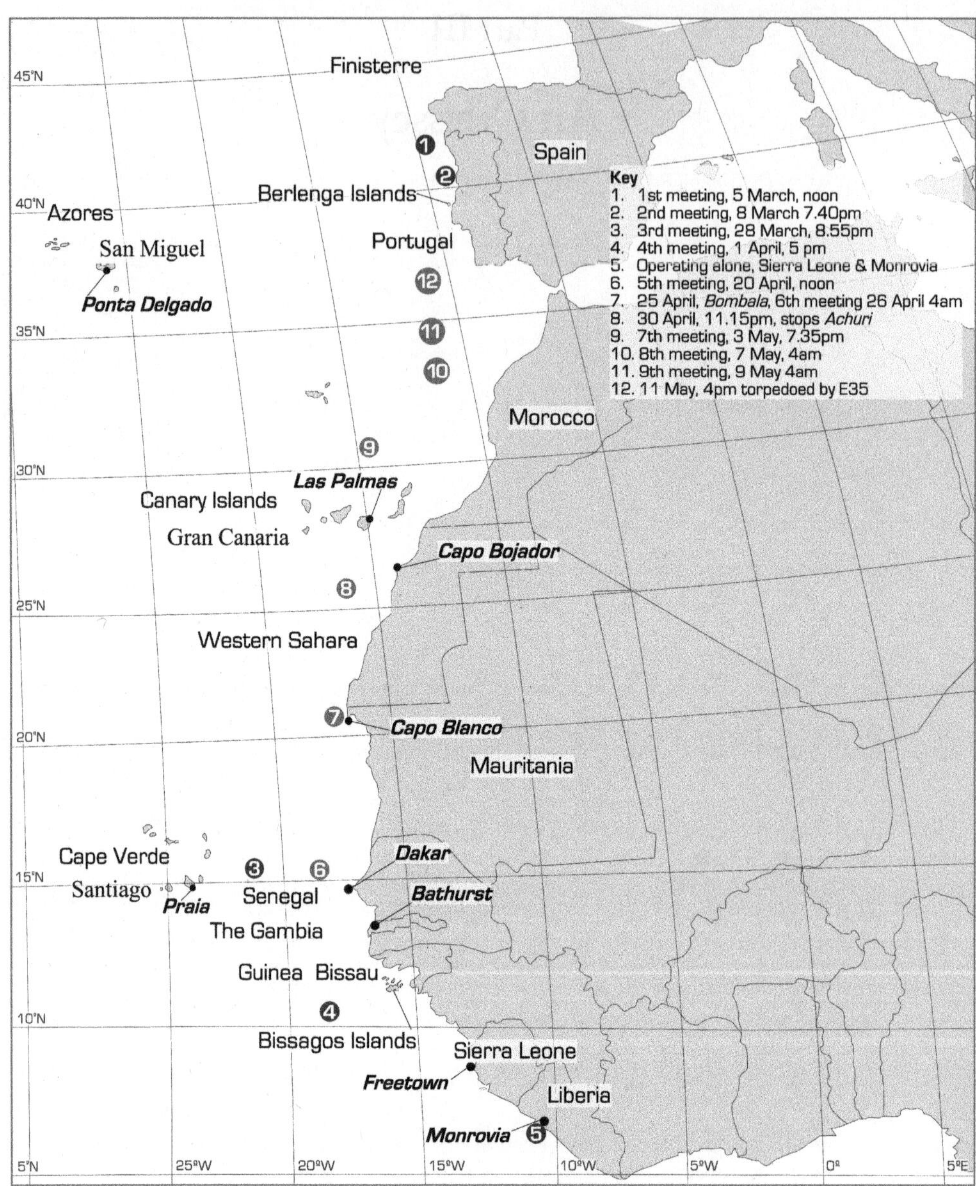

The Voyage of *U-154*.

Chapter 21

The Turning Point: U-Boats

In late May 1916, Winnie wrote:

> I was at home with the boys and Ursula when the doorbell rang. Harry ran after me.
>
> The postman handed me a telegram. I opened it. My legs wobbled so I sat down. My throat dried up even before I read the message. When I gasped the one word, 'Georg', a weird, distorted croak came out. I heard it as if it had been uttered by someone else. Harry put his arms around me.
>
> There had been so many losses and here they were, still piling up. They wouldn't stop. Later that year, our friend Heinrich Mathy[1] was shot down in his Zeppelin over Potters Bar. He had been flying knowing, all along, that he would die on the job. His last postcard? Just one sentence. 'We can only do our best.' That's what we all felt.

Every day, more sons, husbands and fathers, were killed. The 'In Memoriam' pages in the newspapers grew longer and longer. Was there a single household which hadn't endured loss? Hermann was deeply saddened. Beyond the death of so many of his good friends and comrades, he had to absorb the inexorable and terrible loss of both his brothers. Younger brothers. Boys he had always tried to protect. Why had they died and not him? Had they been taking greater risks?

Winnie wrote that Hermann had long been advocating that Germany should offer a generous peace settlement:

> When last in Danzig,[2] Hermann told me that the time had come for a negotiated peace. I agreed with him. Germany had nothing to gain from prolonging the war. We were occupying a large part of Belgium, including the important European port of Antwerp. We held the Baltic provinces as far as Windau.[3] We had new allies: Turkey (which had joined us early on) and, more recently, Bulgaria.[4] We should quit while ahead. We should give back the territory we had taken in the east and set out on a path for peace.

But no peace came. Instead, life got worse, especially during the severe 'Turnip Winter' of 1916/17. People were starving, and food was rationed: one tiny pat of butter per person per week. Clothes? Three pairs of coarse cotton stockings per woman per year. Some things were unobtainable, others in short supply. Everyone tried to find a patch of soil to grow their own vegetables. A pot on the balcony would do, or an old tin. Otherwise, it was out and about to pick weeds growing along the roadside. Fat Hen[5] for spinach, nettles for soup, and strawberry leaves for tea. The particularly desperate, pregnant women for example, sometimes stole. One woman Winnie knew was reduced to stealing potato peelings. But Winnie herself and her children were, relatively speaking, well-off. They feasted on prunes boiled with barley, carried up every day by cheerful sailors from the depot. They grew to love this dish beyond all others.

But finding clothing was another problem, one which could not be solved by Grandfather at the depot. Winnie's children, once smart and plump, were now ragged and thin. They were looking much like the refugee children streaming in from the Russian empire. Children there were also suffering from hunger and lack of clothes, but they had the additional terror of living under the daily threat of violence from one invading side or the other. Yes. Germans living in the Russian borderlands were less well off than children in Germany. But then, there was always somebody less well-off than oneself.

As the children grew, Winnie was grateful for hand-me-downs, and when these ran out, often as not there was nothing at all. Shoes were a particular problem. The boys wore hinged, wooden-soled sandals until Winnie found a kind Swedish skipper in Warnemünde harbour who promised to bring them proper shoes from Sweden on his next trip.

By the end of 1916 Hermann saw that the war in the Baltic was becoming something of a stalemate. With the High Seas Fleet largely inactive, U-Boats were now Germany's only hope – if not for victory, then at least for a better negotiated peace. U-Boats did indeed offer the best chance of success, but they also offered the greatest danger to their crews. Few returned. Nevertheless, with both his brothers dead, Hermann was considering the submarines as the only option for himself. But what would happen to his wife and children if he was killed? The state would provide generously for them, as long as the country survived the war with its economy more or less intact. But that didn't help his heart, which broke for Winnie and for his children. What should he do? He decided that he would either volunteer for the U-Boats and live for a short while but with a clear conscience, or he would not. In this way, he gradually argued himself into believing that, by offering his own life, he was doing the best all round. For them, for himself and for his country. 'I could not love thee dear so much, loved I not honour more.'[6]

But what about his parents? His father, for all his bluffness, was on the point of physical and emotional collapse. And his mother? She would look after whoever was left, but was there not a limit, even to her steely determination? Hermann, the born carer in the family, had to learn to let go. He began looking to Lenchen as the only one of the four siblings who would likely be left to take care of their parents in their old age. The only one to accompany them through whatever heartache lay ahead.

Many years later, Lenchen wrote:

> My eldest brother was special, if only because, towards the end of the war, out of the four of us, we were the only two left. We bore our grief in silence but at least we had each other. In those years, I often heard my usually serene Hermann sighing heavily. Without saying a word, he would turn his face, sorely troubled, and gaze at me.

Things were dire at the national level as well. On 9 January 1917, the Kaiser called a high-level meeting to discuss the situation. At that meeting, he and his advisers came up with the same idea as Hermann. The only answer was the U-Boat. The decision was to revive an earlier, but short-lived policy of unrestricted submarine warfare.

While the British Grand Fleet was holed up in Scapa Flow for most of the war, there were still plenty of other British ships to patrol the waters around Britain and the oceans of the world. They attacked enemy ships, protected the British merchant navy, blockaded Germany and hoped to starve it into submission. They gave Britain a good chance of winning the war.

The Germans saw it like this: if the Royal Navy was trying to starve Germany, why not turn the tables? Why not starve Britain? Why not start fighting (as the British had done from the very beginning) a war on commerce?

Vice-Admiral Scheer had understood the situation ever since the Battle of Jutland.[7] At Jutland, he had inflicted more damage on the Royal Navy than the British had inflicted on the Imperial Navy, but the result did not gain Germany any real advantage. No one acknowledged defeat.[8] The only way forward was to starve the people of Britain into forcing peace negotiations on their government. This had to be achieved before Britain forced the German people to do the same.

In his report on the Battle of Jutland to the Kaiser, Scheer wrote:

> There can be no doubt, that even the most successful result from a high seas battle will not compel England to make peace … A victorious end to the war, at a not too distant date, can only be achieved by crushing English economic life through U-Boat action against English commerce.[9]

German economists agreed. They had worked out that if Germany could sink around 600,000 tons of British shipping a month, the British would be brought to the negotiating table.[10] So this was the aim. And the tool? Given that the Royal Navy was the stronger force, Germany needed something unexpected. It needed David's small sling to tackle Goliath. It needed a stealth weapon to undermine the supremacy of a well-armed, superior surface fleet. It needed to revive the earlier submarine campaign. Submarines were stealth weapons only insofar as merchant ships were unlikely to see them coming. Submarines at this time generally carried guns on deck as well as torpedoes, and actual combat was often on the surface. Once on the surface, of course, the U-Boat no longer had the advantage. The rules established by the Imperial German Navy and governing unrestricted submarine warfare generally required submarines to surface. On meeting a merchantman, the U-Boat surfaced, hailed it and reviewed its papers to discover if it were aiding the enemy or not. If it were, its crew would be put into its lifeboats and the ship would be sunk. So-called 'unrestricted submarine warfare' did not mean that U-Boats sank all shipping regardless. It required that all merchantmen, whether neutral or not, be challenged.

This high-handed approach (of stopping one and all) naturally angered neutral countries, especially the United States, which had objected strongly when the British, using surface ships to do the challenging, launched a more extensive but similar policy in 1914. From the start, British ships challenged all foreign merchantmen, whether neutral or not, and forced them, if they were carrying cargo for Germany, to sail to Allied ports instead and unload there.

Since no one was powerful enough, or perhaps sufficiently motivated, to call Britain to account, the British got away with it. Ironically, when, in February 1915, Germany launched a similar programme, only using submarines, no one objected more fervently than the British.[11]This objection often took the form of strong anti-German propaganda. Propaganda of this kind had begun before the outbreak of the war, but with this new threat, the gloves were off. Submarines were sneaky, and the Germans sailors who sailed them, barbarous. This kind of language had begun with the scandalous writings of William le Queux,[12] strongly supported by Lord Northcliffe, owner of the *Daily Mail*. Lord Northcliffe found le Queux's sensational stories sold newspapers. In 1906, le Queux produced a series of articles under the heading 'The Invasion of 1910'. In these stories, he sensationalized a world which Erskine Childers had explored in his 1903 *Riddle of the Sands*. Historian Andreas Rose writes that le Queux's stories were far more melodramatic and brutal than Childers'. He 'imposed on Germans the worst of enemy stereotypes …Germans burnt and pillaged; they massacred women and children and they forced their victims to dig their own graves.'[13] Once the war began, especially once unrestricted submarine warfare began, the tone of such propaganda intensified. U-Boats threatened Britain's ability to feed and arm itself and to keep in touch with its empire. Admiral John

Fisher, First Sea Lord in 1914, wrote, 'The British Empire and the German submarine cannot co-exist.'[14]

No event was more successful in fuelling anti-U-Boat propaganda than the sinking of the liner *Lusitania* on 5 May 1915. Carrying passengers as well as 173 tons of munitions, she was sailing from New York to Britain when she was sunk, without warning, by a U-Boat. Around 1,200 lives were lost. The submarine had not surfaced beforehand, possibly because the target was too large and too fast for it to take the risk, or possibly because that particular commander, Lieutenant Walter Schwieger, weighed risks differently to others. The only warning passengers were given were notices placed by the German Embassy in Washington in New York newspapers. New York was the *Lusitania*'s departure point. 'Travellers intending to embark on the Atlantic voyage are reminded that a state of war exists between Germany … and Great Britain … and that travellers sailing in the war zone on ships of Great Britain or her allies do so at their own risk.' Once hit, *Lusitania* sank in only eighteen minutes, possibly because a torpedo struck the munitions room.[15] There wasn't enough time to launch all of the ship's forty-eight lifeboats. Her sinking provoked general outrage. A few months later, the Kaiser cancelled this, his first attempt at unrestricted submarine warfare. He always had difficulty dealing with criticism. Especially from Britain. Especially about his navy. British propaganda had had exactly the impact intended.

The Kaiser's 1917 decision to revive the earlier campaign initially met with stunning success. By June, his submarine fleet had sunk more than enough tonnage to seriously threaten Britain's ability to continue the war. Britain was in such severe danger that American Vice-Admiral, William Sims,[16] Commander of the United States Forces in Britain, commented to First Sea Lord Admiral Jellicoe that it looked as if Germany was actually winning the war. Jellicoe's reply was chilling but to the point: 'They will win unless we can stop these losses, and stop them soon.'[17]

By that time, Hermann had already made his decision. He had decided as early as the end of 1916 that the submarines were the future. If Winnie agreed, he would train as a U-Boat Commander. Once again, she was torn in two, but this time, his request was even more painful than before. She hated submarines. She hated the idea of death in a small container at the bottom of the sea. Of course she didn't want him to go. But what could she say? 'You must do what you feel is right,' she said.

Next hurdle? His commander, Admiral Hopman was also extremely reluctant to let Hermann go. He had long known of his growing frustration with the Baltic War. They had discussed it for hours in their Libau headquarters. It wasn't going anywhere. German successes were marginal, and anyway, Russia was increasingly unstable. Would she end up solving the problem for Germany by simply imploding?[18] Hopman wrote that, towards the end of 1916, 'I lost my first Admiral Staff Officer, Lieutenant Hermann Gercke because he believed U-Boats would determine the outcome of the war. With a heavy heart, I yielded to his request. I knew that I lost, with him, one of the most gifted and capable of all my young officers.'[19]

In January 1917, Hermann signed up for the submariner school. Classes were held in Kiel and Eckernförde, about 30km up the coast. The course included theory and practical work such as underwater 'marches', diving and artillery practice. Hermann's good friend and crewmate Gernot Goetting[20] signed up on the same day.

The government's January decision included the addition of a new kind of submarine to the existing fleet. These were big, bulky, long-distance cargo U-Boats. Two such boats already existed. Privately built, they had completed their maiden voyages the previous year; at least, one of them had, the *Deutschland*. Her sister ship, the *Bremen*, had disappeared without trace. Their purpose was twofold: firstly, to allow Germany to trade safely, regardless of the blockade enforced by surface ships, and secondly, to take the war further afield, to British trade routes in the Atlantic and off the coast of Africa. Able to stay at sea for four months or more, the new boats extended the U-Boats' normal operational range tremendously. Until their arrival, U-Boats had operated only in the waters around the British Isles or, if based in the Austrian port of Pola on the Adriatic, in the Mediterranean Sea.

The January 1917 decision was to arm the *Deutschland*, include her in the Imperial Navy's submarine fleet, and build more like her. These became known as the Deutschland class of U-Boat. The first of these were *U-154* and *U-153*. They would be ready for service by the end of that year, or so it was hoped. One was assigned to Hermann and the other to Goetting.

This was not good news for Hermann. He had always disliked the clumsiness of big vessels, and these cargo U-Boats were nothing if not clumsy. They were broad in the beam, cumbersome and slow.[21] They were difficult to manoeuvre. They could not dive quickly. They were also unstable, possibly because, as Hermann and Goetting both pointed out, their hydroplanes were too small and failed to balance the craft effectively. This made firing torpedoes a chancy business. Lastly, being big, they were easily seen and presented sizeable targets. If a regular submarine and a cargo U-Boat both surfaced at the same time, the cargo boat was always spotted first.

Hermann's boat carried twenty torpedoes and two 10.5cm deck guns, one on either side of the fo'cs'le, with four smaller guns (8.8cm), two fore and two aft. Hermann preferred his deck guns. When he met a merchant ship he surfaced, fired a warning shot (possibly a star shell) over the bows of the target vessel and ordered the captain to bring the ship's papers on board. If these were in order (i.e. if they showed that the ship was not carrying cargo to benefit the enemy), the vessel would be allowed to resume its voyage. If not, its crew was ordered to take to the lifeboats, the ship was set with explosives and sunk. Both Goetting and Hermann followed this procedure rigorously, thereby putting themselves at a disadvantage, since every ship they challenged and released reported their position.

These two commanders were following the procedure taught in the Eckernförder submariner school. It was a matter of honour. So much for British propaganda which even Admiral Jellicoe countenanced: 'Between the beginning and end [of the war], how far did they [German naval officers] travel in ways of dishonour and what infamies did they achieve!'[22] Such statements riled Winnie. They riled her a great deal, and she wrote:

> I am an English woman, the widow of a German officer in the Imperial Navy and living in London. Since Hermann's death, I have endured endless anti-German British propaganda denigrating the honour of men like my husband. I write these notes to show that Germany, like Britain, had a brave, highly disciplined and honourable navy. The British are slow to understand this. Propaganda has become entrenched. No one notices it.

Propaganda does indeed bite deep. It sets limits to our way of thinking which later generations find hard to escape.

The fact is that, in spite of what was said in public, the First Lord of the Admiralty, Winston Churchill, implicitly agreed one hundred per cent with Winnie. He was *utterly* confident in the good behaviour of German naval officers. His infamous Q-ship campaign would never have worked had German officers not been honourable. Q-ships were Royal Navy warships which sailed under a false flag. They pretended they were merchant vessels with a merchant navy crew and offered themselves up as bait, hoping to be hailed by a U-Boat. When this happened, the Q-ship's crew simulated panic and launched lifeboats, so that the U-Boat's captain, fully aware of a sailor's duty to save life at sea, would be lured ever closer to assist. Once the U-Boat was entirely vulnerable, false hoardings along the Q-ship's decks were lowered to reveal rows of guns, Royal Navy gunners beside them. Like a fly in a web, the U-Boat was done for. There wasn't a shred of honour in it. At least, not on the British side.

The use of these Q-ships was secret, but rumours were rife, especially after the *Baralong* scandal.[23] In January 1915, the captain of a British Q-ship, the *Baralong*, disguised as an American vessel and flying the Stars and Stripes, trapped a U-Boat and then proceeded to summarily execute captured German sailors. In September 1915, the same British Q-ship, again flying the Stars and Stripes, shot shipwrecked German sailors who were seeking rescue. Britain had lowered the bar. This was indeed 'dirty tricks warfare'.[24] Given the use of Q-ships, it is all the more remarkable that Hermann and Goetting stuck to the rules.

When Hermann signed up in 1917 for U-Boat school, German submarines were winning the war, but by June that year, the initial momentum was waning. The project was in decline. As with poison gas, as with flamethrowers, so with submarines. A new threat impelled the enemy to develop counter-measures. Effective ones. By 1917, the Allies had devised enough successful anti-submarine strategies and enough new anti-submarine weapons that they were able to stem the tide once noted with such dismay by Admiral Sims and Admiral Jellicoe. The new strategies included the highly successful use of armed warships to escort convoys. The new weapons included the development of more effective British mines and their more extensive use, the deployment of submarine nets, and the use of hydrophones and depth charges.

Hermann and Goetting didn't set sail till February 1918. They were launching their careers as submariners when the tide of success had already turned. Worse still, by this time, extra thick barrages of mines and submarine nets stretched across both the North Sea and the English Channel. Perhaps the most dangerous moments for any U-Boat captain as he sailed out of the Baltic Sea were simply getting round the vast British breakwater which was the British Isles.

But in 1917 all this lay well ahead. Winnie's first experience as a submariner's wife was moving back to Schleswig-Holstein:

> To stay close together while Em was 'at school', we rented a small family cottage, with a garden, close to the tiny fishing village of Borby, near Eckernförde. With the help of Langheinrich,[25] his loyal and lanky batman, Hermann started growing vegetables, which saved us from eating 'Fat Hen'. Everyone was using substitutes. My neighbours drank tea made from strawberry leaves. Talking of tea, sometimes the children and I were invited to a royal tea by Princess Irene. She was living nearby in Hemmelmark. Those were true red-letter days for on the whole, life in Borby that winter was dull, cold and boring. My greatest thrill was buying a pair of black silk stockings. I remember seeing some for sale. Such a surprise. We never usually got anything of the kind. I'm afraid I rushed into the shop and bought them.
>
> Most of Hermann's fellow trainee officers were unmarried and younger. They lived on board an old warship in the harbour, while Hermann came home every night. At the tender age of thirty-three, he was known

among the sailors as 'The Old Man'. During his training period there was an unforgettable and awful submarine accident. We heard, first of all, that a training boat had gone down in a fjord during a practice run. Four aeroplanes immediately flew out to search for it. The pilots spotted a large dark hull sitting in white ooze near the fjord's exit. The school's *Mutterschiff* [mother ship] was called the *Vulkan*. It was a weird kind of vessel in two pieces, with an open space with a windlass in the middle to haul up stricken boats. The *Vulkan* and the *Meteor* [another mother ship] were sent out to the site, and divers set to work. They tried to slide hawsers round the boat's hull. Because of the mud, this wasn't easy. It took hours to get the cables in position.

Meanwhile, divers communicated with the seamen inside the stricken vessel by tapping on the hull. The men inside tapped back. Twice the hawsers were in place. Twice the crane started to lift the shattered boat. Twice they hauled it right up to the surface but twice, at the very last minute, the ropes broke and the submarine sank once more, very slowly, to the bottom. Eventually, the tapping stopped and, in the end, it was months and months before that boat was hauled to the surface. Hermann attended the funerals. We handled danger by not talking about it. He would come home every evening with jokey stories about the funny things that had happened during the day.

At the best of times, Schleswig-Holstein is wearisome, bleak and damp in winter. That winter, the children all succumbed to bronchitis and pneumonia, one after the other. Life was far better in the summer. Being right on the fjord, we could watch the boats, including Hermann's, from our cottage garden. And when his own submarine's fat, iron body bobbed against the Eckernförde quayside, he took us on a conducted tour. The boys were delighted. Submarines were cutting edge technology, '*Heldenboote*' [boats for heroes]. Having a father as a U-Boat commander made my eldest (the only one then at school) a bit of a hero himself.

Hermann's boat had relatively spacious living quarters. I made cotton curtains for its few portholes and a silk shade for the lamp in his cabin. This was just beyond the wardroom, where his brother officers played cards, read, ate and slept. I felt sorry for the crew. Many of them slept in hammocks suspended over the torpedoes.

The excitement was premature. The Admiralty had other plans for Hermann. At least, in the short term. To his utter disgust, in late 1917, he was assigned to work with the army.

Chapter 22

Operation Albion

The German Eighth Army, under General Oskar von Hutier[1], planned to take the strategically key Russian port of Riga in September 1917 and would follow this up with a joint army and navy operation to take the Baltic Islands to the north of the Gulf of Riga. The largest of these were Ösel, Dagö and Moon.[2] They lie close to a little-known channel[3] which gives access to the Gulf of Finland. This new plan would bring enormous pressure to bear on St Petersburg. As ever, the idea was to force Russia out of the war and enable Germany to fight on only one front.

The joint operation was given the code name Operation Albion. The moment was ripe. Unrest in Russia was bringing the country to its knees. In early 1917, food shortages had led to mass protests in St Petersburg against rationing. After the February Revolution the Tsar abdicated, and the liberal Alexander Kerenski[4] took over the reins of power. From the German point of view, the chances of closing down the Russian front were improving, except for one thing: Kerenski. He wanted to keep Russia in the war, so Germany set about undermining him.

Vladimir Lenin,[5] a first-rate disruptor, was in exile in Switzerland. The German government agreed to let him return to Russia that April, travelling without let or hindrance through Germany by train, and on to St Petersburg. But before Lenin had time to launch his Bolshevik Revolution in October (it started, according to the Gregorian Calendar, on 7 November), Germany had already implemented Operation Albion.

The army was in overall command of the operation, while the navy was under the command of Vice-Admiral Erhard Schmidt, who had led the failed 1915 attempt to take Riga. Once again, Schmidt brought with him from Wilhelmshaven a large part of the High Seas Fleet: ten dreadnoughts and a large number of minesweepers, cruisers, torpedo boats, submarines, cargo ships, coalers and hospital ships. Aircraft and airships joined in. Practically every vessel of war known to man seems to have had a role in Operation Albion. The column was so long that, once underway, it stretched for 37km. It sailed through the Kiel Canal, with reconnaissance aircraft flying overhead, and crossed the Baltic Sea from west to east, some 1,600km. Minesweepers took the lead. It was a mighty procession and one that Winston Churchill would have admired.

The minesweepers did a first-rate job. They swept the route so efficiently that although the Baltic was studded with thousands and thousands of Russian mines, not one German craft was damaged. Not one life was lost. In addition, the Germans enjoyed an unaccountable stroke of luck in that there were no attacks by British submarines,[6] and this despite the fact that there were eight of them in the Baltic at the time. Also, there were no attacks by the Russians. But then they had other issues to deal with. The Russian Fleet had to prioritize with care. Revolution was its first concern.

As a result, the Russian navy watched helplessly as an enemy navy with ten dreadnoughts advanced towards their own country. They watched in full knowledge that Russia was falling apart, that the government was shaky, that they had no dreadnoughts, and that their naval command system was under attack from within; Russian officers could give orders, but ratings were free to ignore them. There was little trust, anyway, in orders emanating from an uncertain government in St Petersburg. These were indeed desperate circumstances for Russia, but in spite of this, the Russian navy and army, as far as it could, held its ground, putting up some fight for as long as possible, and with courage.

Operation Albion was huge and groundbreaking. It required major logistical control both between the services and within each service itself. The two had never before depended on each other so completely. The Baltic Fleet was, of course, as part of the armada, under Schmidt's overall control, but its own commander was Admiral Hopman. It is almost certainly because of Hopman's presence that Hermann was pulled out of his submariner school and roped in to help. He was appointed Liaison Officer to General Hutier and Co-ordination Officer for the Imperial Navy, a very important position, a key position, and one which Hermann did not enjoy in the least. Co-ordination was essential, yet both he and Hopman knew, from the joint army and navy attack on Libau in 1915, that co-ordination between the two services was not easy. They had different priorities, and complicating everything was the army's belief that, as the senior service, it was the superior of the two. Fortunately, Hermann had all the diplomatic skills needed to handle the delicate egos of generals and admirals alike.

Brilliantly planned and brilliantly executed, this was the first ever major, modern, joint operation, so of course, by the end of it, the Germans were purring with delight. They won one battle after another. It went like clockwork. It was, in fact, so successful that they could easily have gone on to take the Russian capital itself, but they didn't. Perhaps the thinking was, as Hermann suggested in one of his letters home, that it wasn't necessary because Russia was on the point of imploding regardless.

The first three of the letters from Hermann which follow are to his father and deal with military and naval matters. The fourth is to his wife, and does not.

12 October 1917
General Army Office
Dear Father,
Do you know what a Pilako is? Or an Afl, an Ifl or a Grufl?[7] No? Really! Three weeks ago I wouldn't have thought it necessary to know either. Nor would I have thought I would ever become a General Staff Officer. As of today, that is, since our troops (brilliantly transported here and landed by part of the High Seas Fleet) set firm foot on Ösel, I can say that I too have been bought into this operation. I have been made Naval Advisor to the Commander-in-Chief, General von Hutier, of the Eighth Army High Command. As such, I sit here, sometimes down, sometimes up, with my magnificent General, in Riga. What gets me down is that I am a submariner, a frontline man, and no office manager, lubricating things in the background. If they ever assign me again on such a special mission, they might at least put me up on board a ship. What cheers me is that, in spite of what all the misery-sayers predicted, the operation has worked brilliantly. I have never before experienced such a well-organized operation (in its preparation, deployment and the opening attack), nor would I even have thought it possible.

As a submariner, I am ashamed half to death of my English and Russian fellow seafarers. Not a single soldier of ours was harmed during the journey here, nor on landing, by any enemy submarines nor enemy mines. Shameful! Our transport fleet was 20 nautical miles long. As I watched it, I thought myself in some kind of trance.

What was almost incomprehensible was the speed with which the Russian coastal batteries were silenced. In the Dardanelles, the Franco-British fleet spent a month shelling the *Goeben*,[8] with its single 15cm gun, when it was anchored on the Asiatic side of the Dardanelles. And still they didn't manage to damage it. However, unlike the English, we didn't use old tubs against the coastal forts which then, like erupting volcanoes, flew into the air. No, we used the best of the best. They did the job.

Now, with the first troops of the advance party on land, the harbour and landing place are firmly in our hands and I fear no further difficulties. I suspect that tonight the Russians are clearing the town of Arensburg which is severely threatened, and the Sworbe peninsula. Both of these sites are key. They control the entry to the Bay of Riga. Once we gain Riga, the Russians will be unable to hold Moon and the rest of Ösel.[9]

It's good to witness something like this close to, even when it has to be witnessed from a sadly limiting desk. And who knows, perhaps I can one day use what I am learning from this experience. That is to say, I have some little things in mind.

You know, in the summer of 1915 (when I was last here) I complained because we didn't go on to take Ösel.[10] At that time it was not fortified and easy to take. This time, it was still a relatively simple affair. The well-laid Russian roads, airports, facilities, and part of the defence batteries have readily fallen to us. With any luck, we will harvest more of what the Russians have sown.

Now it's really late. My Adjutant (yes, I have one of these as well) has gone on watch and I will lie down on my bunk.

With a thousand hugs to you, Mama and Lenelein,

Your true son, Hermann

Riga 16 October 1917

Dear Father,

Now the most difficult part is completed and in the most remarkable way. Yesterday evening we took the strongly fortified Island of Ösel after only four days of fighting. In the long history of sea warfare, no army and navy combined operation has ever worked more brilliantly.

Granted the Russians ran as soon as our troops landed. Granted we had enormous good luck in experiencing a spell of the best weather we have had all autumn (extremely important for the minesweepers). And granted, our transport fleet, with its many steamers, cargo ships, coalers, hospital ships etc, etc, slipped unharmed through the only gap in a very well laid-out offshore mine defence barrier. But this good luck was also earned. Von Levetzov[11] (the man who did it) bided his time, waiting for the right moment. He waited with astonishing resolve, waited, waited and waited till the weather was exactly as he needed it to be. And he waited in spite of pressure from above, from even higher than above, from both sides and from underneath. Withstanding everybody else's point of view – even that of your dear son – he stood firm and he was right. Bravo.

In the battle, our torpedo boats did extremely well. Indeed, our penetrating into the Kassar Wiek through the Soelo Sound[12] – a waterway we didn't know existed up to this point – was a masterpiece and the attack on the torpedo boat *Grom*[13] was well executed. A pity the boat sank in the process.

It is also a pity that the Russians ran away so quickly. A large number of them escaped across the causeway to Moon, in spite of fire from our torpedo boats. They had entered the small sound from the north.

Yesterday evening, the Sworbe peninsula, the best defended place in Ösel, was the last place to fall. It was defended by four 30.5cm guns with a range of 27 kilometres which, together with an extremely dense offshore minefield, completely blocked the entrance to the Bay of Riga from the direction of Zerel. If only Tsingtau[14] had been protected by guns like those. They could have held out for a long, long time, and yet our ships of the line softened them up in an astonishingly short time. The night before last, the Russians on Sworbe must have been feeling pretty unsure. Yesterday at midday, they were yelling for help from their fleet. When it didn't come, they began at 3.00 in the afternoon to blow up and burn their equipment.

I think this is the first time that a fleet has been able to defeat a strong land battery from the sea. I am just thrilled by the actual impact of our ship's guns. Perhaps it's actually around zero. Perhaps the success was more due to low Russian morale than to anything else. If it were really that easy to damage shore batteries from the sea, then our guns in Flanders would have been turned to dust long ago.

Booty so far includes one division staff and two brigade staffs –we've been capturing enemy divisional staff for a long time – also a war chest (hopefully with English money in it) and five sea planes together with their flight station which were taken by our own sea planes during their operations. All pretty good really. Have you heard the awful story about Kerenski? He wired his troop ships that 'the time for the supreme test had arrived. Russia was waiting to be saved through the bravery of the entire Russian navy. As your Commander-in-Chief, I call upon the Russian forces to sacrifice themselves.'[15]

The Russian forces will cough up something for him. But they will do so by pretending to be heroes, as did those men manning the Toffri battery[16] who claimed they had sunk four German torpedo boats when in fact, all they could boast of was one hit on a boat without even putting it out of action. Heroism of this kind is fine by us.

It's interesting here in Riga. The German Balts[17] seem to be pretty pleased about developments. The city scarcely fought at all and there is plenty still in the stores, only everything is on sale for eye-watering prices (one lemon costs two roubles). The ordinary poor Prussian officer can't afford even a quick drink in a pub! I hope to see the Chancellor[18] the day after tomorrow and further hope, in about three week's time, to be finished with my job here. Meanwhile, the Commander-in-Chief, I think, is going over to Arensberg and is taking me with him. I would like to see the Russian batteries there. After that I will have had quite enough of my army duties which smother me in paper and ink. These duties keep me away from seawater and fresh air. They also, last but not least, cost me me a pile of money. This is because they are eating away at my submariner skills and, at the same time, imposing considerable expenses. Hey. So what.

With a thousand heartfelt hugs to you, Mother and Lenelein, your true son, Hermann.

17 October
Dear Papa,
I have just received your dear letters of the 27th and 28th September which Winnie forwarded to me. I also received a letter addressed to Field Post 168 (I receive a lot of letters, far more than I am entitled to). Many are actually destined for a certain Oberleutnant zur See Bernhard Gerke (no 'c').[19] He seems to have got his promotion the same time as me, and his suppliers seem to have been left in the dark about his address. Well. I think that is fine, but I was a little bit surprised when today I received a registered express letter from his Mama. It was addressed to me but meant for him. Well, I didn't read it, but you know, to leave his Mama in the same state of ignorance as his creditors. I find that's a bit thick. Though, at the same time, I have to admit that one is a constant debtor in relation to one's mother.

In your letter to Field Post 168 (4 August 1917), you complain about the noisy rumour mill in Warnemünde.[20] Well, this time it did no damage. The Russians seem to have been taken completely by surprise. At least, judging from the way things proceeded. I expect the rest of the Ösel crew stationed on Moon will fall into our hands today.

Every day, the navy and army have been working together in a new and exemplary way. I am convinced that we could reach St Petersburg if we wanted. But perhaps the porridge there will cook well enough without our help.

I am sorry to hear that little Mrs G. Recke has fallen apart. Nothing will happen to her husband.

On my side, there is nothing to report. I'm fine except for the fact that I am worried at having to fight (by telegram) to get my salary handed over to Winnie. Of course, no one is 'responsible' for the problem. Oh, the Imperial Navy, such a magnificent weapon! But so poor at organisation and administration.

Well. Heaven be praised. What really matters is the first.

What is your view on Capelle?

With a thousand greetings to you, Mama and Lenelein,

Your faithful son, Hermann

Deutsche Feldpost 689
5 November 1917
Darling,
I would love to tell you a thousand different things but of course I cannot write those that are really interesting, such as who I am with, or what I am doing. Only this much can out: it is all very interesting and I am, as ever, learning a lot. But whether what I learn is pleasant or not remains to be seen.

I am fine. Physically, I am in very good shape. Unfortunately, I am not sailing and out at sea, from which statement you will deduce that I am still, as far as is humanly possible, captivated by every opportunity for dangerous situations. This is something my parents also accuse me of. It could always turn out that I, like poor von Pappenheim[21] who died three days ago, will fall ill with appendicitis. Others are pursuing a life on the ocean wave including Ihem, Ehrhardt, Tillchsen, Faulborn, Heinecke, Heinrich[22] and other old friends whom I see from time to time.

The one thing that worries me is the thought of you with your terrible tasks of moving house and registering the children in a new school. Be sure to give Langheinrich a hard time if he lets you down in any way whatsoever!

Did you get my last letter of the 3rd? Do everything I ask you to do exactly.

Darling, I long for you with all my heart. It already seems to me as if it was an eternity since I last saw and kissed you. [In English] Win I am so longing for you. Do you feel the same sometimes?

[In German again] I still have no idea how long I have to stay so far away from you. Tomorrow I am travelling to where, in peacetime, we got to know Frau Lange. I am very excited at the opportunity to check on how things are there today.

[In English) Write to me soon at Feldpost 689 Do write a sweet letter!

[In German again] Please pay Frau Bastian[23] a visit (Feldstrasse 125.III). I am with her husband until tomorrow.

With thousands of kisses, your Hermann

These letters show Hermann's playful, teasing character. They show his love and concern for his parents, his sister and his wife. They show his passion and immediacy. His letter to Winnie sounds as if they were newly-weds. In fact, they were in the eleventh year of their marriage. We hear his disdain for pomposity, for office work and bureaucracy; his deep preference for adventure and for an open-air life on board ship. He takes the broader view and is interested in the war as a whole, comparing and contrasting events in the Far East, the Mediterranean and the English Channel. And lastly, he searches for the positive, promising himself that he will learn useful things even when carrying out a deeply unloved assignment. A intelligent, diligent, optimistic man.

During the course of Operation Albion, one of the navy's greatest successes lay in its finding pathways through extensive and largely unknown minefields. There were thousands of Russian mines in the Irben Straits, and strings of them in the waterways between the islands. This success was due to the level-headedness of one man, the indomitable Levetzov. He earned his reward and, as Hermann pointed out, much of the operation's success was similarly earned. But much too was unearned. The Germans were lucky in that the four British E-Class submarines in the Baltic at this time did not attack; and that none of the four C-Class submarines, also in the Baltic, were able to damage the German fleet – one was in the Gulf of Riga at the time and tried to fire at them but failed. The Germans were lucky in that the British, who must have known about this operation through Room 40, did not take advantage of the absence of ten dreadnoughts from the High Seas Fleet in the North Sea to attack what remained. And of course, they were lucky in that Russia was in a sorry state of disarray. Last but not least, they were lucky with the weather.

By the end of Operation Albion, Germany had achieved exactly what it had set out to do. Russia was out of the war and Germany was, at last, fighting on only one front. Negotiations were underway in the town of Brest-Litvosk. They had in fact been going on there since long before the Operation started. Hermann joked in a letter written in January 1917 that his voluble two-year old daughter, Ursula, would have fitted in perfectly round 'the negotiating table at Brest-Litovsk!' After the Operation, those negotiations continued, and a punitive treaty was signed in March 1918.[24]

Still untroubled by English submarines, the High Seas Fleet returned safely to its North Sea base. Levetzov was given a *Pour le Mérite*, the highest and most coveted of all German awards, and Hermann didn't do badly either. He was awarded the Order of the Royal House of Hohenzollern, an essential pre-requisite leading to the *Pour le Mérite*.

Hermann returned safely home. By the end of the year he was back with his family in their little cottage in Borby. But not for long. Not even for Christmas. Winnie saw less and less of him. His great odyssey was about to begin.

Chapter 23

Komm Gut nach Hause (Come Safely Home)

They didn't know exactly when it would be, but the day of departure was drawing inexorably nearer and nearer. Hermann decided to send his family to Warnemünde, where his father was harbourmaster and in charge of the naval depot. He could be reasonably certain that, in spite of the hardships endured by one and all, his own small children and his soon-to-be grass widow (now pregnant with their fourth child) would be relatively well fed while he was away. Win recalled:

> The short journey from Kiel to Warnemünde was one of the most dramatic of my life.[1] In early January, one dark, blustery, freezing cold night, Hermann walked the children, the nurse and me down to Kiel harbour, where all of us, save him, embarked on a minesweeper (it was actually a trawler converted into a minesweeper), together with our goods and chattels. Once we were safely on board, he returned to his submarine.
>
> The nurse turned green as soon as she stepped on board. Diving below deck, she reappeared only at the end, when we landed. The boys, the baby and I stayed in the fo'c'sle, under a tarpaulin, with one side open to the elements. A kind of tent. The boys lay on benches around the sides and were sick. The baby slept. I tried to warm myself on a small coke brazier in the centre. There was a blackout all along the north German coast. No lights shone in the town or in the harbour, and our own space was lit only by a single oil lamp dangling from a pole propping up our tent. The sea was rough. As we drew away from harbour, with a loud clatter, a bottle of paraffin fell over on deck and started rolling towards the coke fire. I pushed it aside with my foot and yelled. How thankful I was when, after eight long hours, I saw the quayside at Warnemünde,
>
> I caught sight of my parents-in-law waiting for us. It was very dark. Here, as everywhere else, there was a blackout. After some sleepy hugs and murmurs of '*Omi! Opa!*' [Granny! Grandad!], we all set off for our new home, which was a flat above a shop on the harbour side of the quay. We would be near to their own place. Cosy and warm again, with the boys tucked up in bed and Ursula in her cot, Mila put the kettle on to make us

tea. My parents-in-law were, as always, bright, open-armed and welcoming. In return, Hermann's children, in their innocence and neediness, distracted them from their own sorrows.

Warnemünde is a tiny fishing town where, every summer, the tourists arrive. They fill the hotels and cover the beaches with high-backed, wicker chairs with canopies. These provide some shelter from strong winds. But now, in January, most of the houses and villas were boarded up and the winds blew freely, no chairs to break the gusts. Only the houses right on the harbour showed any signs of life. Food was scarce and coal more so. True to his son, my father-in-law sent sailors up from the depot every day. They carried pails of coal in one hand and terrines of barley boiled with prunes in the other. Oddly enough, this was a dish I grew to love, as did the children. It became our mainstay.

How blest we were, not only did we have supplies, but the cook at the naval centre had been, in peace time, chief chef of the main Leipzig railway station restaurant. If anyone could make something out of nothing, it was him. And he did. That cook had many skills. He was chief tenor in the small choir the Captain organised at the depot. They sang at Christmas concerts and other celebrations, both he and the Captain. Yes, in spite of everything, my father-in-law kept singing. He was well-loved. And not just because he held the keys to the larder.

On 15 February, sailors from the depot brought us the news that the *U-154* was coming into harbour that evening. She would be leaving before sunrise the next day, 16 February, Mila's birthday. I was a bundle of nerves. I wanted to see Hermann so much, but not in these circumstances. To say goodbye? No.

Hermann duly arrived and went, first of all, to see his parents. Then he came to us. The children greeted him with joy, dragging him to sit on the floor and play. He did so. Harry and Georg got out their toy battle ships, while Ursula toddled about unsteadily. How delighted they all were. Then the children went to bed.

When I think back to the many things I could have said, and about the stupid nonsense I actually spouted, I am mortified. The remembrance of it has haunted me ever since. How I regret my waste of those few, fleeting, precious hours. Meaningless trivia came out of my mouth. How long will you be away? Will you write? Can I write to you?

He said that if he did not return he hoped the boys would be educated in Germany, in the Plön School for the sons of naval officers. We talked about what I should do with his few possessions. Who should get what. He told me to give his warm naval great coat to Langheinrich. There was no need for such things on a U-Boat anyway. From now on he would wear a black leather jacket, woollen sweaters, warm trousers, sea boots, oilskins and a sou'wester.

He told me once again, as he had often done before, that he was doing what he had to do. And he was doing it for us and for the children. 'If I don't return, don't forget to tell them this, and to tell the other one as well, the one who is coming. I am sure we will have another girl and that she will be a great comfort to you. If it is a girl, let's call her Ingrid, you always liked that name. And as for you my sweetest Win. The Navy looks after its own. You will be well provided for. And if I do return, what a wonderful time we will have together.'

I wept and leant against him. Tears were the last thing he wanted to see.

'Remember what Papa says – I have an enchanted life. I have been lucky so far. Don't despair. All will be well.'

We hugged each other. Towards morning, long before it was light, he left. I think his last word was 'darling'.

It was so hard on the children. What they wanted was their father and the sense of safety which he brought with him. I remember one evening I caught sight of my youngest boy, four-year-old Georg. He was alone in his bedroom, standing at the open window and gazing at the night sky. It was filled with a million tiny star specks. He spoke to the star specks. '*Lieber Gott, geh Du in den Krieg und schicke Vater nach Hause.*' (Dear God, go to war yourself, and send Father home.)

Hermann walked to the harbour mole alone. His father joined him a little later. This is what Philipp wrote:

On 15 February, Hermann's submarine lay in the harbour. We brought him water and supplies. We gave his boat a final refuelling. In fact, we did everything we could to make sure the *U-154* was in tip-top shape. We knew, all too well, some of its defects – problems which had shown up during trial runs. We tried to fix his two broken cog-wheels and checked to see that he had all the kit needed to fix things himself, if anything went wrong again. With what love and devotion we all worked! If only I could have gone in his place.

I snatched a few hours' sleep at home and then, at 4.00 in the morning, returned to the harbour. Hermann was already there. He was standing on the mole, chatting to a group of sailors. With a sober smile, he said goodbye to us all, and stepped onto the gangway. As he joined his crew, they gave him three 'Hurrahs', determined, but quiet (appropriate to the hour). The gangway was pulled noisily back onto the quayside. Chains rattled on concrete. My men cast off the ropes and threw them onto the submarine's deck. It was 4.25 am.

The last time I saw him, he was standing in the conning tower with two others. After a brief word of command, the diesel engines started. The boat quivered and drew away from the quayside. As it got up speed, the handsome Imperial Navy flag, with its strong black cross, fluttered from the radio mast. The boat reached the harbour entrance, and I walked along the mole waving my cap. Right to the end.

'Success be yours and a happy home-coming.'

He turned briefly, gave me a smart salute, then returned to face the sea. His boat drew further and further away. It passed the harbour entrance and disappeared on a north-easterly course.

Chapter 24

The Kingpin

Admiral Sir William Milbourne James[1] was de facto head of Room 40 when Hermann went to sea in *U-154*. Room 40 in the Old Admiralty Building was not so much a room as a series of cubby-holes. This was the Admiralty's intelligence department for cryptanalysis. Responsible predominantly for the decryption of intercepted German naval messages, it was where an extraordinarily mixed staff of forty men and women, each in his or her own idiosyncratic way, worked at deciphering German codes. The group included a lawyer, a theologian, a publisher, a schoolteacher, a papyrologist (who claimed to do his best work in the bath), a mild-mannered Etonian known as 'The Dormouse' and an Olympic hockey player. They worked under the authority of the Director of Naval Intelligence, Admiral Sir William Hall, who was himself something of an eccentric. He had extra-bushy eyebrows, beneath which one eye, possibly because of a facial twitch, flashed like a Navy signalling lamp. They called him 'Blinker'. The work these men and women did was deadly serious and of national importance. Its value could not be overestimated. It determined the movements of the fleet and was the lynchpin, or 'kingpin' as Sir James calls it, of the naval war effort.[2] It saved thousands of British lives and cost countless German ones, including that of my grandfather.

The unit foreshadowed work done at Bletchley Park in the war which followed. Anyone entering the decoding room in Bletchley Park would probably have met cryptanalysts who had spent the First World War in Room 40. This allowed Britain to benefit in two world wars from vital, secret information which twice gave it a winning hand.

Since the 1917 decision in Germany to relaunch the 'unrestricted submarine warfare' programme, Room 40 had been busier than ever. More and more submarines. More and more signalling. British spies within Germany reported that in one German shipyard alone, one new U-Boat was being delivered every seventeen days.[3] Among these new boats were the two long-range cargo submarines, the *U-154* and the *U-153*. Because they were new and because they were long-range, British Intelligence wanted to know as much about them as possible. Their strong points, their weak points and above all, their task. In order to find out, Room 40 started tracking Hermann and Goetting long before they ever began their mission. They tracked them as they went on trial runs in Kiel Bay. They checked Hermann's reports on the efficiency, or otherwise, of his equipment. How serious a threat were these new submarines going to be?

The development of long-range German submarines put a spotlight on the Azores which lie at an oceanic crossroads. Britain's trade, whether with the south or west, often passed through or close to the Azores so British anxiety was high. Would these new submarines threaten trade with the British Empire and beyond? It was this anxiety which helped drive a January 1918 decision by Britain's ally, the United States, to build a new US naval base near Ponta Delgada, capital of the Azores and the main town on the island of São Miguel. The base would house a contingent of US Marines manning a battery of 179mm guns. They would run a new airfield for some eighteen spotter planes and be charged with patrolling the Azorean seas. The base was meant to keep people like Hermann and Goetting in check. Fortunately for them, the base does not appear to have been fully operational at the time of their mission. Goetting saw no American planes and Hermann met only one US ship in the area, an armed steamer, the *Chincha*, on 18 March.

The *U-154* and *U-153* were among the first of the long-range submarines to implement Germany's new campaign. They were ordered to operate largely off the coast of West Africa and they were fitted with cable-cutting equipment. Their job was twofold. Firstly, to cut those communications cables which kept Britain in touch with its Empire and with the Americas, and secondly, to attack trade supporting the Allied war effort. Fisher's comment comes to mind: 'The British Empire and the German submarine cannot co-exist.'

In the First World War, there were three main ways of locating a U-Boat. The first was by transmitted radio signals. In 1902, an American scientist discovered that the location of a radio source can be determined by measuring the direction of signals it emits from two or more locations.[4] The British took the discovery further, developing SIGINT, or signals intelligence, in other words, information derived from electronic signals. In 1914, SIGINT was just emerging as a field of study and it was British-led.

The second way to determine an enemy boat's location is by decoding actual messages sent to and from the boat in question. From these you could learn not only where the boat was, but why it was there and what it was planning, and this system worked perfectly once Russia and Britain both held the key to the German codes. The third method of tracking a U-Boat was through direct reports, coded from spies or uncoded when sent by other vessels at sea. All such reports were immediately transmitted by the nearest British embassy or consulate, to the Admiralty in London.

The first two systems (radio direction finding and decoding) both depended on picking up electronic signals, which is why Britain, only hours after war was declared, ordered cable-cutting ships to sever German undersea cables. The move ensured that German messages to the outside world could now only be sent using a telegraph line connected through the British network, which therefore could be tapped, or by using radio signals, which the British could intercept. During the First World War, intercept stations sprouted up all over Britain, especially on the east and south coasts.

The German scientific world was well aware of developments in direction-finding. Individuals in the German Navy were working on it too. Hermann and his father were in the process of setting up a radio direction-finding station in Warnemünde in 1918. But its implications had not permeated the body of the Imperial Navy as a whole. Little had changed in the way it conducted itself, or in the way it expected its officers to conduct themselves. The Navy never discouraged radio chatter[5] and in fact probably inadvertently encouraged it. Nauen, the German home base radio transmitting station near Berlin, was constantly asking U-Boats to report their location and the tonnage sunk.[6] The only way to escape such demands was by keeping the long-range radio mast down as much as possible, which Hermann did. This is why home base resorted to asking his sister U-Boat, the *U-153*, for the same information. Hermann was perhaps extra cautious because he had been in the eastern Baltic the night the *Magdeburg* went down. He knew the danger. He knew Admiral Behring's concerns. He knew Prince Heinrich's. To communicate with Goetting, he used his two short wave radio masts or, if they were within sight of each other, blinker signals. For any significant discussion of strategy, Hermann insisted that the two commanders meet face-to-face, and he was right in his insistence. Even today, after all these years and after so many improvements in communications, the only truly secure way to communicate is still in person.

Towards the end of their voyage, the *U-62*, a new *Kreuzer* (cruiser) type of longer-range U-Boat was sent out to meet them. Before setting out on their return journey, *U-153* and *U-154* were ordered to supply *U-62* with any spare fuel and spare torpedoes they might have. Such a rendezvous required planning, and there was much chat between *U-153* and *U-62* about where and when the meeting was to take place. *U-62* asked *U-153*, more than once, to repeat the coordinates of their meeting place, and Goetting felt forced to reply. Hermann, on the other hand, didn't even know these exchanges were taking place until Goetting told him about them in person. His own communications with Germany were few and far between and generally limited to reports on particularly serious situations, such as the deaths of crew members.

Hermann was so right. Electronic signalling was dangerous. Room 40 was reading their messages and following up the intelligence gathered by systematically neutralizing their work. It sent telegrams to embassies and consulates ordering them to stop, delay or re-route shipping if a U-Boat was on the hunt. This is why Goetting and Hermann, sailing the busiest areas in the Atlantic Ocean, saw remarkably few ships. Little did they know that troop ships had been re-routed, that shipments of gold bullion had been halted and that convoys had been delayed or re-routed. No wonder the oceans appeared well-nigh deserted.

And there were still other ways of neutralizing Hermann's and Goetting's work. When the U-Boats laid mines, the Admiralty sent minesweepers to clear them. When they cut cables, the Admiralty sent out repair crews. When they first bombed a signalling station, signalling engineers were dispatched to fix it. Lastly, and most frustrating of all from the U-Boat commander's point of view, when Nauen informed its U-Boat commanders about where they might locate gaps in the mine barrages in the North Sea and the Channel, the British, picking up those reports, sent out minelayers to close them.

The only other option open to the Admiralty in finding ways to deal with the news gathered by Room 40 was to send out British submariners to ambush and destroy enemy submarines. This the Admiralty was reluctant to do, because it would almost certainly signal to the German side that their codes had been broken. And this is, in fact, exactly what happened when the Admiralty broke its own unspoken rule. In May 1918, it sent out a direct command for the ambush of two long-range U-Boats meeting in the Atlantic, between Gibraltar and Morocco, the *U-154* and the *U-153*. Trade disruptors, they threatened the Empire. A step too far. For this, Room 40 was prepared to risk discovery. After *U-154* was targeted, the captains of the *U-153* and of the *U-62* (which was also at the meeting) both signalled that their codes might be compromised. The head of the U-Kreuzer Flotilla, Commander von Koch wrote that he thought it highly likely that here had been a compromise of key *Gamma Ulli*, though conclusive proof was hardly possible. He urged immediate change in the use of that key and extreme caution on the part of all U-Kreuzer commanders. This slow and cautious reaction to a very present intelligence threat was typical of the German navy during the First World War. Commander Koch suspects, but his reaction is limited.

The commanders of *U-154* and the *U-153* left on their missions a couple of days apart, with a plan to meet up off Cape Finisterre in Spain. There they discussed the weakness of their boats and decided to protect each other to counter those weaknesses. They spent their entire mission working closely together, thereby forming the first U-Boat Wolf Pack – a small one, but still a pack. This approach came into its own during the Second World War and, in both cases, it was chosen because it offered the U-Boats greater safety and a greater chance of success. Given that working together required frequent consultation, and given Hermann's distrust of wireless signalling, the two of them met on each other's boats frequently. They met nine times[7] during the nine weeks that they were 'on the hunt' (from the date of their first rendezvous in the Atlantic on 5 March, till the day that the *U-154* was torpedoed on 11 May, 1918). Generally, it was Hermann who was rowed over to visit Goetting. Each time, their crews were delighted. Drawn up alongside each other in calm waters and on a sunny day, this was a welcome chance to greet old shipmates. The men stood in the sunshine on their respective decks yelling messages to each other, while one captain in a jolly boat (a seaman at the oars) rowed over to meet his friend. The meetings were far more than moments for secure discussion. They were morale-boosters.

Goetting was less stringent than Hermann about his long-range radio mast, but what could he do in the face of demands from Nauen? And what could either of them do if brother officers treated the wireless system as a veritable chat line?

Chapter 25

The *U-154*

When Admiral Lord Jellicoe told US Rear-Admiral William Sims that the rate of British losses due to German submarine activity would likely force an end to the war, he was thinking about the amount of tonnage sunk. Ships bringing food and raw materials to the British Isles were going down. People might starve. Factories close. But he knew that to win a modern war, you needed to manage the politics of war as well as the economics. You had to argue for loans and spread propaganda. To this end, Germany's communications system with the world must be shut down and Britain's kept open. The First World War was the first global information war.

Acknowledging this from the beginning, an order to cut Germany's undersea telegraph cables went out at just past midnight on 5 August 1914, roughly twenty-five hours after war was declared. A few hours later, and Britain had hamstrung Germany's communications system with the outside world. The telegraph company which had laid the cables in the first place did the job. They used their own fleets and their own men.

It took Germany a long while to catch up (or rather to attempt to catch up, for it never succeeded), but in February 1918 *U-154* and *U-153* were dispatched on their mission with grappling hooks on board. Part of their work was to rip up British cables lying off the coast of West Africa. Dakar in Senegal and Bathurst (now Banjul) in Gambia were at a junction of undersea telegraph cables. West-east ones passed through the Cape Verde Islands and linked the Americas with the rest of the world and north-south cables connected Cape Town and the south with Britain. *U-154* and *U-153* were charged with breaking these links.

This was challenging, for although the crews had practised cable-cutting in Kiel harbour, it was not one of their well-honed skills born of years of experience, nor was the equipment they used up to the same standards as that available on the cable ships owned by the British telegraph company.

The West Coast of Africa was of course, also important for shipping, especially routes connecting Britain with its empire. It had long been the route used for shipments of gold bullion from the Gold Coast (Ghana) and the Cape (South Africa) to Britain. With a mounting war debt and dire need for ever greater loans, these shipments were important. This, too, was the route for troop ships from India, Africa, Australia and New Zealand. The *U-154* and *U-153* were to fulfil Fisher's prediction and break the links between Britain and her Empire.

The West African route was growing in importance, partly because of significant U-Boat successes in the Mediterranean. Voyages through the Suez Canal to India and the East had become increasingly dangerous. The outstanding commander in the Mediterranean was Winnie's and Hermann's good friend, Arnauld de la Perrière. Working from the Austro-Hungarian port of Pola in the Adriatic, between November 1915 and 1918, he sank 453,716 tons of shipping. In response, the Allies began sending ships round the Cape instead of through the Suez Canal. This increased traffic in West African ports used for re-supplying and refuelling: Dakar (Senegal), Bathurst (Gambia) and Freetown (Sierra Leone). Allied naval bases along the coast were expanding and this is why the *U-154* and *U-153* carried mines to sow in the waters around those bases.

And, lastly, the two U-Boats were tasked with the classic job, the one expected of all submarines, namely, to sink enemy war vessels and all merchant shipping working to support the enemy.

Germany knew that the area to which they were sending *U-154* and *U-153* was important, but Berlin had no idea that the United States, which had officially entered the war on 4 April 1917, also had interests there, and that those interests were expanding. In 1917, the US negotiated with Portugal (initially neutral) to establish an American naval base in São Miguel, one of the islands in the Portuguese Azores. Even more significantly, the same month that it declared war on Germany, the US passed an emergency act (the Liberty Loan Act). This enabled it to lend money to neutral foreign governments, 'encouraging' them to come over to the Allied side.

At the start of the war, 75 per cent of Liberia's foreign trade was with Germany. German engineers went there to build and man a telegraph signalling and cable station in the capital, Monrovia. It was no surprise when, in 1914, Liberia chose neutrality. But as the war progressed, its foreign trade collapsed, and in 1917 the US offered $500m in the form of an American loan under the new Loan Act to Daniel Edward Howard, President of Liberia. He accepted, and Liberia joined the Allied side. Howard expelled the German workers at the telegraph station and agreed to the presence of Richard Bundy, the US chargé d'affaires, at his side as his 'adviser'.[1] Germany may have known about the Loan Act, but it had no idea that countries like Liberia would be more or less taken over by American interests.

The submariners set out two days apart, met almost three weeks later off Cape Finisterre in Spain and worked together from then on. I have no evidence to suggest that they had been ordered to work as a team, but they did so. They were firm friends, both Crew 1902. They had signed up for submariner school together and they graduated together. They were sailing sister boats, both difficult to manoeuvre and therefore vulnerable to enemy attack. They not only met frequently, but often sailed within sight of each other, either abreast of in scouting line, usually with *U-154* in the lead. As well as joint planning, the two commanders supported each other with men and machinery and they supported each other tactically. *U-154* signalled to *U-153* when danger threatened in the form of a Q-ship and they attacked it together.

Setting on one side for a moment the disaster which eventually befell *U-154*, neither U-Boat sustained major damage from enemy fire during their mission, but they both experienced serious mechanical failures. On the final leg of its journey home, *U-153* ran with only one of its diesel engines functioning, but *U-154* had the worst of it. Hermann sustained two serious accidents, both associated with his deck guns, which he preferred to his torpedoes. On 18 March, he lost three men because the breech block on one of the deck guns flew out and backfired on being opened. On 25 April, he lost eight men, with two badly wounded.[2] In that second case, Hermann reported that the accident was the result of careless loading, which allowed the gun's sometimes shattering recoil to set off ammunition stacked behind it. Following that event, he hailed a passing Spanish merchantman, the *Achuri*, and asked the captain if he would take both wounded men to the military hospital in Las Palmas, Gran Canaria. Once restored to health, the men remained on the island as prisoners of war until 1919, when they returned home to Germany. One of these two, Hans Hinrichsen, serves here as a mouthpiece to give an imagined description of the voyage of the *U-154*. The description is based on reports from other U-Boat mariners taking a similar route, on the War Log Book of the *U-153*,[3] on newspaper reports and on Goetting's and Winnie's notes.

Hinrichsen's story is intertwined with contemporary reports from Room 40 and related telegrams sent by the Admiralty in London. Room 40 kept a ledger in which each U-Boat had a page (or pages) listing decoded and translated messages.[4] These were generally messages between Nauen and the U-Boat in question, or from other U-Boats or accompanying vessels. It is impossible to establish an absolute 'cause and effect' link between Room 40's intelligence and the Admiralty's subsequent actions, but we can be reasonably certain in some cases. To indicate such links, I include Admiralty telegrams wired subsequent to Room 40's decoding work.[5]

In this way, we have two accounts, one from the hunted (in the person of Hinrichsen), and one from the hunter (Room 40). The two are linked inexorably as they move together towards the final explosion.

In addition, I include a section sub-titled 'Shipping News', which offers details of the ships that Hermann sank, or tried to sink. Tonnage sunk is, from the Admiralty's point of view, a key element in the entire exercise. I have seized this opportunity to make this report more accurate than in the German archives, where the sinking of the *Willow Branch* is attributed entirely to *U-153*. Since that battle was a joint affair, I have divided the *Willow Branch*'s tonnage between the two of them.

* * *

(Hinrichsen)

It was pitch black as we left harbour and entered the Baltic. An escort vessel was waiting for us at Gjedser with a minesweeper. 'The Old Man' as we called him, put our red-bearded Oberleutnant Baden in charge with a skeleton crew. He invited the rest of us to the wardroom. We were such a crowd, seventy-seven men in all, that he left the door of his cabin open so some of us could stand in the doorway. None of us knew at that point, what the mission was, nor how long it was to take.

'We are on a three-month mission', he said. '*U-153* has a similar one. You probably all know she left harbour two days ago. All being well, in about three weeks, we will rendezvous with Commander Goetting off Cape Finisterre.

'We are going somewhere where it is nice and warm, to the Azores, the Canaries and the Cape Verde Islands. To the seas off the west coast of Africa. Enough of Kiel's cold and sleet. By the time we get back we will all be as brown as berries. We are going to an area which is a crossroads. A meeting place of trade routes and of submarine telegraph cables. Our job is to cut cables and harry merchantmen. We will sink those which carry cargoes bound for the enemy. There should be a lot of shipping around. We will mine allied ports in West Africa where enemy ships refuel and re-supply. We will loosen Britain's grip on its Empire. We will help bring the enemy to the negotiating table. We will stop them starving our families. The better we do our job, the sooner we get home.

'But … until we reach our first rendezvous, always remember that the enemy has good directional finding systems. No wireless messages!'

We were all pleased to hear this. Firstly, it meant we would be meeting our mates on *U-153*, and secondly, it reminded us that our Old Man was super-careful. That's why many of us had volunteered to serve with him. Also, I have to say, we were quite pleased to be going somewhere warm.

At the end of his briefing, the Old Man smiled and we gave him three hurrahs. We were happy. It was a relief, after all those months of intense preparation, after the heartache of goodbyes, to finally be on our way. Outward bound.

As we approached the straits between Copenhagen and Malmö, our escort boat slowed down. Its captain saluted us and the Old Man thanked him through the megaphone. We were on our own.

(Room 40, Admiralty Old Building. *U-154* ledger)

Decrypted transmission: *16 February at 23.00 we dismissed* U-154 *at Lappa Grund Light House. Have turned back. Signed, Escort Boat.*

Room 40 has recorded a message sent by the *U-154*'s escort boat. There was nothing to record from Hermann himself because he kept silent. But the escort's message was enough. It told Room 40 that the mission of two long-range U-Boats aiming to disrupt British trade along the west coast of Africa had begun. Room 40 had known about the mission for months. They had been following both submarines and recording their messages, even while they were training in Kiel harbour. Following receipt of the 16 February transmission, the Admiralty wired relevant contacts (consuls and embassies) ordering an immediate but temporary halt to all shipments of gold bullion along the west coast of Africa, whether or not they were to be accompanied by convoys.

(Hinrichsen)

We entered The Sound, passing Hven island and Helsingør, and exited to see the Kullen lighthouse on the Swedish shore. The Gulf of Kattegat lay before us.

We worked four-hour watches, separated by four-hour rest periods. The last two watches of the day, the 'dog watches' were shorter. An erratic life it was, but it's surprising how quickly you get used to it.

In the North Sea, for fear of the British mine barrage, we sailed north, well within the safety of Norwegian waters. Once north of 60 degrees, we surfaced and changed course for the west. In the conning tower, the watch officers stood back to back, scanning the sea through their Zeiss binoculars, each turning a half circle on his own axis. The Old Man, aft of the conning tower, stared straight ahead. Now and again, when the glasses became clouded, they whipped pieces of chamois leather out of their pockets and wiped them. Then they resumed searching the horizon for those fateful smudges of smoke. Enemy shipping.

Night fell. A moonlit night. This was fine by us. The full moon acted as a searchlight, and we needed one because we had reached the area between Shetland and Scandinavia where a convoy route connected Britain with Archangel in Russia. If we spotted the smallest puff of smoke on the horizon, the cry went out, 'Diving stations!' Then came the piercing, bone-rattling noise of the alarm bell. Everyone on the conning tower hurled themselves at the open hatchway, clattered down the steel ladder and scrambled to their diving stations. Last of all came the Old Man. He jammed the iron hatchway closed behind him.

'Conning-tower hatch closed!'

'All hands at diving stations. All clear for diving,' yelled the Chief Engineer.

'Flood!' ordered the Captain.

Levers spun. The engineer gave the sign for petty officers to turn big hand wheels under the deck of the Control Room to open the vents. Compressed air in the tanks was driven out and sea-water poured in. The floor gently sank beneath our feet, and the boat tilted forward as the depth gauge needle rose.

A few feet down and the periscope was our only eye. In the dim glow of a single electric light, the commander stood on a pedestal in the Control Room, both hands on the periscope's handles. He gazed intently at the reflection of the scene above the surface. The helmsman in front of him stood at the wheel. The only noise was the quiet thump of the periscope as the captain adjusted it for height.

We had a few portholes, each with a heavy iron cover. If you raised this as you dived, you'd see a foaming mass of water crash over the bows. You'd see the forward deck gun disappear in a surge of chaotic eddies. But the deeper you went, the calmer the water became, until, at last, total calm. That's when the bow gun looked as if it was magically suspended in green light. Once below periscope level, the boat was blind. The compass and depth gauge were all we had to guide us.

'Take her down to five fathoms!' the captain would say, and down we went, ever further.

We'd have continued going down till we reached the bottom if it wasn't for the electric motors. They came to life and drove us forwards. Their beguiling hum replaced the roaring clank of the diesel engines. We were wafting our way through an ethereal underwater world.

The two trawlers we'd spotted were possibly the escort to some convoy. Once we'd given them time to disappear, the whole process was repeated in reverse order.

'Surface stations!'

And the boat rose slowly, bow first. We'd emerge, our guns draped with jelly fish, and seaweed strung like washing along the hawsers which connected our fore and aft short-distance wireless masts. As soon as we could, we opened the conning tower hatch, and fresh sea air swept through the boat. What joy. What pleasure.

At the northernmost tip of the Shetland Islands, a storm was brewing. Long rollers raced down on us, smashing onto the deck. Whenever they saw another massive rolling wave approaching, the watchmen, lashed in place, automatically ducked below the conning tower's low wall. It was terrifying, but also exhilarating, awe-inspiring. And it was far better than being down below. That's where glistening green faces told your eyes a story which your nose had told you as soon as you opened the hatch. The pitching and heaving of a U-Boat is far worse than that of a big ship.

That day, the storm was too much. We had to dive to escape it, and hours later, we resurfaced into a transformed world. The clear, northern sky was washed clean. Light mauve flecked with pink. The sea was pearl. Clouds of puffins winged their way over soft seas. Whales glided past towards the Faroe Islands, which rose to the far west. Beyond them, in the reddish glow of a setting sun, were the desolate Flannan Islands. And beyond these, the sudden high cliffs of St Kilda.

Sailors were on deck assessing the damage. The boom for lowering and raising the dinghy had been smashed and some upper deck railings bent. Otherwise nothing too serious. We celebrated. Cigars and cigarettes. In all the trip round the British Isles, apart from those trawlers in the far distance, we hadn't met a single British ship.

Right on time, nineteen days out at sea, we reached our pre-arranged meeting point off Cape Finisterre. It was 5 March 1918. A glorious sunny day. Blue skies and calm seas. Every man who could be out was up on deck, treading the warm boards in bare feet. We waved and cheered when we saw the crew of *U-153*. Meanwhile, the Old Man, wearing his regulation black leather jacket, jumped into a dinghy with a sailor and rowed over. He and Captain Goetting compared notes on storm damage and about how the boats had handled. Both agreed that the horizontal rudders were too small. They made it difficult to hold the ship steady at periscope level.[6] The two of them decided that, as far as possible, they would work together and keep within sight of each other. Co-operation would offset our individual weaknesses.

The first stretch of our plan was to sail south, along the Portuguese coast, past the Berlenga Islands (south of Porto and north of Lisbon). That's where we'd meet and confer again. The Old Man rowed back, and off we sailed, the *U-153* following in our wake. We saw Finisterre's lighthouse, then Silleiro's, then Montedor's. Lastly, the next day, we saw the lighthouse near Porto.

We met again, off the Berlenga Islands. The Old Man went on board *U-153* and together he and Commander Goetting decided that, starting from the north-east corner of the Azores' blockaded area, we would head south, towards the Canaries.[7]

This was it. The start of our mission proper.

Next day, our lookouts spotted a four-master on the horizon. We dived and approached at periscope level, surfacing when near. It was a handsome vessel flying the Norwegian flag.[8] We signalled for her to stop, and the captain brought his papers aboard. Her cargo was within the rules. Much relieved, we let her steam onwards. No one wanted to sink a fine old wooden ship like that! We took photographs.

Three days later, south of Gibraltar and off the coast of Africa, smoke smudges again on the horizon. We dived to periscope level. The Navigation

Officer, armed with a pair of compasses, a pencil, two set squares and a large sheet of paper, traced the course of the ship and checked his bearing apparatus. He calculated the ship's speed. The chase was on. Nerve-wracking hours were spent underwater as we positioned ourselves to challenge her. Our boat was silent as the grave. Every man at his post.

'She has a gun on deck. She has two guns, fore and aft!'

We surfaced and, since it was getting dark and she was still unaware of our presence, we fired a star shell.[9] But instead of stopping, she changed course and put on speed.

'She is flying the red ensign![10]

We dived again. No one moved. The bulkhead doors and the heavy iron hatches were closed tight. The gun crew waited in the wardroom and the torpedo men waited beside their brass, red-tipped eels. The most important question was the size and tonnage of this steamer. Would she be too quick for us? Were her guns bigger than ours? We kept a copy of Lloyd's Shipping Register to hand. As soon as we saw her name, we looked her up. The SS *Nellore*. She had a top speed which exceeded our own.

'*Los*!' (Fire!), says the Old Man, and two torpedoes were let loose. All eyes were on the second hand. Will we hear a dull, far-off crash?

Number One torpedo passed below her, the other close to her bows.

We had more luck next day, when we sighted an old Norwegian steamer, the *Nordkyn*. As soon as she was challenged she hove to. Her first officer brought her papers across. She was carrying wheat from Philadelphia to Italy via Gibraltar, which meant her cargo was destined to support the enemy.[11] We ordered the crew into lifeboats and sank her with gunfire.

It was five days before we sighted anything further. The next one was a Spanish steamer, the *Guadalquivir*. She was carrying cotton, rubber and wax to an enemy port. We took some of her rubber and wax on board, thinking it might be useful back home. Her crew took to the lifeboats and made for the coast. She too went down with gunfire.

(Shipping News)

The SS *Nellore*, 6,853 tons, was a British passenger/cargo liner, built in Greenock in 1913. She was the last of eight sister ships in what was known as the 'N'-class, ships owned and operated by the Peninsular and Oriental Steam Navigation Company (P&O). She encountered *U-154* on 11 March 1918. She was eventually sunk by a Japanese submarine in 1944. *Nellore* may have been the first ship to report the whereabouts of the *U-154* to London.

The *Nordkyn*, 3,244 tons, a Norwegian cargo steamer, was built in Stockton-on-Tees in 1895. She was sunk by the *U-154* on 12 March 1918. I do not know if there were any casualties.

The SS *Guadalquivir*, 2,078 tons, a Spanish cargo steamer built in 1897 in Sunderland, was carrying steel billets, rubber, wax and cotton from New York to Genoa and was sunk by *U-154* on 17 March 1918. There were no casualties.

(Room 40)

On 11 March, following intelligence gathered by Room 40, a telegram went out to Gibraltar: 'U-154 *may be expected in position 34N 10W on March 13th.*' Hermann had not signalled his position. But some other ship obviously had. Possibly the *Nellore.*

Hermann had to take for granted that every ship that sighted him, whether challenged or not, would send a message back to London giving the U-Boat's location. A Danish ship, for example, reported to Gibraltar that it had been stopped by what was almost certainly the *U-154*. It described the dimensions and appearance of the submarine and then gave this description of two officers: 'Captain short, thick-set, dark, spoke English. Second Officer tall, well-built, red hair and moustache.'[12]

The news was instantly relayed to the Admiralty in London.

(Hinrichsen)

18 March. Leaving the blockaded area, we met the *Chincha*, an American ship, armed and modern (therefore speedy). We surfaced, but she did not respond to our signals. Instead, a heavy artillery battle ensued. She suffered considerable damage but it wasn't good for us either, not because of the skill of her gunners, but because the breech block on one of our own after-guns flew out and backfired on being opened. We lost three men. The *Chincha* limped off and made for the coast.

We continued south till we came to the Cape Verde Islands.[13] These, like the Azores, are Portuguese, within the Allied fold and surrounded by a blockaded area. Our wireless officer intercepted a message from a Portuguese warship warning all shipping that an enemy submarine had been sighted. They were onto us.

On our way to our third rendezvous with *U-153*, we stopped an old Portuguese wooden schooner, the *Beira Alta*. Her captain told us she was carrying saltpetre to an enemy port. Her crew escaped in lifeboats, but before planting explosives on her, our boarding party loaded the jolly boat with bacalao,[14] soap and cigarettes. Not to take home this time, but for us.

(Shipping News)

The *Chincha*, 6,371 tons, a US cargo steamer, was built in Sunderland in 1912. She met *U-154* on 21 March 1918. Four of her crew were killed in this encounter.[15] The *Beira Alta*, 101 tons, a wooden Portuguese cargo schooner built in Portugal in 1893, was carrying saltpetre and general cargo from Lisbon to Madeira. She met *U-154* on 26 March 1918. I do not know if there were any casualties.

(Hinrichsen)

The third rendezvous took place on 28 March, off Boa Vista Island in the Cape Verde group. We would sail together to the Bijagós Archipelago, off Guinea Bissau and there separate. *U-153* would sail north to lay mines off Dakar, while we sailed south to attack the French wireless station in Monrovia.

Then we intercepted a message from Porto da Praia: 'Enemy submarines seen today.'

Off the coast of Guinea Bissau, our commanders held a fourth meeting. Commander Goetting would cut submarine telegraph cables off Bathurst and running past the Bolama and Orango Islands, in the Bijagos archipelago. We'd cut cables off Freetown, Sierra Leone. After a brief initial success, we lost our grappling hooks. So did the *U-153*. Not much luck there! But we both laid our mines without any problem.

(Room 40)

12 April: Admiralty telegram to Dakar:

> *Most Secret. Notbywit.*[16] *Submarine attack may shortly be expected in the vicinity of Sierra Leone and possibly along the coast of Guinea. Cruise of the 'Bacchante'*[17] *should be abandoned.*

Room 40 talks about an 'attack', but actually, *U-154* and *U-153* were, at this point in the business of cable-cutting and mine-laying.

(Hinrichsen)

The next ship we met was the armed French steamer, *La Bruyère*. A tugboat was towing her towards Dakar. On sighting us, the boat fired, so we dived and let loose two torpedoes. It was about 14.30 on a bright, sunny day and the water was clear. The crew on *La Bruyère* could see the bubbles on our bronze eels as they sped towards them. But both torpedoes missed. One passed between the boat and the tug, and the other just under the rudder. So we moved to place ourselves with the sun behind us and resurfaced. We were about to use the deck cannon, but before we could fire a shot, the tugboat dropped its tow line and fled. At the same time, the crew of *La Bruyère* lowered her lifeboats. They also fled.

(Shipping News)

La Bruyère, 2,198 tons, a French sailing boat built in Nantes in 1899, was sailing from Melbourne to Dakar when she met *U-154* on 7 April 1918. She was later found abandoned, about 160km off the coast of Senegal. Her lifeboats were within sight of shore when they were spotted by a tug and towed for the last part of their journey. There were no casualties.

During a later hearing related to taking possession of the wreck, the second in command of *La Bruyère* claimed that the *U-154* had fired first and that his own crew had heroically returned thirty shots with their cannon. But then, he explained, perhaps too carefully, the port gun seized up, while the starboard one was out of range. So they decided to abandon ship. This hearing was followed by a French commission of inquiry. Its report described a different state of affairs. It said that *La Bruyère*'s guns were not out of action and that the flight of crew and captain had been precipitate. The judge's comment? '*Le capitaine a totalement manqué de sangfroid.*' (The captain completely lost his nerve.)[18]

The difference between Hinrichsen's report and that of the crew of *La Bruyère* is a reminder that, in war, the side which is ultimately victorious is free to interpret battles in whichever way shows them in the best light. This happened again, when Hermann arrived off Liberia.

(Hinrichsen)

We were on our way to shell the wireless and cable station in Monrovia when we came across an armed motor boat, the *President Howard.* We took off the crew and sent them ashore in a lifeboat with a letter for their President asking him to evacuate the wireless and cable stations which we would be targeting. We sank the *Howard.*

Liberia lies between Sierra Leone and the Ivory Coast. The country's one gunboat was named after the President, *President Howard.* Hermann's orders were to destroy the wireless and cable station in Monrovia, built by Germany and run by Germans, until very recently. But Hermann didn't want to harm any innocent civilians so he first asked the President to clear the station. In the correspondence which followed, it is clear that Hermann thought he was talking to the President of Liberia, but he wasn't. He was, in effect, talking to Woodrow Wilson, President of the United States. As each of Hermann's letters arrived, Richard Bundy, the US chargé d'affaires, standing at President' Howard's elbow, relayed Hermann's messages to the State Department in Washington and asked what to do.

Hermann's appearance was misreported from the start. A Reuters news story on 15 April 1918 reads:

> Reuters Agency learns that on Tuesday last, a German submarine appeared off the coast of Liberia (the negro republic on the West Coast of Africa) and seized the small armed Liberian vessel *President Grant* [sic]. Those on board were taken prisoners and the vessel sunk. On the following day, the German commander dispatched the Liberian crew with an ultimatum to the Liberian Government in which he threatened that failing the dismantling of the wireless station and the closing of the French cable office, the town of Monrovia would be bombarded.

The name of the boat is wrong. So is the claim that Hermann threatened to bomb the town. He pointed out that in his opinion Monrovia was vulnerable, but his threat is to shell the wireless station without the station being first evacuated, not to bomb Monrovia.

Hermann's first letter reads:

> Sir,
> I have no wish to do any unnecessary damage to the Liberian people, being sure that you were driven into this war against your true interests, therefore I return the prisoners I took from your armed ship the *President Howard*. At the same time, I draw your attention to the fact that the capital of Liberia is, at present, helpless under German guns. Like many others, in this moment of critical danger, you find that neither England nor France are offering you any support. If the wireless and cable stations of Monrovia do not cease their work at once, I regret that I shall be obliged to open fire on them. If you wish to avoid this, you will send me a boat bearing the white flag of truce, and declare that you intend to stop the station yourself.
> Your obedient servant,
> Gercke
> Kapitän Leutnant und Commandant S.M.U. Kreuzer U.[19]

The fact that Hermann wrote at all bears witness to his almost painful adherence to Eckernförde rules and his own too. He and his crew would have been far safer if they had bombarded the station and left, without trying to talk to anyone first. In this case, with a wireless transmitter station as the target, he was putting himself and his crew in extra danger. The station would be used to summon help and Hermann well knew it. The *U-154*'s wireless operator tried to jam transmissions, but he wasn't successful, since Bundy sent two reports to the Secretary of State in Washington.

Delaying till the last minute, President Howard finally replied to Hermann's first letter by asking, rather coyly, how he was to stop the station from functioning.

At 9.17a.m., Hermann wrote again. A note of tetchiness has crept in:

> *Extrême urgence, dernier ultimatum.* I have the honour to acknowledge receipt of your answer to my note this morning. Being sure of your earnest goodwill to comply with my demands, I will not open fire on the cable and wireless stations which I was in the act of doing when, just in time, your boat was sent out. I am glad to be able to do so because my gunfire might have hurt innocent people. I put forward the following demands:
>
> (1) The French flag is to be removed from its current site
> (2) All the houses belonging to the wireless and cable stations are to be set on fire and the apparatus in each station destroyed
> (3) Points one and two are to be executed within one hour of your emissaries reaching shore.
>
> I have the honour to be, Sir, your obedient servant,
> Gercke,
> Kapitän Leutnant und Commandant S.M.U. Kreuzer U.

Hermann wisely put a time limit on the President's response. Bundy complied, but only partially. They evacuated the stations, but that was all. They were playing for time, waiting for rescue.

The chargé d'affaires cabled Washington:

> The Liberian Government has not yet given its final answer to these demands but, in any case, it looks as if the wireless and cable stations at Monrovia will be put out of commission accordingly. This is probably the last message I will be able to send the Department. It is urgently requested that assistance be sent at the earliest possible moment.

At 4.00 that afternoon (none too soon), Hermann's patience ran out. The *U-154* shelled the site and, according to Bundy, two people were killed and two wounded. Accounts of the occasion today not only claim that Hermann threatened to bomb Liberia's capital city but that he was responsible for the deaths. He wasn't. Bundy and Washington were responsible.

By the time Hermann lost his patience, the SS *Burutu*, an armed British ship, was heading his way.

(Hinrichsen)

Not surprisingly, as we sailed north towards Freetown we met a British armed steamer. She was flying the red ensign. We dived and fired two torpedoes. They missed. We changed position, surfaced and an hour-long artillery battle took place during which the *Burutu* took two hits. In the end, the ship, as so often happened, being faster than our own, escaped back to Freetown. Fortunately, no losses on our side.

(Shipping News)

The *President Howard*, a 73-ton Liberian warship built in Hamburg, was named after the Liberian President, Daniel Edward Howard. She had a crew of twenty-six men who, as Hinrichsen reported and Hermann's letter to the President confirms, were freed and returned unharmed to Liberia, together with Hermann's message. The boat was scuttled on 9 April 1918.

SS *Burutu*, 3,863 tons and built in 1902 in Glasgow, was an armed British cargo/passenger steamship. She belonged to the Elder Dempster & Co. line and had in 1914 operated as a special service vessel for the British government and, later, as an army transport. In 1918, she was said to be carrying palm oil, kernels, tin ingots and copper from Lagos to Liverpool. In her battle with the *U-154*, the *Burutu* was holed only half a metre above her waterline, and she lost two men. Time and again, Hinrichsen reported that the *U-154*'s torpedoes missed their mark. Both Hermann and Goetting found their torpedoes unreliable. Goetting wrote that his torpedoes took an 'irregular' course, veering to one side or to the other.

(Room 40)

12 April, Admiralty telegram to the Royal Navy's 9th Cruiser Squadron (off the Gold Coast):

> Notbywit. Secret
> *We have reason to believe that an enemy submarine will continue to operate to the westward of Sierra Leone and to the westward of Dakar for the present.*

Convoys were warned to take special routes to avoid contact with the two U-Boats. On 21 and 22 April, Room 40 noted that the German signalling station in Nauen had sent the following messages to *U-153* and *U-154*:

> It is reported that a Brazilian convoy of troops is taking place on a former German steamer from a Brazilian port to France.
> It is reported that an important convoy will sail from Dakar to Marseilles on 24 April.

U-154 and the *U-153* never saw either of these convoys. Either the information was incorrect or the convoys were delayed or re-routed.

(Hinrichsen)

We reached the southernmost limit of our trip when we were off Monrovia. Hurrah! We were now on our way home. Euphoria enveloped everyone on the submarine except the Old Man. He became more cautious than ever. He said we mustn't let down our guard. The last bit of any journey is a risky moment.

Our commanders met for the fifth time. Commander Goetting reported that he had sighted a large three-masted steamer (one funnel), about 7,000 tons, off the West African coast, near Sierra Leone. It looked like the *Carisbrook Castle*, one of the Union Castle Line's mail and passenger ships. He was preparing to challenge it when he realised it was 'correctly painted' as a hospital ship. He broke off the attack but was left wondering what a hospital ship was doing in these waters. When we heard about this, we all wondered. Are the British moving troops in hospital ships? No one knew for sure. The *U-153* didn't stop the ship to inspect it. They didn't want to reveal their presence.

The Old Man and Commander Goetting decided that, for our return journey, it would be safest to keep even closer together. We would sail abreast, 10nm apart by day and fewer at night. The *U-154* would take the inside course. And so we sailed northwards, just off the African coast. Past Cape Blanco, then up to Cape Corveiro and Cape Bojador.[20]

The Canary Islands, like the Azores, stand at a junction of trans-Atlantic and north-south trade routes. We hoped to see lots of shipping, but we didn't. On our way north, we only came across the *Michelet*, a three-masted French sailing vessel. We challenged her. Her crew got into lifeboats and headed for shore. We scuttled the ship. That was on 21 April. Some days later, on 25 April, we heard that a Japanese merchant steamer, the *Kawachi Maru*, had struck one of the mines we had laid off Sierra Leone.

(Shipping News)

The *Michelet*, 2,636 tons, a French sailing boat built in 1902 in Saint-Nazaire, was scuttled on 21 April 1918.

The *Kawachi Maru*, 5,749 tons, a Japanese cargo steamer built in 1897 in Glasgow, hit one of the mines the crew of *U-154* had laid. She returned to Japan for repairs.

The *Carisbrook Castle*, 7,626 tons, built in Glasgow in 1894 by the Fairfield Shipbuilding and Engineering Company, was one of the Union Castle Line's passenger and mail ships. She plied the Cape Town route but was commandeered during the war as a hospital ship bringing soldiers wounded on the Western Front home to England. Later, she worked as an Army Troop Ship in the Mediterranean. I can find no record of her sailing the Cape Town route in 1918, nor do I know if she kept her hospital ship designation even after taking on work as a troop ship.

(Hinrichsen)

Our wireless operator reported a message from Bathurst. 'Two enemy submarines reported off El Hierro Island on the afternoon of 21 April.' They are onto us again.

That's when the trouble started – trouble which took me out of the war. We saw an armed merchant steamer accompanied by a tug. She was flying the Australian flag. This was just off Cape Blanco. We surfaced and fired a warning shot but the steamer took no notice. Instead it lowered screens on deck to reveal rows of conspicuously long cannon fore and aft, with a team of gunners lying beside each. They started firing at us and taking a zigzag, defensive course. We radioed *U-153* who was to the south of us, to warn her. She surfaced so that now the enemy lay between the two of us. We both fired at her and she fired at both of us, from her fore and aft guns simultaneously.

The name on the steamer read the *Bombala* which, according to our Lloyds Register, was an Australian vessel, but this was no Australian ship. She was sailing under a false flag. This was one of the Royal Navy's infamous Q-ships, military ships disguised as merchantmen. Her true name was *Willow Branch* and she was manned by Royal Navy servicemen. A British ship. And a largely British crew.

(Shipping News)

The real *Bombala* was built in 1904 in Sunderland, a merchantman which sailed as a passenger steamship along the coast of Australia. The false flag *Bombala* was actually a 3,314-ton converted collier, built in 1892 in Sunderland. She carried a crew of around seventy-eight men. Her captain was Lieutenant Cecil Henry Mee, Royal Navy Reserve (RNR), the second-in-command was Lieutenant Bernard Anderson, RNR. Also on board was Sub-Lieutenant Eric Hugh Allan, RNR.

On 25 April 1918, probably alerted to the presence of U-Boats, the *Willow Branch* met *U-154* off the Cape Verde islands and started firing. Warned by *U-154* of what was happening, *U-153* advanced from the south, and Lieutenant Mee found himself facing two submarines. This was not the scenario for which he had been trained. Q-Ships were supposed to act out scenes of panic to lure a single boat nearer to them. With a submarine on either side, the 'show' would be exposed for what it was. A two-hour battle ensued. During the fight, the greater part of the *Willow Branch*'s crew were killed and the ship herself was severely damaged, but the two submarines suffered little. The fact that the Q-Ship resisted so long was at worst reckless stubbornness or at best blind heroism. Goetting described Mee's approach as 'tenacious'. The captain of the tug, the *John O'Gaunt*, cut the tow line and fled.

At the end of it all, one *Willow Branch* officer, Sub-Lieutenant Eric Hugh Allan, brought the wounded Captain Mee alongside *U-154* in a lifeboat. The other three lifeboats, loaded with survivors, set off for shore. Two of them disappeared, while the third, with only twenty-five men on board, drifted for four days before being picked up by a tug. Some of them had gone mad from drinking sea water, some had died, and only two survived to make landfall near the mouth of the Senegal River.

Meanwhile, *U-153* gave the *Willow Branch* its *coup de grâce*, while Allan and the wounded Mee, defiant to the last, were taken on board *U-154*. Although undamaged in the battle, *U-154* had suffered a second severe blow. In March, Hermann had lost three men, now he lost eight. He described it in one of his rare telegrams to Nauen: 'As a result of the careless loading of a No. 1 shell, an explosion occurred owing to which eight men were killed and two wounded.'

Hinrichsen was one of the wounded. As soon as he could, Hermann stopped a passing Spanish steamer by firing a star shell across her bows. It was the *Achuri* and she was carrying rice from India. He asked her captain to take Gunner Böttger and Able Seaman Hinrichsen on board and drop them off at the military hospital in Las Palmas, Gran Canaria. Making the best of a bad situation (as always), Hermann also asked for five bags of rice and gave the Captain two letters, one for Winnie and one for his parents. Both letters arrived long after Hermann had died.

In her letter, Winnie learnt about the fight with the *Bombala*. She learnt that Hermann had taken two Englishmen on board and that Mee was truculent and difficult. In the letter to his parents, Hermann popped in a photo of the glorious Norwegian three-master which the *U-154* had met on the first day of their mission. It was the kind of boat his father knew well.

With Hinrichsen now out of the picture, Gernot Goetting takes up the story:

(Goetting)

After the fight with the Q-ship, the whole course of our adventure changed. We held our sixth rendezvous on 26 April, shortly after the *Bomabala/ Willow Branch* battle. I went on board Hermann's ship, bringing with me four of my crew to make up for some of those he had lost.

We decided that *U-154* would lead *U-153* in line formation, heading directly for the Canary Islands. During the day, we would keep about 9nm [nautical miles] apart (which meant we could still see each other), and we'd lie closer at night. A message from Germany told us that Hermann and I had both been promoted to the rank of Korvettenkapitän.

We rendezvoused again on 3 May, our seventh meeting. It was a hot, sunny, tropical day. Our crews went up on deck. Men sat with their feet in the water. They stretched their almost naked bodies out on the hot boards. Some just stood around, yelling messages to their mates on the other boat. We decided to head northwards, to the blockaded area around the Azores. I went aboard *U-154* on 7 May for our eighth meeting, held at my request. I was having trouble with one of my diesel engines and needed to borrow spare pistons. Hermann gave me two. We agreed to continue in line formation with *U-154* in the lead. We would keep about 10nm apart by day and lie closer at night.

Hermann came on board for our ninth and last meeting at 6.00 am on 8 May. I told him that I had been receiving messages from Nauen. Nauen had given us new orders. Before setting out on our return journey, we were to rendezvous with the Kreuzer [Cruiser] U-Boat, *U-62*. We were to hand over spare fuel and any remaining torpedoes. I also told him about numerous contacts I had been having with *U-62*, a swift, easy-to-manoeuvre, fighter submarine. It was under the command of a loquacious and rather swashbuckling figure of a man, Ernst Hashagen.[21] During his exchanges with me, Hashagen had asked me, several times, to repeat the exact coordinates for our rendezvous. I had also received several messages from Nauen asking me to report our positions. I was beginning to feel very uncomfortable indeed. I knew Hermann's views. We had often discussed the possibility that the British had broken our codes. Hermann traced it back to the loss of the *Magdeburg*. No one was ever sure what had happened. Had the code books been destroyed or not? We just couldn't be sure, but one thing we did know for certain was that directional findings could locate a boat through its wireless messages. That's why we kept signalling to a minimum. He far more than I.

Hermann was dismayed at the news about the *U-62*. I knew he would be. He pointed out that it would be foolish to hand over fuel when neither of us knew how much we needed for the return journey. As for handing over torpedoes, how could we do that at sea? I suggested that we sail to a nearby island with the encouraging name of Deserta Grande, but of course, even that was risky. Someone might see us. And anyway, all these new plans were playing havoc with our own schedules. We agreed we would meet to discuss the situation with *U-62* at Lat 36°45N, Long 12W.

(Room 40)

The noose was tightening. Intercepts were coming in thick and fast showing Room 40 and the Admiralty Intelligence Division that there was about to be a meeting of German submarines at a specific location. The temptation was too much. Up to now, the Admiralty had always kept its hand hidden. No direct attacks. It was about to change its policy.

26 April radio message intercept from Nauen to *U-153*: *Report as soon as possible whether you have received order for returning to the barred zone of the Azores, and at the same time, cite your position and results as well as those of* U-154. U-62 *will arrive in the barred zone of the Azores in the middle of May.*

7 May radio message intercept from Nauen to *U-153*: U-62 *will arrive in the barred area about 10 May.* U-153 *is to arrange to meet* U-62 *then* U-153 *is to occupy the area south of Madeira or south of the Azores.* U-62 *to occupy the area west of Gibraltar, the eastern part of the barred area.*

9 May radio message intercept at 4.50 from *U-153* to *U-62*: *Meeting place will be 36.45N 12.00W.*

10 May radio message intercept at 22.30 from *U-62* to *U-153*: *Shall be at the rendezvous at 1800 on Saturday (11th). Request agreement. Signed,* U-62.

10 May radio message intercept at 22.50 from *U-153* to *U-62*: *Agree. Am coming from the south with* U-154 *in scouting line: 10 miles part.*

Telegram 9 May from the Admiralty to Gibraltar 11.32 am: *Priority. Clear the Line, Most Secret. Two enemy submarines are expected to meet about noon on 11 May in Lat. 36°45N, Long. 12W. Make every effort to send* J1 *and* E35 *to intercept them.*

(Goetting)

When Hermann left that last time, for some reason, I took out my camera, I don't know why. I took a photo of him as he left in the little dinghy, a sailor at the oars and Hermann's leather jacket on the seat behind him. He is looking back at me and smiling. He reached his boat safely, and we both sailed off, in line formation. He in the lead. He always was.

It is difficult for me to recount the events that followed. I feel so guilty. I called Rugia [a radio receiver station on board a ship in Germany] to report our position and tonnage sunk. They didn't understand, so I repeated the message. I also signalled the meeting site to Hashagen. If only I hadn't exchanged so many messages with Hashagen. He was having ridiculous trouble working out where to meet us and, even then, he arrived late. It turned out that one of his lookouts reported seeing 'white stars' on the horizon, so he took a 20-minute detour to check it out. Unbelievable. The 'white stars' turned out to be spray from a pod of whales shimmering in the sunlight. Curiosity satisfied, Hashagen deigned to resume his course, only now he was heading for a rendezvous which he knew he would never make in time. He also knew that he was demanding that two slow and difficult-to-manoeuvre submarines hang around and wait for him.

On 11 May at noon, Hermann and I exchanged blinker signals. All was on course for our meeting with *U-62*. Hermann arrived first. It was around 4.00 pm. We were at Latitude 36°45′N, 12°36′W.

I could see *U-154*. She lay tranquil on the surface of a shining sea. Then, boom! A massive explosion, a flash of flame. This was instantly followed by a huge column of water surging upwards, like a geyser. A dense cloud of black smoke sat on top of it. My lookouts gasped. I gasped. My blood ran cold.

We saw an enemy submarine surface, a British E-class. It sat there for a second or so. Both he and I could see flotsam and jetsam from the explosion and two or three men floundering in the water – Hermann and two lookouts? But we could also see each other, so we both dived, abandoning the survivors to their fate. There was no choice.

My mind and my will separated. I signalled *U-62*: 'Danger. Enemy submarine!' But my mind was floundering in the water with Hermann. To tell the truth, I feel as if I have been floundering ever since.

It was almost impossible not to conclude that, since the enemy submarine, the *E-35*, was in exactly the right place at exactly the right time, our code had been compromised. Here surely, at last was absolute proof of what Hermann and I had so often discussed. Yes. The enemy had broken our code.

When Hashagen saw the enemy submarine, he dived, as I did. And we both stayed under for as long as we could. On 13 May, we surfaced and positioned ourselves within hailing distance. I told him that I had two torpedoes left, but no spare fuel.

Hashagen replied, somewhat acidly, that that being the case, the whole exercise had been pointless. Without more fuel, his mission would have to be curtailed and therefore he wouldn't need the extra torpedoes. So there we were. A pointless exercise which cost many lives, including that of my good friend Hermann. I find this almost as difficult to digest as the memory of the column of water, the black cloud and the floundering men.

We limped home with our stricken engines, down at heart and nervous. Nauen warned us that the minefields in the North Sea were worse than ever. Normally, when a returning U-Boat arrives home, the docks are decorated with garlands, a band plays, a cheerful crowd gathers and happy sailors cheer with joy and relief. When we came into dock that day, my men stood on deck in silence. They did not cheer. We could scarcely smile. No one shouted, 'Hurrah'.

(Room 40)

E-35, captained by a Guy d'Oyly-Hughes[22] was waiting for the *U-154* on its own. The *J1* was not deployed. His first torpedo missed, but *U-154* could not manoeuvre quickly enough to get out of the way of the second, which hit the U-Boat's torpedo room. Hence the massive explosion.

Telegram, 11 May from the Admiralty to the Gold Coast: *Bullion shipments from Secondee*[23] *should be resumed and transmitted to England as soon as circumstances permit.*

Telegram, 13 May from the Admiralty to the C-in-C, 9th Squadron, the Cape: *Shipments of bullion to United Kingdom are to commence forthwith at the rate of three to four millions per month, under the same conditions as before (i.e. with escort ships).*

(Goetting)

When I got home my first duty after seeing my own family, was to visit first Hermann's parents and then his wife. They knew of course, but how was I to describe it to them? There were two things I would never mention. That I saw three men floundering in the water. And that the *U-62*'s captain had remarked, 'What a bit of luck that the whales were there with their "white stars". Otherwise Germany might well have lost more than one submarine that day.'

* * *

The thought of Hermann's death haunted Goetting for the rest of his life. In a daze of grief and anxiety, he managed to pick his way through the minefields to reach home. On 3 June 1918, *U-153* made fast alongside SMS *Mecklenburg* in Kiel harbour. Many among the *U-153* crew were awarded Iron Crosses in recognition of their courage in enduring a four-month-long cruise.

Once the war was over, Goetting spent much time in the Admiralty archives, a sad and lonely man. He sought out Hermann's War Log Book, the one that ended on 16 February. Over the next few years, he added to it so that it also covered the period up to his death. He carefully stuck in press clippings on *U-154*'s exploits, and dated each addition. His last entry is dated 1941. I am told, through a friend of the Goetting family, that shortly after the Second World War began, he committed suicide. War does not end for the combatants, with the cessation of hostilities.

Goetting was right of course. Hermann's family knew the story long before he reached home himself. Philipp noted in his Family Chronicle:

> Was it the 12th or the 13th May when I came across a number of naval flying cadets? They were visiting the depot in Warnemünde to see the layout of our Navy aerodrome (complete with hangars and pilot accommodation). I also showed them my new wireless-based direction-finding equipment at the airport (Hermann and I had planned it together). They came to our apartment first, then we all drove together to the depot. On the way, one of the young men got out a newspaper. I glanced at it and saw a story about a battle off Gibraltar. It had been between an English submarine and two German cargo U-Boats. The English submarine had won. One of the two German boats exploded.
>
> My heart shrank. I said nothing. And I said nothing to Mila when I got home, but my spirit had drained out through the soles of my boots. About fourteen days later, a telegram arrived at the depot radio station. The telegraphist went pale when she read it. She handed it to me without a word. I too was silent. I walked home and gave it to Mila. We stood there, together, each consumed by shock and grief. We could not speak. We could not weep. There was nothing. Only the regular tick-tock of the clock on the kitchen wall. It ticked as if nothing had happened.

Winnie also noted the moment:

> There was a phone call from Frau Goetting. She asked if I had had any news of Hermann. She said she had recently heard that Gernot was all right and suggested I go to the navy depot and ask for news. Then she

hung up. I looked out of the window. I saw my father-in-law walking up the street. His head was down. His step heavy.

It was May. The world could not have looked more beautiful. The sky was bright blue. Cotton wool clouds floated by, exactly as they do in children's picture books. The trees were in new leaf. Blackbirds sang. I stood on the balcony, watching my father-in law coming closer to our house.

Even now, all these years later, when I hear the blackbirds sing after winter, I live that moment. I am standing on that balcony, one hand on the iron railing. Overhanging branches from the lime trees in the street brush against my cheek. Their tiny young leaves are creased, just like a new born baby's palms. Inside me, little Ingrid gives a sudden kick. This is how it is. Beginnings and endings. They are all connected.

The happiest days of my life were spent with Hermann.

Chapter 26

Victory of Another Kind

Many years later, 'little Ursula' was a 72-year old woman living in England. She had spent most of her life speaking foreign languages. First French in Lausanne (Winnie moved the family to Switzerland in the 1920s). Then English in Kent. Wherever she was, she kept her father's photo on her bedside table. In terms of the time she spent with him, she scarcely knew her father. In terms of his importance in her life, he was her guiding star. And all this without ever having read the books I unearthed which mention him, the testimonies I read, the log books, the letters, the archive material. Her love for her father and his for her were things she was sure of. She must have felt it when he carried her as a baby, or when, aged two, she sat on his lap in that deck chair in the garden in Borby. Her image of him had carried her through life. Her inner strength came from him. Perhaps this is what they mean when they say, 'He did not die in vain.' His valiant death helped her, and more besides. Me, for one.

I took her to see, for the first time in her life, the Mariners' Memorial in Laboë, near Kiel. It is a tall brick tower, built like the prow of a ship. It stands on the south shore of the *Kieler Bucht* (Bay of Kiel) and faces northwards, out to sea. Before reaching it, driving along that south bank, we came across another, unexpected, memorial. This one was for submariners only. It consisted of a series of walls lined with metal plaques. Each plaque gave the number of the U-Boat and the name of its captain, with a list of crew names following. We walked along a paved path at the foot of the walls. There it was. *U-154.* We stopped and read it. Her father's name.

A short, paunchy old man came up behind us, the guardian of the memorial. For some reason, he made me think of the porter guarding Macbeth's castle. Do you remember the scene? Duncan has just been horribly murdered. His body is somewhere in the castle, but the comic old porter who goes to answer the knocking at the door has no idea. He shuffles. So did our man. He mumbles. So did our man. He was guarding a terrible truth. So was ours. He talked wisdom. So did ours.

My mother looked at him, pointed at her father's name, and said, 'My father. Now I live in England. My daughter lives in Canada. *Es war alles umsonst* (It was all pointless).'

She stopped herself. Why was she was babbling to a stranger?

Shakespeare's porter looked at her. '*Nichts ist umsonst* (Nothing is pointless)', he said firmly.

I don't remember what happened next. Did he disappear? Maybe he did. But his words stayed behind. I will always remember them.

Bereft, we returned to the car.

The next place was much grander. A cathedral as opposed to a church. We crossed a huge open courtyard. This memorial is for all seamen, but the two world wars are the object of everyone's attention. Each is treated separately. 35,000 seamen died in the First World War, 120,000 in the Second. There were a few people visiting, alone or in small groups. Each was wrapped in thought. So were we. We climbed the stairs to a balcony, where we found two books of remembrance, one for each war. The one on the right was ours. The First World War. One page per boat. It was in a glass case. Locked. And there it was. Open. We leaned over it.

'*Unterseeboot U-154. Hermann Gercke, Korvettenkapitän.*' The names of his crew followed.

Of all the boats that sank in the First World War, on the first and only day that Hermann's daughter visited, the book was open at the page with her father's name on it. Whenever I look back on that moment, I am in awe. She needed something, and it was given to her.

The inscription on the Tomb of the Unknown Warrior in Westminster Abbey reads in part: 'Thus are commemorated the many multitudes who, during the Great War of 1914–1918, gave the most that man can give, Life itself, for God, for King and Country, for loved ones, home and Empire, for the sacred cause of justice and the freedom of the world.' Grandfather didn't die for king or empire. He didn't die for a sacred cause, or for justice, or for freedom. He was on the wrong side. What did he die for then?

He died in part for his country. He stood the watch. He did his duty. But his duty extended also to his brothers, parents, wife and children. And above all it extended to himself. He was true to his own idea of honourable behaviour. Straight as a die, he got it right. So did many others. Mathy for example: 'We can only do our best.' Yes, you can be on the losing side, even on the wrong side, but still come out victorious. The victory is personal.

> This above all: to thine own self be true,
> And it must follow, as the night the day,
> Thou canst not then be false to any man.[1]

This book, Grandfather, is a minuscule thank-you. It is also a thank-you to Philipp, the diligent, humorous recorder; to Mila, that pillar of strength; to elegant Georg and staunch Waldemar; to indignant Winnie; to bereft Ursula. A sober celebration. A quiet victory. But nevertheless, a victory.

Notes

Introduction

1. 'Time became non-existent. To me, at any rate, it seems less real than space, though both are vague enough. The past is never quite the past.' Freya Stark, *The Lycian Shore*, 1956.
2. This was a German empire folk song (an adaptation of an even older song) which celebrated the independence of the northern Hansa port-cities, leading players in the life of the medieval, trade-orientated towns of the Hanseatic League. The first lines (which Ursula almost certainly did not sing) were, '*Hamburg, Lübeck, Bremen, die brauchen sich nicht zu schämen, denn sie sind eine freie Stadt, wo Bismarck nichts zu sagen hat.*' (Hamburg, Lübeck, Bremen. Proud cities, free cities, where Bismarck has no say).

Chapter 1

1. Hermann Philipp Gercke carried the same first name as his eldest son. To make the distinction clear, in this book, I call the elder man Philipp, and his son Hermann.
2. Ilya Repin (1844–1930), a contemporary of Philipp's, was a famous painter well known for his vivid portrayal of Russian peasants and their way of life. One of the engravings Philipp owned was *Barge Haulers on the Volga*, painted in 1873.
3. Wirballen was formerly part of the Russian Empire and is now Virbalis in Lithuania. It lay close to the border with Prussia and on a rail route built in 1861 from Vilnius to Königsberg, making it an important link between the Russian Empire and the Prussian. The town had large German and Jewish populations.
4. The Polish Uprising, 22 January 1863 – 8 June 1864, was an uprising in Russian-occupied Poland.
5. Königsberg is today Kaliningrad.
6. Ironclads were steam-propelled warships protected by iron. Isambard Kingdom Brunel's ship *Great Britain*, built in 1843, was the first to be built entirely of wrought iron.
7. Steel began to be used in ship-building from the 1880s, though it was not generally used in the construction of battleships till the Second World War.
8. The first steamship to cross the Atlantic was the *Savannah* in 1819.
9. From the 1900s, oil-fired engines began to replace the coal-fired engines of the early steam-ships.
10. Alfred Thayer Mahan (1840–1914), a United States naval officer and strategist, believed national greatness was inextricably linked with sea power and empire. He was particularly influential in Germany.
11. Louis XIII and Louis XIV took Elsass-Lothringen in stages during the seventeenth century and thereafter pursued 'francization' policies. Ethnic Germans were deported and ethnic French introduced. I call the provinces by their German name in this book, just to remind readers of this double heritage. They are of course, today officially known as Alsace-Lorraine.

12. The Battle of Sedan was fought between Prussia and France on 1 and 2 September 1871. It resulted in the German army capturing the French monarch, Napoleon III, as well as about 100,000 French troops. It effectively decided the war, though fighting continued, ending with the siege of Paris (19 September 1870 to 28 January 1871), when the people took a heroic stand against a professional army. The pattern set at this time led to the mistaken hope on the German side that France could again be conquered with a single decisive battle.
13. Friedrich Graf von Wrangel (1784–1877), also known as Papa, or 'Olle' Wrangel, was a tough nut both as a general and as a husband. He was governor of Berlin and Commander-in-Chief of Brandenburg during the riots of 1848–49, during which, for a short time he left the city, leaving his wife behind. Philipp refers in his Chronicle to the rumour that when he returned to Berlin 'as conqueror of his own people' on 9 December 1848, he asked his Adjutant, '*Ob sie sie wohl gehängt haben*?' (Had they hanged her?)
14. Albrecht von Roon (1803–1879) was a statesman, modernizer of the army and national hero. He played a key part in the victory over France in 1871.
15. Graf Helmuth von Moltke (1800–1891), another national hero and army modernizer, and also key to the 1871 victory, is often referred to as von Moltke the Elder to distinguish him from his great-nephew, Helmut von Moltke the Younger (1848–1916). The Younger was Wilhelm II's Chief of General Staff from 1 January 1906 till 14 September 1914 and is most remembered for his indecision. He was no national hero.
16. A carriage drawn à la Daumont was an elegant, open carriage without a coach box. It was drawn by four or more horses, ridden by mounted coachmen. This style, on fine days, allowed passengers to enjoy an unobstructed view, as well as allowing the crowd a good view of the passengers.
17. The Empress Augusta of Saxe-Weimar-Eisenach (1811–1890), wife of Wilhelm II.
18. This was an Englishwoman, Victoria or Vicky (1840–1901), Princess Royal, eldest daughter of Queen Victoria of England, and wife of the German Crown Prince, later Emperor, Friedrich III. Her eldest son was the Emperor Wilhelm I and her second eldest, Prince Heinrich.
19. Admiral Albrecht von Stosch (1818–1896), the grand old man of the German navy was originally a general in the army. He was appointed chief of the Admiralty when the Imperial German Navy was created in 1872.
20. The yard is a spar or mast from which sails are set. The royal yard is the smallest one at the top.
21. SMS (*Seiner Majestät Schiff*, His Majesty's Ship) was the prefix for Imperial German Navy vessels. For yachts, it is SMY. SMS *Arcona* has been variously described as a German warship, or war frigate, or war training ship. She was a three-masted, 2,400-ton ship built in 1858. Her captain for Philipp's journey was Freiherr von Reibnitz. As well as serving to train cadets, the journey from 1873 to 1875 was used for scientific research. Her greatest claim to fame is that she was one of the ships which took part in Prussia's first trade mission to Japan in 1859.

Chapter 2

1. Cixi, the Dowager Empress Cixi of China (1835–1908) was effective ruler of China from 1861 until her death.
2. See Cord Eberspächer, 'Arming the Beijing Navy, Sino-German Naval Cooperation 1879–1895', *The International Journal of Naval History*, April 2009, Vol. 8, No.1
3. The first major blow to the Chinese Empire came with the outbreak of the First Opium War (1839–1842), fought between China and Britain. The second (1856–1860) was

between China and Britain together with France. In each case, the foreign powers were victorious and as a result, gained commercial privileges and legal and territorial concessions from China. The conflicts ended with 'unequal treaties', exposing the weakness of the Chinese government and its inability to protect its people. The conflicts were called 'Opium Wars' because a key bone of contention was the insistence by some European countries that their merchants be allowed to sell opium in China. This undermined Chinese efforts to stamp out widespread addiction among its people.

4. In 1897 Germany managed to join the general land grab. The German Navy took the land around Kiautschou Bay, an area which was eventually granted to Germany on a ninety-nine year lease. The site was on the Shantung Peninsula. Its main city, Kiautschou, had previously been a small fishing village called Tsingtao. Germany invested huge sums in the area and in Kiautschou laid out wide streets, built solid housing and government buildings, installed electricity throughout, a sewage system and a safe drinking water supply. The territory had the highest density of schools and the highest per capita student enrolment in all of China. The protectorate was a source of great national pride in Germany. It seemed as safe as houses. It wasn't. All was lost when the Japanese invaded shortly after the First World War broke out in 1914.
5. Li Hongzhang (1823–1901) was a Chinese statesman, general and diplomat. He was Viceroy of the province of Zhili, a northern administrative region which included the capital of China and the port of Tientsin.
6. In 1859, a Prussian-organized trade mission, led by Friedrich zu Eulenberg, set out for Japan. One of the ships in that successful mission was SMS *Arcona*.
7. A better known German expression about a wife's role is *Kinder, Küche, Kirche* (children, kitchen, church). Philipp's version, while still definitely giving the wife a domestic role, suggests attributes rather than function. Much pleasanter.
8. Duelling was illegal in Germany at this time, but the law was rarely enforced. Duelling with pistols, even to the death, was accepted among the upper classes. It seems incredible that this challenge was serious, but from Philipp's reaction it seems that it was.
9. When war broke out, Guido von Usedom (1854–1925) was brought out of retirement and, since the German government feared an assault by the Allies on the Dardanelles, was seconded to the Turkish Navy and appointed Commander-in-Chief of the Straits. Together with the Turkish army, he successfully repelled the Allied invasion at Gallipoli.
10. From the poem by Johann Wolfgang von Goethe (1749–1832)

Freudvoll
Und leidvoll,
Gedankenvoll sein,
Langen
Und bangen
In schwebender Pein,
Himmelhoch jauchzend,
Zu Tode betrübt;
Glücklich allein
Ist die Seele, die liebt.

Full of joy,
Full of sorrow,
Thoughtful,
Yearning,

Trembling
In the anguish of uncertainty;
Buoyed by joy,
Flattened by grief.
Happy alone
Is the soul that loves.

11. *Marine Humoresken*, published by Deutsches Verlagshaus Bong & Co., Berlin and Leipzig, 1909, and various articles including a book of anecdotes on the Kaiser's *Nordlandreisen*. This last was written in Plattdeutsch to disguise its author and origin. It is now lost.
12. *Die Torpedowaffe, Ihre Geschichte, Eigenart, Verwendung und Abwehr*, published by Ernst Siegfried Mittler und Sohn Berlin, 1898 (and republished in 2012) and numerous articles on naval matters, especially in the naval reviews *Marine-Rundschau* and *Überall.*
13. Hermann/Arminius (18/17 BC – AD 21) was a Germanic chieftain who commanded an alliance of Germanic tribes at the Battle of the Teutoburg Forest in AD 9. The legions were reportedly marching in single file along a forest path and, starting at the rear, the forces of Arminius began to pick them off, without the vanguard of the column becoming aware of the attack until it was too late. Three Roman legions under the command of General Publius Quinctilius were destroyed. Arminius' victory precipitated Roman withdrawal from Germany east of the Rhine and is regarded as one of Rome's greatest defeats or, conversely, one of the Germanic people's greatest victories.
14. *Stein* was a Bismarck-class corvette with three masts and one funnel.
15. The Sino-French War (1884–85) ended with China ceding what is now central and north Vietnam to France.
16. Japan's targets were not modest. They included Taiwan, Kiautschou, Korea and Manchuria.
17. Kobe was an important Japanese port, and in 1890 there were about 2,000 foreigners, a good proportion of them German, living in its foreign quarter.
18. Halmahera Island, today part of Indonesia, is the largest of all the Maluku (fomerly Molucca) Islands in the Malay Archipelago. It lies roughly halfway between Borneo and New Guinea. It was once the centre of the spice trade and nearby lie numerous islands which were once the world's only source of nutmeg and mace. The area is also famous for its active volcanoes, translucent waters and palm-lined beaches. The Maluku Sea lies to the west of Halmahera Island, the Pacific Ocean to the east. The Banda Sea lies to the south, and south of the Banda Sea lies the Arafura Sea.
19. Ambon Island is part of the Maluku Islands in Indonesia.
20. Cooktown lies on the east coast of Queensland, close to its northernmost tip.
21. Germany's possessions in West Africa were recent. It had only gained control of German South West Africa the year before Philipp's trip, in 1884. In the same year, it established protectorates in Togo and Cameroon.
22. Port Louis is the capital of Mauritius, a British colony at the time of Philipp's visit.

Chapter 3

1. The first submarine, the *U-1*, docked in Kiel as part of the Imperial Navy in 1906.
2. The Kiel Naval School, founded in 1866, provided rigorous training for naval officers.
3. The Naval Academy, founded in 1872 by Admiral von Stosch, was a graduate school to prepare naval officers for higher duties in the Imperial Navy. The curriculum consisted of naval history and general educational courses. In addition, participants learned two modern foreign languages. Initially, the training lasted for three years but, beginning

in 1883 this was shortened to two. From 1888, the Naval Academy was in the same building as the undergraduate level *Marineschule* (Naval School). In 1910, the Academy moved to the Mürvik Naval School near Flensburg, where it still serves as the academy for the German navy.

4. Prince Heinrich von Preussen, the Kaiser's younger brother, lived in the official residence in Kiel Castle, but in 1894, after his marriage on 24 May 1888, he built himself an English-style manor in Hemmelmark, near Kiel. He popularized the sailor's cap which was named after him and was one of the founders of Kiel's Imperial Yacht Club. A keen aviator, he was one of the first Germans to qualify for a pilot's licence. He was also a keen motorist and, in his honour, a race, the precursor to the German Grand Prix, was established in 1908. In 1911, Vauxhall Motors produced a model called the Vauxhall Prince Henry. War put a stop to that particular model.
5. The three grandchildren on New Year's Eve 1886 were Thusnelda, Hermann and Georg.
6. The Emperor Friedrich III (1831–1888) was the only son of Wilhelm I. He had waited a long time before acceding to the throne. That time allowed for the formation of a pro-Friedrich clique around him and a bigger, stronger, anti-Friedrich clique around his eldest son Wilhelm, who eventually became Wilhelm II. There were plenty who disliked Friedrich because he openly criticized the highly conservative Chancellor Otto von Bismarck, a national hero, a founding father of the German Empire and a man close to the old Emperor Wilhelm I. One of the few things father Friedrich and his eldest son had in common was a dislike of Bismarck. Friedrich had married Victoria, or Vicky, eldest daughter of the Queen of England, for love. Both of them much admired Vicky's father, Prince Albert, and they shared many ideas for reform. These included replacing the office of Chancellor with a British-style cabinet. They supported religious toleration and once attended a synagogue service to demonstrate their support for the Jewish community. They also called for greater freedom of the press. In short, they did everything which put them out of favour with Wilhelm I's conservative supporters and those of their eldest son. Unfortunately for Friedrich (and perhaps for many others), by the time he acceded he was seriously ill with cancer of the larynx. He was called 'the ninety-nine-day emperor', dying only ninety-nine days after his accession. Even his illness caused ructions, because his eldest son, Wilhelm, blamed his mother, Vicky, for calling on an English doctor, Morell Mackenzie, to treat him. Mackenzie (with some others) came to the mistaken view that Friedrich did *not* have cancer, and Wilhelm II saw this as a wicked English plot against the House of Hohenzollern. As a result, Friedrich's last days, and the remaining life of his widow Vicky, were made all the more miserable by a lively feud with their eldest son. Friedrich's early death was a turning point in German history. A popular discussion point among historians is what would have happened if he had lived. The discussion is similar to that around Wilhelm II and his younger brother Prince Heinrich. What if Heinrich had been the heir, and not Wilhelm? Tantalizing but fruitless 'what ifs'.
7. Admiral Gustav Freiherr von Senden-Bibran (1847–1909) became Naval Adjutant to Wilhelm II in 1888 and, the following year, Chief of the German Imperial Naval Cabinet. His influence waned after Admiral von Tirpitz was appointed in 1897 to head the Imperial Naval Office. The two of them disagreed. Tirpitz wanted to build a fleet of big battleships, and von Senden-Bibran favoured light cruisers. The Tirpitz brigade won the argument. Senden-Bibran retired from the Naval Cabinet in 1906 and was succeeded by Georg von Müller, a man for whom Philipp had little time.
8. Friedrich Graf von Baudissin's (1852–1921) naval career flourished under Wilhelm II, though he retired early in 1909, having served on occasion as *Admiral à la suite* in Kaiser

Wilhelm II's entourage; that is to say, he carried the rank but not an official position. He was appointed *Chef des Admiralstabes* (Head of Admiralty Staff) and promoted to Admiral in 1908, just one year before he retired.

9. Ratty was one of the heroes in Kenneth Grahame's *The Wind in the Willows.*
10. Toad, another character in *The Wind in the Willows,* was known for his love of bragging.
11. The royal yacht *Hohenzollern I* had a coal-fired steam engine which drove two side-mounted paddle-wheels to propel the vessel. When steam, rather than wind-filled sails, was first used to propel ships, it was often used in combination with paddle-wheels, but in the late nineteenth century, paddle propulsion was superseded by the screw propeller. The old-fashioned nature of the first *Hohenzollern* must have been something of a thorn in the Kaiser's side because he was particularly keen on all things new in the shipping world, as evidenced by the number of ultra-modern racing yachts which he had built.
12. Commanders of the *Hohenzollern* often held office for very short periods. Prince Heinrich was appointed commander on 5 July 1888 and was replaced on 8 August. Obviously, the Kaiser wanted him in that position expressly for his first visits to foreign monarchs. On the whole, during the Kaiser's reign the main commander of *Hohenzollern* was Kapitän zur See Volkmar von Arnim. The boat was brought into service every spring (April/May), and manned with a reduced crew and another, less senior commander, over the winter period, which usually started in October.

Commanders of *Hohenzollern I*

5 July–8 August 1888	Korvettenkapitän Heinrich von Preussen
28 May 1889–December 1889	Kapitän zur, See Volkmar von Arnim
December 1889–March 1890	Kapitänleutnant Alfred Breusing (reduced crew)
April 1890–September 1890	Kapitän zur, See Volkmar von Arnim
September–16 December 1890	Kapitänleutnant Oskar von Truppel (reduced crew)
2 June 1891–September 1891	Kapitän zur, See Volkmar von Arnim
September 1891–April 1892	Kapitänleutnant Hermann Gercke (reduced crew)
April 1892–June 1892	Kapitän zur, See Volkmar von Arnim

13. Each summer, he spent two to three weeks on holiday, mainly in Norwegian waters. He often attended Cowes Week in the Isle of Wight, followed by some time with his grandmother, Queen Victoria, and Kiel Week. These excursions represented over a month on board each year, mainly in holiday mode. In addition, he used the yacht for foreign family and state visits. In 1889, to take one example, he was away on the yacht from October till December visiting different Heads of State.
14. Paulmann, J. (1999). *'Dearest Nicky...': Monarchical Relations between Prussia, the German Empire and Russia during the Nineteenth Century*. In Bartlett, R., Schönwälder, K. (eds), *The German Lands and Eastern Europe. Studies in Russia and East Europe*, Palgrave Macmillan, London.
15. At this time, Norway and Sweden were ruled by a single Swedish monarch. In 1905 this union was dissolved and Norway chose its own royal family.
16. This war, February to October 1864, was the second of two with Denmark over the Duchy of Schleswig-Holstein. It had been controlled by Denmark, but after the second war it was ceded to Germany.
17. King Leopold of the Belgians had claimed the Congo as his personal fiefdom in 1885 and had come under much criticism for doing so. His regime had a reputation for brutality, as portrayed in Joseph Conrad's *Heart of Darkness,* first published in 1899, ten years after Philipp's visit. The King must have been quite perturbed by the situation to

have raised it with an unknown foreign visitor. Perhaps the subject came up because Philipp had been to West Africa, though not to the Congo.

18. The Training Squadron was renamed the Manoeuvre Squadron in 1889. Summer/autumn manoeuvres were held by the fleet in Kiel every year.
19. Friedrich von Hollmann (1842–1913) was an admiral who became Secretary of State for the Imperial Naval Office but resigned in 1897. He opposed Admiral Tirpitz's policy of building a heavy battle fleet. He would have preferred a navy mainly of cruisers.
20. Kiel Week was first so-called in 1894. It is held in the last week of June.
21. 'Yachting in this country, as well as in Germany, is under a deep obligation to H.I.M. Wilhelm II.' *British Yachts and Yachtsmen*, published in 1907.
22. In a letter from the Kaiser to Sir Edward Mallet, 14 June 1889.
23. From the Kaiser's speech thanking Queen Victoria during his August 1889 visit.
24. The Warnow joins the Baltic Sea at Rostock. Philipp was, in a sense, looking out to sea.

Chapter 4

1. Empress Elisabeth of Austria and Queen of Hungary (1837–1898), also known as Sissi, was a beautiful young Bavarian brought up in a relaxed, informal household. She married Kaiser Franz Josef and found life close to impossible at his formal court in Vienna with his domineering and tactless mother. Her unhappiness was compounded when her only son committed suicide in 1889. After his death, she bought land in Corfu which was later sold to Wilhelm.
2. Trieste, an important port and naval centre, was the Austro-Hungarian Empire's fourth largest city. It was in Trieste and in the nearby port of Fiume (four kilometres away, now called Rijeka and in Croatia) that Robert Whitehead, an engineer from Bolton, Lancashire, developed the first self-propelled torpedo for the Austrian Imperial Navy.
3. This is quoted by Philipp as one of Stosch's favourite sayings. I have been unable to find any corroboration for Stosch's insistence on thrift, but it fits the character of the man who was the son of a Prussian general and had been brought up in the strict tradition of duty and service. Philipp's English daughter-in-law noted that Prussians were not naturally given to extravagance. She was surprised, on her arrival from Britain, to find that the evening meal, *Abendbrot*, was, more or less, exactly that: bread eaten at supper time (with gherkins and cold meats). Also, see Neil MacGregor, *Germany, Memories of a Nation* p.251 (Allen Lane, 2014): 'In Prussia the nation itself was personified in iron: no frippery, no nonsense. This was the Iron Nation.'
4. Full dress uniform.
5. King Umberto I (1878–1900) was the colourful King of Italy; authoritarian and a self-declared warmonger, he said of Crispi, who was accompanying him to that dinner on board *Kaiser*, 'Crispi is a pig but a necessary pig.'
6. Francesco Crispi (1893–1896) was another man with a colourful life (he was said to be a bigamist). Part liberal, part authoritarian, he was a prime mover in the unification of Italy and an admirer of Bismarck.
7. Siemens, the modern German technology conglomerate, was founded in 1847 with the formation in Berlin of the Telegraphen Bau-Anstalt von Siemens & Halske.
8. The Order of the Red Eagle, 4th Class (German), Officer's Service Cross, the Royal Belgian Order of Leopold, Knight of the Royal Order of the Netherlands Lion and the Imperial Russian Order of St Stanislaus, 2nd Class.
9. The Greek Order of the Holy Redeemer, the highest order of the Greek state that can be awarded to foreigners, still exists.

10. A *caïque* is a long, narrow wooden rowing boat, so shaped that it can be rowed in either direction without turning it around. It is traditional to the Bosphorus. In this case, the Kaiser was almost certainly sitting in one of the highly-decorated Imperial Caïques, which had a deck pavilion for the Sultan. They were used for ceremonial and daily excursions. The word can also refer to a fishing boat used in the Ionian or Aegean.
11. The Order of Medjidie was a high Ottoman honour offered to civilians and officers for distinguished service. It was first instituted by Sultan Abdulmejid I, hence its name.
12. Adelsberg, once part of the Austro-Hungarian Empire, is now Postojna, Inner Carniola, Serbia. It is famous for its vast, evocative and inspiring caves, full of stalactites dripping with water. These were visited by the Archduke Ferdinand in 1819 and, ever since, have been a popular tourist destination. A small railway for tourists was installed in 1872 and electric lighting in 1884.
13. Prince Louis of Battenberg (1854–1921), grandfather of the late Duke of Edinburgh, apparently exercised the same charm. Dedicated to a naval career but related to various warring royal houses across Europe, he had difficulty being accepted by any navy. He was royal, and no one was sure which side he would be on. He eventually found a sometimes reluctant home in the Royal Navy.
14. Skat is a popular and difficult German card game. The Kaiser and Philipp played it for money.
15. Imperator Rex. Wilhelm was Emperor of Germany and King of Prussia.
16. The Kaiser, like his mother and grandmother, was a fan of Gilbert and Sullivan operettas. For obvious reasons, the Admiral's song from *HMS Pinafore* especially appealed to him. He could quote from it freely (see Arthur Jacobs, *Arthur Sullivan: A Victorian Musician* Oxford University Press, New York, 1984, p.160). Philipp also loved the song and its biting humour. I have no direct evidence that Philipp actually sang this song for the Kaiser, but there is evidence that the Kaiser was particularly fond of it. There is also evidence that Philipp was fond of operetta, that he sang and that he entertained the Kaiser on board *Hohenzollern*.
17. The Kaiser went into exile in Holland on 10 November 1918. He travelled with his retinue, in a convoy from German headquarters in Spa, Belgium to the Dutch border station of Eijsden, where the imperial train was waiting for him. The day before, a Republic had been proclaimed in Berlin. The Kaiser requested political asylum in the Netherlands. He stayed for almost two years with a member of the Dutch aristocracy, then moved on 15 May 1920 to an estate he had bought near Apeldoorn with a lavishly furnished country house, Huis Doorn,where he lived with his family until his death in 1941.

Chapter 5

1. *Kaiserliche Marine-Kabinets betreffend, Auszüge aus den Qualifikationsberichten über Offiziere. Band I von 1889*
2. Otto von Bismarck (1815–1898) came from a Prussian land-owning family and was the architect of the German Empire. He was intelligent, wily and Machiavellian. Instinctively conservative, he was willing to compromise to achieve his ends. These were the consolidation of Germany as a single state with Prussia the dominant power, and loyalty to the Emperor. In foreign affairs he applied the same principles of *Realpolitik*,and his level-headed self-interest seems to have earned him the trust of those with whom he negotiated, even if they didn't like him personally or Germany.
3. The decline in power of the Ottomans left their empire, particularly those parts which lay in the Balkans, vulnerable to aggression from ambitious, land-hungry western

powers. Bismarck, through the *Dreikaiserbund*, attempted to neutralize Russian/Austro-Hungarian rivalry in the Balkans by agreeing on respective 'spheres of influence'. But by 1887 that rivalry could not be suppressed any longer, and the *Dreikaiserbund* fell apart. In its place, in 1887, Bismarck arranged for a secret Reinsurance Treaty between Russia and Germany. After Bismarck lost power, his enemies in the Foreign Ministry convinced the Kaiser that the treaty was too favourable to Russia and should not be renewed. It was secretly cancelled in 1890. The Kaiser believed that he himself could establish a genial relationship with Tsar Alexander III, and that this personal friendship could provide the security which Germany had lost with its failure to renew diplomatic agreements.

4. Graf Alfred von Schlieffen (1833–1913) Chief of the Imperial General Staff 1891–1906.
5. The visit was to Alexander III, Tsar of Russia, King of Congress Poland and Grand Duke of Finland.
6. The many German speakers living within the Russian Empire, especially along the Baltic coast, were largely the descendants of German merchants and of the Teutonic Knights and their retinues who had invaded in the thirteenth century and established the State of the Teutonic Order.
7. SMY *Kaiseradler* commanders from June 1892 to October 1893: June 1892 to October 1892: Kapitän zur See Volkmar von Arnim. October 1892 to October 1893: Kapitän Hermann Gercke (operating with a reduced crew)
8. Male descendants of Philipp suffer from the same problem.
9. Adolf Stoecker (1835–1909), a Lutheran.
10. There are various reports on Philipp, from January 1894 onwards, which refer to his problem. See Bundesarchiv, Freiburg Auszüge aus den Qualifikationsberichten, BA-MA=RM2/v.827.
11. Admiral Hans von Koester (1844–1928) later became the first active-duty naval officer to attain the rank of *Grossadmiral* (Grand Admiral).
12. Hermann Gercke, *Der Torpedo (1898), Geschichte und Entwicklung* (The Torpedo, its History and Development), reprinted in 2012 by The Maritime Press, Bremen.

Chapter 6

1. *Jugendstil*, which literally means 'style of the young', was known in other parts of Europe as *Art Nouveau.*
2. Albertopolis is the nickname given to the area around Exhibition Road in South Kensington, after Prince Albert, consort of Queen Victoria. He gathered together a number of cultural institutions in that one place, an arrangement similar to the *Museumsinsel* in Berlin.
3. Alfred Peter Friedrich von Tirpitz (1849–1930), Secretary of State of the German Imperial Naval Office from 1897 until 1916. He believed in big battleships rather than light cruisers. A Mahan enthusiast, he thought the German navy was in direct competition with the British. The two countries competed in empire-building and trade.
4. The three main Berlin naval offices under the 1889 reorganization were the Marine Kabinett (Navy Cabinet) responsible for promotions, appointments, administration and issuing orders to naval forces; the Reichsmarineamt (Naval Office), responsible to the Chancellor and for advising the Reichstag on naval matters; and the Oberkommando der Marine (Naval High Command), which only survived till March 1899 when, at the instigation of Tirpitz, the Kaiser took over supreme command of the navy himself.
5. Bismarck first used this phrase in a speech he made to the Prussian House of Representatives on 30 September 1862. The 'blood and iron' he was talking about was

the blood and iron Prussia would have to use against other German states in order to unify Germany. The speech begins, 'The position of Prussia in Germany will not be determined by its liberalism but by its power.'

6. Ernst Graf von Reventlow (1869–1943), a difficult and undistinguished man.
7. The Heberlein brake is a continuous railway brake that is applied by means of a mechanical cable. It was used on narrow-gauge railways running at low speeds.
8. Henry James Pryce (April 1852–13 August 1918)
9. John Rushworth Jellicoe (1859–1935), 1st Lord Jellicoe, Admiral of the Fleet and Commander of the Grand Fleet till December 1917. He commanded the Grand Fleet during the 1916 Battle of Jutland, after which Winston Churchill said that Jellicoe was the only man on either side who could 'lose the war in an afternoon'. An amusing remark but completely untrue: the battle was (mostly) lost, but not the war.
10. Eduard von Capelle (1855–1931) worked, from 1897, with Tirpitz in the Reichsmarineamt but retired in 1915, when both he and his wife suffered ill health after their daughter was killed in Japan. She was the wife of Kapitänleutnant von Saldern, an officer with the Matrosen Artillerieabteilung (Naval Artillery Division), and the family with two children had been stationed in Kiautschou, on the Shantung Peninsula, China. They were captured by the Japanese when Japan captured the German colony of Kiautschou (Shantung peninsula) in October 1914. The von Salderns were held in separate prisons in Japan, and she was permitted to travel by train once a fortnight to see her husband. It was on one such trip that she was attacked, and her husband committed suicide on hearing the news, thereby orphaning the children, who were brought back to Germany by a German doctor who happened to be in Japan at the time. In spite of this tragedy and his wish to be at home, Capelle was recalled to service in 1916. He became Secretary of State for the Navy, replacing Tirpitz. His wife was Luisa Maria Matilde Kruge.
11. Sixty-six and skat are both peculiarly German card games, the first for six hands and the second for three. Skat is considered to be especially difficult. Piquet and bézique are two-handed French games, the first dating from the fifteenth century and the latter from the nineteenth.
12. Lenchen's charmed, protected childhood did little to prepare her for a tough life. She married a doctor, Otto Ehlers, had three sons, Heinrich, Georg and Otto, and lived in an apartment in Gehlsdorf, near Rostock. After the war, Philipp and Mila took an apartment in the same house. Her husband died young and she was left, with Mila (also widowed), to bring up the three children.
13. A Droschke is a four-wheeled, horse-drawn carriage, with the passengers sometimes protected by a black hood with sides over the back seat. They were particularly popular in Russia.
14. A light, open carriage, sitting on two extravagantly large wheels, and pulled by one or two horses.
15. Sophienhof is a small village near Tiefenbachmühle in Thuringia.
16. Deep, a fishing village on the Baltic Sea, formerly in Prussia, is now in Poland and called Mrzezyno. It is where the River Rega enters the Baltic.
17. Anton Alexander von Werner (1843–1915) was appointed Director of the Berlin Academy in 1875.
18. Berlin's cathedral was built on the orders of Kaiser Wilhelm II between 1894 and 1905. It is a heavy baroque pile, and under it, the Hohenzollern crypt contains ninety-four sarcophagi and burial monuments which span four centuries of Brandenburg-Prussian history. Wilhelm disinterred as many ancestors of his as he could and brought them there as evidence of Hohenzollern power and royal continuity. Ironically, he himself

turned out to be the last one to rule. And, being in exile when he died, he is not buried there. He lies in Holland.

19. Die Siegesallee (Victory Walk) was a broad boulevard begun in 1895 and finished in 1905. It was adorned with ninety-six marble statues depicting the Kaiser's predecessors and nicknamed by Berliners the *Puppenallee* (Dolls' Walk). The figures were used to teach history to schoolchildren. The Kaiser once gave a prize to the winner of an essay competition for Joachimsthaler Gymnasium boys. The subject was determining the character of the personalities depicted in the Siegesallee from the position of their legs. Again, this provoked much derision from the public at large.
20. *Kladderadatsch* (the name is onomatopoeic, 'a crash') was founded in Berlin in 1849 and was originally a liberal satirical magazine, although after the First World War it became increasingly conservative, eventually supporting national socialism and antisemitism. It closed in 1944.
21. *Simplicissimus* was a satirical magazine founded in Munich in 1896 and ceased publication in 1964. It combined politically daring content with a modern graphic style and poked fun at the Kaiser and the Prussian class system.
22. Max Liebermann (1847–1935) was a Berliner and a leading proponent of Impressionism in Germany and beyond.
23. Secessionist art movements sprang up in Vienna, Munich, Berlin and elsewhere during the Wilhelmine period. They were all formed in reaction to academic and governmental restrictions on what could, or could not be included in national exhibitions.
24. Hans Grisebach (1848–1904) was an architect whose buildings reflect Gothic, *Jugendstil* and Arts and Crafts influences. He built his own family house on Fasanenstrasse, a wonderland of medieval turrets, romanticized Dutch gables, delicate filigree iron work and Wilhelmine horned devil heads.
25. There is little agreement on how to define the two movements. I see the Arts and Crafts movement as one which was more influenced by the Gothic.
26. Emil Nolde (1867–1956) was an Expressionist painter born in Schleswig-Holstein.
27. Ernst Barlach (1870–1938), an Expressionist who worked mainly as a sculptor. His fame rests, for me, on his ability to interpret grief. Among his most famous works is the *Schwebender Engel* (Floating Angel), a symbol of peace and acceptance. It hangs in Güstrow Cathedral, with a second version in the Cathedral in Cologne. He also built the Hamburg Ehrenmal (War Memorial), which focusses on the widows and children left behind.
28. Wassily Kandinsky (1866–1944), a Russian artist and pioneer of Abstractionism, was studying art in Munich at the same time as Georg.
29. Bruno (1872–1941), a publisher, and Paul Cassirer (1871–1926), an art dealer and editor, both made a huge contribution to Berlin's artistic life in the 1900s. The Kunstsalon represented the Berlin Secessionists and, notably, Paul Cézanne and Vincent van Gogh, among many others. It was one of the first galleries in Germany to display Cubist art. Bruno and Paul Cassirer acted as secretaries to the Berlin Secessionist Movement when it was first formed.
30. Paula Modersohn Becker (1876–1907) died at the age of only thirty-one, shortly after giving birth to her daughter. She studied art at a time when women, except for by the Académie Julian, were generally not accepted in art schools; and even when they were, they had to take lessons separately from men. Having little choice as to models, she often used her own body as a study for her nudes.

31. Henry van de Velde (1863–1957) was a Belgian artist, architect and interior designer, one of the founders of *Jugendstil* or *Art Nouveau*.
32. Charlottenburg Technische Hochschule produced numerous distinguished scholars over the years, including Ludwig Wittgenstein and Wernher von Braun.
33. Fritz Haber (1868–1934) won the Nobel Prize in Chemistry in 1918 for his invention of the Haber-Bosch process, a method used in industry to synthesize ammonia from nitrogen and hydrogen. The invention is important for the large-scale synthesis of fertilizers and explosives. He also invented the poison gas which was first used by the German army in the Second Battle of Ypres in 1916.
34. Carl Bosch (1874–1940), a chemist and engineer, won the Nobel Prize in Chemistry. He was a pioneer in the field of high-pressure industrial chemistry and founder of IG Farben, at one point the world's largest chemical company.
35. Captain Vladimir Ivanovich Semenov (1867–1910) was a Russian naval officer who served in several positions throughout the course of the critical Russo-Japanese War (1904–05). He sailed with the Baltic Fleet during its long voyage to Tsushima and was one of very few Russian officers to be present at both major naval encounters of the war: the Battle of the Yellow Sea and the Battle of Tsushima.
36. Fritz Mackensen (1866–1953), painter and co-founder of the Worpswede artists' colony.
37. Otto Modersohn (1865–1943), painter and co-founder of the Worpswede artists' colony.
38. Académie Julian was a private art school in Paris particularly popular with non-French students because it did not require them, as did *l'École des Beaux-Arts* (School of Fine Arts), to pass a strict French-language exam in order to attend. It also offered a more liberal approach to art.
39. Poppe Folkerts (1875–1949) was born on the Frisian island of Nordeney, the son of a master builder. He won a scholarship to the Berlin Academy and became a student of Carl Saltzmann. With permission from the Kaiser, he travelled widely on Imperial Navy ships. After returning to Kiel to work with Emil Nolde and Hans Arp, he left in 1909 to study at the Académie Julian in Paris, then spent the remainder of his life in the place where he was born.
40. Arthur Johnson (1874–1954) is mainly remembered today for his work with the satirical magazine *Kladderadatsch*. During and between two world wars, he presented a strongly anti-British, anti-American and antisemitic point of view.
41. Arnold Böcklin (1827–1901) painted wildly imaginative and romantic pictures of literary and mythological subjects. He was called a Symbolist and is perhaps best known for his many versions of 'The Isle of the Dead'. Philipp was a great enthusiast for Böcklin's work and used it frequently to illustrate his Family Chronicle. Böcklin's paintings seem to reflect the romantic, pained view Philipp had of the world. Böcklin who was Swiss, came from a wealthy family of silk merchants.
42. Artists, by choice or fate, tended to be non-conformists. Edvard Munch, for example, lived with a woman to whom he was not married. Paul Cézanne married his model. Van Gogh frequented brothels and committed suicide. Philipp almost certainly wanted an ordinary, happy, middle-class life for his son, which was unlikely if he was going to be an artist.
43. Carl Saltzmann (1847–1923), the son of a shoemaker, was a marine artist who taught art to Prince Heinrich and to Wilhelm, his elder brother, both when he was Crown Prince and after he became Emperor. He was a great friend of the Kaiser, accompanying him on most of his *Hohenzollern* trips, both when those were voyages of state and when they were holidays, or *Nordlandreisen*. He illustrated a book, *Kaiser Wilhelms II Reisen*

nach Norwegen in den Jahren 1889-92 (1892), written by the geologist, mountaineer and explorer Paul Güssfeldt (1840–1920), who was also on board.

44. Hans Bohrdt (1857–1945) was a largely self-taught artist who had fallen in love with the sea when he first saw it at the age of fifteen. He painted heroic, nationalistic marine pictures, often featuring the distinctive and dramatic German Imperial Navy flag – a black cross on a white background. He accompanied the Kaiser on many of his sea voyages and gave him lessons. The Kaiser was very fond of him. They saw eye to eye on the importance of the navy and its role as a symbol of the nation.
45. Willy Stöwer (1864–1931), the son of a sea captain, began life working in the shipyards but moved into painting. He often accompanied the Kaiser on his sea voyages, giving him lessons on board.
46. The Grand-Ducal Saxon College of Fine Arts, completed in 1906, had just been built to a design by Henry van de Velde when Georg arrived. Hans Olde (1855–1917) was the Director.
47. Paul Klee (1879–1940) had a highly individual style connected to Expressionism, Cubism and Surrealism.
48. Franz Marc (1880–1960), an Expressionist painter, founded, together with Wassily Kandinsky, the pioneering modern art review *Der Blaue Reiter* (The Blue Horseman) in 1912.

Chapter 7

1. Winifred Alice Bessie Pryce (14 June 1880–1961).
2. Rumty and Bella Pilfer appear in Charles Dickens' *Our Mutual Friend.*
3. Elizabeth Mary Collins (8 July 1858–15 July 1946).
4. Wilfred Pryce (1888-1977), Winnie's younger brother.
5. Pumpernickel, a dense, dark bread with no crust, is made with a sourdough starter and coarsely ground rye. At one time, it was traditional peasant fare.
6. In Germany in the early twentieth century, men were liable for military service from the age of seventeen. It was usually a two year programme, but *Einjärig-Freiwilliger* (One-Year Volunteers) – not in fact volunteers but conscripts – could qualify to serve only one year. Qualification for this shorter term of service depended on educational level and wealth. Usually anyone taking their *Arbitur* could qualify, but such recruits had to pay for their own equipment, uniform and living expenses. On completion of this one-year's service, the recruit hoped to become a reserve officer. For the five years following, he had to return to barracks each year for a fortnight's refresher course. *Einjährig-Freiwilliger* wore twisted wool piping along their epaulettes, and this remained there throughout their military service, whatever rank they finally achieved.
7. Literally, 'little Mother'. Adding '-chen' to the end of a name forms an affectionate diminutive.
8. Königliches Bau- und Verkehrsmuseum (Royal Museum of Building and Transport) was opened in 1906 in the disused neoclassical building which had been the Hamburger Bahnhof.
9. Lothar (1866–1936) and Gertrud (1877–1960) Kunkowski were a highly talented artistic couple who founded an art school in Berlin. They both taught and wrote books on art. She was particularly gifted.
10. The Kaiser's consent was necessary for officers to marry since he was Commander-in-Chief.
11. Winnie and Hermann had to formally register their intention to marry on 31 December 1908, before the Charlottenburg Royal Court. The contract they signed is a wonder

of practicality and a sobering counterbalance to romance: '1. We are engaged to each other and intend to marry in March 1909. We hereby agree to complete separation of property for the duration of our marriage, so that the husband is not entitled to any usufruct or administration of the current or future assets that the wife brings into the marriage or acquires during the same. 2. I, the person appearing at 1, give my future wife the following shares in the securities belonging to me (a) 12,000M government bonds, (b) 3,000M Bonds of the Provincial Association of the Province of Schleswig-Holstein and (c) 11,000M Bonds for the Province of Schleswig-Holstein the usufruct for her lifetime. This right ceases to apply if the marriage ends. 3. Stamps and costs will be borne by the first person appearing. Please send two copies to retired Corvette Captain Hermann Gercke, Nachodstr 18. This protocol was read to those appearing, approved by them and executed by hand as follows: Hermann and Winnie signed.'

12. Defeat in the Russo-Japanese War was followed by Bloody Sunday (St Petersburg, 1905) when unarmed workers, led by priests with a petition for the Tsar, were fired on by the imperial guard. This marked the beginning of the October Revolution as reformists tried to elicit concessions from the Tsar to bring an element of constitutionality to a wholly autocratic system. He did, in fact, make some concessions, but retracted these in his heavy-handed coup of June 1907, which paused but did not stop momentum for change. Life in the Russian Empire had long been marked by an extraordinary number of assassinations and sporadic outbursts of violence, but these intensified in the years shortly before the outbreak of the First World War. In January of the year of Winnie's dinner, Lenin fled Russia and went to live in Switzerland. Disturbances culminated in the 1917 Russian Revolution.
13. The poem is called *Beherzigung* (A Reflection).
14. Heinrich Mathy (1883-1916) an officer in the Imperial Navy, belonged to the same Crew as Hermann and was one of his best friends. As well as being best man at their wedding, he was godfather to their second son, Georg.
15. Hans Eberius (Crew 1890) was promoted Rear Admiral in 1920.
16. Milk was pasteurized (heated to kill off harmful bacteria) in Germany in the 1880s, much earlier than in Britain, where pasteurization was introduced from the 1920s onwards.
17. Winnie's birthday was 9 June. She was twenty-six when she married and twenty-eight in 1911, when her first child was born.
18. As a child Hermann had pronounced his own name as 'Em', and the name stuck throughout his life.
19. Erskine Childers (1870–1922) was a bright, eccentric, upper-class, London-born Anglo-Irishman, addicted to adventure. He was a keen yachtsman and as an undergraduate at Cambridge enjoyed sailing from the Norfolk Broads to Nordeney, the Frisian Islands and the Baltic. He later used this experience in his novel *The Riddle of the Sands*,published in 1903, which is set largely in the Baltic and imagines a German plot to invade England along its east coast. Very critical of the British Empire, he became an ardent Irish nationalist, but was shot by firing squad on the orders of the new nationalist Irish Government for carrying firearms without permission.
20. Lothar von Arnauld de la Perrière (1886–1941), a colleague of Hermann's, was working in the Admiralty in Berlin when war broke out, but later joined the submarine fleet in the Mediterranean. His record for the amount of tonnage and the number of ships sunk is unsurpassed to this day. He was promoted Vice-Admiral in 1941 (Crew 1903).
21. There were indeed good relations. A joint British-German naval review was held in Kiel, starting on 24 June 1914, when a squadron of British super-dreadnoughts was anchored in the midst of the German High Seas Fleet. The Kaiser, dressed in his British

Admiral's uniform (which his grandmother had given him) boarded a British warship and bonhomie reigned supreme. The assassination of the Archduke on 28 June cast a pall over proceedings, but still when the review came to an end, there was no sense that the two countries would be at war five weeks later.

22. Hermann's translations were:
    1. *Die Schlacht bei Tsuschima* (The Battle of Tsushima) Published in Berlin 1907, a translation of a book by Vladimir Semenov about the final battle of the Russo-Japanese war, which ended with a devastating defeat for Russia.
    2. *Raßplata* (The Reckoning) a translation of a book by Vladimir Semenov about the author's experiences during the voyage of the Baltic Fleet to the Far East. Published in Berlin, 1908.
    3. *Unser Lohn* (Our Reward), a translation of a book by Vladimir Semenov, published in Berlin, 1910. It is about his time as a Japanese prisoner of war, his return home and the unrest in the Russian military which followed.
    4. *Von Libau bis Tsuschima*, a translation of letters from Eugen Sigismundowitch Politowski to his wife, published in Berlin, 1911. Politowski was a naval engineer who accompanied the Russian fleet to the Russo-Japanese war and drowned during the Battle of Tsushima at the age of thirty. He was an engineer, not a naval officer, and offers a completely different view point to that of Semenov. He was responsible for ongoing repairs, including repairs to torpedo boats while at sea. He (and others) considered the Russian mission doomed from the start.
23. Hermann Harry Gercke (11 September 1911–1997) was a psychiatrist in Hamburg for most of his life.
24. Raymond Poincaré (1860–1934) was, in 1912, Prime Minister of France.
25. Sergei Sazonov (1860–1927), Russian Foreign Minister.
26. On 17 August 1912, Poincaré sailed to St Petersburg to meet the Russian Tsar Nicholas II (Alexander III had died in 1894) and Sergei Sazonov. France and Russia had begun discussions about a possible alliance almost as soon as Germany failed to renew its secret Reinsurance Treaty with Russia in 1890. In August 1892, shortly after William II's wooing of the Tsar at the Kiel naval review, representatives of the Russian and French general staffs signed a military convention (August 1892), which provided for mutual military aid in the event of a German attack. But negotiations continued. On 17 August Poincaré was indeed, as Hermann surmised, going to St Petersburg to confirm their alliance. But it was far worse than Hermann knew. Poincaré was also going to tell the Tsar about a secret deal he had just reached with Britain, the Anglo-French Naval Convention, only just signed (23 July 1912). That Convention might oblige the British to take France's side in a war with Germany. I say 'might', because the words used in the Convention are ambiguous. Poincaré told the Russians that England had stated her readiness, in the event of an attack on the part of Germany, to give assistance to France with both her naval and her military forces. But the British saw it differently. The news shifted the balance of power, and Russia and France may have both felt that this agreement meant they now had the upper hand. Before the agreement it was roughly two against two: Russia and France against Germany and Austria-Hungary. With Britain in the game, it was now three against two. The British Prime Minister, H.H. Asquith, was keen that any assurance of British support should not be generally known, for fear it might harden French and Russian attitudes towards Germany, which it did.
27. Amusingly enough, the British Foreign Secretary, Sir Edward Grey, also informed Sazonov of this so-called secret agreement. See Andreas Rose, *Between Empire and*

Continent; British Foreign Policy before the First World War (Berghahn, New York and Oxford, 2017) p.2.

Chapter 8

1. *Das Königen Elisabeth Garde-Grenadier*, or The Elisabeths, as they were known, were the third of four élite Prussian Guard Corps regiments based in Berlin, all named after foreign and German royals. The four regiments were the Franz (Regiment no. 1), after the Austrian Emperor; the Augustas (Regiment no. 2), after Wilhelm I's wife; the Elisabeths, after Queen Elisabeth, wife of King Friedrich Wilhelm IV of Prussia; and the Alexanders (Regiment no.4), after the Russian Tsar. At the beginning of the war, soldiers in these regiments were all Berliners, but as casualties soared, increasing numbers of new recruits arrived from other parts of Germany, and these famous 'Berlin regiments' became, less and less, regiments of Berliners.
2. An ocarina is a round-shaped flute, generally made of clay.
3. Professor Heinrich Müller-Breslau (1851–1925) was both a practising engineer and a theoretical researcher. He brought the previously separate elements of classical structural analysis together in a unified theory of beams and frames. He systematized computational methods, in particular the principle of virtual displacements, and applied energy sets systematically. He also calculated structures for airships.
4. Wilhelm Hauff (1802–1827) was a poet and novelist. The story Georg illustrated comes from the book *Märchen Almanach für das Jahr 1826* (Fairytale Almanac of 1826).
5. Franz Leuwer, with his wife Rosa (the first female dentist in Bremen), owned a book store-cum-art exhibition space in Bremen. They were Jewish and their store, rented from Norddeutschen Lloyd, was a cultural hub in the city. When the Nazis came to power, the company told Rosa, by then a widow, to vacate the premises. Her children had already left Germany and they urged her to do the same, but she said, 'It's difficult to transplant an old tree.' Wearing a yellow star, she was killed in Theresienstadt concentration camp.
6. Bremen is one of the fiercely proud *Hansestädte* of North Germany, cities which acquired independent status within the Holy Roman Empire. Its merchants and guilds were at the centre of the Hanseatic League that sought to monopolize North Sea and Baltic trade.
7. Emigrants usually sailed on steamships belonging to the big shipping company, Norddeutschen Lloyd. Founded in Bremen in 1857, it became one of the world's leading shipping companies. The company's emblem was an anchor and the crossed keys of Bremen. The company was ruined in the two world wars.
8. Max Neumark, Rosa's brother and an artist.
9. Carl Schünemann, a publisher and writer in Bremen.
10. Hans am Ende (1864–1918), a painter with the Worpswede community who died during the war.
11. Heinrich Vogeler (1872–1942), a painter with the Worpswede community and a political activist.
12. Walter Bertelsmann (1877–1963).
13. Friedrich Blau (1831–1899).
14. Daniel-Henry Kahnweiler (1884–1979). German-born, he was one of the most notable of all French art collectors of the twentieth century. He rose to prominence in 1907 as the champion of the Cubist work of Pablo Picasso and Georges Braque.
15. The *Siebenbürger* Saxons were German immigrants invited to settle in Transylvania by the ruler of Hungary in the mid-1100s to protect the borders of Hungary. They built

strongly fortified cities, many of which remain to this day, though many if not most of the Germans living there have left.

16. Christel married Lt. Kurt Happe, also from Berlin, on 15 May 1919. See the *Osnabrücker Zeitung*.
17. Christopher Andrew, *The Origins of the Secret Service* (2009) p.9.
18. Winnie and Hermann's second son, Georg Wilfred Gercke, was born on 9 August 1913.
19. The Lutheran Auenkirche was built between 1895 and 1897, a direct response to Berlin's growing population. It is built in a neo-gothic style out of brick, with single gothic arches and many beautiful details, such as red and black brickwork and fine art-nouveau roses and vines on decorative tiles. A pretty stone font stands in front of the chancel.
20. On 18 January 1913 Admiral Alfred von Tirpitz, Secretary of State of the German Imperial Naval Office, persuaded the Kaiser to agree to a five-year expansion programme of German naval airship strength. A contract was placed for the first airship on 30 January, one requirement being that the craft should be capable of bombing England, though there were no actual plans to do this. The L-2, the second airship purchased by the Imperial Navy, blew up on 17 October 1913. An inflight engine fire ignited the ship's hydrogen, killing all aboard. The loss of the L-2 occurred six weeks after the loss of the L-1 with most of its crew. The two disasters deprived the navy of most of its experienced personnel and led to the temporary suspension of a planned expansion programme.
21. Libau is today the Latvian port of Liepāja.
22. The Kurland or Courland Peninsula, on the south shore of the Baltic, projects to form the southern shores of the Irben Straits.
23. Irben (or Irbe) Straits lead from the Baltic into the Gulf of Riga.
24. Reval, nowadays Tallin and the capital of Estonia.
25. Nevski Prospekt is one of the main streets in St Petersburg and its most famous. Its name comes from the Alexander Nevski Lavra, the monastery which stands at the eastern end of the street and which commemorates the Russian Prince and soldier saint, Alexander Nevski, Prince of Novgorod, Grand Prince of Kiev and Grand Prince of Vladimir, a key figure in medieval Russian history. He rose to legendary status on account of his military victories over Swedish invaders.
26. Count Friedrich de Pourtalès (1853–1928) was a German aristocrat and diplomat who served as Ambassador to the Russian Empire in St Petersburg from 1907 to 1914.
27. I cannot locate Stealka, but it may be a St Petersburg ferry departure point for Helsinki. The distance is 175 nautical miles, and the ferry today takes thirteen hours. It may have taken Winnie and Hermann two days to complete the journey. They must have stopped en route. No such trips are available today. The Gulf of Finland is navigable from May to October.
28. The port of Kronstadt is located on an island at the head of the Gulf of Finland and is linked to St Petersburg by a combination causeway-seagate. It is of great strategic importance since it guards the sea approaches to St Petersburg. It was the main base for the Russian Baltic Fleet. The second most important base was at Riga.
29. A *dacha* is a Russian holiday home.
30. Admiral Henning von Krusenstierna (1862–1933) was a senior Swedish naval officer who served as head of the Military Office of the Ministry of Naval Affairs (1906–1909), Flag Captain (1909–1915), Minister for Naval Affairs (1910–1911) and Chief of the Naval Staff (1916–1927). He worked extensively on military coastal geography, inaugurating a surveillance and signalling system operating along the entire Swedish coast, later called the coastal signalling service.

31. I have been unable to locate Lieutenant von Bahr and his wife but I do know that they were kind to Winnie during the war. She kept in touch with her father in letters forwarded through them. He was also able to forward money.
32. Claës Olof Lindstrom (1876–1964) was a Swedish naval officer and one-time Chief of the Naval Staff. In 1913, he was Adjutant to King Gustaf V and served from 1917 to 1919 as a naval attaché in Berlin and Copenhagen. He was also a member of the Swedish Naval Studies Commission which, in the autumn of 1917, visited Germany and Occupied Belgium.
33. Trelleborg is a ferry terminal and the southernmost town in Sweden. The first ferry connection to Germany opened in 1897.This was replaced with a train-ferry line to Sassnitz in 1909 as a part of the line Malmö–Berlin.
34. The fishing village-cum-seaside resort of Sassnitz is the terminal for the ferry from Sweden. Rail links connect it to Berlin. It lies on the north-east coast of the island of Rügen, off the German Baltic coast. Winnie and Hermann were taking the same crossing (Sassnitz–Trelleborg) as Vladimir Lenin and his party took three years later, in 1917.
35. The Royal Swedish Order of the Sword was awarded to officers, and originally intended as an award for bravery and particularly long or useful service. For Hermann it would have been for bravery and useful service.
36. *Roter Adlerorden* (Order of the Red Eagle) was an order of chivalry of the Kingdom of Prussia awarded to both military personnel and civilians, to recognize valour in combat, excellence in military leadership, long and faithful service to the kingdom, or other achievements.

Chapter 9

1. Hugo von Pohl (1855–1916) was, like Philipp, a member of Crew 1872. In 1914, he was a vice-admiral, Chief of the Admiralty Staff and involved in deliberations during the July Crisis.
2. Germany declared war on France on 3 August 1914.
3. By the beginning of the twentieth century half of the oil sold in international markets was extracted in Baku.
4. Julia Karlovna was one of the daughters of Philipp's uncle, Karl Gercke. She was thus Hermann's first cousin, once removed. Most relations not in the immediate family circle, and of a certain age, were referred to as either 'uncle' or 'aunt'.
5. Prince Lichnowski (1860–1928) was German ambassador to Britain from 1912 to August 1914. He had warned Berlin that Britain might intervene in the event of a continental war. On 25 July, he asked the German government to accept an offer of British mediation in the Austro-Serbian dispute and in a cable on 28 July he relayed an offer from George V to hold a conference of European ambassadors to avoid a general war. But from von Müller's comments, it is clear that even on 3 August, Lichnowski had left his staff with the impression that he thought war was avoidable. He must have been a poor reader of the public mood. Philipp's description of London that day is of a city on a war footing. On 3 August, at 4.00 pm British Foreign Secretary, Sir Edward Grey addressed the House of Commons. Members cheered loudly as he said Britain would take a stand over Belgium. War was declared on 4 August at 11.00 pm.
6. Carl Hans Lody (1877–1914), a reserve officer with the German merchant navy, was hanged in November 1914 for spying on the Royal Navy. He had arrived in England as a spy in late August 1914, the same month that Philipp was sent there in a similar capacity. Lody was sent by the *Nachrichten-Abteilung* and Philipp, by von Pohl and possibly by the Kaiser.

7. This was the Kaiser's last sea-trip, not just on the *Hohenzollern* but on any ship. It was also the final voyage of SMY *Hohenzollern*. She was scrapped in 1923.
8. Winston Churchill, *The World Crisis 1914–1918* p. 255.
9. Formerly belonging to the Habsburg Monarchy and now Karlovy Vary in the Czech Republic, this Bohemian town has many thermal springs and is one of Europe's most famous spas.

Chapter 10

1. Prince Heinrich was humble, unobtrusive and apparently without ambition except to be with his family and to sail as much as possible. Yet he had enemies at court in Berlin, enemies who interceded against him with the Kaiser. Hermann liked him but laughed at his inability to see the big picture. He allowed himself to worry about things of no importance. One of his great concerns in 1914 was whether or not, if a British airman was shot down over Germany, he should be given a funeral with full military honours. He tended to get bogged down in detail. Perhaps he was too self-effacing. Perhaps he deferred too readily to his elder brother.
2. The German army crossed the Belgian frontier on 4 August 1914 which contravened the 1839 Treaty of London (which Prussia had signed) to guarantee the Belgian frontiers. In spite of this aggression, the war was viewed in Germany as a defensive war against encirclement.
3. The British embassy is still located at 70–71 Wilhelmstrasse, though the building is a replacement of the one which stood there in 1914. The building Winnie knew was a grand neo-classical edifice called the Palais Strousberg.
4. They had just returned from London.
5. The blockade is considered one of the key elements in the eventual Allied victory. In December 1918, the German Board of Public Health concluded that 763,000 German civilians had died from starvation and disease because of it. Part of the issue was that German manufacturers had turned to military production and abandoned the manufacture of civilian products.
6. Arnaud de la Perrière (1886–1941) was initially *Admiralsstabsoffizier* to Admiral von Pohl but later transferred to train in Pola, the Austro-Hungarian Mediterranean port and submarine centre. As captain of the *U-35* he made fourteen voyages, sinking 189 merchant vessels in the Mediterranean. In 1918 he transferred to the *U-139* and sank a further five ships. This record remains unsurpassed to this day. He was awarded the *Pour le Mérite* in 1916, the highest award that Germany could offer.
7. Prince Heinrich's birthday was 14 August. In 1914, he was celebrating his fifty-second.
8. From August 1914 to 20 April 1915, Ehler Behring (1865–1918) was *Detachierter Admiral der östlichen Ostsee beim Oberbefehlshaber der Ostseestreitkräfte* (Detached Rear-Admiral). He was 'detached' in the sense that he reported directly to Prince Heinrich, thus being freed from intermediary paperwork.
9. Danzig is now Gdansk and is in Poland; Königsberg is now Kaliningrad and in Russia; Swinemünde is now Swinoujscie and in Poland; Memel is now Klaipeda and in Lithuania; Libau is now Liepāja and in Latvia; while Windau is now Ventspils and is in Latvia.
10. Germany's alternatives to its High Seas Fleet were its Baltic Fleet and its developing Submarine Flotilla.
11. John Rushworth Jellicoe (1859–1935) was appointed Commander of the Grand Fleet in August 1914 and First Sea Lord (the professional head of the entire Royal Navy) in November 1916. He was dismissed on Christmas Eve 1917. His and Admiral Tirpitz's decision to avoid direct confrontation between the two fleets caused frustration on both

sides. See Iain Ballantyne, *The Deadly Trade* (Weidenfeld & Nicolson, 2018) p, 200: 'In the Grand Fleet's battleships – swinging at anchor while the army did the bulk of the fighting and dying – there were many frustrated sailors itching to get at the enemy.' Many in the big battleships at Wilhelmshaven felt the same way.

12. The Russian Baltic Fleet in 1914 consisted of: 2 large warships, 4 ships of the line, 5 ironclads, 4 gun cruisers, 62 old destroyers and 1 new, 12 submarines plus English E-class submarines (2 in 1914, 3 in 1915, 4 more in 1917).The German Baltic Fleet consisted of 7 small Cruisers, 6 old destroyers and 3 new U-Boats.
13. Nelson (1758–1805) was a hero to the German navy as well as the British. Hermann's prize for that essay he wrote in 1909 was a large engraved portrait of him. Nelson was admired because he abandoned traditional strategy in favour of whatever new idea might give him an advantage. Also, rather than direct a battle as it was occurring, through the use of signals, he would gather his captains together prior to action and tell them his plan, allowing them leeway in how they carried out their individual orders. He worked on the basis of trust.
14. Matti E. Mäkelä, *Das Geheimnis der Magdeburg* (The Secret of the Magdeburg) (Bernard und Graefe Verlag, 1984) p. 17. See also for general interest, Commander H. Frost, in *The Battle of Jutland* p.516: risk is 'the very foundation of naval and military greatness'.
15. *Auf See unbesiegt*, material gathered by Eberhard von Mantey, Vizeadmiral a. D., in a story written by Kapitän zur See Franz Wieting, *Torpedoboosfahrten in der Ostsee* (J. F. Lehmanns Verlag München, 1921) Vol 1, p. 64.
16. *Auf See unbesiegt*, material gathered by Eberhard von Mantey, Vizeadmiral a. D., in a story written by Korvettenkapitän Werner Grassmann, a gunner on board the *Augsburg* at the time, *Torpedoboosfahrten in der Ostsee* (J. F. Lehmanns Verlag München, 1921) Vol 2. p. 196.
17. *Auf See unbesiegt*, material gathered by Eberhard von Mantey, Vizeadmiral a. D., in a story written by Kapitän zur See Franz Wieting, *Torpedoboosfahrten in der Ostsee* (J. F. Lehmanns Verlag München, 1921) Vol 1, p. 64.
18. Admiral Mantey, *Unsere Marine im Weltkrieg* (Vaterländischer Verlag C.U. Weller, Berlin, 1927) p.169.
19. *Signalbuch der Kaiserlichen Marine* (SKM), a key German naval codebook, big and weighty (38cm x 30.5cm x15cm). Difficult to handle. Difficult to dispose of.
20. The phrase is used in a typewritten and unsigned letter to Admiral Sir Doveton Sturdee (1859–1935), formerly Chief of War Staff at the Admiralty), dated 25 May 1917. It is one of two unsigned typed letters in a file (ADM223/768 National Archives, Kew) which have been incorrectly labelled as 'Correspondence to Sir J. A. Ewing'. Clearly they are not. One is dated 18 May 1917 and begins, 'My dear Commander in Chief" (Admiral Jellicoe); the other dated 25 May 1917, begins, 'Dear Sir Doveton Sturdee'. Until an unknown date in May 1917, the head of Room 40 was Sir James Ewing, not a Royal Navy man, though he had worked for the Admiralty since 1903. He may well have left by the time these letters were written, and of course he was certainly not the man to whom the letters are addressed. Given the familiarity of the address to Jellicoe, the familiarity of the writer with officers in the Royal Navy and the ingrained respect for RN officers ('The "team" is composed of some forty civilians who are as able and keen as possible but require (and want) the leadership of a Naval Officer'), they were both almost certainly written by Admiral Sir William Hall, Director of the Naval Intelligence Division. He was at this time in overall charge of operations in Room 40. Hall is asking that Commander William James be released from his existing duties

in order to assist Captain Herbert Willis Webley Hope, the then head of Room 40, who had had a nervous breakdown as the result of overwork. (ADM223/768 National Archives, Kew.)

Chapter 11

1. Oberst (Colonel) Böhm, later Generalmajor, was a professional soldier who, after the war, started writing the history of the 201st. He died when he reached the year 1915, at which point others took over.
2. General Axel von Petersdorff (1861–1933) came from an old Prussian military family.
3. General Karl von Bülow (1846–1931), also from an old Prussia military family, commanded the Second Army from 1914 to 1916.
4. General Alexander von Kluck (1846–1934), the son of an architect, joined the Prussian Army and commanded the First Army 1914–1916.
5. Helmuth von Moltke (1848–1916) Chief of General Staff, August 1906–September 1914.
6. It was customary for soldiers to mark any special moment with three hurrahs, equivalent to our 'Hip, Hip, Hurray!' as well to sing what was called the *Deutschlandlied* (Germany's song). The lyrics were written in 1841 and it later became the German national anthem. Wilhelm II encouraged this because he wanted Germans to stop thinking of themselves in their local context (as Bavarians, Württemburgers and so on) but as a single nation. The first line of the song is, '*Deutschland, Deutschland, über alles*', meaning 'Germany first'.
7. The Zouaves were French colonial troops from North Africa. When war broke out in 1914, the French made immediate use of their colonial troops.
8. The Geneva Convention (1906) and the Hague Land Warfare Convention (1907) governed the treatment of civilians and the behaviour of invading armies. The Geneva Convention dealt strictly with the treatment of the military. It aimed at ensuring respect and humanitarian treatment for those in uniform and states that it is obligatory for combatant authorities to inform their populations of the rules. Article 26 states: 'The signatory governments shall take the necessary steps to acquaint their troops, and particularly the protected personnel, with the provisions of this convention and to make them known to the people at large.' Limiting humanitarian protection to those in uniform could imply that civilians who kill are guilty of murder. The Hague Land Warfare Convention states under Article 2: 'The inhabitants of a territory which has not been occupied, who, on the approach of the enemy, spontaneously take up arms to resist the invading troops without having had time to organize themselves ...shall be regarded as belligerents if they carry arms openly and if they respect the laws and customs of war.' It could perhaps be argued that individual civilians who shot spontaneously at the German invaders were not belligerents because they did not carry arms openly. As so often with international law, it only applies if parties want it to.
9. General Joseph Joffre (1852–1931) Commander-in-Chief of the French forces, ordered General Charles Lanzerac (1852–1925), commander of the French Fifth Army, to attack regardless of what the British Army on his left flank was up to.
10. Lanzerac commanded the French Fifth Army at the beginning of the First World War, fighting to the right of the British Expeditionary Force. He had a poor relationship with the British commander General Sir John French. He was replaced in September 1914, prior to the Battle of the Marne.
11. The Battle of St Quentin also known as the First Battle of Guise (29–30 August 1914).

12. At the beginning of the war, French army uniform included bright red trousers.
13. The First Battle of the Marne was fought between the French, English and Germans between 5 and 12 September 1914. It is difficult to separate the casualties in the Battle of the Marne from the casualties in other related battles of August and September 1914. Over two million men fought in the campaign leading to the First Battle of the Marne, and although there are no exact official casualty figures for the battle, estimates for the actions of September along the Marne front for all armies are often given as around 500,000 killed or wounded.
14. *Majestät, wir haben den Krieg verloren.*' Otto-Ernst Schüddekopf, *Der Erste Weltkrieg* (Bertelsmann Lexikon-Verlag , 1977) p.18. Historians argue ad infinitum about von Moltke's decision. Was it a good one? Was it disastrous? On the one side, you might say that the German lines were overstretched, on the other, that the railway lines from Waimes through Belgium into France were either ready or would shortly be ready. Whatever the arguments, the result remains the same. It was the turning point for Germany in the First World War. By choosing retreat, Germany transformed its war from one of attack to one of defence. It kept hoping the Allies would sue for peace. And they didn't. In spite of this turn for the worse, Germany went on fighting for another four years.

Chapter 12

1. Many German nationals living in France had their possessions sequestered by the French state and sold by the government at auction. Georg's possessions were most likely sold off by his landlady. Many artists lost their work through looting, bombing and fire.
2. Eric von Falkenhayn (1861–1922) was Chief of General Staff from 14 September 1914 till 29 August 1916. That is, from just after the First Battle of the Marne (5–12 September 1914) until shortly after the Battle of Verdun (21 February–18 December 1916).
3. Alfred von Loewenfeld (1848–1927) came from an old Prussian military family and had served in the 1870 War against France. During the First World War he was local commanding officer of the Guard Corps in Berlin.
4. Oberst von Kuczkowski was a retired Prussian colonel.
5. Oberleutnant von Frantzius later became a major and was one of the three authors who edited and produced the regimental history, *Der Geschichte des Reserve Infanterie Regiments Nummer 201,* (Verlag Bernard & Graefe, Berlin 1940).
6. The Battle of the Yser, 16–31 October 1914. The British official historian, James Edmonds, wrote in 1925, in the second 1914 volume of the *History of the Great War*, that from October to 30 November 1914, between Gheluvelt and the coast, the Germans suffered an estimated 76,250 casualties.
7. Generalmajor Hugo von Seydewitz (1849–1915) was a Prussian general brought out of retirement.
8. King Albert I of Belgium (1875–1934) had a German mother and a German wife, but he was a popular king. He was known during and after the First World War as *le Roi Chevalier* for his spirited defence of his country in the face of overwhelming odds.
9. The standard approach to trenches was one front line trench with parallel trenches behind for support troops and a zigzag communications trench running at right angles to those trenches and leading to the rear. The zigzag course was to minimize the impact of enemy shells falling into the trench.
10. From the very beginning, the French were using their colonial troops, mainly *zouaves*, light infantry from North Africa.

11. There were three costly battles round Ypres in the First World War. The First Battle of Ypres ran roughly from 19 October to 22 November 1914, the Second from 22 April to 25 May 1915 and the Third (also known as the Battle of Passchendaele) from 31 July to 10 November 1917. Georg saw action during the Second Battle.

Chapter 13

1. Admiral Georg Alexander von Müller (1854–1940) was an enemy of Prince Heinrich and possibly, as Philipp hints, a sycophant of the Kaiser. In 1906, he succeeded Gustav von Senden-Bibran as Chief of the Imperial Naval Cabinet and remained in this post until 1918.

Chapter 14

1. Libau is now known as Liepāja and is in Latvia.
2. Windau is now known as Ventspils and is in Latvia.
3. When the British submarines first arrived in the Baltic, the Russians were in the process of dismantling their submarine and other military installations in Libau for fear of a successful German assault. The British submarines therefore diverted and eventually operated alongside the Russian fleet out of Reval.
4. *Auf See unbesiegt*, material gathered by Eberhard von Mantey, Vizeadmiral a. D., *Torpedoboosfahrten in der Ostsee*, by Kapitän zur See Franz Wieting, (J. F. Lehmanns Verlag München, 1921) Vol 1, p. 64.
5. Memel, now called Klaipeda and in Lithuania, was, in 1914, the last German port before the border with Russia. In November 1914, it was the nearest German port to the sinking *Friedrich Carl.*
6. This is an adaptation of a story by Korvettenkapitän Werner Grassman in *Auf See unbesiegt,* Zweiter Band, stories edited by Eberhard von Mantey Vizeadmiral a.D., *Die Brave Alte Augsburg,* (J.F. Lehmanns Verlag, München, 1922) Vol. 2, p.196. I have combined Grassman's story with Gernot Goetting's report to Winnie.

Chapter 15

1. It is interesting to compare *Die Liller Kriegszeitung* to the British *Wipers Times*. The former is serious and its cartoons tend to be bitter. The latter is mostly comic.
2. This was done by the *Volksbund Deutsche Kriegsgräberfürsorge*, without contacting relatives first. In Germany, graves in cemeteries are not bought but rented. If rental payments cease, the grave is re-used. Only those who died in war have permanent resting places so, in a way, we are lucky to have any place at all to remember those we have lost. Those who died in battle, but whose bodies were irrecoverable, have no grave. There is no comprehensive list available in German cemeteries giving the names of all those killed, only of those whose bodies were recovered.
3. The quote is from Virginia Woolf's diary for 1927. She was referring to Knole, the country seat of the Sackville West family. 'All the centuries seemed lit up, the past expressive, articulate; not dumb and forgotten; but a crowd of people stood behind, not dead at all; not remarkable; fair faced, long limbed; affable; and so we reach the days of Elizabeth quite easily.'

Chapter 17

1. Menen is a Belgian town near the border with France.
2. The Kaiser's birthday fell on 27 January. He was born in 1859 in Berlin and died in 1941 in Apeldoorn, Holland. He reigned from 1 June 1888 till 9 November 1918, when

he went into exile. As Commander-in-Chief of the Armed Forces, his birthday was celebrated by the military, both in Germany and throughout the German Empire.

3. *Lebkuchen* are traditional and unique German Christmas biscuits.
4. *Feldmarschall* Paul von Hindenburg's victories on the Eastern Front were making him a national hero. He had won the Second Battle of Tannenberg in the first month of the war (26–30 August 1914) and the First Battle of the Masurian Lakes (2–14 September 1914). He also won (and this is the victory Georg and the 201st were celebrating in Menen), the Second Battle of the Masurian Lakes (7–28 February 1915). The Russians had invaded East Prussia just over two weeks into the war in 1914, and by this 1915 battle they were pushed back for good. Von Hindenburg eventually became so strongly associated with victory that, after disastrous mismanagement during the Battle of Verdun in 1916, the Kaiser called on him to take over as Chief of the General Staff from von Falkenhayn.
5. Although Kaiser Wilhelm II did not get on with Otto von Bismarck (1815–1898), and in fact chased him out of office, he remained, and remains, a national hero. His main achievements came when he served under Kaiser Wilhelm I when he was key to Germany's victories over Denmark, Austria and, most importantly, France at Sedan in 1870. He was appointed to the new post of Chancellor of the German Empire.
6. Poison gas was first used by the Germans at Ypres on 22 April 1915. It had been developed based on the work of Nobel prize-winning chemist, Fritz Haber, who had attended the Charlottenburg Technische Hochschule.
7. A Belgian village also known as Bikschote.
8. *Geschichte des Reserve Infanterie Regiments Nummer 201*, written and complied by Oberst Hayner, Major von Frantzius and Otto Zarn. Published by Verlag Bernard & Graefe, Berlin 1940, p.104.
9. Ibid. p.126.
10. General Ferdinand Foch (1851–1929) was, in 1915, Assistant Commander-in-Chief for the Northern Zone, while General Joffre was the Commander-in-Chief.
11. Artois is now part of Pas-de-Calais. There were three battles in the area during the First World War: the First, from 17 December 1914 to 13 January 1915, the Second from 9 May to 18 June 1915, and the Third from 25 September to 4 November 1915. Georg and the 201st took part in the Second Battle, called in German *Die Lorettoschlacht* (the Battle of Loretto Heights).
12. Periscopes were in use in the First World on both sides as early as December 1914, but no mention is made of their use by the 201st Reserve Regiment. On the contrary, the talk in 1915 is of the frequent death of lookouts using only branches to hide them as they peered over the parapet.
13. The French suffered horrendous casualties during the Second Battle of Artois – 102,500 men, twice the number lost by the Germans. The use of colonial troops for these incredibly costly assaults seems to imply another case of Allied mistreatment of colonial forces.
14. *Geschichte des Reserve Infanterie Regiments Nummer 201*, op. cit. p.31.
15. Ibid. p.161.

Chapter 18

1. In his Chronicle Philipp repeats here Voltaire's famous quote: 'Lord protect me from my friends; I can take care of my enemies.' There was a strong belief that Prussian order and discipline produced the best soldiers in the world, but there is no suggestion, judging from the experiences of the three Gercke men in the First World War, that this extended to the leaders.

2. The Kosava wind is a cold north-easterly which starts in the Carpathian Mountains and follows the Danube through the narrow Iron Gate gorge. This gives the wind a powerful jet effect as it blows on to Belgrade.
3. Kraljevo is an important city in central Serbia.
4. German iron rations in 1914 consisted of: 250g biscuit, 200g preserved meat or 170g bacon, 150g preserved vegetables, 25g coffee, 25g salt. This is the food that each soldier carries with him, for use in the field when the kitchen unit fails.
5. *Geschichte des Reserve Infanterie Regiments Nummer 201*, written and compiled by Oberst. Hayner, Major von Frantzius and Otto Zarn. Published by Verlag Bernard & Graefe, Berlin 1940, p.186.
6. Over 200,000 soldiers and civilians died on the three-month journey through the Alps that winter. Some called this trek a 'strategic withdrawal', others an Albanian Golgotha. Among those that survived was the King.
7. Neu Karlovitz was in Austria-Hungary and is now Novi Karlovci in northern Serbia.
8. *Geschichte des Reserve Infanterie Regiments Nummer 201* op. cit. p.195.
9. Verdun is a city in north-eastern France, about 80km from the German border. It sits at a crossing over the River Meuse.

Chapter 19

1. Admiral Albert Hopman (1865–1942) published two books about his war-time experiences, *The Logbook of a German Naval Officer* (Berlin 1924) and *The War Diary of a German Naval Officer* (Berlin 1925).
2. Germany's torpedo boats were numbered, not named. Each number was prefixed by an initial letter to denote the builder.
3. Hopman's diary entry for 31 July 1915 reads: 'Gercke's birthday. He is 32 years old. We celebrated at lunch. I hope this great and capable man stays with us.'
4. Admiral Erhard Schmidt (1863–1946), in 1915 *Chef des IV Geschwaders in der östlichen Ostsee* (Commander of the IV Squadron in the Eastern Baltic), and in 1916 *Befehlshaber der Aufklärungsschiffe in der östlichen Ostsee* (Commander of Reconnaissance Ships in the Eastern Baltic Sea).
5. Hermann always took great care when communicating by wireless.
6. This is an adaptation of an article, '*Weltkrieg in der Irbenstraße*' by Korvettenkapitän Max Bastian, in *Auf See unbesiegt* vol. 1, Stories selected by Eberhard von Mantey (Berlin 1921), pp. 307–18.
7. *Dobrowoletz*,also known as *Dobrovoletz*,was a 580-ton Russian torpedo boat destroyer carrying three artillery pieces, four machine guns, two torpedo tubes and a crew of ninety-seven, thirty-seven of whom died when she sank. She was built in Helsingfors and St Petersburg. See *Taschenbuch der Kriegsflotten 1914–15*, p. 86.
8. For the torpedoeing of the *Prinz Adalbert* by *E-9*, see Gary Staff, 'The Sea Battle off Ostergarn' in *Battle on the Seven Seas* (Pen & Sword Books, 2001) pp. 1–13.

Chapter 20

1. The Battle of Verdun, between the French and the Germans, was one of two extensive and costly battles in 1916. The other was the Battle of the Somme, fought against the British and the French. The Battle of Verdun, from 21 February to 18 December, was one of the longest battles of the war and one of the most brutal. The French suffered over 400,000 casualties and the Germans 350,000. In all, 300,000 men were killed.

2. The grim name of *Toter Mann* or *Homme Mort* may derive simply from the shape of the hill. When it is not covered in trees, it is easier to see, perhaps, the outline of a man lying on his back with his head where the two summits are.
3. Lt. Kurt Schweitzer is an imaginary figure used here to describe accounts of the fighting in *Geschichte des Reserve Infanterie Regiments Nummer 201*, written and compiled by Oberst Hayner, Major von Frantzius and Otto Zarn (Verlag Bernard & Graefe, Berlin 1940) pp. 211–26.
4. Oberst a. D. Hayner, brought out of retirement, had been promoted from Major to Colonel by the end of the war. He was one of several who later compiled and wrote *Der Geschichte des Reserve Infanterie Regiments Nummer 201* (The History of Reserve Infantry Regiment Number 201).
5. Lipperweg is one of the German communications trenches in this area.
6. German maps show numbered points to denote company locations. Georg stood between 153 and 154. Oddly enough, these were the same numbers as those of the two U-Boats which his brother Hermann, and Hermann's friend Gernot Götting, commanded in 1917–1918.
7. *Der Geschichte des Reserve Infanterie Regiments Nummer 201,* p. 225.
8. Ibid. p. 226.
9. Max von Gallwitz, General der Artillerie, *Erleben im Western 1916–1918*, p. 36.
10. General von Falkenhayn, *The German General Staff and its Critical Decisions, 1914–1916.*
11. The French information board quotes a text from *Die Tragödie von Verdun*, third volume of *Die Zermürbungsschlacht* (The War of Attrition), III Teil, 'Toter Mann-Höhe 304', III Teil, by Ludwig Gold. From Volume 13, *Schlachten des Weltkrieges.*

Chapter 21

1. Leutunant Heinrich Mathy (1883–1916), Crew of 1900, was killed on 1 October. He was Hermann's best man and godfather to Hermann and Winnie's second son. He joined the Imperial Navy's Zeppelin Division and commanded fifteen raids over Britain, starting in 1915 with an attack on London, a city he knew slightly from having visited in 1908 as Hermann's best man. The Army's Zeppelin Division was planning to bomb London as early as August 1914, but the Kaiser hesitated for fear of bombing his relatives (it was almost impossible to aim bombs dropped from Zeppelins especially as, for safety reasons, they flew at night). The Imperial Navy launched its own Zeppelin programme in 1915, but by that time the British were developing effective defences. By 1918, when Mathy flew his last flight, the British used searchlights, anti-aircraft guns, incendiary bullets and a patrol plane to bring him down. Mathy, Commander of the L-31, and his crew of eighteen came down over Potters Bar on the night of 1/2 October 1916. Once his Zeppelin had been hit, Mathy jumped out. The impact of his body on landing pushed it several inches into the ground. He was first buried in the local churchyard and now lies in Cannock Chase German Military Cemetery, Staffordshire, Memorial ID: 105783037
2. Winnie was last in Danzig in November 1915.
3. Germany occupied Libau on 7 May 1915, and Windau on 18 July 1915.
4. Turkey entered the war on Germany's side on 31 October 1914, Bulgaria on 14 October 1915.
5. Fat Hen, *Chenopodium album*, also known as White Goosefoot, was once grown as a food for pigs, sheep and chicken.
6. Richard Lovelace (1617–1657), his poem, *To Lucasta, Going to the Wars.*

7. Admiral Reinhard Scheer (1863–1928) Commander of the High Seas Fleet, fought alongside Admiral Franz von Hipper (1863–1932), Commander of the 1st Scouting Group, at the Battle of Jutland. Scheer realized that the only pressure which could lead to negotiations to end the war was from a public suffering from food shortages. He was right, but ironically, it was this pressure, exerted on the German public, which was largely responsible, towards the end of 1918, for taking Germany out of the war.
8. The story of the Battle of Jutland (31 May to 1 June 1916) is one of those wartime stories which was manipulated at the time by the British government for propaganda purposes. The truth has only emerged with difficulty since. It was reported as a German victory by the *Manchester Guardian* on 3 June 1916, but thereafter, the story was shifted to imply a more favourable outcome to Britain. See Gary Staff, *Skagerrak: The Battle of Jutland Though German Eyes* (Pen & Sword Books, 2016) pp.141–2.
9. Ibid., p 141.
10. Iain Ballantyne, *The Deadly Trade, a Complete History of Submarine Warfare from Archimedes to the Present* (Weidenfeld & Nicolson, 2018) p.171.
11. Germany first ordered its U-Boats to sink commercial shipping carrying war materiel for the benefit of the Allies in February1915. The order was rescinded in May, after the sinking of the *Lusitania.*
12. William le Queux (1864–1927) was an Anglo-French, real-life version of Baron von Munchausen. His series of *Daily Mail* articles, purporting to describe the invasion of Britain by Germany, made much money both for himself and for Lord Northcliffe out of what would today be called 'fake news'.
13. Andreas Rose, *Between Empire and Continent; British Foreign Policy before the First World War* (Berghahn, New York and Oxford, 2017) p. 52.
14. Admiral John 'Jacky' Fisher (1841–1920), briefly First Sea Lord in 1914, made this perceptive statement in a letter to Reginald McKenna, a former First Lord of the Admiralty. It is quoted in *Fear God and Dread Nought, the Correspondence of Admiral of the Fleet Lord Fisher of Kilverstone*, edited by Arthur J. Marder, vol 3, p.414. Fisher's life as a sailor much resembled Philipp's in that it spanned an era which saw wooden boats exchanged for steel submarines.
15. *Lusitania* was a British luxury Cunard transatlantic liner. It was sunk by a U-Boat in British waters on 7 May 1915. Before she left New York, the German Embassy in the US put the following in fifty American newspapers:

Notice!

Travellers intending to embark on the Atlantic voyage are reminded that a state of war exists between Germany and her allies and Great Britain and her allies; that the zone of war includes the waters adjacent to the British Isles; that, in accordance with formal notice given by the Imperial German Government, vessels flying the flag of Great Britain, or any of her allies, are liable to destruction in those waters and that travellers sailing in the war zone on the ships of Great Britain or her allies do so at their own risk.

Imperial German Embassy
Washington, D.C., 22 April 1915

She was carrying 1,997 passengers, crew and stowaways, as well as 4.2 million rounds of rifle ammunition, almost 5,000 shrapnel-filled artillery shell casings and 3,240 brass percussion fuses. The passengers were, unwittingly, providing cover for the British war effort.

16. Vice Admiral William Sowden Sims (1858–1936) was born in Port Hope, Canada to a Canadian mother. His father was American. See Ballantyne, op. cit.
17. Ballantyne, op. cit. p.173.
18. Popular discontent had been growing in Russia for many years. It had increased after the ignominious defeat in the Russo-Japanese war and, as Winnie heard at her dinner with the admirals in Berlin in 1908, many had long been expecting revolution. In 1916, food shortages, food rationing, and mismanagement of the war led to bread riots and the February 1916 revolution, followed by the abdication of the Tsar on 15 March 1917 and the establishment of a Provisional Government.
19. Admiral Hopman, *Das Kiegtagesbuch eines deutschen Seeoffiziers* (August Scherl, Berlin, 1925) p.230.
20. Gernot Goetting (1882–1943?) was an officer on board SMS *Augsburg* when she rescued the crew of the *Friedrich Carl*. He remained close to Hermann throughout the war and to his family thereafter.
21. The cargo U-Boats could only make 11 knots on the surface, far less than a steamboat. They took at least three minutes (as opposed to seconds) to dive. Once underwater, their battery-powered engines had a limited life. They could not stay submerged for more than twelve hours, by which time not only would the batteries be flat, but the crew would be sleepy from lack of oxygen. They were unstable because they carried overly small hydroplanes (the little rudders at the side which acted like fins). As a result, it was difficult to hold the boat steady at periscope level. Goetting writes in his logbook that his torpedoes used to break the surface several times before reaching their target. Sometimes they veered to the right, sometimes to the left. He described their course as 'irregular'. Hermann preferred to use his deck cannon, which were easier to aim, but they too seem to have had problems associated with recoil.
22. R.H. Gibson and Maurice Prendergast, *The German Submarine War 1914–1918*, with a foreword by Admiral of the Fleet, Earl Jellicoe (Constable and Co. Ltd, London) 1931.
23. The use of Q-ships led to accusations that Britain had committed war crimes.
24. 'Dirty tricks' is the description used by Iain Ballantyne, op. cit., p.163.
25. Langheinrich was Hermann's devoted batman. He wanted to join *U-154*'s crew but was turned down because he was unsuitably tall. ('Langheinrich' means 'Long John' and was probably a nickname). When the war ended he visited Winnie several times, brought her food and tried to help her. He told her that he wished he had died with Hermann.

Chapter 22

1. General Oskar von Hutier (1857–1934) was Commander of the German Eighth Army which took Riga in early September 1917. The navy was then called in for a joint army and navy assault to take the Baltic Islands. Operation Albion followed, running from 12 October to 3 November 1917. It has since become a model of how to organize amphibious military operations and is still used as a model in military staff colleges all over the world.
2. The Gulf of Riga is entered from the Baltic through the Irben Straits, but it can also be accessed from the Gulf of Finland by sailing south past various islands and along the Moon Sound. The biggest island is Ösel (Saaremaa), which includes the Sorbe (Sorve) Peninsula, with Zerel Point lying at its southernmost tip on the Irben Straits. The town of Arensburg (Kuressaare) stands just north of Zerel. North of Ösel lies the island of Dagö (Hiiumaa), and north-east lies the smaller island of Moon (Muhumaa). Moon Sound is the stretch of water between the island of Moon and the mainland. Today the

mainland and islands belong to Estonia, while Riga and the land around it belongs to Latvia.

3. Little known to navies other than the Russian.
4. Following the abdication of the Tsar, Alexander Kerenski (1881–1970) led the Provisional Government of the short-lived Russian Republic from late July to early November 1917. He was deposed by Lenin, leader of the Bolsheviks, in the October Revolution.
5. Vladimir Lenin (1870–1924) returned to St Petersburg on 16 April 1917.
6. Four E-Class British submarines were operating in the Baltic at this time (*E-1*, *E-8*, *E-9*, *E-19*). Also four C-Class submarines (*C-26*, *C-27*, *C-32*, *C-35*). The former had entered the Baltic via The Sound, the latter had arrived overland from Archangel. The C-Class submarines were not operational till 1917. *C-32* and the *C-27* were in the Gulf of Riga when the Germans arrived, and *C-26* was sent to join them. None of them succeeded in torpedoing any of the German boats. One fired two torpedoes and missed. One was stranded on a sandbank. All they did, as submarines in the Baltic did from the start, was make the German navy nervous and extra-cautious. Every night, the German navy extinguished the lit buoys which marked the cleared channel.
7. I don't know either. Hermann is mocking some bureaucratic acronyms: 'Pilako', 'Afl', 'Ifl' and 'Grufl'.
8. SMS *Goeben* was in the Mediterranean when war broke out and sailed to Constantinople for safety. The British tried to damage her when she was anchored off the Dardanelles, but failed. She was transferred to the Imperial Ottoman Navy, became its flagship under the name of *Yavuz Sultan Selim* and sank two small British warships. After the war, she carried Kemal Attaturk's remains from Istanbul to Izmir in 1938. She remained the flagship of the Turkish navy till 1950.
9. Hermann is referring to the Gulf of Riga when he mentions the word Riga.
10. Hermann is referring to the August 1915 failed German assault on Riga. It seems at the time that he favoured a broader attack.
11. Magnus von Levetzov (1871–1939) was Chief of Operations of the High Seas Fleet in 1917. He was awarded the *Pour le Mérite* for his work during Operation Albion and went on to become an admiral.
12. Soelo Sound lies at the entrance to the waterway between Ösel and Dagö. The water beyond that Sound is called the Kassar Wiek.
13. The *Grom*, a Russian destroyer built in 1915, was captured by the Germans in the Kassar Wiek on 14 October 1917. They found maps on board showing the distribution of mine barrages in the area and possibly charts showing water depths. The area was shallow, and depths changed rapidly. The Russians had dredged critical shipping channels in particular areas such as Moon Sound.
14. Hermann is recalling the long siege (27 August–7 November 1914) of the German fortified town of Tsingtau on the Shantung Peninsula in China. After it fell, Germans on the peninsula, who included the Gerckes' friends, von Capelle's daughter, son-in-law and grandchildren, were interned in Japan. Von Capelle's daughter was later murdered, and her husband committed suicide in prison.
15. The request or order, was not unusual. Falkenhayn asked the same thing of his men before they left for the Battle of the Yser in 1914. Field Marshal Joffre asked it of his men before the First Battle of the Marne.
16. Toffri lies at the southernmost end of the island of Dagö.
17. The Balts are those living on the Baltic Sea, usually those on its south-eastern shores: Letts, Lithuanians, Estonians, Curonians, Wends and many Germans.

18. The German Chancellor was Georg Michaelis (1857–1936), who had succeeded Theobald von Bethmann Hollweg during the summer of 1917. Michaelis fell from grace on 31 October, only days after his meeting with Hermann. The actual rulers of Germany at this time were the two generals who had been successful in the east, Paul von Hindenburg and Erich Ludendorff. They had engineered both the fall of Bethmann Hollweg (who was interested in a stronger rather than a larger Germany) and the appointment of Michaelis, a man who, without their support, was powerless. At their behest, he evaded every move towards peace. They were the driving force behind the group which refused to let go of territory gained by force of arms in the east. They were also behind the punitive Treaty of Brest-Litovsk which followed Operation Albion.
19. To this day there is confusion between those who spell the surname 'Gercke' with a 'c' and those who spell it without.
20. Philipp often attributes German military disasters, including the eventual death of his eldest son, to treachery. In order to hide the work of Room 40, the British Admiralty deliberately spread rumours that Germany was being betrayed by spies. Their work was effective. Here Hermann is expressing pleasure that for once the German plans have not been betrayed and they took the Russians by surprise. We know that the Russians could read the German messages and act on them. It is more likely that the Russians did not act because they were too engrossed with internal politics to deal with the enemy in October 1917. The failure of the British, on the other hand, to take advantage of the absence of the dreadnoughts from Wilhelmshaven is a puzzle.
21. There were several von Pappenheims fighting in the First World War. A distinguished military family, the one Hermann refers to had the misfortune to die young and off the battlefield. These sentences suggest that poor Winnie had been expressing anxiety about her husband's safety. As we know from Hermann's earlier letter to his father, some women went to pieces with the stress of it all.
22. I am unsure about the spelling of all these names except for Ehrhardt. Hermann Ehrhardt (1881–1971), who was a colleague of Hermann's in the Imperial Navy. After the war, he led one of the most notorious of the Freikorps Brigades. He was fighting communists, but eventually had to flee Germany because he also opposed Adolf Hitler.
23. Frau Bastian was the wife of Max Bastian (1883–1958) a crewmate and colleague of Hermann's in the Imperial Navy. He later became an admiral.
24. The punitive Treaty of Brest-Litovsk was the first peace treaty signed in the First World War. It was a precursor (did it set the tone?) for a second punitive document, the Treaty of Versailles. The first was between Soviet Russia and the Central Powers (Germany, Austria-Hungary, the Ottoman Empire and Bulgaria). It was signed 3 March 1918. Under Brest-Litovsk, the former Russian Empire lost 34 per cent of its populations, 54 per cent of its industrial land, 89 per cent of its coalfields and 20 per cent of its railway lines. In addition, it had to pay six billion marks in war reparations. With it, Hermann's hopes of Germany giving back any of the land which it had gained became more unlikely than ever.

Chapter 23

1. The distance by sea is about 207km.

Chapter 24

1. Admiral Sir William Milbourne James, the man Admiral Sir William Hall had been lobbying for in letters (quoted earlier) dating from May 1917, was the grandson of the

beautiful pre-Raphaelite model Effie Millais and her second husband, the painter Sir John Everett Millais. As a curly-haired boy, the Admiral had posed for his grandfather dressed in velvet and lace, most famously in the painting known as 'Bubbles'. It was a start in life which the Admiral was never allowed to forget.

2. See the letter from Admiral Sir William Hall to the Commander-in-Chief, dated 18 May 1917: 'in view of the extreme importance of the work, the value of which really cannot be overestimated', and 'I would not approach you in this matter were I not convinced that it is a matter of national importance.' In a letter to Sir Doveton Sturdee dated 25 May 1917, he described Room 40's work as 'The provision of the intelligence on which all operations depend' and said that Room 40 'is now a great organisation and is the king-pin of everything ... the movements of the fleet depending on it.'
3. Hans Joachim Koerver, *German Submarine Warfare 1914–1989 in the Eyes of British Intelligence* (LIS Reinisch, A-7441 Steinbach) p.684.
4. The potential for locating ships from their electronic signals was studied in 1902 by the American John Stone, although a German, Heinrich Hertz, in 1888, had also worked in this field. It was an emerging technology much discussed in the scientific community regardless of nationality.
5. This was not voice chatter because radios as such did not exist. Communication was by Morse code transmitted over the air waves.
6. The German Admiralty's chief radio transmitter station in Nauen was founded in 1903 by the Telefunken Company, one of the world's two giant wireless companies, the other one being Britain's Marconi Company. During the war, Nauen was run by the German Admiralty.
7. They met on 5, 6 and 28 March, 1, 20 and 26 April; and 3, 7, and 8 May 1918.

Chapter 25

1. https://history.state.gov/historicaldocuments/frus1918Supp01v01/d715. Papers Relating to the Foreign Relations of the United States, 1918, Supplement 1, The World War, Volume I. File No. 763.72/9592. January 1918, the USA. Half a billion dollars in 1918 is about $11 billion today.
2. These were *Matrose* (Able Seaman) Hinrichsen (I have given him the Christian name of Hans) and *Steuermannsmaat* (Helmsman's Mate) Böger.
3. Hermann had two Log Books for 1918. One ended on 16 February, when he left Warnemünde. This still exists. But his War Log Book from 16 February to 11 May does not. Goetting's Log Book remains in the Bundesarchiv, Abteilung Militärarchiv, Freiburg.
4. U-Boat ledger, ADM 137/4155 Submarine History Sheets, U-Cruiser section, National Archives, Kew.
5. Admiralty special telegrams ADM 137/869 and ADM137/1935 Secret packs, for the *Willow Branch,* National Archives, Kew.
6. Hermann and Goetting's challenges: unsteadiness due to the small size of the horizontal rudders; poor manoeuvrability; slow diving capacity; slow speed; and high visibility.
7. Waters round countries associated with the Allies were said to be 'blockaded', meaning that enemy shipping should keep out, but there was hardly any enforcement, so the designation implied little except that enemy shipping should exercise caution. In 1914, the Azores were part of the Portuguese Empire. Portugal was initially neutral during the First World War. At the outbreak of war, there were thirty-six German and Austro-Hungarian ships moored in Lisbon's harbour. These were interned by a neutral Portugal but, in late 1915, Britain put financial pressure on Portugal by offering her

a large loan, and Portugal felt bound to seize the ships, which she did. At this point, Germany declared war on Portugal (9 March 1916). South of the Azores, the Canary Islands were part of the Spanish Empire, and Spain remained neutral throughout the war, one of the most important countries in Europe to do so. Seven larger islands make up the Canary Islands. Among them is El Hierro, which is the second smallest and most westerly. Gran Canaria lies roughly in the middle, while Fuerteventura and Lanzarote are the easternmost isles. Only about 100km of water separates the Canaries from Morocco and the west coast of Africa. Las Palmas, Gran Canaria, was one of the most important transatlantic re-fuelling and re-supply centres. A submarine telegraph cable linked it with Spain, with Dakar in Senegal, and with Brazil, via the Cape Verde Islands.

8. Norway, with the fourth largest merchant fleet in the world, had declared itself neutral at the outbreak of the First World War, but it was pushed, following trade threats from Britain, to favour the Allies. It became known as the 'Neutral Ally'. Hermann took a photo of this boat and sent it home to his parents when, in April that year, the captain of the Spanish steamer *Achuri* took two letters from Hermann and posted them in Spain.
9. A star shell is like a firework. It is designed not to damage, but to attract attention.
10. The Red Ensign is the flag of the British Merchant Navy.
11. On 23 May 1915, Italy declared war on Germany and Austria-Hungary.
12. A disconcerting but ultimately accurate description of Hermann and Oberleutnant Baden.
13. The Cape Verde Islands, then part of the Portuguese Empire, include five larger islands, São Tiago, Santo Antão, São Vicente, São Nicolau and Boa Vista. The islands were important in 1918 as a refuelling spot for transatlantic shipping and as a submarine telegraph cable link point. Submarine telegraph cables linked the Cape Verdes to Brazil, the Cameroons (via Bathurst in the Gambia), Spain and Britain. For a map of the global undersea cable system in 1914, see the Norman B. Leventhal map centre's 'Carte Générale, Grandes Communications Télégraphique', 1914.
14. *Bacalao* is dried cod, the main ingredient of some traditional Portuguese dishes. The fish was dried to preserve it on the voyage from where it was caught (off Canada) to the market in Portugal.
15. USS *Chincha* suffered four casualties in this encounter. See *American Ship Casualties of the World War Including Naval Vessels, Merchant Ships Sailing Vessels, and Fishing Craft.* https://www.history.navy.mil/content/history/nhhc/research/library/online-reading-room/title-list-alphabetically/a/american-ship-casualties-world-war.html
16. 'Notbywit' precedes some of these telegrams. It means that the message is to not to be transmitted using wireless telegraphy, and is therefore less likely to be intercepted. An alternative form of transmission was using cables, to which Germany had no access.
17. HMS *Bacchante* was a Royal Navy armoured cruiser. From mid-1917 till the end of the war she was flagship to the 9th Cruiser Squadron and on convoy escort duties off the African coast.
18. The report of what happened to *La Bruyère* comes from *La Bruyère: trois mâts barque, René Guillon & René Fleury*. See https://forum.pages14-18.com/viewtopic.php?t=44857
19. Hermann, when he wrote to the President of Liberia, signed himself off as 'Commandant S.M.U. Kreuzer U'. That is to say, *Commandant Seine Majestäts Unterseeboot Kreuzer U-Boot* (Commander, His Majesty's Cruiser Submarine Flotilla).
20. Cape Blanco, today called Ras Nouadhibou, lies at the northernmost end of the Mauretanian coast, immediately south of the border with its neighbour, Western

Sahara. Cape Corveiro lies on the coast of Western Sahara, just north of its border with Mauretania, and Cape Bojador is a dangerous reef-lined stretch of coast lying towards the north of Mauretania, near its border with the Western Sahara. Western Sahara lies between Mauretania to the south, and Morocco to the north.

21. Ernst Hashagen (1851–1947), Commander of the *U-62*. For the story of *U-62* and its failed rendezvous with *U-154* and *U-153*, see Ernst Hashagen, *The Log of a U-Boat Commander* (Putnam, 1931) pp. 210–2.
22. Captain Guy d'Oyly-Hughes (1904–1940), an American with a British father, had lived in Britain from the age of nine and joined the submarines in the First World War. He was awarded the Distinguished Service Cross and the Distinguished Service Order for heroic deeds in the Middle East before he was ordered, in 1918, to blow up a U-Boat in the Atlantic. He did not know which U-Boat it was. He fired his first torpedoes at 18.17 hrs but missed. He fired two more at 18.23 hrs and both hit. One hit *U-154*'s magazine causing a catastrophic explosion which was so close that the lights went out in the English submarine. A tremendous water column, smoke and flame rose 60m into the air. The *E-35* surfaced, D'Oyly saw three men floundering in the water and then he also saw *U-153,* about four nautical miles distant. Fearing it might come under attack, *E-35* dived and left the scene. The commander of *U-153* did likewise. During the inter-war period, when Hermann's eldest son Harry was visiting his grandmother in London, d'Oyly-Hughes heard of the visit through a mutual acquaintance (Admiral Sir William Goodenough) and invited the young man to have lunch with him at Simpsons in the Strand. A compassionate and homely touch and evidence that no one (or almost no one) likes to kill. D'Oyly-Hughes himself died in the Second World War when his ship and two escort ships were sunk by *Gneisenau* and *Scharnhorst.*
23. Secondee or Sekondi, also known as Fort George, was a fort on the Gold Coast, now Ghana.

_U-154_ – Activity plus Enemy and Neutral Tonnage sunk in 1918

11 March	*Nellore* (torpedoes missed), 6,853 tons, Britain
12 March	*Nordkyn* (sunk), 3,244 tons, Norway
17 March	*Guadalquivir* (sunk), 2,078 tons, Spain
21 March	*Chincha* (damaged), 6,371 tons, USA
26 March	*Beira Alta* (sunk), 101 tons, Portugal
	Mines laid off Sierra Leone
7 April	*La Bruyère* (damaged), 2,198 tons, France
	President Howard (sunk), 73 tons, Liberia
	Monrovia wireless station and cable installation shelled
10 April	*Burutu* (damaged), 3,902 tons, Britain
21 April	*Michelet* (sunk), 2,636 tons, France
25 April	*Karachi Maru* (damaged), 5,749 tons, Japan
25 April	*Willow Branch/Bombala* (sunk jointly with *U-153*), 3,314 Tons, Britain

Total tonnage sunk 9,789 (giving half *Willow Branch*'s tonnage to U-154).
By comparison, on the same voyage, *U-153* sank 6,112 tons.

Chapter 26

1. Polonius saying farewell to his son Laertes in *Hamlet*, Act I, Scene 3.

Bibliography

Books cited in the text and those used for factual research and to invoke the mood of the times.

Anon, *British Yachts and Yachtsmen: a Complete History of British Yachting from the Middle of the Sixteenth Century to the Present Day* (*The Yachtsmen's Magazine*, 1907)

Appel, F., *Das Reserve-Infanterie-Regiment Nr. 205 im Weltkrieg* from *Deutsche Tat im Weltkrieg* vol 82 (Verlag Bernard & Graefe, 1937)

Ballantyne, I., *The Deadly Trade; a Complete History of Submarine Warfare from Archimedes to the Present* (Weidenfeld & Nicholson 2018)

Bartlett, R., Schönwâlder, K., (eds), *The German Lands and Eastern Europe: Essays on the History of their Social, Cultural and Political Relations* (Palgrave Macmillan, 1999)

Bergen, C. et al., *U-Boat Stories: Narratives of German U-Boat Sailors* (Constable & Co. Ltd. 1931)

Böhm, Oberst, *Erinnerungsblätter deutscher Regimenter, herausgegeben unter Mitwirkung des Reichsarchivs, Infanterie Heft 2. Das Königin Elisabeth Garde Grenadier Regiment Nr 3.* (Verlag Gerhard Stallung 1923)

Bracken, J., *The Verdun Regiment. Into the Furnace: the 151st Infantry Regiment in the Battle of Verdun 1916* (Pen & Sword, 2018)

Brittain, V., *Testament of Youth* (Virago, 1978)

Brown, M., *Verdun 1916* (Tempus Publishing Inc., 1999)

Childers, E., *Riddle of the Sands: a Record of Secret Service* (Smith Elder & Co., 1903)

Churchill, W., *The World Crisis 1911–1918* (Thornton Butterworth and Charles Scribner's Sons, 1923–1931)

Clark C., *The Sleepwalkers: How Europe went to War in 1914* (Harper Collins, 2012)

DiNardo, R., *Invasion: The Conquest of Serbia, 1915* (ABC-CLIO, 2015)

Ertan, Irfan, 'The Orient Journey of Kaiser Wilhelm II (1898)', thesis for the Technical University, Ankara, Turkey, September 2018

Fisher, J., *Fear God and Dread Nought: the Correspondence of Admiral of the Fleet Lord Fisher of Kilverstone*, edited by Arthur J. Harder (Jonathan Cape, 1952)

Frost, H.H., *The Battle of Jutland* (United States Naval Institute, 1964)

Gercke, H. P., *Die Torpedowaffe, Ihre Geschichte, Eigenart, Verwendung und Abwehr* (Mittler, 1898)

Gercke, H.P., *Marine Humoresken* (Verlagshaus Bong & Co., 1909)

Gibson, R.H. and Prendergast M., *The German Submarine War 1914–1918* (Constable & Co. Ltd, 1931)

Gottschall, T.D., *By Order of the Kaiser: Otto von Diederichs and the Rise of the Imperial German Navy 1865–1902* (Naval Institute Press, 2003)

Gray, E., *The Killing Time: the German U-Boats 1914–1918* (Charles Scribner's Sons, 1972)

Grimmer-Solem, E., *Learning Empire: Globalization and the German Quest for World Status, 1875–1919* (Cambridge University Press, 2019)

Hashagen, E., *The Log of a U-Boat Commander* (Putnam, 1931)

Hedin, S., *With the German Armies in the West* (Naval and Military Press, 1915)

Hopman, A., *Das Kriegtagesbuch eines deutschen Seeoffiziers* (August Scherl, 1925)

Hopman, A., *The Logbook of a German Naval Officer* (August Scherl, 1925) and *The War Diary of a German Naval Officer* (August Scherl, 1925)

Hoyer, K., *Blood and Iron: the Rise and Fall of the German Empire 1871–1918* (The History Press, 2001)

Jacobs, A., *Arthur Sullivan: a Victorian Musician* (Oxford University Press, 1984)

Jankowski, P., *Verdun: the Longest Battle of the Great War* (Oxford University Press, 2016)

Jünger E., *In Stahlgewittern* (Storm of Steel) (Klett Cotta Verlag, 2015)

Keegan, J., *The First World War* (Hutchinson, 1998)

Koerver, H. J., *German Submarine Warfare in the Eyes of British Intelligence* (LIS Reinisch, 2010)

Koerver, H. J. (ed.), *Room 40: German Naval Warfare 1914–1918, Vol.1 The Fleet in Action* (2007)

MacGregor, N., *Germany: Memories of a Nation* (Allen Lane, 2014)

MacMillan, M., *The War that Ended Peace: The Road to 1914* ((Penguin, 2013)

Mäkelä, M.E., *Das Geheimnis der 'Magdeburg'* (Verlag Bernard und Graefe, 1984)

Moiser, J., *Verdun, the Lost History of the most Important Battle of World War I* (Calber, 2014)

Röhl, J.C.G., *The Kaiser and his Court: Wilhelm II and the Government of Germany* (Cambridge University Press, 1994)

Röhl, J.C.G., *Kaiser Wilhelm II: New Interpretations* (Cambridge University Press, 1982)

Röhl, J.C.G., *Wilhelm II: Into the Abyss of War and Exile, 1900–1941* (Cambridge University Press, 2014)

Röhl, J.C.G., *Young Wilhelm: The Kaiser's Early Life 1859–1888* (Cambridge University Press 1998)

Rose, A., *Between Empire and Continent; British Foreign Policy before the First World War* (Berghahn, 2017)

Scheer, R., *Germany's High Sea Fleet in the World War* (The Naval and Military Press Ltd., first published in 1919)

Schüddenkopf, O. E., *Der Erste Weltkrieg* (Bertelsmann Lexikon-Verlag, 1977)

Semenov, V. I., books translated from the original Russian by H. Gercke: *Die Schlacht bei Tsuschima* (Mittler, 1907), *Rassplata* (Mittler, 1908), *Unser Lohn* (Mittler, 1910)

Sheldon, J., *The German Army at Ypres 1914 and The Battle for Flanders* (Pen & Sword, 2010)

Staff, G., *Battle on the Seven Seas: German Cruiser Battles 1914–1918* (Pen & Sword, 2001)

Staff, G., *Skagerrak: The Battle of Jutland through German Eyes* (Pen & Sword, 2016)

Steven, D., *1914–1918: the History of the First World War* (Penguin Books, 2005)

Unruh, K., *Langemarck: Legende und Wirklichkeit* (Bernard und Graefe Verlag, 1997)

von Falkenhayn, E., *General Headquarters 1914–1916 and its Critical Decisions* (Creative Media Partners, 2021)

von Forstner, *The Journal of Submarine Commander von Forstner* (Cambridge University Press, 1917)

von Frantzius, Hayner and Otto Zarn, (editors and compilers), *Der Geschichte des Reserve Infanterie Regiments Nummer 201* (Verlag Bernard & Graefe, 1940)

von Gallwitz, M., *Erleben im Westen 1916-1918* (Mittler, 1932)

von Mantey, E, (compiler and editor), *Auf See Unbesiegt* Vols I and II (J.F. Lehmanns Verlag 1921, 1922) von Mantey, E.(compiler and editor), *Unsere Marine im Weltkrieg* (Vaterländischer Verlag, 1927)

Reichsarchiv, Schlachten des Weltkriegs, (various authors) *Das Marnedrama 1914, Die Schlacht bei St. Quentin 1914* Vols I and II and *Die Tragödie von Verdun 1916* Vol 1 (Ludwig Gold and Martin Reymann), (Verlag Gerhard Stalling, 1924, 1926, 1928).

von Rosenberg-Lipinsky, H.O., chief editor of *Das Königin Elisabeth Garde Genadier Regiment Nr 3 im Weltkriege 1914-1918* (Verlag Bernhard Sporn, Zeulenroda, 1933)

Weyer, B., *Taschenbuch der Kriegsflotten 1914–1915* (Lehmanns Verlag, 1914)

Zweig, A., *Outside Verdun: a Novel from the First World War* (Freight Books, 2014)

Websites

https://history.state.gov/historicaldocuments/frus1918Supp01y01/d715

Papers relating to the Foreign Relations of the United States, 1918, Supplement 1, The World War, Vil. L1, File No. 763.72/9592.

https://www.history.navy.mil/content/history/nhhc/research/library/online-reading-room/title-list-
alphabetically/a/american-ship-casualties-world-war.html

American Ship Casualties of the World War including Naval Vessels, Merchant Ships, Sailing Vessels and Fishing Craft

https://forum.pages14-18.com/viewtopic.php?t=44857

La Bruyère: trois mâts barque, René Guillon & René Fleury

Index